Third Workshop on Natural Language Processing for Indigenous Languages of the Americas (AmericasNLP 2023)

Toronto, Canada
14 July 2023

ISBN: 978-1-7138-8182-7

Printed from e-media with permission by:

Curran Associates, Inc.
57 Morehouse Lane
Red Hook, NY 12571

Some format issues inherent in the e-media version may also appear in this print version.

Association for Computational Linguistics
209 N. Eighth Street
Stroudsburg, Pennsylvania 18360

Phone: 1-570-476-8006
Fax: 1-570-476-0860

acl@aclweb.org

Additional copies of this publication are available from:

Curran Associates, Inc.
57 Morehouse Lane
Red Hook, NY 12571 USA
Phone: 845-758-0400
Fax: 845-758-2633
Email: curran@proceedings.com
Web: www.proceedings.com

ACL 2023

Third Workshop on Natural Language Processing for Indigenous Languages of the Americas

Proceedings of the Workshop on Natural Language Processing for Indigenous Languages of the Americas (AmericasNLP)

July 14, 2023

The ACL organizers gratefully acknowledge the support from the following sponsors.

Gold

Google

Order copies of this and other ACL proceedings from:

Association for Computational Linguistics (ACL)
209 N. Eighth Street
Stroudsburg, PA 18360
USA
Tel: +1-570-476-8006
Fax: +1-570-476-0860
acl@aclweb.org

Introduction

Welcome to AmericasNLP 2023, the Third Workshop on Natural Language Processing for Indigenous Languages of the Americas!

AmericasNLP aims to...

- ...encourage research on NLP, computational linguistics, corpus linguistics, and speech around the globe to work on Indigenous American languages.
- ...connect researchers and professionals from underrepresented communities and native speakers of endangered languages with the machine learning and NLP communities.
- ...promote research on both neural and non-neural machine learning approaches suitable for low-resource languages.

In 2023, AmericasNLP is being held in Toronto, Canada, on July 14. There will be 3 invited talks, an overview of this year's AmericasNLP shared task, a poster session, and multiple paper as well as shared task system presentations.

We received a total of 33 submissions this year: 22 research papers, 1 extended abstract, 3 previously published papers, and 7 shared task system description papers. 15 research papers were accepted (acceptance rate: 68%) – as well as all extended abstracts, previously published papers, and system description papers. In addition, two Findings of ACL papers will be presented at the workshop.

We would like to extend our gratitude to everyone who helped make AmericasNLP happen: First, we thank our gold sponsor, Google. In addition, AmericasNLP would not be possible without all the work that went into the reviewing process. Thus, we thank the program committee members for committing their time to help us select an excellent technical program. Finally, we thank all the authors who submitted their work to the workshop and all participants who will be at the workshop to exchange their ideas around NLP for Indigenous languages of the Americas!

Manuel Mager, Abteen Ebrahimi, Arturo Oncevay, Enora Rice, Shruti Rijhwani, Alexis Palmer,
and Katharina Kann
AmericasNLP 2023 Organizing Committee

Organizing Committee

Organizing Committee

Mager Manuel, AWS AI Labs, USA
Abteen Ebrahimi, University of Colorado Boulder, USA
Arturo Oncevay, University of Edinburgh, UK
Enora Rice, University of Colorado Boulder, USA
Shruti Rijhwani, Google Research, USA
Alexis Palmer, University of Colorado Boulder, USA
Katharina Kann, University of Colorado Boulder, USA

Program Committee

Program Committee

Eduardo Blanco, University of Arizona
Jie Cao, University of Colorado
Paulo Cavalin, IBM Research - Brazil
Luis Chiruzzo, Universidad de la Republica
Rolando Coto-solano, Dartmouth College
Ruixiang Cui, University of Copenhagen
C.m. Downey, University of Washington
Cristina España-bonet, DFKI GmbH
Luke Gessler, Georgetown University
Héctor Jiménez-salazar, Universidad Autónoma Metropolitana, Cuajimalpa
Kartik Kannapur, Amazon Web Services
Zoey Liu, Department of Linguistics, University of Florida
Arya D. Mccarthy, Johns Hopkins University
Ivan Vladimir Meza Ruiz, Insituto de Investigaciones en Matemáticas Aplicadas y en Sistemas, Universidad Nacional Autónoma de México
Daniela Moctezuma, Centrogeo
Sarah Moeller, University of Colorado
Manuel Montes, INAOE
John E. Ortega, Northeastern University
Shiva Kumar Pentyala, Salesforce AI
Angeles Belem Priego Sanchez, Universidad Autónoma Metropolitana
Amit Sah, Department of Computer Science, South Asian University
Elizabeth Salesky, Johns Hopkins University
Shabnam Tafreshi, UMD:ARLIS
Atnafu Lambebo Tonja, Instituto Politécnico Nacional (IPN), Centro de Investigación en Computación (CIC)
Ivan Vulić, University of Cambridge
Ekaterina Vylomova, University of Melbourne
Koichiro Watanabe, pluszero, inc
Adam Wiemerslage, University of Colorado Boulder

Keynote Talk: No Language Left Behind: Scaling Human-Centered Machine Translation

Angela Fan
Meta AI Research
2023-07-14 09:15:00 – Room: **TBD**

Abstract: Driven by the goal of eradicating language barriers on a global scale, machine translation has solidified itself as a key focus of artificial intelligence research today. However, such efforts have coalesced around a small subset of languages, leaving behind the vast majority of mostly low-resource languages. What does it take to break the 200 language barrier while ensuring safe, high-quality results, all while keeping ethical considerations in mind? In this talk, I introduce No Language Left Behind, an initiative to break language barriers for low-resource languages. In No Language Left Behind, we took on the low-resource language translation challenge by first contextualizing the need for translation support through exploratory interviews with native speakers. Then, we created datasets and models aimed at narrowing the performance gap between low and high-resource languages. We proposed multiple architectural and training improvements to counteract overfitting while training on thousands of tasks. Critically, we evaluated the performance of over 40,000 different translation directions using a human-translated benchmark, Flores-200, and combined human evaluation with a novel toxicity benchmark covering all languages in Flores-200 to assess translation safety. Our model achieves an improvement of 44% BLEU relative to the previous state-of-the-art, laying important groundwork towards realizing a universal translation system in an open-source manner.

Bio: Angela is a research scientist at Meta AI Research in New York, focusing on research in text generation. Currently, Angela works on language modeling. Recent projects include No Language Left Behind (https://ai.facebook.com/research/no-language-left-behind/) and Universal Speech Translation for Unwritten Languages (https://ai.facebook.com/blog/ai-translation-hokkien/). Before translation, Angela previously focused on research in on-device models for NLP and computer vision and text generation.

Keynote Talk: From fieldwork to "data" - A behind-the-scenes look from Brazilian Amazonia

Kristine Stenzel
Federal University of Rio de Janeiro / University of Colorado Boulder
2023-07-14 11:00:00 – Room: **TBD**

Abstract: This talk offers an overview of one linguist's experience in language documentation with two indigenous groups in the northwest Amazon. Based on over twenty years of fieldwork, it aims to provide broader perspective on what goes into the collection, organization, and annotation of "data" from endangered or low-resource languages.

Bio: Kristine Stenzel was an Associate Professor of Linguistics at the Federal University of Rio de Janeiro, Brazil from 2009-2022 and is currently at the University of Colorado as Coordinator of the Computational Linguistics, Analytics, Search, and Informatics Professional Master's Program. She has conducted research with the Kotiria and Wa'ikhana language communities since 2000, receiving grants from NSF, NEH, ELDP, as well as CNPq and CAPES in Brazil. Her scientific contributions include *A Reference Grammar of Kotiria* and publications in English and in Portuguese on diverse topics in phonology, morphosyntax, discourse, multilingualism, contact phenomena, and language documentation. She has developed language maintenance and revitalization materials for the Kotiria and Wa'ikhana, including practical orthographies, pedagogical publications, documentary films, and audiovisual archives (ELAR, open access).

Keynote Talk: From doctoral thesis to the classroom: The case of San Juan Quiahije Chatino

Emiliana Cruz Cruz
CIESAS-CDMX
2023-07-14 16:00:00 – Room: **TBD**

Abstract: In this presentation I will address an issue that is very important to us as speakers of indigenous languages: how to ensure that linguistic studies on indigenous languages reach the hands of the speakers of these languages. Over the last 20 years, the Chatino Language Documentation Project (CLDP) has resulted in seven doctoral theses in the three Chatino languages, all written in English. For the Eastern San Juan Quiahije Chatino, there are four doctoral theses. The theses are of great importance for the speakers. However, generating pedagogical products based on these doctoral theses has been a slow process. It is not just a translation issue, as CLDP linguists have tried to make teaching materials out of their research. So, what are the challenges when we are dealing with a "well-studied" Chatino language? In this talk I will present some reflections around this question based on a project in the municipality of Quiahije.

Bio: I am a linguistic anthropologist and assistant professor at CIESAS-DF. I primarily work on language treatment and revitalization, with a focus on the Chatino language of Oaxaca, Mexico; cultural identity and maintenance through language programs and curriculum development; orthography development; and, finally, issues related to sovereignty and decolonization. One aspect of my research is the application of anthropological methods in the documentation of naturally occurring discourse in indigenous languages. An essential contribution of the anthropological perspective is the recognition of the crucial role to be played by native speaker linguists in all phases of research. My linguistic work centers on the complex tonal structure of Chatino languages, and I developed the San Juan Quiahije variety's alphabet. An important result of this project has been the creation of pedagogical materials that will enable members of the Chatino community to preserve their language and cultural integrity. I am a native speaker of Chatino and founder of The Chatino Language Documentation Project, a team of linguists which aims to document and revitalize Chatino languages.

Table of Contents

Use of NLP in the Context of Belief states of Ethnic Minorities in Latin America

Olga Kellert and **Md Mahmud Uz Zaman**
University of Göttingen, Germany
olga.kellert@phil.uni-goettingen.de and
mail.mahmuduzzaman@gmail.com

Abstract

The major goal of our study is to test methods in NLP in the domain of health care education related to Covid-19 of vulnerable groups such as indigenous people from Latin America. In order to achieve this goal, we asked participants in a survey questionnaire to provide answers about health related topics. We used these answers to measure the health education status of our participants. In this paper, we summarize the results from our NLP-application on the participants' answers. In the first experiment, we use embeddings-based tools to measure the semantic similarity between participants' answers and "expert" or "reference" answers. In the second experiment, we use synonym-based methods to classify answers under topics. We compare the results from both experiments with human annotations. Our results show that the tested NLP-methods reach a significantly lower accuracy score than human annotations in both experiments. We explain this difference by the assumption that human annotators are much better in pragmatic inferencing necessary to classify the semantic similarity and topic classification of answers.

1 Introduction

Indigenous people belong to the particularly vulnerable groups in the COVID-19 era and are disproportionally affected by epidemics and other crises, as acknowledged by the United Nations (United Nations and Affairs, 2020). Beyond the general problems related to the socio-economic marginalization and the concomitant inaccessibility of health-care services (in particular in rural regions and remote communities), a major threat for indigenous people arises through miscommunication, either due to the sparsity of information material in indigenous languages or due to cultural differences hindering the interpretation/application of the recommended health measures(García et al., 2020) (Afifi et al., 2020). Dissemination of reliable COVID-19- related information, adapted to cultural and linguistic background of indigenous peoples, is a major priority in epidemic crisis; (García et al., 2020) (Afifi et al., 2020) (UN, 13 April 2020). Several initiatives of the European Union (EU) and World Health Organization (WHO) address the problems in communication of health related information (Baccolini, 2021). These initiatives target communication of key health-related terms and concepts underlying them such as understanding of medical instructions. In the recent covid pandemic, it was documented that misconceptions about preventive measures against the spread of covid had a strong impact on the severity of the pandemic (UN, 13 April 2020). In order to reduce health-illiteracy and avoid unnecessary spread of infectious diseases, it is necessary to observe people's understandings of infectious diseases and their treatments. For instance, some individuals have the perception that antibiotics are a "cure-all" drug and might take antibiotics to cure diseases caused by viruses, which is an improper use of antibiotics and can lead to severe damaging effects(Calderón-Parra J, 2021).

Given the urgency of measuring the accuracy of health-related concepts and uses, it is necessary to develop NLP tools that can ease and speed up the process related to health education measurement. The key outcome of our research project is testing NLP methodology targeting measurement of health education related to the COVID-19 pandemics.

2 State-of-the-art

Accuracy measurement of medical terms uses like *antibiotics* is **currently missing** due to two main reasons: a) missing **data sources and methodologies** that enable researchers to identify, characterize and measure **actual** uses of health related topics and concepts and b) **missing statistical** (in)accuracy measures of actual information status related to infectious diseases. It is thus not surprising that the initiative *the Social Media Mining 4*

Proceedings of the Workshop on Natural Language Processing for Indigenous Languages of the Americas (AmericasNLP), pages 1–5
July 14, 2023

Health (#SMM4H) is addressing these problems in its agenda(Klein, 2021) (Magge et al., 2021). This initiative uses social media data as a data source for solving health-related tasks and problems such as finding disease mentions and symptoms(Klein, 2021) (Magge et al., 2021) (Weissenbacher et al., 2019). However, this rich data source does not have demographic information necessary for the statistics on social variation in the health literacy study. In addition, social media does not represent all social groups including indigenous population that often has low internet access or uses other tools for communication. As a consequence, data from indigenous communities related to Covid pandemics is very rare (Ojha et al., 2021). In order to address these problems, we used a traditional methodology in social sciences in order to access the information about the health education status, namely the survey methodology. We asked health-related questions such as questions about virus propagation and treatment to our participants. In order to be able to measure the accuracy of health-related concepts and uses of our participants', it is necessary to compare their information status with "expert" knowledge or uses.
In recent years, big progress has been made in semantic comparison of linguistic units such as words and sentences due to recent developments in **neural language models** such as BERT(Devlin et al., 2019) (Giulianelli et al., 2020). BERT is a language model trained on a large amount of natural language data to predict words that have been masked out as shown in Table 1 for the word *coach* (Devlin et al., 2019).

BERT has been used to find out which word vectors are responsible for lexical meaning variation such as *coach* used as 'trainer' and 'vehicle'. A word vector is essentially a mathematical representation of the meaning of a word based on learning or memorizing the frequency at which a word appears in a particular linguistic context. The differences or similarities of word vectors have been used to predict semantic (dis)similarity of words (Giulianelli et al., 2020) and sentences (Reimers and Gurevych, 2020). However, previous approaches mainly focus on meaning differences in Big Data sources such as social media and very few of them address meaning differences in survey questionnaires of ethnic minorities. It is thus not known yet how well these models work in the low resource scenario given the specific topic domain and the specific format of answers. This paper presents results from testing vector-based approaches in the measurement of answer similarity in the low resource domain.

3 Methodology

We carried out a survey study with our cooperation partners from Latin America (Marleen Haboud, Claudia Crespo, Fernando Ortega Pérez), in which indigenous groups speaking Quechua or Kichwa from Peru and Ecuador (around 150 people from each country) answered questions about Covid-19 (10 yes-no questions and 10 open-ended questions). Our task was to measure the accuracy of key concepts related to health. We tested how well the information status of indigenous groups matches the information and suggestions from reliable sources such as the World Health Organization (WHO), henceforth our Reference Corpus. For instance, according to the WHO, the virus COVID-19 is distributed through contact, hence the suggestion to keep social distancing. We asked our participants about how the virus COVID-19 is distributed in order to see how well their answer matches the information from WHO. The answers were collected in rural areas via free interviews by a local person knowing indigenous communities. The method of free interviews was particularly important in order to include individuals who are less accustomed to performing highly controlled tasks such as older and/or illiterate participants. Due to lack of time and resources we did not transcribe the interviews. Instead, the local interviewer summarized the answers to the questions in a digital form in Spanish. Consequently, the answers in this survey study do not **directly** reflect the information state of indigenous minorities.

4 Experiments and Results

We ran two experiments. The data and the code for both experiments can be found on GitHub[1]. In our first experiment, we tested the SBERT Model for measuring the semantic similarity between the participants' answers and the "expected" answers from the reference corpus via cosine similarity (see Sentence Transformers based on Reimers and Gurevych, 2020). The following examples demonstrate some results of cosine similarity from the chosen method:

[1] https://github.com/mahmuduzzamanDE/ACLAmericaNLP

Word	Before mask	After mask
coach 'vehicle'	I have driven my coach into the garage.	I have driven my <mask> into the garage.
coach 'trainer'	I have a female coach.	I have a female <mask>.

Table 1: MASK TASK

Question : 8. When should a mask be used?
Reference text : Especially in closed public places, but it is also useful in outdoor public places."
Answers by participants:
"['Whenever we are in contact with another person.'] # participant 1
"Similarity: tensor([[0.1775]])", # similarity between reference text and participant 1

"['All the time when leaving home.'] # participant 2
"Similarity: tensor([[0.0477]])", # similarity between reference text and participant 2

"['Especially in closed public places, but it is also useful in outdoor public places']", "Similarity: tensor([[0.9961]])", match between reference text and reference text

"['When we are in public places where social distancing cannot be maintained.']", participant 3
"Similarity: tensor([[0.2265]])", # similarity between reference text and participant 3

In order to evaluate the validity of the similarity measure by SBERT, we asked human annotators to annotate participants' answers from 0-5 as not similar (0) or similar (5). The annotators were four students of linguistics and one expert in medical anthropology. We divided the human ratings into three categories: similar (4-5), dissimilar (0-2), ambiguous (3) and selected the answers with high inter-speaker agreement. We translated the human ratings into correspondent cosine similarity scores: similar (>0.6), dissimilar (<0.4), ambiguous (> 0.4 and < 0.6). Our results show that the semantic similarity measured by cosine similarity using SBERT is significantly lower **(mean 0.2)** than the semantic similarity acquired by human annotation **(mean 0.7)**.

Our second experiment had the goal to find a computational method to classify a topic of an answer to an open-ended question. Here is an example. Survey question: Why do you not want to be vaccinated? Topics: a) afraid of side effects, b) my own decision, c).... An automatic classification of answers under the correspondent topics can ease the process of survey data analysis and provide a uniform way of measuring answers to open-ended questions. We asked human annotators to create topics for the interview questions and then to annotate answers according to these topics, e.g. "I can get thrombosis" was classified by human annotators as a) afraid of side effects.

We tested automatic methods to classify answers under suggested topics. The underlying idea was to look for key words in the answers that semantically correspond to suggested topics. For this aim, we performed a synonym-based similarity task without stemming (Task 1) and with stemming (Task 2). In the first task, if the topic was a synonym of one of the tokens in the given answer, the classification was TRUE. In the second task, if the topic stem was a synonym of the token stem in the given answer, the classification was TRUE. The latter case ignores morphological variation of words and focuses only on the lexical stem. We preprocessed the given answers by tokenization, removing stop words and case lowering. The synonyms were taken from the NLTK wordnet.

```
print(set(synonyms))
{'impinging','contact','reach',
'get_through',                'inter-
group_communication'    ,'contact_lens',
...}
```

We used a Stemmer from NLTK, to stem the synonym words:

```
print(Stem)
{contact|saliv|aglomer|tos|segur|
mascarill|distanci|comun|familiar|
friccion|intim|relacion|roc|
tocamient|....}
```

Table 2 demonstrates which answers the synonym-based approach by stemming correctly identified and which answers the system did not correctly identify.

Our results in Table 3 show that stemming gives slightly better results than the absence of stemming, namely a correct classification of additional 10 answers. However, despite this light improvement, the accuracy is still very low, or more precisely, the system could not make a link between a given

Used Sentence (Spanish)	Translated (English)	w/o Stem	Stem
por no seguir medidas de bioseguridad	*for not maintaining social distancing*	✓	✓
mediante contacto de persona a persona	*through contact from one person to another*	✓	✓
por saliba secreciones nasales, tos, falta de aseo	*through salive, secretion, cough, no cleanliness*	✗	✓
cuando estamos juntos	*when we are together*	✗	✓
transmisión aérea de persona a persona, vias respiratorias principalmente.	*through air transmission from person to person, mostly through respiration*	✗	✗
no acercándose mucho a otras personas	*we should not come too close to other people*	✗	✗

Table 2: Example Sentences

answer and a topic in around 50 % of the cases.

5 Discussion

The computational approaches we tested have shown much lower accuracy compared to human annotations. The biggest problem we have identified is the lack of pragmatic inferencing humans are good at, but automatic models we tested are not. For instance, people answered to the question about how the virus distributes by saying "through crowd". Due to a pragmatic inference human annotators can evaluate this answer as similar to the answer given by the reference corpus. "A crowd" implies pragmatically that social distancing cannot be obtained adequately and this can promote virus infection. However, none of our automatic models was able to predict a high similarity between the reference answer "through contact" and the participant's answer "through crowd". Another example illustrating problems with pragmatic inferences is the annotation of vaccination side effects. While human annotators had no difficulties to classify "thrombosis" as a possible vaccination side-effect, our automatic methods were not able to do it. To sum up, one of the biggest challenges in our tasks was the lack of Natural Language Understanding and Inferencing (NLI and NLU) by the computational models we tested. Using NLI and NLU in the context of low resource is reserved for future research. In the near future, we will test models trained on health-related topics, fragmented answers that represent the majority of our answers and models trained on NLI-and NLU-datasets (Kochkina et al., 2023).

Future Work

There are several issues of our methodology that need to be addressed in future research. The absence of good resources for indigenous languages has forced us to work with local translators who digitized the answers the way they perceived them. In future we will use transcribed oral data for our experiments.

Another issue is the use of few human annotations that have provided us the human similarity score necessary to evaluate computational models. Even though the inter-speaker agreement was comparatively high in our study due to very explicit training and discussion of annotation guidelines, we suspect that the inter-speaker agreement will show a much higher variation in the perception of semantic similarity if the annotation guidelines are missing as is often the case in crowd-sourced human annotations. The trade-off between expensive human annotators with long training for annotation and cheap crowd-sourced human annotations without any training is an issue that needs to be addressed in the future research.

Ethics Statement

Scientific work carried out in our project complies with the ACL Ethics Policy and with the ethic guidelines from the German Research Foundation (DFG). We have informed our participants about the goals of our project and they signed an agreement with us. In addition, the data acquisition by interviewing indigenous people was approved by Ethic committees at the universities of our cooperation partners.

Task	Cosine sim.	Synonym-token-sim.	Synonym-token-sim.+ stemming
Value	0.2	0.4	0.5
Human Annot.	0.7	1	1
Accuracy loss	0.5	0.6	0.5

Table 3: Accuracy values and accuracy loss per task

Acknowledgements

We acknowledge the funding support from the German Research Foundation (DFG) (Grant number: 468416293).

References

Rima A. Afifi, Nicole Novak, Paul A. Gilbert, Bernadette Pauly, Sawsan Abdulrahim, Sabina Faiz Rashid, Fernando Ortega, and Rashida A. Ferrand. 2020. 'most at risk' for covid19? the imperative to expand the definition from biological to social factors for equity. *Preventive Medicine*, 139:106229.

Rosso A. Di Paolo C. et al. Baccolini, V. 2021. What is the prevalence of low health literacy in european union member states? a systematic review and meta-analysis. doi: 10.1007/s11606-020-06407-8. epub 2021 jan 5. pmid: 33403622; pmcid: Pmc7947142. *Journal of General Internal Medicine*, 36:753–761.

Bendala-Estrada AD Ramos-Martínez A Muñez-Rubio E Fernández Carracedo E et al. Calderón-Parra J, Muiño-Miguez A. 2021. Inappropriate antibiotic use in the covid-19 era: Factors associated with inappropriate prescribing and secondary complications. analysis of the registry semi-covid. *PLoS ONE*, 16.

Jacob Devlin, Ming-Wei Chang, Kenton Lee, and Kristina Toutanova. 2019. BERT: Pre-training of deep bidirectional transformers for language understanding. In *Proceedings of the 2019 Conference of the North American Chapter of the Association for Computational Linguistics: Human Language Technologies, Volume 1 (Long and Short Papers)*, pages 4171–4186, Minneapolis, Minnesota. Association for Computational Linguistics.

Gerardo M. García, Marleen Haboud, Rosaleen Howard, Antonia Manresa, and Julieta Zurita. 2020. Miscommunication in the covid-19 era. *Bulletin of Latin American Research*, 39(S1):39–46.

Mario Giulianelli, Marco Del Tredici, and Raquel Fernández. 2020. Analysing lexical semantic change with contextualised word representations. In *Proceedings of the 58th Annual Meeting of the Association for Computational Linguistics*, pages 3960–3973, Online. Association for Computational Linguistics.

G. Gonzalez Hernandez Klein, A.Z.; A. Magge; K. O'Connor; J.I. Flores Amaro; D. Weissenbacher. 2021. Toward using twitter for tracking covid-19: A natural language processing pipeline and exploratory data set. *Journal of medical Internet research*, 23.

Elena Kochkina, Tamanna Hossain, Robert L. Logan, Miguel Arana-Catania, Rob Procter, Arkaitz Zubiaga, Sameer Singh, Yulan He, and Maria Liakata. 2023. Evaluating the generalisability of neural rumour verification models. *Information Processing Management*, 60(1):103116.

Arjun Magge, Ari Klein, Antonio Miranda-Escalada, Mohammed Ali Al-Garadi, Ilseyar Alimova, Zulfat Miftahutdinov, Eulalia Farre, Salvador Lima López, Ivan Flores, Karen O'Connor, Davy Weissenbacher, Elena Tutubalina, Abeed Sarker, Juan Banda, Martin Krallinger, and Graciela Gonzalez-Hernandez. 2021. Overview of the sixth social media mining for health applications (#SMM4H) shared tasks at NAACL 2021. In *Proceedings of the Sixth Social Media Mining for Health (#SMM4H) Workshop and Shared Task*, pages 21–32, Mexico City, Mexico. Association for Computational Linguistics.

Atul Kr. Ojha, Chao-Hong Liu, Katharina Kann, John Ortega, Sheetal Shatam, and Theodorus Fransen. 2021. Findings of the LoResMT 2021 shared task on COVID and sign language for low-resource languages. In *Proceedings of the 4th Workshop on Technologies for MT of Low Resource Languages (LoResMT2021)*, pages 114–123, Virtual. Association for Machine Translation in the Americas.

Nils Reimers and Iryna Gurevych. 2020. Making monolingual sentence embeddings multilingual using knowledge distillation. In *Proceedings of the 2020 Conference on Empirical Methods in Natural Language Processing (EMNLP)*, pages 4512–4525, Online. Association for Computational Linguistics.

News UN. 13 April 2020. During this coronavirus pandemic, 'fake news' is putting lives at risk: Unesco.

Department of Economic United Nations and Social Affairs. 2020. Indigenous peoples and the covid-19 pandemic: considerations.

Davy Weissenbacher, Abeed Sarker, Ari Klein, Karen O'Connor, Arjun Magge, and Graciela Gonzalez-Hernandez. 2019. Deep neural networks ensemble for detecting medication mentions in tweets. *Journal of the American Medical Informatics Association*, 26(12):1618–1626.

Neural Machine Translation through Active Learning on low-resource languages: The case of Spanish to Mapudungun

María Begoña Pendas
National Center for Artificial Intelligence, Santiago, Chile

Andrés Carvallo
National Center for Artificial Intelligence, Santiago, Chile

Carlos Aspillaga
National Center for Artificial Intelligence, Santiago, Chile

Abstract

Active learning is an algorithmic approach that strategically selects a subset of examples for labeling, with the goal of reducing workload and required resources. Previous research has applied active learning to Neural Machine Translation (NMT) for high-resource or well-represented languages, achieving significant reductions in manual labor. In this study, we explore the application of active learning for NMT in the context of Mapudungun, a low-resource language spoken by the Mapuche community in South America. Mapudungun was chosen due to the limited number of fluent speakers and the pressing need to provide access to content predominantly available in widely represented languages. We assess both model-dependent and model-agnostic active learning strategies for NMT between Spanish and Mapudungun in both directions, demonstrating that we can achieve over 40% reduction in manual translation workload in both cases.

1 Introduction

Over the course of history, South America has been home to numerous indigenous cultures and languages (Campbell et al., 2012), reflecting the region's rich linguistic diversity and heritage. Unfortunately, the dominance of the Spanish language in this region has threatened many indigenous languages, often leading to their decline or even extinction. This has resulted in an immeasurable cultural and historical loss for humanity, as language diversity vanishes (Ostler, 1999). Among the last remaining native languages is *Mapudungun*, spoken in Chile and Argentina by nearly 1.8 million people (Mapuches), but only 10% of them handle the language correctly and barely another 10% understand it. In the same spirit, the Conadi Indigenous Languages Program[1] predicts that this language will become extinct in a few generations, mainly due to the lack of individuals that can speak this language. Despite this, there are still groups within Chile that only speak *Mapudungun*, leaving them sometimes excluded from the rest of society. Furthermore, the social tension over the past few years has raised native indigenous people to the forefront of discussion, attracting high interest in the community to find ways to include them in society as equals. Unfortunately, the availability of human translators fluent in those languages is minimal, and no automated translators exist today supporting those languages. In this work, we present an active learning setting to improve the efficiency and efficacy of machine translation for low-resource languages, in this case, *Mapudungun*. In other words, we aim to reduce the effort made by human translators given that the quantity of people fluent in *Mapudungun* is scarce. Given this, the task of translating and reviewing large amounts of text is unattainable. One of the main tasks of active learning is choosing the appropriate data points (texts) to be translated by human translators to train a neural machine translation (NMT) model with as few examples as possible. To evaluate our approach, we utilized an open-source corpus from the AVENUE project (Levin et al., 2000) and supplemented it by scraping the web for Spanish-Mapudungun sentence pairs. We assembled a dataset of approximately 30,000 pairs, creating a comprehensive corpus for our research. We simulate an offline active learning setting to measure the amount of work that can be reduced by using different active learning strategies. The main contributions of this paper are: (1) Proposing active learning training strategies to reduce low-resource language speaker translators workload by more than 40%, (2) Finetuning a *Mapudungun* NMT model capable of obtaining competitive results and (3) Sharing our code for research reproducibility[2].

[1] https://www.conadi.gob.cl/noticias/conadi-lanzo-aplicaciones-y-realizara-cursos-online-de-mapuzungun-para-que-miles-de-indigenas-aprend

[2] https://github.com/OpenCENIA/al4mt

Proceedings of the Workshop on Natural Language Processing for Indigenous Languages of the Americas (AmericasNLP), pages 6–11
July 14, 2023

2 Related work

Active learning

Active learning is an effective machine learning training approach where the algorithm actively selects informative data to learn from, resulting in improved performance with fewer labeled instances (Settles, 2009). While initially applied to text classification, information retrieval, classification, and regression tasks (Tong and Koller, 2001; Zhang and Chen, 2002; Carvallo et al., 2020; Carvallo and Parra, 2019; Houlsby et al., 2011), active learning has recently been extended to tasks such as Named Entity Recognition, Text Summarization, and Machine Translation (Shen et al., 2017; Zhang and Fung, 2012; Zhao et al., 2020; Zhang et al., 2018). This study investigates unexplored potential of active learning in machine translation for untranslated examples in Mapudungun, a low-resource language.

Machine translation for low-resource languages

Efforts to overcome resource scarcity in low-resource language translation have proposed pretraining strategies for data generation and performance improvement. Methods include cross-lingual language model pretraining on high-resource languages data, then finetuning on low-resource languages (Zheng et al., 2021), multilingual sequence-to-sequence pretraining (Song et al., 2019; Xue et al., 2020; Liu et al., 2020), dictionary and monolingual data augmentation (Reid et al., 2021), and back-translation data augmentation (Sugiyama and Yoshinaga, 2019). However, these strategies lack human-in-the-loop components and don't guarantee human approval of the model's iterative translations under active learning.

Data selection in NMT

The data selection problem in NMT has received attention from several authors. Some propose weighted sampling methods to improve performance and accelerate training (Van Der Wees et al., 2017; Wang et al., 2018a), while others focus on filtering noisy data (Wang et al., 2018b; Pham et al., 2018) or selecting domain-specific data for back-translation (Fadaee and Monz, 2018; Poncelas et al., 2023; Dou et al., 2020). Furthermore, Wang et al proposed a method to select relevant sentences from other languages to enhance low-resource NMT performance (Wang and Neubig, 2019). As in using data augmentation the task of selecting data for training a NMT model do not include a user in the feedback loop.

3 Methodology

In this section we describe in detail the active learning framework proposed for NMT on low-resource languages and the type of active learning strategies depending if there is or not a machine learning model involved in the selection of examples for being labeled. In Figure 1, we show the active learning setting used in this work. In the first step, we initialize an NMT model, then given a monolingual corpus in Spanish and an active learning strategy, it chooses examples for being translated by an oracle to *Mapudungun*. After obtaining the translated sentences, we fine-tune the NMT model, update its parameters, and then use this updated version to select new sentences for labeling. We use four active learning strategies to select sentences for an oracle's translation: entropy sampling, margin sampling, confidence sampling, and decay logarithm frequency. The strategies chosen are pertinent to both Spanish to Mapudungun and Mapudungun to Spanish translations in low-resource scenarios. They address key issues such as uncertainty, data diversity, and model reliance, thus optimizing translation models and aiding language preservation. The strategy's reliance on the model varies; model-agnostic strategies don't need it for selecting sentences, while model-related ones use its certainty level. The number of active learning iterations and oracle translation requests is user-determined at the start of training.

3.1 Model-related strategies

These strategies use the model to choose the examples for being labeled and rely on the model's confidence level in untranslated examples.

Entropy sampling

In this strategy we consider entropy as a measure of uncertainty, where the higher entropy indicates higher uncertainty and more chaos. Therefore this strategy consists in sampling examples with higher average entropy given by equation 1.

$$\frac{1}{m}\sum_{i=1}^{m} entropy(P_\theta(.|x, \hat{y}_{<i}) \quad (1)$$

Minimum margin sampling

This strategy calculates the average probability gap between the model's most confident word ($y^*_{i,1}$)

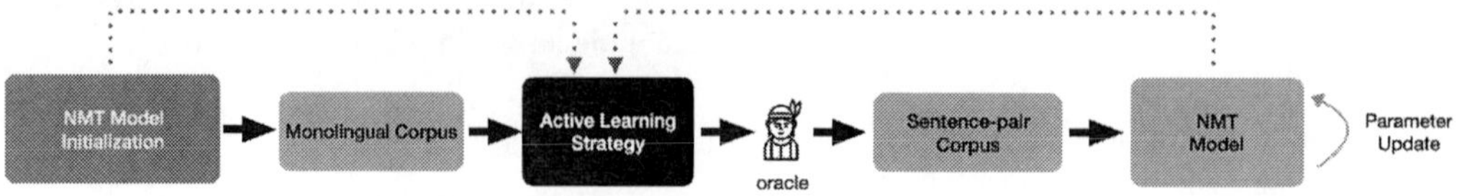

Figure 1: Illustration of the active learning approach.

and the second most confident word ($y^*_{i,2}$). If the margin is small, the model cannot identify the best translation from an inferior one, so we sample sentences with a lower margin as shown in the equation 2.

$$\frac{1}{m}\sum_{i=1}^{m}[P_\theta(y^*_{i,1}|x,\hat{y}_{<i}) - P_\theta(y^*_{i,2}|x,\hat{y}_{<i})] \quad (2)$$

Least Confidence sampling

This strategy estimates the model uncertainty by averaging the predicted probability of each word the translator generates. We sample those sentences with a lower level of confidence to force the model to learn harder sentences, as shown in equation 3.

$$\frac{1}{m}\sum_{i=1}^{m}[1 - P_\theta(\hat{y}_i|x,y_{<i})] \quad (3)$$

3.2 Model-agnostic strategy

In this case, we use the decay logarithm frequency strategy (Zhao et al., 2020) that does not require a NMT model to choose examples for being labeled by an oracle. The intuition behind this strategy is to choose sentences different from the ones that have already been translated in terms of linguistic features.

Decay logarithm frequency

We define two sets of sentences: U that are untranslated and L translated sentences on the current active learning iteration. In the first step, we define the logarithm frequency of a word w in U, namely $F(w|U)$ shown in equations 4 and 5.

$$G(w|U) = log(C(w|U) + 1) \quad (4)$$

$$F(w|U) = \frac{G(w|U)}{\sum_{w' \in U} G(w'|U)} \quad (5)$$

Where $C(w|.)$ measures the frequency of a word w in a given sentence set that can be U or L. Then we add a decay factor that favors the diversity of words and includes two hiper-parameters (λ_1 and λ_2) that allow giving more or less importance to words from the labeled (L) or the unlabeled sets (U). Also, we normalize by dividing the obtained score over the sentence length (K).

$$fy(s) = \frac{\sum_{i=1}^{K} F(s_i|U) \times e^{-\lambda_1 C(s_i|L)}}{K} \quad (6)$$

Equation 6 if used as threshold to obtain $\hat{U}(s)$ that is the set of all sentences that have a higher lf score than s. In this way, we tend to discard repetitive sentences and filter out insignificant function words. The obtention of the final delfy score is shown in equations 7 and 8.

$$delfy(s) = \frac{\sum_{i=1}^{K} F(s_i|U) \times Decay(s_i)}{K} \quad (7)$$

$$Decay(s_i) = e^{-\lambda_1 C(s_i|L)} \times e^{-\lambda_2 C(s_i|\hat{U}(s))} \quad (8)$$

4 Experiments

4.1 Dataset, preprocessing and NMT model

The dataset consists of 29,829 Spanish to *Mapudungun* sentence pairs considering only sentences length higher than five words, with 50,840 unique words in Spanish, 67,757 unique words in *Mapudungun*, and a vocabulary size of 118,597. We do not remove stopwords, lemmatization, or low-case texts, since we aim to capture both languages' peculiarities, including punctuation and idioms. We used a MarianMT (Junczys-Dowmunt et al., 2018) translation model based on a transformer architecture consisting of 12 encoder layers, 16 encoder attention heads, 12 decoder layers, and 16 attention heads. For training on active learning, we use a learning rate of 0.0002 and a weight decay of 0.01. We train the necessary epochs in each active training round until the validation perplexity remains the same. λ_1 and λ_2 in the delfy are set to 1.0 each. For training on active learning, we

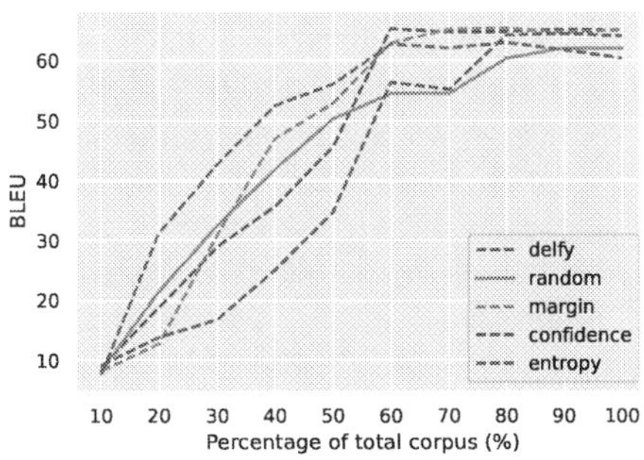

(a) ESP-MAPU

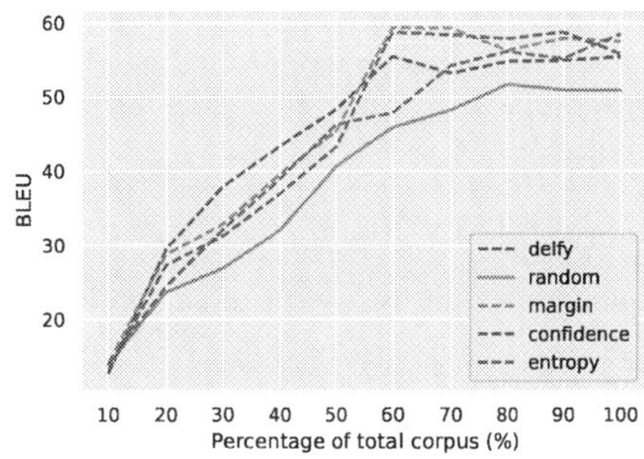

(b) MAPU-ESP

Figure 2: NTM models training on Active Learning. X-axis indicate the percentage of the corpus used to train each model choosing examples based on each active learning strategy. Y-axis indicates the BLEU score.

finetune a MarianMT translator from Spanish to Deutsch. Despite the apparent oddity of linking an Indo-European language, Deutsch with Mapudungun, our approach harnesses shared agglutinative traits to enhance translation.

4.2 Active Learning for NMT

Concerning the active learning setting, we run ten iterations using the 10% of the train set. For evaluating active learning strategies, we used the SacreBLEU[3] library and evaluated the model's outputs with BLEU (Papineni et al., 2002). As we run an offline experiment, we assume the oracle is continuously right, extracting the correct translation each time and adding those examples to the train set. In our offline experiment, we used existing labeled training data to eliminate the need for human annotators. Our goal was to assess which strategy efficiently utilizes a smaller data proportion, reducing manual translation effort while preserving model performance. This approach enables optimization of active learning strategies without added annotation costs.

4.3 Results

The results of this study suggest that for Spanish to *Mapudungun* translation, the most effective active learning strategy is Delfy, which achieved a BLEU score of 65.45 when trained on 60% of the corpus. Margin and entropy sampling were also effective strategies, achieving BLEU scores of 62.92 and 62.72, respectively. For *Mapudungun* to Spanish translation, margin sampling was the most effective active learning strategy, achieving a BLEU score of 59.378. Both settings showed benefits of training on active learning, with a reduction in the workload of approximately 40%. However, there is space for improvement in further reducing workload, as other studies on high-resource or well-represented languages have reduced over 80% (Zhao et al., 2020) of manual translation work. This work demonstrated significant progress in translating a low-resource language such as *Mapudungun*, with both active learning strategies outperforming the baseline strategy of random sampling.

5 Conclusion

In conclusion, this study revealed that Delfy was the most effective active learning strategy for Spanish to *Mapudungun* translation, while margin sampling outperformed in *Mapudungun* to Spanish. In both cases, training with active learning strategies reduced workload by over 40%. Our comparative analysis, driven by the diverse approaches of the chosen strategies, identifies the most efficient methods for low-resource translation tasks. This research is crucial for languages particularly *Mapudungun*, as it fosters information access and reduces language barriers for indigenous communities. Future work will focus on designing active learning strategies specifically for low-resource languages.

Acknowledgements

National Center for Artificial Intelligence CENIA FB210017, Basal ANID.

[3]https://github.com/mjpost/sacrebleu

References

Lyle Campbell, Verónica Grondona, and HH Hock. 2012. *The indigenous languages of South America*. de Gruyter.

Andres Carvallo and Denis Parra. 2019. Comparing word embeddings for document screening based on active learning. In *BIRNDL@ SIGIR*, pages 100–107.

Andres Carvallo, Denis Parra, Hans Lobel, and Alvaro Soto. 2020. Automatic document screening of medical literature using word and text embeddings in an active learning setting. *Scientometrics*, 125:3047–3084.

Zi-Yi Dou, Antonios Anastasopoulos, and Graham Neubig. 2020. Dynamic data selection and weighting for iterative back-translation. *arXiv preprint arXiv:2004.03672*.

Marzieh Fadaee and Christof Monz. 2018. Back-translation sampling by targeting difficult words in neural machine translation. *arXiv preprint arXiv:1808.09006*.

Neil Houlsby, Ferenc Huszár, Zoubin Ghahramani, and Máté Lengyel. 2011. Bayesian active learning for classification and preference learning. *arXiv preprint arXiv:1112.5745*.

Marcin Junczys-Dowmunt, Roman Grundkiewicz, Tomasz Dwojak, Hieu Hoang, Kenneth Heafield, Tom Neckermann, Frank Seide, Ulrich Germann, Alham Fikri Aji, Nikolay Bogoychev, et al. 2018. Marian: Fast neural machine translation in c++. *arXiv preprint arXiv:1804.00344*.

Lorraine Levin, Rodolfo M Vega, Jaime G Carbonell, Ralf D Brown, Alon Lavie, Eliseo Cañulef, and Carolina Huenchullan. 2000. Data collection and language technologies for mapudungun.

Yinhan Liu, Jiatao Gu, Naman Goyal, Xian Li, Sergey Edunov, Marjan Ghazvininejad, Mike Lewis, and Luke Zettlemoyer. 2020. Multilingual denoising pre-training for neural machine translation. *Transactions of the Association for Computational Linguistics*, 8:726–742.

Rosemarie Ostler. 1999. Disappearing languages. *The Futurist*, 33(7):16.

Kishore Papineni, Salim Roukos, Todd Ward, and Wei-Jing Zhu. 2002. Bleu: a method for automatic evaluation of machine translation. In *Proceedings of the 40th annual meeting of the Association for Computational Linguistics*, pages 311–318.

Minh Quang Pham, Josep M Crego, Jean Senellart, and François Yvon. 2018. Fixing translation divergences in parallel corpora for neural mt. In *Proceedings of the 2018 Conference on Empirical Methods in Natural Language Processing*, pages 2967–2973.

Alberto Poncelas, Gideon Maillette de Buy Wenniger, and Andy Way. 2023. Adaptation of machine translation models with back-translated data using transductive data selection methods. In *Computational Linguistics and Intelligent Text Processing: 20th International Conference, CICLing 2019, La Rochelle, France, April 7–13, 2019, Revised Selected Papers, Part I*, pages 567–579. Springer.

Machel Reid, Junjie Hu, Graham Neubig, and Yutaka Matsuo. 2021. Afromt: Pretraining strategies and reproducible benchmarks for translation of 8 african languages. *arXiv preprint arXiv:2109.04715*.

Burr Settles. 2009. Active learning literature survey.

Yanyao Shen, Hyokun Yun, Zachary C Lipton, Yakov Kronrod, and Animashree Anandkumar. 2017. Deep active learning for named entity recognition. *arXiv preprint arXiv:1707.05928*.

Kaitao Song, Xu Tan, Tao Qin, Jianfeng Lu, and Tie-Yan Liu. 2019. Mass: Masked sequence to sequence pre-training for language generation. *arXiv preprint arXiv:1905.02450*.

Amane Sugiyama and Naoki Yoshinaga. 2019. Data augmentation using back-translation for context-aware neural machine translation. In *Proceedings of the Fourth Workshop on Discourse in Machine Translation (DiscoMT 2019)*, pages 35–44.

Simon Tong and Daphne Koller. 2001. Support vector machine active learning with applications to text classification. *Journal of machine learning research*, 2(Nov):45–66.

Marlies Van Der Wees, Arianna Bisazza, and Christof Monz. 2017. Dynamic data selection for neural machine translation. *arXiv preprint arXiv:1708.00712*.

Rui Wang, Masao Utiyama, and Eiichiro Sumita. 2018a. Dynamic sentence sampling for efficient training of neural machine translation. *arXiv preprint arXiv:1805.00178*.

Wei Wang, Taro Watanabe, Macduff Hughes, Tetsuji Nakagawa, and Ciprian Chelba. 2018b. Denoising neural machine translation training with trusted data and online data selection. *arXiv preprint arXiv:1809.00068*.

Xinyi Wang and Graham Neubig. 2019. Target conditioned sampling: Optimizing data selection for multilingual neural machine translation. *arXiv preprint arXiv:1905.08212*.

Linting Xue, Noah Constant, Adam Roberts, Mihir Kale, Rami Al-Rfou, Aditya Siddhant, Aditya Barua, and Colin Raffel. 2020. mt5: A massively multilingual pre-trained text-to-text transformer. *arXiv preprint arXiv:2010.11934*.

Cha Zhang and Tsuhan Chen. 2002. An active learning framework for content-based information retrieval. *IEEE transactions on multimedia*, 4(2):260–268.

Justin Jian Zhang and Pascale Fung. 2012. Active learning with semi-automatic annotation for extractive speech summarization. *ACM Transactions on Speech and Language Processing (TSLP)*, 8(4):1–25.

Pei Zhang, Xueying Xu, and Deyi Xiong. 2018. Active learning for neural machine translation. In *2018 International Conference on Asian Language Processing (IALP)*, pages 153–158. IEEE.

Yuekai Zhao, Haoran Zhang, Shuchang Zhou, and Zhihua Zhang. 2020. Active learning approaches to enhancing neural machine translation. In *Findings of the Association for Computational Linguistics: EMNLP 2020*, pages 1796–1806.

Francis Zheng, Machel Reid, Edison Marrese-Taylor, and Yutaka Matsuo. 2021. Low-resource machine translation using cross-lingual language model pretraining. In *Proceedings of the First Workshop on Natural Language Processing for Indigenous Languages of the Americas*, pages 234–240.

Understanding Native Language Identification for Brazilian Indigenous Languages

Paulo Cavalin, Pedro H. Domingues, Julio Nogima, Claudio Pinhanez
IBM Research
Rio de Janeiro, RJ, Brazil
pcavalin@br.ibm.com

Abstract

We investigate native language identification (LangID) for Brazilian Indigenous Languages (BILs), using the Bible as training data. Our research extends from previous work, by presenting two analyses on the generalization of Bible-based LangID in non-biblical data. First, with newly collected non-biblical datasets, we show that such a LangID can still provide quite reasonable accuracy in languages for which there are more established writing standards, such as Guarani Mbya and Kaigang, but there can be a quite drastic drop in accuracy depending on the language. Then, we applied the LangID on a large set of texts, about 13M sentences from the Portuguese Wikipedia, towards understanding the difficulty factors may come out of such task in practice. The main outcome is that the lack of handling other American indigenous languages can affect considerably the precision for BILs, suggesting the need of a joint effort with related languages from the Americas.

1 Introduction

Brazil is home to about 270 indigenous languages, referred to as Brazilian Indigenous Languages (BILs) hereafter. All of those language are endangered, spoken by at most 30 thousand people, and are quite understudied. Serious effort should be put onto creating resources and tools to help vitalize the culture of such underrepresented communities. The creation of AI tools, in special language models and applications such as language translators, next-word predictors, spell checkers, can be key for this endeavour, since all could be used as learning-aid tools.

One main issue in building AI tools for understudied languages, which is the case of BILs, is the lack of data. There is almost no data available in ready-to-use formats, such as parallel corpora and labelled datasets, even monolingual data is scarce. Finding data for such languages is very difficult, since documents are stored in varied repositories and there is no indexing in search engines for such languages.

Native language identification (LangID) represent of a crucial approach to help in the task of gathering and augmenting data for BILs and many other indigenous languages. Not only LangID can be helpful to mine data from the web, it can be used as a tool to validate data that is generated synthetically with back-translation or self-training (Feldman and Coto-Solano, 2020; He et al., 2020). Before putting a LangID system into practice, though, it is very important to have a clear understanding of its capabilities, such as the expected accuracy on unseen domains.

Apart from an evaluation of LangID with indigenous languages in isolation (Lima et al., 2021), or the addition of some language in a publicly-available LangID dataset (Brown, 2014), in both cases with only Bible data, the potential of LangID for BILs in non-biblical, open-world data is quite understudied. That, again, owns to the lack of data, since the only source of data available to build a LangID for BILs is the Bible. And that is quite limiting in terms of understanding of the usefulness of a LangID for BILs in varied domains.

In this work we focus on expanding the horizons on a LangID for BILs, and present a deeper investigation on the quality and practical issues of Bible data for LangID on such languages. For that, we collected and appended 1.5M sentences from 51 BILs to the existing WiLi2018 LangID dataset, with 235 languages (Thoma, 2018), to train a machine learning-based LangID approach, and test it on different scenarios. We focused on answering two main research questions: **RQ1)** what is the level of accuracy achieved by this Bible-based LangID on a sample of out-of-domain, non-biblical data sets? and **RQ2)** if we apply this LangID on a large set of texts in the wild, what are the main difficulty factors?

Proceedings of the Workshop on Natural Language Processing for Indigenous Languages of the Americas (AmericasNLP), pages 12–18
July 14, 2023 ©2023 Association for Computational Linguistics

For LangID, we implemented an approach considering bag-of-words on tokens computed with SentencePiece, and Support Vector Machines (SVMs) as the classifier. Results show an accuracy of 73.3% and 95.1% for BILs and non-BIL languages, respectively. To answer RQ1, we built a dataset with almost three thousand sentences, comprising seven monolingual dataset in six different BILs. The results indicate that our LangID classifier generalizes quite well to most languages, reaching up to about 90% accuracy. But we see also that there might be a drop to about 37% with Apurinã, for which writing standards are not quite well established. To answer RQ2, we applied our LangID on about 13.5M sentences extracted from the Portuguese Wikipedia. As much as 3,821 sentences were pointed out with a BIL as the most probable class, but most of them with very low probability scores, below 0.1. A further manual inspection showed a precision of 7% only, uncovering a fundamental issue that needs to be overcome in the future to improve the prediction of LangID in in-the-wild data, which the need to handle other american languages to reduce false positive hits.

2 A LangID Dataset for BILs

We built a dataset containing 51 BILs, with data extracted from the Bible. Although this covers only a sample of the total of about 270 existing BILs, according to the last comprehensive assessment of linguistic diversity in Brazil (IBGE, 2010)[1], this set represents about a third of the estimate of 90 languages that have established standards of writing (Diniz, 2007). Additionally, we expect that the results expand to languages that belong to same families and branches in which the BILs are organized (Storto, 2019; Rodrigues, 1986).

Besides the languages spoken solely in Brazil, we include languages that are mostly spoken outside of Brazil but with some speakers in the country, such as the version of Guarani spoken in Paraguay, and languages that are relatives to some BILs, such as the eastern and western versions of Guarani spoken in Bolivia.

For data splitting, the test set was composed of all sentences from the Matthews New Testament book, for which we tokenized all chapters with the NLTK sentence tokenizer. Then we perform the same procedure to create the training set, with all remaining books from the New Testament, and books from the Old Testament, when available. As a result, the total number of training samples is 1,330,457 samples, and 199,128 test examples. The average number of samples per language is of 26,087 for the training set, and 3,904 in the test set.

Additional details are presented in Appendix A.

3 The LangID Classifier for BILs

We developed a LangID system using a linear SVM classifier with Bag-of-words (BOW) features, relying on the SentencePiece tokenizer[2], with 100K tokens. Note that we have evaluated different configurations for vocabulary size and other classifiers, but found that the linear SVM with 100K tokens presented the highest mean accuracy in the two test sets available, i.e. one for the BILs and another from WiLi-2018. Detailed results are provided in Appendix B.

As the training set, we considered the concatenation of our Bible-based dataset for BILs and the WiLi-2018 dataset, which contains 235K samples, evenly distributed over the 235 languages in the dataset. The accuracy on those sets are, respectively, 73.3% and 95.1%. Notice that our LangID approach excels pretty well on the WiLi2018 test set, almost 5 percentage points better than the 89.42% accuracy reported in Thoma (2018). But the accuracy presented on the BILs test set is 22 percentage points lower, which we believe is related to the inherited difficulties of doing LangID for such languages.

4 Accuracy on non-biblical datasets

In order to validate the quality of the LangID system proposed in this work, and to answer RQ1, we performed an evaluation on non-biblical data. We built seven new datasets, comprising six different BILs, to measure the accuracy of LangID on domains that are quite unrelated to the training set. Furthermore, this analysis also helps understand if the orthography of the training samples match what is expected in unseen domains.

This data has been collected either from PDF files, available in repositories in the web, or from annotation efforts such as the Universal Dependencies Parsing (UDP). For the former, the task basically consisted of cleaning up any annotation and generating a file only with the sentences in the corresponding BIL. But for the PDFs, we had to

[1]There is some discussion about the accuracy of those numbers, see Franchetto (2020); Storto (2019).

[2]https://github.com/google/sentencepiece

Table 1: Results on out-of-domain, non-biblical datasets.

Language	Source	#sent	Acc(%)
gun	Books	1,400	88.2
gun	Tales	1,022	88.8
myu	UDP	157	91.7
kgp	Books	146	81.8
urb	UDP	83	72.3
apu	UDP	59	37.3
xav	UDP	20	75.0
mean		412.4	76.4

either copy and paste the contents in the PDF to text files, or even retype the content given the lack of standard in encoding for such languages and the lack of standard for PDFs files. In both cases, tough, manual inspection of the conversion results proved necessary to handle special characters such as some combinations of letters and accents that are not very usual in non-indigenous languages. Once the blocks of texts have been inspected and converted to a text file, we then applied a sentence tokenizer to split paragraphs into individual sentences. Finally, we filtered all sentences with less than three tokens, to avoid dealing with such very short sentences.

In Table 1, we present further details on each dataset, such as the language, the source, and the resulting number of sentences. Note that some datasets consist of groupings of different sources, such Books in gun and kgp, which are composed of sentences extracted from multiple school books in PDF formats, such as Dooley (1985), and Tales in gun, which comprises several PDF files containing short indigenous tales (Dooley, 1988a,b).

The accuracy rates, also presented in Table 1, show that the results vary greatly from language to language. For the datasets in Guarani Mbya (gun), our LangID approach was able to achieve an accuracy of 88.6% on average, which is quite higher than the 73.3% achieved on held-out bible data. And the approach was able to achieve accuracy as high as 91.7% on myu. For urb and xav, we observe accuracy that are comparable to what we found on bible data, i.e. 72.3% and 75%. And for apu, there is a significant drop to 37.3% . We suspect that such drop in accuracy is due to differences in orthography from what is in the Bible and what is in these test sets, but further inspection with linguists or native speakers is necessary to check this assumption. It is worth mentioning that gun and kgp have quite established written forms, and for those languages we do not see such a drastic drop in classification quality.

An additional evaluation was then performed to understand if the classification of BILs is affected by non-indigenous languages. For that, we checked which languages where misclassified the most with gun in the respective datasets for this language. In the Books dataset, from the 162 misclassifications, 63 (39%) were associated to languages belonging to the Tupi-guarani family, which is the same family of gun. From those 63 samples, 38 were detected as kgk, and 25 as gug. Similarly, in the Tales dataset, from the 118 errors, 78 (66%) were from Tupi-guarani family languages: 48 in kgk and 30 in gug. Thus, considering the high similarity of such languages from the Tupi family, it is likely that the results with gun can be improved with further development of the LangID classifier, in order to handle better the classification among these similar languages.

5 Bringing LangID closer to practice

Aiming at answering RQ2, we expanded the evaluation of the previous chapter to a large, unsupervised set. Our goal was to understand the main challenges in a scenario that is closer to practical application, which is applying our LangID on in-the-wild data, to mine for sentences written in one of the 51 BILs. For that, we considered about 13.5M sentences extracted from the Portuguese Wikipedia. Although that data presents limitations, since most pages are supposedly written in Portuguese and a totally open set such as Common Crawl represents better the real world, that is also an advantage since we can discard all sentences detected as Portuguese and manually inspect only the remaining smaller set. And the associated Wikipedia pages can be used as ground-truth for the results of the classifier.

This evaluation considered an exact total of 13,573,101 sentences, from which our proposed LangID was able to identify 3,821 sentences as one of the 51 BILs considered in this work. That corresponds to 0.03% of total sentences in the dataset. We observed, though, the very low prediction score for such detected sentences, with a mean of around 0.03, and decided to discarded all sentences with a prediction score below 0.1, resulting in a set of only 129 sentences. That is a quite small set, but this number was somewhat expected given the data in Portuguese. One the other hand, that allowed us to conduct a manual inspection on the results.

We manually inspected all of the detected 129 sentences, marking all sentences that 'looked like being correctly classified'. That is, we inspected the 129 sentences and marked all sentences that were written in a latin scripts, but with words that did not belong to any of the non-indigenous languages known by the authors, such as Portuguese, English, Spanish, German, and French, to name a few. With that approach, we found a total of 50 sentences that could likely be from a BIL. Then, for each of those 50 sentences, we searched for the original Wikipedia page of the sentence, by using its text as a query on Google, and inspected the resulting pages. The results were, on one hand, disappointing, since very few sentences were correctly classified. But on the other hand, they were quite useful in understanding some particular difficulties of this task, and how to approach this problem better in the future. Details are provided next.

The results were disappointing in the sense that very few sentences were correctly classified, i.e. very low precision. From the 50 sentences that we suspected were correct, only 9 sentences were extracted from a Wikipedia page that related to the actual predicted language. That gives a precision of only 7%. Besides, we uncovered that those nine sentences consisted of samples of the Lord's prayer, which is a content that is very close to what is in the training for such languages, so these results do not help in clarifying the potential of LangID in non-religious content.

Nevertheless, some interesting findings of this study consist of a better understanding of the main difficulties that we may face when applying LangID to mine data for BILs. One clear drawback of our proposed approach, is the limited handling of similar low-resource languages, such as indigenous languages from other South and North American countries besides Brazil. Most of the classification mistakes involved Wikipedia entries of languages spoken in countries such as Peru, Colombia, Mexico, and the United States. Some other few mistakes involved languages from more distant locations, such as Indonesia and the African continent. These results show that, in order to perform accurate LangID for BILs, it is important to include as much languages as possible in the training set to have a more precise classification, or to implement some mechanism to deal with out-of-scope detection.

This evaluation also showed that searching for webpages using sentences in a target language as a query for a search engine can be helpful to find for additional data, such as PDFs with additional content such as the one found for the Amarakaeri language[3]. Even though Amarakaeri is not included in the set of BILs, with more accuracy in LangID, we could search for PDF documents is such languages with greater precision. Furthermore, we found that misclassifications can be useful to find content in additional related languages, such as the language Cocama[4], which is spoken in Brazil and belongs to the Tupi family, but was not included our set of BILs for LangID.

6 Conclusions and future work

In this paper we present an evaluation of LangID for Brazilian Indigenous Languages (BILs), using the Bible as the only source for training data. We demonstrate that on non-biblical, labeled datasets, the approach is able to achieve even accuracy in languages with more establised written forms, such as Guarani Mbya and Kaigang, but the performance may drop considerable for less studied languages. By applying the LangID classifier in an almost in-the-wild dataset, we saw that the precision is quite affected by related American indigenous languages that are not handled by our LangID approach, so a joint effort must be made to handle as much american languages as possible, together, to improve the quality of the LangID in practice.

As future work, we believe that expanding the LangID training set, to consider as much languages as possible, is mandatory. Furthermore, an inspection of the orthography of some languages should also be done, by partnering with linguists and/or native speakers. And we think that we could further develop the study in in-the-wild data, either by searching for BIL data on a more comprehensive dataset, such as Common Crawl[5] and BrWac[6], and by including the search for PDF documents, which is the most commonly used format containing data for such languages.

[3]https://www.ohchr.org/sites/default/files/UDHR/ Documents/UDHR_Translations/amr.pdf

[4]https://pt.wikipedia.org/wiki/Língua_cocama

[5]https://commoncrawl.org/

[6]https://www.inf.ufrgs.br/pln/wiki/index.php?title=BrWaC

Limitations

One limitation of this work is the lack of a more comprehensive study of LangID methods, which could impact slightly the results. Another limitation is the number of non-BIL languages, which can be increased to more than 1,000 languages with the datasets proposed in (Brown, 2014). Furthermore, the use of Wikipedia data limits the search of samples, since all pages are supposedly written in Portuguese. So, relying on a broader set can bring a more realistic estimate on the in-the-wild search for data. In addition, a major limitation of this work is the lack of inspection of the results with native speakers. We are already engaging with one mbya guarani community, but it is quite difficult to extend such engagement to other communities.

References

Ralf Brown. 2014. Non-linear mapping for improved identification of 1300+ languages. In *Proceedings of the 2014 Conference on Empirical Methods in Natural Language Processing (EMNLP)*, pages 627–632, Doha, Qatar. Association for Computational Linguistics.

Kollontai Cossich Diniz. 2007. Notas sobre tipografias para línguas indígenas do brasil. *InfoDesign: Revista Brasileira de Design da Informação*, 4(1).

Robert Dooley. 1985. Nhanhemboe aguã nhandeayvu py [1-5].

Robert Dooley. 1988a. Arquivo de textos indígenas – guaraní (dialeto mbyá) [1].

Robert Dooley. 1988b. Arquivo de textos indígenas – guaraní (dialeto mbyá) [2].

Isaac Feldman and Rolando Coto-Solano. 2020. Neural machine translation models with back-translation for the extremely low-resource indigenous language Bribri. In *Proceedings of the 28th International Conference on Computational Linguistics*, pages 3965–3976, Barcelona, Spain (Online). International Committee on Computational Linguistics.

Bruna Franchetto. 2020. Língua (s): cosmopolíticas, micropolíticas, macropolíticas. *Campos-Revista de Antropologia*, 21(1):21–36.

Junxian He, Jiatao Gu, Jiajun Shen, and Marc'Aurelio Ranzato. 2020. Revisiting self-training for neural sequence generation. In *8th International Conference on Learning Representations, ICLR 2020, Addis Ababa, Ethiopia, April 26-30, 2020*. OpenReview.net.

IBGE. 2010. Censo demográfico 2010. Accessed = 2022-12-30.

Tiago Lima, André Nascimento, Pericles Miranda, and Rafael Mello. 2021. Analysis of a brazilian indigenous corpus using machine learning methods. In *Anais do XVIII Encontro Nacional de Inteligência Artificial e Computacional*, pages 118–129, Porto Alegre, RS, Brasil. SBC.

Aryon Dall'Igna Rodrigues. 1986. *Línguas brasileiras: para o conhecimento das línguas indígenas*. Edições Loyola.

Luciana Raccanello Storto. 2019. *Línguas indígenas: tradição, universais e diversidade*. Mercado de Letras.

Martin Thoma. 2018. The wili benchmark dataset for written language identification. *CoRR*, abs/1801.07779.

A Details on languages and datasets

In Table 2 we present the full list of Brazilian Indigenous Languages (BILs) considered for this work, with the corresponding ISO 639 codes, their geo-linguistc classification in terms of branches and families, the estimated number of speakers, and the number of samples for training and test sets.

B Detailed results on classifier evaluation

In Table 3 we present the detailed accuracy on each methods and dataset evaluated in this work. In terms of classifier, we evaluated two approaches: Logistic Regression and Support Vectors Machines (SVMs). For feature extraction, we evaluate the use of bag of words (BoW) and corpus-based vocabulary extraction with SentencePiece (SP), with varied number of tokens: 10K, 50K, 100K, and 250K.

Table 2: Details on the indigenous languages and datasets used in the study.

Languages					# Aligned Sentences		
Name	**Acron**	**Branch**	**Family**	**Speakers**	**Train**	**Test**	**Total**
Apalaí	apy	No Branch	Karib	252	27,763	4,401	32,164
Apinayé	apn	Macro Jê	Jê	1,386	28,069	4,354	32,423
Apurinã	apu	No Branch	Aruak	824	28,629	4,403	33,032
Ashaninka	cni	No Branch	Aruak	302	19,564	2,943	22,507
Bakairí	bkq	No Branch	Karib	173	27,314	4,206	31,520
Boróro	bor	Macro Jê	Boróro	1,035	32,392	5,206	37,598
Desána	des	No Branch	Tukano	95	26,115	4,019	30,134
Guajajára	gub	Tupi	Tupi-Guarani	8,269	33,188	4,818	38,006
Guarani Eastern Bolivia	gui	Tupi	Tupi-Guarani	NA	22,681	3,342	26,023
Guarani Kaiowá	kgk	Tupi	Tupi-Guarani	24,368	31,523	4,711	36,234
Guarani Mbya	gun	Tupi	Tupi-Guarani	3,248	18,245	2,857	21,102
Guarani Paraguay	gug	Tupi	Tupi-Guarani	2,464	16,891	2,841	19,732
Guarani Western Bolivia	gnw	Tupi	Tupi-Guarani	NA	22,281	3,264	25,545
Hixkaryána	hix	No Branch	Karib	52	37,893	5,797	43,690
Jamamadí-Kanamanti	jaa	No Branch	Arawá	217	21,169	3,121	24,290
Ka'apor	urb	Tupi	Tupi-Guarani	1,241	44,969	6,678	51,647
Kadiwéu	kcb	No Branch	Guaikurú	649	19,773	3,020	22,793
Kaiabi	kyz	Tupi	Tupi-Guarani	673	36,118	5,145	41,263
Kaingáng	kgp	Macro Jê	Jê	19,905	27,778	4,070	31,848
Kanela	ram	Macro Jê	Jê	488	18,342	731	19,073
Karajá	kpj	Macro Jê	Karajá	3,119	22,721	3,646	26,367
Kaxinawá	cbs	No Branch	Pano	3,588	14,590	2,099	16,689
Kayapó	txu	Macro Jê	Jê	5,520	34,066	5,631	39,697
Kubeo	cub	No Branch	Tukano	171	25,216	3,650	28,866
Kulina Madijá	cul	No Branch	Arawá	3,043	27,744	4,318	32,062
Makúna	myy	No Branch	Tukano	6	27,568	4,000	31,568
Makuxí	mbc	No Branch	Karib	4,675	26,942	4,199	31,141
Matsés	mcf	No Branch	Pano	1,144	23,754	3,772	27,526
Mawé	mav	Tupi	Mawé	8,103	27,034	3,035	30,069
Maxakali	mbl	Macro Jê	Maxakali	1,024	20,663	3,045	23,708
Mundurukú	myu	Tupi	Mundurukú	3,563	32,880	5,146	38,026
Nadëb	mbj	No Branch	Makú	326	24,653	3,821	28,474
Nambikwára	nab	No Branch	Nambikwára	951	29,089	4,377	33,466
Nheengatu	yrl	Tupi	Tupi-Guarani	3,771	15,236	2,321	17,557
Palikúr	plu	No Branch	Aruak	925	28,322	4,228	32,550
Paresí	pab	No Branch	Aruak	122	20,759	3,043	23,802
Paumarí	pad	No Branch	Arawá	166	30,389	4,550	34,939
Piratapúya	pir	No Branch	Tukano	81	25,721	4,030	29,751
Rikbaktsa	rkb	Macro Jê	Rikbaktsa	10	35,777	4,841	40,618
Sanumá	xsu	No Branch	Yanomámi	1,788	25,118	3,749	28,867
Siriáno	sri	No Branch	Tukano	2	24,247	3,626	27,873
Tenharim	pah	Tupi	Tupi-Guarani	32	30,277	5,145	35,422
Teréna	ter	No Branch	Aruak	6,314	20,713	3,170	23,883
Tikúna	tca	No Branch	No Family	30,057	20,101	3,218	23,319
Tukáno	tuo	No Branch	Tukano	4,412	26,826	3,952	30,778
Tuyúca	tue	No Branch	Tukano	263	23,973	3,572	27,545
Wanana	gvc	No Branch	Tukano	236	25,487	3,983	29,470
Wapishana	wap	No Branch	Aruak	3,154	20,561	2,930	23,491
Xavante	xav	Macro Jê	Jê	11,733	24,714	3,737	28,451
Yamináwa	yaa	No Branch	Pano	222	24,808	3,680	28,488
Yanomámi	guu	No Branch	Yanomámi	12,301	29,811	4,687	34,498
TOTAL				**176,463**	**1,330,457**	**199,128**	**1,529,585**

Table 3: Detailed results considering different classifiers and feature extraction methods.

		Classifier									
		Logistic Regression					Support Vector Machine				
		BoW	SP10K	SP50K	SP100K	SP250K	BoW	SP10K	SP50K	SP100K	SP250K
Test set	WiLi2018	73.87	93.13	92.30	91.37	89.70	89.45	94.15	94.94	95.07	94.63
	Bibles-BILs	69.59	72.81	72.31	71.96	71.47	72.85	73.18	73.19	73.28	73.14
	mean	71.73	82.97	82.31	81.67	80.59	81.15	83.67	84.07	**84.18**	83.89
	gun Books	71.01	86.67	86.51	85.73	86.06	82.21	89.10	89.25	88.20	89.32
	gun Tales	82.19	83.95	83.66	82.88	83.76	86.20	89.53	90.12	88.85	88.65
	myu UDP	73.97	95.54	91.08	89.81	90.45	87.67	96.18	91.72	91.72	91.08
	kgp Books	73.55	81.25	73.43	70.63	69.23	84.30	89.58	86.01	81.82	81.82
	urb UDP	43.84	60.24	61.45	59.04	62.65	63.01	65.06	74.70	72.29	72.29
	apu UDP	14.29	28.81	33.90	28.81	32.20	25.00	25.42	33.90	37.29	45.76
	xav UDP	47.37	75.00	75.00	60.00	50.00	63.16	75.00	70.00	75.00	18.75
	mean	58.03	73.07	72.15	68.13	67.76	70.22	75.70	76.53	76.45	69.67

Codex to corpus: Exploring annotation and processing for an open and extensible machine-readable edition of the Florentine Codex

Francis M. Tyers
Department of Linguistics
Indiana University
Bloomington, IN 47401
ftyers@iu.edu

Robert Pugh
Department of Linguistics
Indiana University
Bloomington, IN 47401
pughrob@iu.edu

Valery A. Berthoud F.
Department of Philosophy
Humboldt-Universität zu Berlin
Unter den Linden 6, Berlin 10099
valeryberthoud@gmail.com

Abstract

This paper describes an ongoing effort to create, from the original hand-written text, a machine-readable, linguistically-annotated, and easily-searchable corpus of the Nahuatl portion of the Florentine Codex, a 16th century Mesoamerican manuscript written in Nahuatl and Spanish. The Codex consists of 12 books and over 300,000 tokens. We describe the process of annotating 3 of these books, the steps of text preprocessing undertaken, our approach to efficient manual processing and annotation, and some of the challenges faced along the way. We also report on a set of experiments evaluating our ability to automate the text processing tasks to aid in the remaining annotation effort, and find the results promising despite the relatively low volume of training data. Finally, we briefly present a real use case from the humanities that would benefit from the searchable, linguistically annotated corpus we describe.

1 Introduction

The Nahuatl language, an agglutinating and polysynthetic member of the Uto-Aztecan family spoken throughout Mexico by about 1.5 million people today, has a rich literary tradition (Gingerich, 1975; León-Portilla, 1985). With a strong preconquest oral tradition and a hieroglyphic writing system, Nahuatl speakers quickly adopted the Latin alphabet for writing their language after its introduction almost immediately after the Spanish invasion. As a result, the volume of the colonial-era Nahuatl literary canon is unrivalled in Latin America (Olko and Sullivan, 2013). These texts are invaluable resources to scholars interested in the history, culture, and language of colonial and pre-invasion Nahua communities.

Perhaps the most notable Nahuatl text of the early colonial period, the *Historia General de las Cosas de Nueva España* "General History of the Things of New Spain" (Florentine Codex, FC) is an encyclopaedic work in Nahuatl and Spanish compiled by Indigenous scholars from the Colegio de Santa Cruz de Tlatelolco and Franciscan friar Bernardino de Sahagún.

The FC is undoubtedly one of the most valuable manuscripts of the early modern period. However, it was forgotten for centuries until Angelo Maria Bandini described it in 1793. He named it "Codice Fiorentino" after the Biblioteca Medicea Laurenziana in Florence, where it is still kept. But only at the beginning of the 20th century did Francisco del Paso y Troncoso bring it to a wider audience (Martínez, 1982). Charles Dibble and Arthur Anderson published a translation of the books into English throughout the second half of the 20th century. The original manuscript became available in the World Digital Library only ten years ago, thanks to the Library of Congress.

The impetus for the present project was the need of the third author, a humanities scholar, to search the text of the FC for specific linguistic constructions and terminology. This proposition is complicated by a number of factors:

First, there are few fully digitised versions of the FC, and those that do exist are under copyright, constraining the ability of a scholar to reproduce, annotate, and/or re-release any part of the text that results from a given research endeavour.

Second, the FC, having multiple authors and being written in the early years of Nahuatl alphabetic writing, contains numerous orthographic inconsistencies throughout the 12 books, with many words written in multiple distinct ways and decisions about word tokenisation not being standardised. Furthermore, due to constraints on column width in the original manuscript, words are frequently split by line breaks with no indication of whether the following line continues the word from the end of the previous one. Keyword searching this text is a seemingly-futile process involving determining all possible spellings for a given word and all possible tokenisations of a single syntactic

Proceedings of the Workshop on Natural Language Processing for Indigenous Languages of the Americas (AmericasNLP), pages 19–29
July 14, 2023

```
fo. 1

Jc macujlli amuxtli, vncan mo
teneoa: intetzaujtl catca, inqujte
tzammatia, in iehoantin mexica.

Jc ce capitulo, vncan mitoa, inte
tzaujtl inqujtetzammatia: iniquac
ioaltica, aca quicaquja: in chocaia:
itla tequanj, inanoce, iuhquj aca
ilamachocaia: auh iequene, intlejn
qujtoaia, tonalpouhque: in mjtova
ia tlamatinjme catca.

I nievecauh, inoc tlateo
toco: injuh quitoa, ce
qujntin veuetque, ve
ue tlaca: inoc titixca
vitoque, inoc titomattoque, inoc to
tlalpan tiqujtoaia: inaia aque tech
nelotoque: inaiaque totlah onoque,
Yzqujtlamantli, y, in quj tetzamma
tia, inquitetzaujttaia, in tetzaujtl ipan
quimatia innetetzaujloia, in tlatetza
ujaia.

Jnic centlamantli, iehoatl, iniquac
aca quicaquia: in tequanj choca, te
quanj ipan choca: injuhquj tecciztli
qujpitza: tepetl qujnanqujlia: teh
cuiooa, tlaoalanja: iuhqujn ilama
pul choca. Ynjn, qujtovaia ie iaomj
qujz: anoço  ie mjqujz, tlalmiqujz:
anoço , ie itla com monamjctiz, ic
```

Figure 1: On the left: first folio of Book 5 of the Florentine Codex "The Omens". The first paragraph translates as "Fifth book, where are told the omens, which the Mexicans believed". On the right: The transcription of the left-hand column of the folio. [Image credit: Library of Congress]

word into multiple orthographic words.

Finally, Nahuatl is a morphologically complex language with large amounts of inflection and derivation, making querying the surface/inflected form, instead of e.g., a lemma, particularly difficult.

The present project attempts to address these issues by creating an open-source, retokenised, and normalised corpus of the FC with queryable linguistic annotations following the Universal Dependencies framework (Nivre et al., 2020a). In the following sections, we describe the corpus, each component involved in its creation, and an investigation into automating the processing. We conclude by outlining a road map for the project's completion and a vision of future applications.

2 Related work

The FC has been the subject of a great deal of research in the humanities by scholars interested in the cultural beliefs and practices of the Nahua people during the early colonial period (Sullivan et al., 1966; Gingerich, 1988; Sigal, 2007; McDonough, 2020; Olivier, 2021). It has also served as a foundational component for work studying so-called "Classical Nahuatl," or Nahuatl spoken during the period (Launey, 1986; Lockhart, 1992, 2001). Both Olko et al. (2015) and Olko (2018) leverage corpus-based approaches using a multitude of historical Nahuatl documents, but it is unclear how much linguistic information was available in the corpus, and to our knowledge, this corpus has not been released to the public.

Gutierrez-Vasques et al. (2016) released *Axolotl*, a large, Spanish-Nahuatl parallel corpus with a focus on machine translation. It includes Nahuatl from multiple variants and time periods, including the early colonial period, but does not include text from the FC. Furthermore, the text in *Axolotl* is unprocessed and unannotated.

Other corpora that include Nahuatl texts include the Johns Hopkins University Bible Corpus (McCarthy et al., 2020), a parallel multilingual corpus that includes numerous contemporary Nahuatl variants. This corpus has been used to produce morphosyntactically-annotated resources for a large number of languages (Nicolai and Yarowsky, 2019; Nicolai et al., 2020).

The first open morphosyntactically-annotated corpus of Nahuatl was recently released by Pugh et al. (2022) and includes 10,000 tokens of the Western Sierra Puebla variety. Following this work, we also select UD as our annotation schema.

Marc Eisinger was the first to publish a computerised version of the FC, which is not freely available (Eisinger, 1977). The Universidad Autónoma de México (UNAM) hosts a website, *Temoa*, containing a large volume of digitised colonial-era Nahuatl texts, with minimal processing (at the very least, tokenisation problems in the FC appear to be corrected (Universidad Nacional Autónoma de México, 2023). However, the copyright and rights to use for annotation and re-release are retained by UNAM,[1] making it not possible to create derivative works, such as the annotated corpus described in this paper. Furthermore, the original text (before fixing tokenisation) is not available.

Related to the computational processing of colonial Mexican texts, The "Digging into colonial Mexico" project (Murrieta-Flores et al., 2022) involves the creation of a number of processed and machine-readable resources based on colonial Mexican documents, mostly written in colonial-era Mexican Spanish. As for colonial texts written in Mexican languages, the Ticha project (Broadwell et al., 2020), a collaboration between members of Zapotec-speaking communities and academics from universities in the United States of America, offers an "online digital text explorer" for colonial Zapotec texts and includes morphological analyses and translations.

3 Corpus

Our corpus comes from a typed transcription upholding the original layout, published in the open-access repository Zenodo[2] to allow the semantic and computational study of the text from the primary source (de Sahagún, 2022). In Figure 1 we present a folio from the manuscript where the text in Spanish (left) and Nahuatl (right) is seen in two columns, and an example of the transcription output in our corpus.

3.1 Orthography

There is a great deal of orthographic variation in the FC, in both the Nahuatl and Spanish sections, with multiple characters used inconsistently throughout. For example, the letter [v] can represent either /w/, e.g. *veue* /wewe/ 'big' (norm. *huehue*), or a long /oː/, e.g. *vmpa* /oːmpa/ 'there' (norm. *ompa*). [j] is used both for the vowel /i/ e.g., *jnpilhoan* /inpilwaːn/ 'their (pl) children' (norm. *inpilhuan*) and the glide /j/, e.g. *jollochicaoac* /joloːtʃikaːwak/ 'brave' (norm. *yollochicahuac*). The letter [i] is also observed in both of these contexts.

There are also instances where a single sound, e.g. /ʃ/ can be represented by multiple letters, in this case [x] or [s]. For example, the word *axcan* /aːʃkaːn/ 'now, today' can appear as *ascan* or *axcan*. But [s] can also be the voiceless alveolar sibilant /s/ in loan words from Spanish *visorrej* /bisorei/ 'viceroy' (norm. *visorrey*).

4 Processing

A major theme of the processing of the FC is the use of initial detailed hand-annotation in order to bootstrap automated approaches for the remaining text. Crucially, the resulting corpus should be usable for academic research and, as such, must maintain the utmost quality. In this context, then, we consider automation a strategy to assist in human annotation, but still require manual auditing of the entirety of the annotated corpus.

4.1 Sentence segmentation

Full stops (or in dialogue, exclamation marks, and question marks) are used as sentence boundaries throughout the corpus, with the colon symbol often used to separate clauses, making sentence segmentation fairly straightforward. There are a number of abbreviations, such as *xpo.* for Christ and *p.* for Pedro. Table 5 presents the size of each book in terms of sentences, space-separated tokens, and words. Words are only given for the three books we have processed so far.

4.2 Retokenisation

There are a number of tokenisation inconsistencies in the original manuscript, resulting from (1) physical constraints, namely the author running out of room on one line and splitting a word across a line boundary (see Figure 1), (2) inconsistent tokenisation practices by the authors, such as sometimes writing the article subordinator *in* and an adjacent verb together as a single orthographic word, and (3) possible mistakes introduced during the process of manually typing up the manuscript.

[1] https://temoa.iib.unam.mx/creditos

[2] https://zenodo.org/

Y·njqc·oiuh·ipan·muchiuh,	Yn·jqc·oiuh·ipan·muchiuh,	In ihcuac oyouh ipan mochiuh,
·y:·njman·ic·iauh,¶qujttaz·	·y:·njman·ic·iauh, qujttaz·	y: niman ic yauh, quittaz
intonalpouhquj:·vmpa·quella¶	in·tonalpouhquj:·vmpa·	in tonalpouhqui: ompa
quaoa,·qujtlapaloa:·qujlvia.¶	quellaquaoa,·qujtlapaloa:·qujlvia.	quellacuahua, quitlapaloa: quilhuia.

Table 1: A sentence from Book 5 of the FC, the sentence reads "When it happened, he went to see the reader of the day signs, there he encouraged and greeted him and said:" Note that the original tokens *Y·njqc* have been retokenised into *Yn jqc* 'when', the token *intonalpouhquj* has been split into two tokens *in·tonalpouhquj* 'the reader of the day signs' and the tokens *quella¶quaoa* which have been split by a newline have been joined into *quellaquaoa* 'he encouraged him'.

Our first step in processing the codex, after obtaining text files transcribed from the original manuscript, involves "retokenisation": altering the word boundaries in the text to align them with canonical Nahuatl words.[3] An example of the input and output of this process is shown in Table 1, wherein a space is represented by the mid-dot character, ·, and newline is represented by the pilcrow character, ¶.

As with the rest of the processing steps, retokenisation starts as a manual process. For each identified case where retokenisation is necessary, we use the left and right contexts to write a rule for handling that case, ensuring that the contexts are large enough to avoid potential ambiguities (for instance, a minimal-context rule such as "n·c →nc" will likely produce many false positive matches). In the event that a rule produces false positives, we expand its contexts (e.g., "qujn·caoa →qujncaoa"). We use a left-to-right longest-match (LRLM) algorithm to apply the approximately 4,000 retokenisation rules.

4.3 Normalisation

Once the text is correctly tokenised, the next processing step is orthographic normalisation. We use the ACK (Andrews, Campbell, Karttunen) orthographic standard for the target orthography, since it is designed to reflect colonial-era Nahuatl writing (Campbell and Karttunen, 1989; Andrews, 2003; Karttunen, 1992).

For Spanish words we use contemporary orthography, so for example, *gouernadores* is normalised to *gobernadores* 'governors.'

For proper nouns, we also use modern orthographic conventions where available. For example, *tlatilulco* is normalised to *Tlatelolco*, and *motecucoma* is normalised to *Moctezuma*.

The process uses a hand-curated dictionary mapping original word forms to their normalised counterparts (e.g. the normalised form *yaoyotl* 'war' is written variably as *iaoiotl*, *iauiotl*, *iaviotl*, *iaujutl* and *iaujotl*. Thus, our dictionary has an entry for each of these forms mapping to the normalised form). To build the dictionary, we start with a naïve finite-state transducer (FST) model designed using general patterns of colonial-era Nahuatl writing. We then post-edit the output of the FST, adding all correct word pairs to the dictionary. We update the FST weights as we add forms to the dictionary to improve its performance. After processing three books, the dictionary contains 6,515 entries.

The main motivation for performing the normalisation manually is to ensure a high-quality data set with which to train a model for automating the process. We discuss the evaluation of such an approach in §6.2.

4.4 Part-of-speech tagging

The part-of-speech tags are based on the Universal Part-of-Speech categories (UPOS) defined and used in the Universal Dependencies framework (Nivre et al., 2020b).

We accomplish part-of-speech tagging in three steps. We use a lexicon, a morphological analyser (see §4.5) and a set of ordered, regular-expression-based guessing rules applied to the normalised form, in sequence. We refer to this last component as 'the guesser.'

The lexicon is simply a list of normalised surface forms and their part of speech. Of the 10,959 types presently annotated for part-of-speech, 1,478 (6,916 tokens) received their POS from the lexicon.

In the event that a given surface form is not observed in the lexicon, we next run the word through the morphological analyser. This method accounts for 13,762 of the tokens thus far annotated (1,705 types).

[3]Following authoritative resources like Andrews (2003) and Campbell and Karttunen (1989) in identifying "canonical words", which should include subject, object, and aspectual affixes.

Finally, any word not identified in the previous two steps is passed to the guesser. The guesser consists of 36 rules which use regular expressions to look for particular prefixes and suffixes and assign part-of-speech tags with high precision. For example, words beginning with *nimitz-*, a combination of the first person subject marker and second person object marker are categorised as verbs, and words ending in *-tzitzin*, which is the plural reverential marker, are categorised as nouns. These rules are high precision, but low recall: a total of 986 forms out of 10,959 forms (1,471 tokens) in the three processed books receive guessed analyses.

We randomly sampled and manually checked 200 of these guesses and found that 198 were correct. In one case the mistake was due to a mistaken normalisation (*iehoatin* → **yehuatin* instead of *yehhuantin* 'they, them'), which resulted in the word being tagged as a noun due to the *-tin* 'PL' ending (plural). The second case was to do with the same plural rule, which resulted in the word *xixitin* 'it crumbled' (from the verb *xixintini* 'to crumble') being tagged as a noun.

4.5 Morphological analysis

Morphological analysis is the task of producing, for a given surface form, a lemma and a set of morphosyntactic tags describing that form. For example, given the form *tictlamacazque* /ti-c-tla-maca-z-que/ 'We will give something to him' (or 'We will make offerings to him') it would produce,

```
<s_pl1><i_sg3><o_nn3>maca<v><dv><fut>
```

Where <s_pl1> stands for 1st person plural subject, <i_sg3> stands for 3rd person singular secondary object, <o_nn3> stands for 3rd person inanimate indefinite object, <v> stands for verb, <dv> stands for ditransitive and <fut> stands for future. Note that there is a long distance dependency between the prefix *ti-*, which can be 2nd person singular or 1st person plural and the suffix *-que* which marks a plural subject.

A given token can produce more than one analysis, so for example, *quinchihua* 'They made them' or 'He made them' produces,

```
<s_pl3><o_pl3>chihua<v><tv><pres>
<s_sg3><o_pl3>chihua<v><tv><pres>
```

In this case, because of underspecification in the orthography, the plural subject-marking suffix *-h* is not written, resulting in an ambiguous analysis. The omission of this suffix is quite common in Nahuatl texts.

For implementing the morphological analyser we used the Helsinki Finite-State Toolkit (HFST) (Lindén et al., 2009). The analyser was implemented over the normalised forms. Morphotactics and the lexicon were implemented using `lexc`, while any morphographemic constraints were implemented with `twol`. A given surface form, for example, *omoyollochichili* 'He strove strongly' (lit. "he waited for himself on behalf of the heart"), consists of three parts, the surface form (1), the morphotactic form (2) and the lexical form/analysis (3).

```
1. omoyollochichili
2. o>mo>«yollo»chichi>lia
3. <aug><s_sg3><o_ref>«yollotl<n>»
   chichilia<v><tv><past>
```

The morphotactic form is the combination of the morphs before morphographemic rules are applied, it includes symbols to mark segment boundaries, such as '>' for an inflectional boundary, '«...»' for incorporated elements (in this case, the second object), ~ for reduplication and '·' for clitic boundaries. The symbols around the incorporated element allow that part of the surface form to be extracted for use in the representation of incorporation (see §5.1).

5 Representations

In this section we discuss a number of features of Nahuatl that require special attention in the Universal Dependencies framework.

5.1 Incorporation

Incorporation is the process by which a verb can incorporate, that is, be syntactically incorporated with one or more of its arguments or adjuncts. Incorporation has been understudied in the field of natural language processing, and there are few articles that describe annotation projects for languages exhibiting this feature.

In this project, we follow the proposal laid out by Tyers and Mishchenkova (2020) in which incorporated items are exposed in the enhanced dependency graph annotated with the relation of the slot that they fulfill in the argument structure.

sent_id = Book_01_-_The_Gods.txt:87
text = [...] : qujlhuja, timotenoatzaz, titlacatlaquaz, timocujtlaxculcaoaz, naujlhujtl: [...]
text[norm] = [...] : quilhuia, timotenhuatzaz, titlacatlacuaz, timocuitlaxcolzahuaz, nahuilhuitl: [...]
text[orig] = [...] :·qujlhuja·,·timotenoa¶tzaz·,·titlacatlaquaz·,·timocujtlax¶culcaoaz·,·naujlhujtl·:·[...]
[...]

10	:	:	PUNCT	_	_	_	Norm=:
11	qujlhuja	ilhuia	VERB	_	_	_	Norm=quilhuia
12	,	,	PUNCT	_	_	_	Norm=,
13	timotenoatzaz	huatza	VERB	_	Subcat=Tran|Reflexive[iobj]=Yes†	_	Norm=timotenhuatzaz
13.1	ten	tentli	NOUN	_	_	_	Norm=ten
14	,	,	PUNCT	_	_	_	Norm=,
15	titlacatlaquaz	tlacatlacua	VERB	_	Subcat=Intr†	_	Norm=titlacatlacuaz
16	,	,	PUNCT	_		_	Norm=,
17	timocujtlaxculcaoaz	zahua	VERB	_	Subcat=Tran|Reflexive[iobj]=Yes†	_	Norm=timocuitlaxcolzahuaz
17.1	cujtlaxcul	cuitlaxcolli	NOUN	_	_		Norm=cuitlaxcol
18	,	,	PUNCT	_	_	_	Norm=,
19	naujlhujtl	nahuilhuitl	NOUN	_	_	_	Norm=nahuilhuitl
20	:	:	PUNCT	_	_	_	Norm=:

[...]

Table 2: The second clause from the 87th sentence in Book 1. The sentence reads "He said to him: you will dry your mouth, you will fast, you will fast your entrails, four days". The underlined nouns are incorporated. † Feature=Value pairs Number[subj]=Sing|Person[subj]=2|Tense=Fut|VerbForm=Fin and repeated empty columns are left out for reasons of space.

Table 2 demonstrates this with the verb *moyollochichili*, where the verb *chichilia* 'enbitter' takes the incorporated object *yollo-* 'heart.'

5.2 Relational nouns

Relational nouns are nouns which express spatial and temporal relations when used with other noun phrases. These may be used as independent words in a possessive structure (1) or compounded to other words (2).

1. *inepantla in ilhuicatl* 'in the midst of the heavens' (lit. its-midst the heaven)
2. *ilhuicayollotitech* 'in the heart of the heavens' (lit. heavens-heart-on)

The first case is straightforward, each noun is analysed as a separate word, with the relational noun receiving a lexical feature NounType=Relat in addition to the necessary possessive morphology.

In the second, we take advantage of the multi-token word encoding in the CoNLL-U format and analyse the compound as consisting of two parts, the head and the compounded relative noun.

5.3 Lemmas

We also include the lemmas, or the stems, for each word. Lemmas ignore any of the inflectional morphology on the surface form of the word. Lemmatisation is performed first by looking up a surface form in the lexicon and, if the word is not in the lexicon, by the morphological analyser.

6 Automated processing

We experiment with the existing processed FC data to see to what extent we might be able to automate the retokenisation and normalisation steps. Following previous work showing that historical text normalisation can be modelled effectively as a character-based machine translation problem (Bollmann, 2019), we train an encoder-decoder Seq2Seq model with Attention on character sequences for both tasks. While a natural inclination would be to train both retokenisation and spelling normalisation jointly, we are interested in storing each intermediate step for potential future research, and so train a separate model for each task.

For the orthography normalisation model, we treat each word as a training instance, and map the unnormalised word (e.g. *qujchioa*) to its corresponding normalised form (e.g. *quichihua*).

For the retokenisation model, training on each word would not work since the phenomenon we are modelling spans word boundaries. Instead, we split the text on unambiguous punctuation ('.,:;?!'), creating numerous subsequences from each sentence.

Since the objective is to evaluate how well we could automate the text processing for future books, we used two of the three already-complete books (Books 1 and 8) for training, and held out

Book 5 for evaluation. The models used a bidirectional LSTM encoder, and training was done using OpenNMT (Klein et al., 2020). We trained both for 100 epochs.

Results of the experiments are listed in Table 3. They are generally favourable, though perhaps not quite to the point of being able to completely automate the low-level processing of the remaining books.

6.1 Retokenisation

A number of the mistakes we see from the retokenisation model involve a type of 'hallucinations,' where the output contains characters not in the input. This is an effect of treating this problem as one of translation with a relatively low volume of training data. To remedy this problem, we may try adding an additional auto-encoding or "copying" auxiliary task as discussed in Mager et al. (2019), wherein we add training examples that are already correctly tokenised in order to provide more examples of correct outputs.

Alternatively, the task of retokenisation can be straightforwardly modelled as a one-to-one sequence tagging problem, where for each input character the model must assign one of three "retokenisation actions": (1) merge, or remove a token boundary that follows the current character, (2) split, or add a token boundary after the current character, or (3) do nothing. For comparison, we also evaluate this approach, using a bidirectional LSTM also trained for 100 epochs.[4] This approach has a slightly worse word error rate compared to the MT-based approach, but has a lower character error rate. The advantage to this approach is that we don't risk transforming characters or inserting substrings during the tokenisation step.

6.2 Orthographic normalisation

The orthographic normalisation model correctly normalises 87% of the words in the held out book. The errors suggest a similar issue seen in the retokenisation model, namely the insertion of multiple additional characters not corresponding to the input (e.g. converting input *ie*, to **yeyecye* instead of *ye*). This issue, as mentioned above, would likely be alleviated with some data augmentation and/or multi-task training to ensure the model sees enough examples of properly formed output strings. We plan to leverage this model as a backup in the case where we are not able to identify a normalisation via our dictionary-lookup approach. For example, by first checking if we have seen a given word in the training data and, if so, using the corresponding output from training and using the model's prediction on unseen words only, the word error rate drops to 8.3.

7 Use cases

In this section, we provide descriptions of a few research questions that could be informed by our corpus. The use cases are based on information that is available in the corpus and is not found in other editions of the manuscript.

The first use case concerns the status of the *tlamatinimeh* 'sages, wise men' (lit. those who know things). It is widely claimed that there is no philosophy outside Western philosophy (Maffie, 2014), but this claim has been contested by scholars, starting from Ángel María Garibay and his student Miguel León-Portilla who identify the *tlamatinimeh* with philosophers and argue that the precontact Mexicans had long philosophical traditions (León-Portilla, 1956). Analysing individual words has since this work been the basis of understanding Nahua thought. However, to date this process is difficult and error-prone as it involves carefully reading through unannotated concordances of surface forms and it is easy to miss examples that appear in forms that are unknown or unfamiliar to the researcher.

Our corpus will be able to help by allowing scholars to extract examples that are morphologically and syntactically related. For example, by allowing queries based on lemmas (encompassing for example *tlamatini* 'sage', *tlamatinimeh* 'sages', etc.) It will also allow for searching for specific syntactic constructions, such as those where a *tlamatini* is the subject of a speech verb.

The second use case concerns concepts of time. For instance, consider Maffie (2014)'s statement about the Mexica conceiving time and space as a single unit. He argues that the Mexica did not separate time and space but had a perception of a "time-place" . This argument is based on the word *cahuitl*, which means 'time', and the intransitive verb *cahui*, which means "to stay or end". However, Maffie argues that *cahuitl* is also related to

[4] Given our limited data volume and the interest to simulate testing on an unseen book, the results we report here do not include a hyper-parameter tuning step using a heldout development set. With an additional held out book we could tune these models' hyperparameters and improve performance.

Task	Model	Train	Test	CER	WER
Retokenisation:	NMT	5,245	1,264	3.6	23.1
	Sequence labelling	5,245	1,264	2.8	23.9
Orthographic normalisation:	NMT	15,208	3,209	4.3	13.3
	NMT + Dictionary	15,208	3,209	1.7	8.3

Table 3: Results from experiments on automating text processing tasks (retokenisation and normalisation). The training set includes books 1 and 8, while the test set includes book 5.

Ret. Action	Precision	Recall	F1
Merge	0.856	0.952	0.902
Split	0.978	0.926	0.952
Nothing	0.997	0.995	0.996

Table 4: Results on predicting the "retokenisation actions" to correctly tokenise each original sequence. The corresponding word and character error rates are listed in Table 3.

the transitive verb *cahua*, which means "to leave or abandon", among other senses.

The morphological annotations (including lemmas) in our corpus will allow for searching on lemma (to be able to distinguish forms of *cahui* from forms of *cahua*). And the syntactic annotations will allow for the extraction of time and place obliques that are dependents of those two verbs.

8 Concluding remarks

We have outlined the strategies and approaches involved in creating a free and open, linguistically-annotated corpus of the FC. Having nearly completed retokenisation, orthographic normalisation, lemmatisation, part-of-speech tagging, and morphological analysis for 3 of the 12 books, we have established the key linguistic information to include in the corpus, and have engineered the foundations of the annotation process. Results of our preliminary experiments into automatic annotation suggest that some tasks, like orthographic normalisation, can largely be automated with the existing data, whereas others, e.g., retokenisation, likely still require more labelled data and/or a more powerful architecture.

8.1 Future work

Our first priority for the future is to continue the annotation process, automating some of the text normalisation, expanding the lexica, and enhancing the morphological analyser. We are optimistic that with each subsequent book, the additional amount of available annotated data will enable faster future annotation via automation. Finally, adding dependency syntax annotations will enable quantitative analysis of colonial Nahuatl syntax, a field with relatively little prior work.

The study described in §7 is one of many potential uses of an annotated corpus as described here. We expect that the release of this corpus with complete morphosyntactic annotations and an unambiguous free licence will promote future research from scholars in a variety of fields.

Additionally, the tools for automatic processing of the FC will likely be applicable to the numerous additional texts written in Nahuatl during the colonial period, contributing to the advancement of language technology development for Nahuatl.

Finally, another important project related to the development of this corpus involves the translation of the FC into contemporary Nahuatl variants, making the rich cultural heritage of the Nahuatl language more accessible to Nahuatl-speaking communities. It is our hope that the production of this corpus can aid in the translation process.

Acknowledgements

We would like to thank Maira Cayetano Nemecio and Stephanie Berthoud Frías for their valuable contributions. We are grateful to Mitsuya Sasaki and Joe Campbell for fielding numerous questions about language use in the Florentine Codex, and to the anonymous reviewers for their helpful feedback. Finally, a special thanks to Daniel Swanson, Andrew Davis, Zack Leech, and Maria Lucero Guillen Puon, for stimulating discussions about Nahuatl and the Florentine Codex.

References

James Richard Andrews. 2003. *Introduction to classical Nahuatl*, volume 1. University of Oklahoma Press.

Marcel Bollmann. 2019. A large-scale comparison of historical text normalization systems. *arXiv preprint arXiv:1904.02036*.

George Aaron Broadwell, Moisés García Guzmán, Brook Danielle Lillehaugen, Felipe H Lopez, May Helena Plumb, and Mike Zarafonetis. 2020. Ticha: Collaboration with indigenous communities to build digital resources on zapotec language and history. *DHQ: Digital Humanities Quarterly*, (4).

Joe R. Campbell and Frances Karttunen. 1989. Foundation course in Nahuatl grammar.

Bernardino de Sahagún. 2022. Transcript of the florentine codex (nahuatl). In *The General/Universal History of the things of New Spain*. Zenodo.

Marc Eisinger. 1977. *Codex de Florence et informatique: propositions pour l'étude systématique des textes nahua*. Ecole des Hautes Etudes en Sciences Sociales.

Willard Gingerich. 1988. Chipahuacanemiliztli: The purified life, in the discourses of book vi, florentine codex. In *Smoke and Mist: Mesoamerican Studies in Memory of Thelma D. Sullivan*, 402. British Archaeological Reports.

Willard P Gingerich. 1975. A bibliographic introduction to twenty manuscripts of classical nahuatl literature. *Latin American Research Review*, 10(1):105–125.

Ximena Gutierrez-Vasques, Gerardo Sierra, and Isaac Hernandez Pompa. 2016. Axolotl: a web accessible parallel corpus for spanish-nahuatl. In *Proceedings of the Tenth International Conference on Language Resources and Evaluation (LREC'16)*, pages 4210–4214.

Frances E Karttunen. 1992. *An analytical dictionary of Nahuatl*. University of Oklahoma Press.

Guillaume Klein, François Hernandez, Vincent Nguyen, and Jean Senellart. 2020. The opennmt neural machine translation toolkit: 2020 edition. In *Proceedings of the 14th Conference of the Association for Machine Translation in the Americas (Volume 1: Research Track)*, pages 102–109.

Michel Launey. 1986. *Catégories et opérations dans la grammaire nahuatl*. Ph.D. thesis, Paris 4.

Miguel León-Portilla. 1956. *La filosofía náhuatl estudiada en sus fuentes*. Instituto Indigenista Interamericano, Mexico City.

Miguel León-Portilla. 1985. Nahuatl literature. In *Supplement to the Handbook of Middle American Indians, Volume 3: Literatures*, pages 7–43. University of Texas Press.

Krister Lindén, Miikka Silfverberg, and Tommi Pirinen. 2009. Hfst tools for morphology–an efficient open-source package for construction of morphological analyzers. In *State of the Art in Computational Morphology: Workshop on Systems and Frameworks for Computational Morphology, SFCM 2009, Zurich, Switzerland, September 4, 2009. Proceedings*, pages 28–47. Springer.

James Lockhart. 1992. *The Nahuas after the conquest: A social and cultural history of the Indians of Central Mexico, sixteenth through eighteenth centuries*. Stanford University Press.

James Lockhart. 2001. *Nahuatl as written: Lessons in older written Nahuatl, with copious examples and texts*, volume 6. Stanford University Press.

James Maffie. 2014. *Aztec Philosophy*. University Press of Colorado, Boulder.

Manuel Mager, Monica Jasso Rosales, Özlem Çetinoğlu, and Ivan Meza. 2019. Low-resource neural character-based noisy text normalization. *Journal of Intelligent & Fuzzy Systems*, 36(5):4921–4929.

José Luis Martínez. 1982. *El "Códice Florentino" y la "Historia General" de Sahagún*, 1. edition. Archivo General de la Nación, Mexico City.

Arya D. McCarthy, Rachel Wicks, Dylan Lewis, Aaron Mueller, Winston Wu, Oliver Adams, Garrett Nicolai, Matt Post, and David Yarowsky. 2020. The Johns Hopkins University Bible corpus: 1600+ tongues for typological exploration. In *Proceedings of the Twelfth Language Resources and Evaluation Conference*, pages 2884–2892, Marseille, France. European Language Resources Association.

Kelly McDonough. 2020. Intercultural (mis) translations: Colonial static and "authorship" in the florentine codex and the relaciones geográficas of new spain. In *The Routledge Hispanic Studies Companion to Colonial Latin America and the Caribbean (1492–1898)*, pages 393–405. Routledge.

Patricia Murrieta-Flores, Diego Jiménez-Badillo, and Bruno Martins. 2022. Digital resources: Artificial intelligence, computational approaches, and geographical text analysis to investigate early colonial mexico. In *Oxford Research Encyclopedia of Latin American History*.

Garrett Nicolai, Dylan Lewis, Arya D. McCarthy, Aaron Mueller, Winston Wu, and David Yarowsky. 2020. Fine-grained morphosyntactic analysis and generation tools for more than one thousand languages. In *Proceedings of the Twelfth Language Resources and Evaluation Conference*, pages 3963–3972, Marseille, France. European Language Resources Association.

Garrett Nicolai and David Yarowsky. 2019. Learning morphosyntactic analyzers from the Bible via iterative annotation projection across 26 languages. In

Proceedings of the 57th Annual Meeting of the Association for Computational Linguistics, pages 1765–1774, Florence, Italy. Association for Computational Linguistics.

Joakim Nivre, Marie-Catherine de Marneffe, Filip Ginter, Jan Hajič, Christopher D Manning, Sampo Pyysalo, Sebastian Schuster, Francis Tyers, and Daniel Zeman. 2020a. Universal dependencies v2: An evergrowing multilingual treebank collection. *arXiv preprint arXiv:2004.10643*.

Joakim Nivre, Marie-Catherine de Marneffe, Filip Ginter, Jan Hajič, Christopher D. Manning, Sampo Pyysalo, Sebastian Schuster, Francis Tyers, and Daniel Zeman. 2020b. Universal Dependencies v2: An evergrowing multilingual treebank collection. In *Proceedings of the Twelfth Language Resources and Evaluation Conference*, pages 4034–4043, Marseille, France. European Language Resources Association.

Guilhem Olivier. 2021. Teotl and diablo: Indigenous and christian conceptions of gods and devils in the florentine codex. In *The Florentine Codex*, pages 110–122. University of Texas Press.

Justyna Olko. 2018. Unbalanced language contact and the struggle for survival: Bridging diachronic and synchronic perspectives on nahuatl. *European Review*, 26(1):207–228.

Justyna Olko and John Sullivan. 2013. Empire, colony, and globalization. a brief history of the nahuatl language. In *Colloquia humanistica*, 2. Instytut Slawistyki Polskiej Akademii Nauk.

Justyna Olko et al. 2015. Language encounters: Toward a better comprehension of contact-induced lexical change in colonial nahuatl. *Politeja-Pismo Wydziału Studiów Międzynarodowych i Politycznych Uniwersytetu Jagiellońskiego*, 12(38):35–52.

Robert Pugh, Marivel Huerta Mendez, Mitsuya Sasaki, and Francis M. Tyers. 2022. Universal Dependencies for Western Sierra Puebla Nahuatl. In *Proceedings of the 13th Language Resources and Evaluation Conference*.

Pete Sigal. 2007. Queer nahuatl: Sahagún's faggots and sodomites, lesbians and hermaphrodites. *Ethnohistory*, 54(1):9–34.

Thelma D Sullivan et al. 1966. Pregnancy, childbirth, and the deification of the women who died in childbirth: texts from the florentine codex, book vi, folos 128v-143v. *Estudios de cultura Nahuatl*, 6:63–95.

Francis Tyers and Karina Mishchenkova. 2020. Dependency annotation of noun incorporation in polysynthetic languages. In *Proceedings of the Fourth Workshop on Universal Dependencies (UDW 2020)*, pages 195–204.

Universidad Nacional Autónoma de México. 2023. Temoa [en línea]. `http://temoa.iib.unam.mx`; Accessed 4th April, 2023.

Book	Title	Sentences	Tokens	Words
01	The Gods	178	6,066	6,481
02	Ceremonies	664	29,209	–
03	The Origins of the Gods	186	5,794	–
04	The Art of Divination	341	24,283	–
05	The Omens	111	3,546	4,470
06	Rhetoric and Moral Philosophy	1,450	57,021	–
07	The Sun, Moon, Stars, and the Binding of the Years	229	5,189	–
08	Kings and Lords	348	13,711	13,970
09	The Merchants	506	21,022	–
10	The People	1,217	35,196	–
11	Earthly Things	3,074	78,066	–
12	The Conquest of Mexico	667	27,099	–
		8,971	306,202	24,921

Table 5: A breakdown of the FC by book. "Tokens" refers to raw whitespace-separated tokens, prior to the retokenisation process described in §4.2. At present, we have processed approximately 637 sentences containing a total of 25,000 words. We strategically started with the shorter books for manual processing with the idea that we can leverage this data to mostly automate the processing of the longest books.

A Books of the Florentine Codex

Table 5 presents some statistics about the books of the Florentine Codex.

Developing finite-state language technology for Maya

Robert Pugh[†] and **Quetzil Castañeda**[‡◇] and **Francis Tyers**[†]
pughrob@iu.edu, quetzil@osea-cite.org, ftyers@iu.edu
[†]Department of Linguistics, Indiana University
[‡]Center for Latin-American and Caribbean Studies
[◇]Open School of Ethnography and Anthropology (OSEA-CITE)

Abstract

We describe a suite of finite-state language technologies for Maya, a Mayan language spoken in Mexico. At the core is a computational model of Maya morphology and phonology using a finite-state transducer.[1] This model results in a morphological analyzer and a morphologically-informed spell-checker. All of these technologies are designed for use as both a pedagogical reading/writing aid for L2 learners and as a general language processing tool capable of supporting much of the natural variation in written Maya. We discuss the relevant features of Maya morphosyntax and orthography, and then outline the implementation details of the analyzer. To conclude, we present a longer-term vision for these tools and their use by both native speakers and learners.

1 Introduction

Maya[2] is a member of the Yucatecan branch of the Mayan language family (Figure 2[3]). It is the second most widely-spoken indigenous language of Mexico, with around 800,000 speakers primarily in the states of Yucatan, Quintana Roo, and Campeche in southern Mexico (Collin, 2010) (See Figure 1[4]), including a substantial speaker population in California (Mattiace and de Mola, 2015) and a modest population in Belize.

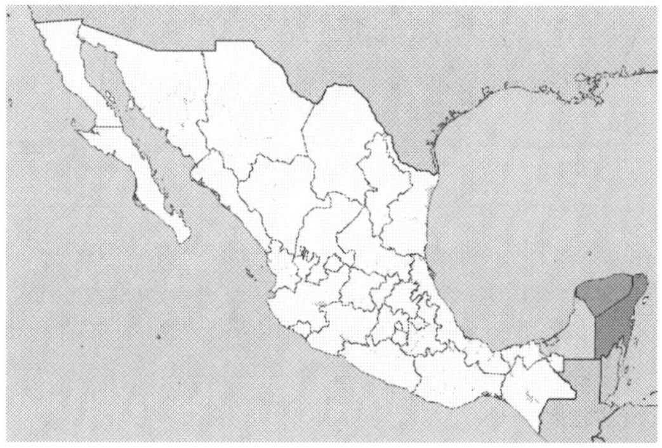

Figure 1: A map highlighting the three Mexican states where Maya is spoken: Yucatan (Orange), Quintana Roo (Purple), and Campeche (Yellow).

Text-based language technologies, ubiquitous for a small number of "mainstream", mostly colonial languages such as English or Spanish, facilitate human-computer interaction and to a large extent computer-mediated communication, and can aid in language learning (Shadiev and Yang, 2020). Furthermore, language technology for endangered languages can play a useful role in language maintenance and revitalization efforts (Reyhner, 1999; Ben Slimane, 2008; Zhang et al., 2022). Unfortunately, there is a paucity of such technology for most of the world's languages, leaving speakers and language learners without potentially valuable resources. Consequently, monolingual speakers face additional barriers to entry in the digital domain, and speakers who are bilingual in a dominant, colonial language for which such technology exists will be more likely to use that language online and on digital devices, further contributing to language shift.

This paper outlines the design and implementation of a finite-state morphological analyzer for Maya. Developed in concert with Maya language educators, the analyzer is intended for use as a writing tool for authors, educators, and students

[1]https://github.com/apertium/apertium-yua

[2]We follow the recommendation of the Open School or Ethnography and Anthropology and the Community Institute of Transcultural Change (see §1.1) with respect to terminology, using the term "Maya," the autonym of the Maya-speaking people, when referring to the language or cultural/ethnic group, instead of "Yucatec Maya," commonly used by linguists, or "Mayan", which should be reserved for referring to the language family or proto-Mayan (Castañeda and Dzidz Yam, 2014).

[3]Figure 2 was created by user Madman2001 (https://commons.wikimedia.org/wiki/File:Mayan_Language_Tree.svg)

[4]Figure 1 is based on work by user Kmusser (https://commons.wikimedia.org/wiki/File:Mexico_States_blank_map.svg)

Proceedings of the Workshop on Natural Language Processing for Indigenous Languages of the Americas (AmericasNLP), pages 30–39
July 14, 2023

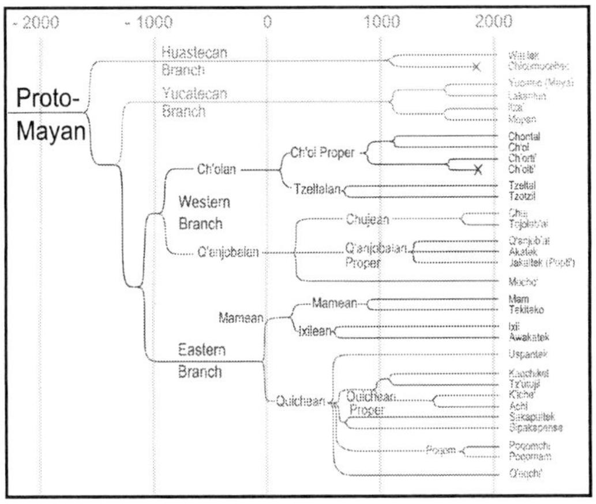

Figure 2: The Mayan language family. Maya ("Yucatec Maya", the focus of this paper) is located on the green "Yucatecan Branch".

(to ensure consistent written resources via a spell-checker), and as a reading-aid that can provide students with lexical information (e.g. the root and/or grammatical features) about an unknown word in a text. We focus primarily on the grammar of Maya and the implementation of the analyzer, and present a prototype of a working spell-checker.

1.1 Motivation and OSEA-CITE

The motivation for the present work stems from a collaboration with the Open School of Ethnography and Anthropology and the Community Institute of Transcultural Change (OSEA-CITE, henceforth OSEA), a Pisté-based organization whose stated focus is "language revitalization, sustainability, cultural ownership, heritage rights, community health and well-being, the innovation of tradition, and the interconnections between local, national, and transnational communities and social forces." While designed with Maya speakers, learners, linguists, and language activists in mind, the technologies described below are particularly informed by and aligned with OSEA pedagogical materials (Castañeda, 2014) for use in the classroom as reading and writing tools for both learners and educators in OSEA programs.

2 Related work

The use of finite-state transducers (FSTs) for modeling human language has a long tradition spanning multiple decades (Kornai, 1996) and proving effective in areas such as morphological analysis (Beesley and Karttunen, 2003), spell-checking (Pirinen et al., 2014), among others. It is particularly attractive in the low-resource case since it requires significantly less data than popular statistical approaches. Furthermore, finite-state systems can also be leveraged in order to generate data to train better statistical machine-learning models (Moeller et al., 2018).

The application of finite-state language technology to indigenous languages of Mesoamerica also has some precedent, with morphological analyzers developed for Nahuatl (Maxwell and Amith, 2005; Pugh and Tyers, 2021; Tona et al., 2023), Zapotec (Washington et al., 2021), Huave (Tyers and Castro, 2023), and K'iche' (Richardson and Tyers, 2021). Nicolai et al. (2020) present the large-scale development of morphological analyzers and generators for over one thousand languages using the Johns Hopkins University Bible Corpus (McCarthy et al., 2020), including some Mayan languages.

Kuhn and Mateo-Toledo (2004) is perhaps one of the earliest published works focused on the development and application of language technology to assist in documenting a Mayan language, Q'anjob'al (spoken in Guatemala), training a maximum-entropy part-of-speech tagger. Palmer (2009) and Palmer et al. (2010) also apply techniques from machine learning and computational linguistics to the documentation of a Mayan language (Uspanteko, also spoken in Guatemala). More recently, Tyers and Henderson (2021) and Tyers and Howell (2021) developed an annotated linguistic corpus of K'iche' and explored approaches to automated tagging and parsing. Maya is also included as one of six Mexican languages aligned with Spanish in the Parallel Corpus for Mexican Languages (Sierra Martínez et al., 2020).

There has also been interest and some work leveraging computational technology to annotate and analyze Classic Maya heiroglyphic writing (Prager et al., 2018; Vertan and Prager, 2022).

Particularly relevant to motivation and aims of the present project, Gasser (2011), outlines useful applications of computational morphological analyzers for learners of morphologically-rich indigenous languages of the Americas.

3 Orthography

The Latin alphabet has been used to write Yucatec Maya since the 16th century, but the first organized efforts to standardize the orthography took place in the mid-20th century (Brody, 2004). The colonial-era writing practices are described thoroughly in Shigeto (2011), and a variant of this orthographic approach is also used in Bolles and Bolles (2001). Many linguistic resources for Maya also use an orthography inspired by the Americanist Phonetic Alphabet (Bricker et al., 1998; Blair and Vermont-Salas, 1965), (e.g. using ʔ for the glottal stop). Today, the commonly (though by no means unanimously) adopted "contemporary orthography" is laid out in the publication *Normas de Escritura Para la Lengua Maya* (SEP & INALI, 2014).

In the classroom, OSEA teaches a writing system similar to the contemporary one, with a few pedagogically-motivated changes, like the explicit marking of low tone on long low vowels. Additionally, there are some differences related to the spelling of specific words. In order to offer students a consistent source for spelling questions (primarily with respect to vowel quantity and tone), OSEA uses Bricker et al. (1998) as an authoritative reference. This is not to say that alternative spellings are incorrect from OSEA's perspective, but rather that it is valuable for students to have a thorough and consistent guide to reference when making spelling decisions[5].

Since the project presented here is intended to be used by students and teachers in the OSEA Maya language program, we follow these orthographic norms while still supporting both the colonial and contemporary orthographies. Details about this are provided in section 6.5.

4 A brief overview of Maya morphosyntax

An important linguistic property of Maya worth mentioning at the outset is that it does not have tenses, per se. Instead, it inflects verbs for aspect to reflect whether a given action has been completed, or how long ago it began (Bricker et al., 1998). Details about this system are explored in greater depth in section 4.2.

Maya is a split-ergative language, i.e. it follows ergative-absolutive alignment in all but the imperfective aspect, where it follows nominative-accusative alignment.

As will become obvious in the discussion below, Maya has a complex derivational system. Most word classes can be derived from other word classes, and the transitivity and voice of a verb is derived morphologically as well.

4.1 Pronouns

Maya has three sets of pronouns: one set (the "independent pronouns") is syntactically independent of verbs while two, called "Dependent Pronouns" are affixes or clitics on the verb.

Independent pronouns, as the name suggests, are independent words (e.g. not affixes or clitics). They may be used to emphasize (Example 1) or topicalize (Example 2) a verbal argument, or after prepositions to express indirect objects.

(1) *k'abéet a bin-e'ex te'ex*
OBLIG S2 go-S2PL PRON2PL
'You all (emph.) must go'.

(2) *te'ex-e k'abéet a bin-e'ex*
PRON2PL-TOP OBLIG S2 go-S2PL
'As for you all, you must go'.

Set A pronouns (*a* in examples 1 and 2) which come before the verb, typically written separated from the verb, and are sometimes written as merged or contracted with a preceding aspectual auxiliary. With respect to case, Set A pronouns correspond to the A argument (as defined in Dixon and Dixon (1994)) except when in the imperfective, in which case they are the subject of both transitive and intransitive verbs, except in copular clauses where a Set B pronoun is used to mark the subject. Set A pronouns are also the possessive pronouns.

Set B pronouns are suffixes used to express the S and O arguments of the verb, i.e. the subject of an intransitive verb and the object of a transitive verb, except in the imperfective. They are also used as the subject in copular clauses.

4.2 Verbs

Verbs are by far the most morphologically complex words in Maya. The specific components of the "verb compound" depend on the verb's transitivity and the aspectual class of the conjugation. The aspectual auxiliaries and Set A pronouns are often written as separate orthographic words from the verb itself.

In the imperfective, verbs typically must be preceded by an aspectual auxiliary followed by a Set A pronoun. For example, *k* (habitual), *táan* (progressive aspect), *laili'...e'* ("still doing X"), etc. Note that some of these auxiliaries, such as *laili'* above,

[5] It should be noted that our implementation is also flexible and can be easily-updated to be applied to other writing conventions and pedagogical environments.

Orthography	Notes	Example text
Colonial-style	*cħ*, *pp*, *dz* for /tʃ'/, /p'/, and /ts'/, no tone or length marking on vowels	Le chochlin, tumen chen kay cu betice ti le yax kino, ma tu bin u caxte u yoch.
Contemporary (INALI)	*j* for /h/, marks long high and re-articulated vowels	Le ch'och'lin, tumen chen k'aay ku beetike' ti' le yáax k'iino', ma' tu bin u kaxtej u yo'och.
Modified contemporary (OSEA)	Similar to Contemporary. Marks long high, long low, and rearticulated vowels, *h* for /h/	Le ch'och'lin, tumèen chen k'àay ku bèetike' ti' le yáax k'ìino', ma' tu bin u kaxteh u yo'och.

Table 1: An example of three different orthographic styles in written Maya. The original text is from Bolles and Bolles (2001) and is written in a style inspired by colonial-era orthography, which we refer to here as "Colonial-style." Note the differences in character choice (e.g. *j* vs. *h*), as well as minor spelling differences like *tumen* vs. *tumèen* (the latter's vowel quantity and tone coming from a particular reference dictionary). The descriptions of the orthographies are by no means exhaustive, as a complete breakdown of the similarities and differences of each is beyond the scope of this paper.

Person/Num.	Set A	Set B	Indep.
1Sg	*in*	*-en*	*tèen*
2Sg	*a*	*-ech*	*tèech*
3Sg	*u*	Ø	*leti'*
1Pl	*k*	*-o'on*	*to'on*
2Pl	*a...-e'ex*	*-e'ex*	*te'ex*
3Pl	*u...-o'ob*	*-o'ob*	*leti'o'ob*

Table 2: A table of the three sets of Maya pronouns: dependent pronouns (Set A, Set B) and independent pronouns. Note that the second- and third-person plural Set A pronouns consist of both a prefix and a corresponding suffix

have a corresponding terminal enclitic that is attached to the end of the verb (Example 3). The aspectual auxiliaries often combine with the adjacent Set A pronoun to form a contraction, e.g. *táan+in* →*tin*.

(3) *laili' u xòok-o'ob-e'*
still s3 study.APS-3PL-CONT.
'They (pl.) are still studying'.

There are three important features of verbs that determine how they are inflected: transitivity, the derivational processes undergone to achieve that transitivity (e.g. is the verb a transitive root or an intransitive/nominal/adjectival root that has become transitive via derivation), and voice (Maya has four distinct voice categories: active, passive, antipassive, and middle).

Intransitive verb stems often take one of a set of aspectual "status" suffixes[6] depending on the aspect and/or mood: *-Vl* suffix in the imperfective, where *V* matches the vowel in the root, a null suffix in the perfective, *-a'an* in the present perfect, and *-Vk* in the subjunctive.

Root	Deriv.	Asp. status	SetB	SetA Pl.
hóok	*-s*	*-ah*	*-en*	*-e'ex*
go.out	CAUS	PERF	O.SG1	S.PL2

Table 3: A simplified template of the verbal compound in Maya, with each slot's corresponding value for the word *hóoksahene'ex* "You (pl) took me out." Not all of the possible verbal morphemes are represented in this table. To the left of the verb, the verbal compound can also include a negation marker, an aspectual auxiliary, and/or a Set A pronoun. These are omitted from the template above since they are typically written as separate orthographic words, and thus are treated as such in our analyzer. On the right side, there can also be a "terminal enclitic" (Bricker et al., 1998) corresponding to a previous part of the phrase, such as a negation or locative particle (*-i*).

Transitive verb stems in the active voice take aspectual status suffixes *-ik*, *-ah*, and *-mah* in the imperfective, perfective, and present perfect aspects, respectively. In the subjunctive mood, no suffix is added, unless the verb is phrase final, in which case it takes *-eh*.

The majority of root transitive verbs follow a CVC phonological template, which changes systematically to produce changes in voice: CVVC for

[6] Bohnemeyer (1998), Brody (2004), and others have referred to these suffixes as "status suffixes", and they go by various other names in the literature. In the OSEA-CITE pedagogical literature, these suffixes are referred to as "primary suffixes". We use the term "status" in this paper for the sake of consistency with previous linguistic work.

antipassive, CV'VC for passive, and CVVC for the middle voice. The status suffixes for these verbs are listed in Table 5. Transitive verbs can become reflexive with the addition of a suffix of the formula 'Set A + bah' (Example 4).

(4) *táan in wil-ik-**in-bah***
PROG S1SG.A see-STATUS-S1SG.A-REFL
'I am seeing myself.'

Intransitive roots can be transitivized with either the *-t* suffix or the causative *-s* suffix. They typically use the same status suffixes as transitive roots.

A third class of verbs with a distinct morphological pattern is that of Positional verbs. These verbs take status suffixes *-tal*, *-lah*, *-la'an*, and *-lak* in the imperfective, perfective, present perfect, and subjunctive, respectively.

Note that the discussion here is limited only to regular intransitive roots, regular transitive roots, and positionals. There are other verb root classes that follow slightly different inflectional patterns, but a complete description of them is beyond the scope of this paper.

4.3 Nouns and adjectives

Nouns and adjectives have notably less morphologically-complex than Maya verbs. They inflect for number, with the suffixes *-o'ob* and *-tak* (the latter for expressing a plurality of types vs. simply plural in number). Both Nouns and Adjectives can also behave as intransitive predicates, taking a Set B pronoun as the subject (Example 5. Commonly, Nouns that are core arguments of the verb can be topicalized by placing them at the front of the sentence with the topic suffix *-e*. Deixis can also be expressed using nominal morphology. Gender, while not a required feature of Nouns, can be indicated with the prefixes *x-* and *h-* (*x-* is also used as an instrumental nominalizer on verbs). Verbs can be derived from either nouns or adjectives using *-tal / -chahal* for intransitives (e.g. *ma'alob* "good" →*ma'alobtal* "to improve") and *-kuns / -kins* for transitives (e.g. *wíinik* "man" →*wíinikkunsik* "make someone into a man/human").

(5) *kòolnáal-o'on*
farmer-S1PL
'We are farmers'.

4.4 Phrase-level morphology

There are a number of cases of words in Maya which require a corresponding terminal suffix at some point later in the phrase. These include the negation marker *ma'a*, which typically requires that the end of the negated word or phrase have a *-i* suffix, certain aspectual auxiliaries like *laili'* which has a corresponding *-e* at the end of the verb phrase, and numerous other cases. Deictic suffixes *-a* "this", *-o* "that", and *-e* "this right here" also correspond to a prenominal article *le* (See Example 6).

(6) *ti' **le** yáax k'ìino'*
ADP ART first day-DEM3
'At the beginning of that day'.

Title	Sentences	Tokens
Simple Sentences	103	553
Tsikbalo'ob	200	1,099
Xkùuruch	85	710
Mam Ku'ukeba	41	376
Hun túul xnùuk òoch	11	129
Ch'och'lin yéetel síinik	11	166
Total	451	3,033

Table 4: A breakdown of the different works that make up the corpus.

5 Data

For development, we use a small corpus consisting primarily of pedagogical texts used in the classroom by OSEA. They include lists of sentences and a number of *tsikbalo'ob* (dialogues). We also include four short stories from Bolles and Bolles (2001), for which we changed the orthography to reflect the writing norms of OSEA-CITE (with permission from the author). Sentence and token counts are listed in table 4.

6 Implementation

The morphological analyzer is developed within the Apertium project (Forcada et al., 2011; Khanna et al., 2021), and is made up of three principle components: a model of Maya morphotactics, a model of phonological processes, and an analysis disambiguation step. A sample of the type of analysis that is produced can be seen in Table 6.

One major advantage of using the Apertium platform is that a single morphological model can trivially be extended to additional applications, such as spell-checking and machine translation. Here, we describe the development of the morphological analyzer, and briefly discuss a spell-checking application prototype.

Aspect/Mood	Trans.	Intr.	Positional	Aps	Derived Trans Pss
Imperfective	*-ik*	*-Vl/Ø*	*-t-al*	Ø	*-a'al*
Perfective	*-ah*	Ø	*-l-ah*	*-nah*	*-a'ab*
Present perfect	*-m-ah*	*-a'an*	*-l-aha'an*	*-naha'an*	*-a'an*
Subjunctive	*-Ø/-eh*	*-Vk*	*-l-ak*	*-nak*	*-a'ak*

Table 5: Some of the common aspectual "status suffixes" ("primary suffixes") for different types of Maya verbs. Trans. and Intr. refer to transitive and intransitive root verbs, "Aps" = Antipassive, and "Derived Trans Pss" refers to intransitive roots that are transitivized and then passivized (e.g. *hóoken* "I went out" →*a hóoksahen* "You took me out" →*hóoksa'aben* "I was taken out.")

Word	**Analysis**
Ma'	`"ma'" neg`
ta	`"t" aux pfv`
	`"a" s_sg2 pron`
kaxtah	`"kax" v tv pfv o_sg3`
ba'al	`"ba'al" n sg`
hanteh	`"han" v tv subj o_sg3`

Table 6: An example of the output from our analyzer for an example sentence from the story "Ch'och'lin yéetel síinik": *Ma' ta kaxtah ba'al hanteh?* "You didn't find something to eat?" The tagset corresponds with common abbreviations used in Apertium: neg=Negation, aux=Auxiliary, pfv=Perfective s_sg2=Second-person singular subject, pron=Pronoun, v=Verb, tv=Transitive, o_sg3=3rd-person singular object, n=Noun, sg=Singular, subj=Subjunctive.

6.1 Morphotactics

Morphotactics are defined using `lexc`. For verbs, we separate intransitive roots, transitive roots, and positionals. We encode lexical information about the root, e.g. whether an intransitive root takes the *-Vl* ending in the imperfective, in the lexicon entry. When a word undergoes derivation, we maintain the original lemma. For example, the CVC transitive root *xok* has in its lexicon entry the two additional voice derivations:

```
! Study, read
xok<v><tv>:xok TransActive;
xok<v><iv><aps>:xòok TransAps;
xok<v><iv><pss>:xo'ok TransPss;
xok<v><iv><mv >:xóok TransMed;
```

Each continuation lexicon reflects the specific set of status suffixes for the given root, aspect, and mood.

The lexicon entries for intransitive verbs also include lexical information, e.g. whether a given verb's transitive derivation takes the transitivizer *-t*, the causative *-s*, or nothing.

Noun stems are optionally preceded by the gender/agentive prefixes *h-* or *x-*, and are followed by either the nominal inflections (e.g. diminutive, plural, possessive suffixes) or by denominalizing verbal morphology (e.g. the *-tal* / *-chahal* status suffixes).

Since the aforementioned terminal clitics can be appended to most words, each word optionally ends with them.

6.2 Phonology

Phonological processes are modeled with `twol` rules (Karttunen et al., 1987). As an example, take vowel harmony, a common process in Maya. In cases where a morpheme's vowel harmonizes with that of the previous morpheme (e.g. the *-Vl* suffix for many intransitive roots), we represent these vowels as archiphonemes, and define the harmony process in `twol` as follows:

```
"Vowel harmony"
V:Vx <=> Vx [Cns | >:0 | ']+ >:0 _
; where Vx in UnaccVow ;
```

This component is also where we handle common contractions. For example, the intransitive verb *tàal* "come", when transitivized with the causative *-s*, usually drops the last consonant in the root (*tàal-s-ik* →*tàasik*). There are a number of verbs for which this is the case, irrespective of which transitivizer they take. For these verbs, we represent the root with an archiphoneme (e.g. `{l}` as the last consonant of the root, which is surfaced as either 'l' or 'Ø').

6.3 Analysis disambiguation

Given the complexity of Maya morphology, our model of morphotactics often produces a number of potential analyses for the same form. As a simple example, take the second-person Set A pronoun *a*. This is used for both singular and plural subjects/possessors, and the number of the subject is determined by the presence or absence of the second-person plural suffix on the adjacent verb/noun. Similarly, the phrasal terminal suffixes *-i* and *-e* on a verb could signify negation, agreement with one of a subset of aspectual auxiliaries, or a locative analysis.

We use Constraint Grammar (Karlsson et al., 2011) to disambiguate analyses using the analyses and lemmas of words in the surrounding context. For example, to disambiguate the *a* Set A pronoun, we use the following rules:

```
REMOVE PRO + 2Sg IF (1 VN + SP12);
REMOVE PRO + 2Pl IF (1 VN - SP12);
```

Any time the Set A pronoun *a* is seen, it will include both plural and singular analyses. The first rule above removes the singular analysis if the following (right-adjacent) word is a verb with a second-person plural subject analysis. The second rule removes the plural analysis if the right-adjacent word is a verb without a second-person plural analysis.

The example above is one of a large number of Constraint Grammar rules needed to effectively narrow-down the morphological analyses using the surrounding words as context.

6.4 Spell checking

While the ability to automatically provide a morphological analysis is both interesting and valuable in itself, our system, thanks to the infrastructure set up by the Apertium project, is also easily extensible to a number of other applications. Here, we briefly discuss how we integrated the morphological analyzer to make a spell-checker and spelling-corrector for a word processor.

The use of finite-state models for efficient spell-checking of morphologically-rich languages has a long history (Beesley and Karttunen, 2003; Pirinen et al., 2014). As a prototype spell-checker and corrector, we use an FST which transduces incorrectly-spelled words within a fixed edit-distance to the words in our model. This FST can then be integrated with a spelling and grammar extension developed by the Voikko[7] project to be used with LibreOffice Writer[8], a free and open source, multi-platform word processor that is part of the LibreOffice suite of software[9]. Figure 3 shows a screenshot of the spell-checker in action. Its current status is a working prototype, but we plan to improve it by adding common misspellings to the model and weighting it using proofread written text.

6.5 Supporting variation in written Maya: normative and descriptive models

An important intended feature of our model is the ability to simultaneously support a normative model for pedagogical purposes, and a descriptive model for other natural language processing tasks. Specifically, the spell-checker, insofar as it is used by a language teacher to write pedagogical material or to encourage uniformity in writing practices among students, should adhere to the principles taught and followed by the educators. The morphological analyzer on the other hand, which can be used to help understand, analyze, or segment a Maya text from a number of potential sources/authors, should be flexible to common written variation in the language.

The Apertium platform allows for precisely this flexibility via "Direction" flags in our morphotactics file, and a `spellrelax` file. The "Direction" flags are simply commented annotations on a specific line in the `lexc` file that specify which direction that line should be included in at compile time. As an example, take the case of the nominal classifier. It is commonplace to see the number, such as *hun* "one", and the following nominal classifier, e.g. *p'éel* for inanimate nouns, written as a single orthographic word (in this case with nasal place assimilation): *hump'éel*. The OSEA program teaches its students to write these as two separate words: *hun p'éel*. Thus, we would like for our spell-checker to identify hump'éel as "incorrectly" spelled, while still recognizing this form in the analyzer so as to cover common variation in contemporary Maya writing. We can achieve this by including the annotation `Dir/LR` on the entry for this variant. This is a very minor example, but is one of many, and is illustrative of the type of flexibility we want to maintain in our system.

The `spellrelax` file allows for orthographic variation in the input of the morphological analyzer, and the ability to map it to the canonical written forms used in our lexicon. We use this file to support the large amount of orthographic variation that is characteristic of Maya writing.

[7] https://voikko.puimula.org/

[8] https://www.libreoffice.org/discover/writer/

[9] https://www.libreoffice.org/

The following three lines illustrate how we handle (1) the common use of [j] where the OSEA orthography uses [h], (2) the omission of tone marking on long low vowels also characteristic of the contemporary INALI orthography but dispreferred for pedagogical purposes by OSEA, and (3) the use of [dz] for [ts'] in texts using the colonial style:

```
[ h (->) j ] .o. ! j for h
[àa (->) aa] .o. ! opt low mark
[ts' (->) dz] ! colonial ts'
```

Figure 3: Screenshot of spell-checking for Maya based on the analyzer discussed in this paper. The spellchecker correctly identifies the misspelling of "tàak" (which in our normative spelling requires marking of the long low vowel) and "wilike'exi'" in the incorrectly-spelled sentence "ma' taak in wilikeexi" "I don't want to see you (pl)." Note that the form *wilike'exi'* is not explicitly listed in a spelling lexicon. Instead, the analyzer contains the root verb *il*, and the morphological model enables the suggestion of the correct inflected form *w-il-ik-e'ex-i'*.

7 Coverage

On our modest-sized corpus, the morphological analyzer's coverage is about 96% on tokens and 85% on types. Of the forms currently not covered by the analyzer, many are interjections that may be author-specific (e.g. "kikiriki", the sound of a rooster crowing), and foreign loans (e.g. "cinco", "greedy"). Currently, all of the missed words by our analyzer are hapax legomena.

8 Concluding remarks and future work

We have described in detail a finite-state morphological analyzer for Maya, and demonstrated its utility outside of merely performing morphological analysis by using the model to build a spell-checker.

	N	Coverage (%)
Tokens	3,033	96
Types	734	85

Table 7: Current coverage of our analyzer on the corpus. All of the words not yet covered have a frequency of one.

For the near future, our first priority is growing the corpus. We are in the process of normalizing the orthography for a number of additional texts which we will then add and use to update the analyzer lexicon. Outside of simply improving the vocabulary and coverage of the analyzer, we plan to explore the numerous ways this tool can be of use to students by incorporating it into a browser-extension that aids the user's understanding of Maya texts read in the browser.

We also hope to improve the spell-checker by adding a better-informed error model that takes into consideration common spelling mistakes. Adding support for the spell-checker in other popular word processors is a longer-term goal, as this would greatly improve accessibility of the tool for teachers and students.

9 Acknowledgements

We are grateful to David Bolles for his permission to use, modify, and release his texts. We also extend a sincere thank you to Meesum Alam, Laura Merino Hernández, Héctor Figueroa, Matthew Fort, and Alex O'neil for their careful reading and thoughtful feedback of drafts of the present paper, and to the anonymous reviewers for their helpful comments.

References

Kenneth R Beesley and Lauri Karttunen. 2003. Finite-state morphology: Xerox tools and techniques. *CSLI, Stanford.*

Mourad Ben Slimane. 2008. *Appropriating new technology for minority language revitalization: The Welsh case.* Ph.D. thesis, Freie Universität Berlin.

Robert Wallace Blair and Refugio Vermont-Salas. 1965. *Spoken Yucatec Maya.* University of Chicago Library, Chicago.

Jürgen Bohnemeyer. 1998. *Time relations in discourse. Evidence from a comparative approach to Yukatek Maya.* Ph.D. thesis, Tilburg University.

David Bolles and Alejandra Bolles. 2001. *A grammar of the Yucatecan Mayan language*. Labyrinthos.

Victoria Reifler Bricker, Eleuterio Po ot Yah, and Ofelia Dzul de Po ot. 1998. *A dictionary of the Maya language: As spoken in Hocabá, Yucatán*. University of Utah Press.

Michal Brody. 2004. *The fixed word, the moving tongue: Variation in written Yucatec Maya and the meandering evolution toward unified norms*. The University of Texas at Austin.

Quetzil E Castañeda. 2014. Ko'ox Tsíikbal Màayat'àan: Beginning and Intermediate Level Maya. Volume One (Introduction Essential Grammar), Volume Two (Beginning Maya Workbook), Volume Three (Intermediate Maya Workbook).

Quetzil E Castañeda and Edber Dzidz Yam. 2014. Ko'ox Kanik Màaya: Grammar and Workbook for First Year Maya.

Richard Oliver Collin. 2010. Ethnologue. *Ethnopolitics*, 9(3-4):425–432.

Robert MW Dixon and Robert MW Dixon. 1994. *Ergativity*. Cambridge University Press.

Mikel L Forcada, Mireia Ginestí-Rosell, Jacob Nordfalk, Jim O'Regan, Sergio Ortiz-Rojas, Juan Antonio Pérez-Ortiz, Felipe Sánchez-Martínez, Gema Ramírez-Sánchez, and Francis M Tyers. 2011. Apertium: a free/open-source platform for rule-based machine translation. *Machine translation*, 25:127–144.

Michael Gasser. 2011. Computational morphology and the teaching of indigenous languages. In *Indigenous Languages of Latin America Actas del Primer Simposio sobre Enseñanza de Lenguas Indígenas de América Latina*, page 52.

Fred Karlsson, Atro Voutilainen, Juha Heikkilae, and Arto Anttila. 2011. *Constraint Grammar: a language-independent system for parsing unrestricted text*, volume 4. Walter de Gruyter.

Lauri Karttunen, Kimmo Koskenniemi, and Ronald Kaplan. 1987. A compiler for two-level phonological rules. *Tools for morphological analysis*.

Tanmai Khanna, Jonathan N Washington, Francis M Tyers, Sevilay Bayatlı, Daniel G Swanson, Tommi A Pirinen, Irene Tang, and Hèctor Alòs i Font. 2021. Recent advances in apertium, a free/open-source rule-based machine translation platform for low-resource languages. *Machine Translation*, 35(4):475–502.

András Kornai. 1996. Extended finite state models of language. *Natural Language Engineering*, 2(4):287–290.

Jonas Kuhn and B'alam Mateo-Toledo. 2004. Applying computational linguistic techniques in a documentary project for Q'anjob'al (Mayan, Guatemala). In *Proceedings of the Fourth International Conference on Language Resources and Evaluation (LREC'04)*, Lisbon, Portugal. European Language Resources Association (ELRA).

Shannan Mattiace and Patricia Fortuny Loret de Mola. 2015. Yucatec maya organizations in san francisco, california: Ethnic identity formation across migrant generations. *Latin American Research Review*, 50:201 – 215.

Mike Maxwell and Jonathan D Amith. 2005. Language Documentation: The Nahuatl Grammar. In *Computational Linguistics and Intelligent Text Processing: 6th International Conference, CICLing 2005, Mexico City, Mexico, February 13-19, 2005. Proceedings 6*, pages 474–485. Springer.

Arya D. McCarthy, Rachel Wicks, Dylan Lewis, Aaron Mueller, Winston Wu, Oliver Adams, Garrett Nicolai, Matt Post, and David Yarowsky. 2020. The Johns Hopkins University Bible corpus: 1600+ tongues for typological exploration. In *Proceedings of the Twelfth Language Resources and Evaluation Conference*, pages 2884–2892, Marseille, France. European Language Resources Association.

Sarah Moeller, Ghazaleh Kazeminejad, Andrew Cowell, and Mans Hulden. 2018. A neural morphological analyzer for Arapaho verbs learned from a finite state transducer. In *Proceedings of the Workshop on Computational Modeling of Polysynthetic Languages*, pages 12–20.

Garrett Nicolai, Dylan Lewis, Arya D. McCarthy, Aaron Mueller, Winston Wu, and David Yarowsky. 2020. Fine-grained morphosyntactic analysis and generation tools for more than one thousand languages. In *Proceedings of the Twelfth Language Resources and Evaluation Conference*, pages 3963–3972, Marseille, France. European Language Resources Association.

Alexis Palmer, Taesun Moon, Jason Baldridge, Katrin Erk, Eric Campbell, and Telma Can. 2010. Computational strategies for reducing annotation effort in language documentation: A case study in creating interlinear texts for uspanteko. *Linguistic Issues in Language Technology*, 3.

Alexis Mary Palmer. 2009. *Semi-automated annotation and active learning for language documentation*. Ph.D. thesis, University of Texas, Austin.

Tommi Pirinen et al. 2014. *Weighted Finite-State Methods for Spell-Checking and Correction*. Ph.D. thesis, Helsingin yliopisto.

Christian Prager, Nikolai Grube, Maximilian Brodhun, Katja Diederichs, Franziska Diehr, Sven Gronemeyer, and Elisabeth Wagner. 2018. 5 the Digital Exploration of Maya Hieroglyphic Writing and Language. *Crossing Experiences in Digital Epigraphy: From Practice to Discipline*, pages 65–83.

Robert Pugh and Francis Tyers. 2021. Towards an open source finite-state morphological analyzer for Zacatlán-Ahuacatlán-Tepetzintla Nahuatl. In *Proceedings of the 4th Workshop on the Use of Computational Methods in the Study of Endangered Languages Volume 1 (Papers)*, pages 80–85.

J. Reyhner. 1999. Some basics of indigenous language revitalization. `http://jan.ucc.nau.edu/~jar/RIL_Contents.html`.

Ivy Richardson and Francis M Tyers. 2021. A morphological analyser for K'iche'. *Procesamiento del Lenguaje Natural*, 66:99–109.

SEP & INALI. 2014. *U nu'ukbesajil u ts'íibta'al maayat'aan (Normas de escritura para la lengua maya)*.

Rustam Shadiev and Mengke Yang. 2020. Review of studies on technology-enhanced language learning and teaching. *Sustainability*, 12(2):524.

Yoshida Shigeto. 2011. *Guía gramatical del maya yucateco para los hispanohablantes*. Ministerio del Educación, ciencia y Cultura del gobierno japonés, Japón.

Gerardo Sierra Martínez, Cynthia Montaño, Gemma Bel-Enguix, Diego Córdova, and Margarita Mota Montoya. 2020. CPLM, a parallel corpus for Mexican languages: Development and interface. In *Proceedings of the Twelfth Language Resources and Evaluation Conference*, pages 2947–2952, Marseille, France. European Language Resources Association.

Ana Tona, Guillaume Thomas, and Ewan Dunbar. 2023. A morphological analyzer for Huasteca Nahuatl. In *Proceedings of the Sixth Workshop on the Use of Computational Methods in the Study of Endangered Languages*, pages 112–116.

Francis Tyers and Samuel Herrera Castro. 2023. Towards a finite-state morphological analyser for San Mateo Huave. In *Proceedings of the Sixth Workshop on the Use of Computational Methods in the Study of Endangered Languages*, pages 30–37.

Francis Tyers and Robert Henderson. 2021. A corpus of k'iche'annotated for morphosyntactic structure. In *Proceedings of the First Workshop on Natural Language Processing for Indigenous Languages of the Americas*, pages 10–20.

Francis Tyers and Nick Howell. 2021. A survey of part-of-speech tagging approaches applied to k'iche'. In *Proceedings of the First Workshop on Natural Language Processing for Indigenous Languages of the Americas*, pages 44–52.

Cristina Vertan and Christian Prager. 2022. From inscription to semi-automatic annotation of maya hieroglyphic texts. In *Proceedings of the Second Workshop on Language Technologies for Historical and Ancient Languages*, pages 114–118, Marseille, France. European Language Resources Association.

Jonathan Washington, Felipe Lopez, and Brook Lillehaugen. 2021. Towards a morphological transducer and orthography converter for Western Tlacolula Valley Zapotec. In *Proceedings of the First Workshop on Natural Language Processing for Indigenous Languages of the Americas*, pages 185–193.

Shiyue Zhang, Ben Frey, and Mohit Bansal. 2022. How can NLP help revitalize endangered languages? a case study and roadmap for the Cherokee language. *arXiv preprint arXiv:2204.11909*.

Modelling the Reduplicating Lushootseed Morphology with an FST and LSTM

Jack Rueter
University of Helsinki
first.last@helsinki.fi

Mika Hämäläinen
Metropolia University of Applied Sciences
first.last@metropolia.fi

Khalid Alnajjar
Rootroo Ltd
first@rootroo.com

Abstract

In this paper, we present an FST based approach for conducting morphological analysis, lemmatization and generation of Lushootseed words. Furthermore, we use the FST to generate training data for an LSTM based neural model and train this model to do morphological analysis. The neural model reaches a 71.9% accuracy on the test data. Furthermore, we discuss reduplication types in the Lushootseed language forms. The approach involves the use of both attested instances of reduplication and bare stems for applying a variety of reduplications to, as it is unclear just how much variation can be attributed to the individual speakers and authors of the source materials. That is, there may be areal factors that can be aligned with certain types of reduplication and their frequencies.

1 Introduction

A significant proportion of the world's languages face the threat of endangerment to varying degrees. This endangered status poses certain constraints on the extent to which modern NLP research can be conducted with such languages. This is due to the fact that many endangered languages lack extensive textual resources that are readily accessible online. Furthermore, even with available resources, there is concern about the quality of the data, as it may be influenced by various factors such as the author's level of fluency, accuracy of spelling, and inconsistencies in character encoding at the most basic level (see Hämäläinen 2021).

Reduplication appears in many languages of the world (Raimy, 2000). While full reduplication is observed as a repeated word form, partial reduplication is associated with extensive variety both regular and irregular. This paper focuses on a finite-state description of the partial reduplication patterns found in the Lushootseed language forms (lut) and (slh). The most predominant forms of reduplication in Lushootseed are distributive (Distr) and diminutive (Dim), which can, in fact, appear in tandem, but there are restrictions delimiting their use (see Broselow 1983, Bates 1986, Urbanczyk 1994). In addition to Distr and Dim, however, we also find a third and slightly less frequent random or out of control distributive (OC) (see Bates et al. 1994, Urbanczyk 1996).

The base of these three types of reduplication can be found in the initial two to three phonemes of the word root most often referred to with the notation C_1VC_2, but the authors of this paper will surround the vowel with parentheses to indicate the possibility of its absence: $C_1(V)C_2$ and thus accommodate the radical CC mentioned in (Beck 1999:24; Crowgey 2019: 39, 42).

The radical consist of simple and compound letters alike, e.g., q́ʷ, gʷ, ƛ', all of which add to the issues of facilitating the extensive variation in Lushootseed reduplication. First, the concept of compound letters involved in regular reduplication segments is a very import part of finite-state description for Lushootseed. Although the 46 phonemes canonize the extensive alphabet, they create their own demands on the description.

Our facilitation of Lushootseed reduplication with a finite-state machine[1] is based on the use of a five-place holder segement concatenated directly before the radical. We number these right-to-left away from the radical {p5}{p4}{p3}{p2}{p1} where the odd-numbered place holders represent consonants, and the even-numbered ones vowels. The system is set up so that the place holders {p3}{p2}{p1} are used with Distr, Dim and OC reduplication, whereas the more remote place holders {p5}{p4} are used to deal with Distr + Dim combinations. Albeit, theory sees the distributive losing the third phoneme due to a principle of antigemination (see Broselow 1983: 326–329, and Urbanczyk 1994: 515) referencing also (Hess

[1] Our code is published in https://github.com/giellalt/lang-lut

Proceedings of the Workshop on Natural Language Processing for Indigenous Languages of the Americas (AmericasNLP), pages 40–46
July 14, 2023 ©2023 Association for Computational Linguistics

1967: 7) and (Snyder 1968: 22). We have assumed the absence of geminates and therefore have left them out of the equation. Perhaps, further studies will require their addition to our finite-state description of reduplication in permeating the Lushootseed vocabulary.

2 Related work

Several different methods are currently in use to model morphology of endangered languages computationally. In this section, we will covers some of the existing rule-based, statistical and neural approaches. Our method embraces the rule-based tradition because machine-learning based methods rely on a lot of annoated data we currently do not have for Lushootseed.

In the rule-based research, morphology has mainly been modelled using a finite-state transducer (FST) using one of several technologies such as HFST (Lindén et al., 2013), OpenFST (Allauzen et al., 2007) or Foma (Hulden, 2009). Such an approach has been successful in describing languages of a variety of different morphological groups such as polysynthetic languages (e.g. Plains Cree (Snoek et al., 2014), East Cree (Arppe et al., 2017) and Odawa (Bowers et al., 2017)), agglutinative languages (e.g. Komi-Zyrian (Rueter et al., 2021), San Mateo Huave (Tyers and Castro, 2023), Skolt Sami (Rueter and Hämäläinen, 2020), Sakha (Ivanova et al., 2022) and Erzya (Rueter et al., 2020)) and fusional languages (e.g. Akkadian (Sahala et al., 2020) and Arabic (Shaalan and Attia, 2012)).

For statistical approaches, Tang (2006) has done research on English morphology by an approach that comprises two interrelated components, which are morphological rule learning and morphological analysis. The morphological rules are acquired by means of statistical learning from a list of words. On another line of work, Kumar et al. (2009) has developed a machine learning technique that utilizes sequence labeling and kernel methods for training, which enables the model to effectively capture the non-linear associations between various aspects of the morphological features found in Tamil.

With the emergence of UniMorph (McCarthy et al., 2020), which continues to include only partial morphological descriptions of each language, a great deal of neural based research has emerged to conduct morphological analysis. The typical models that are used are LSTM (Matteson et al., 2018; Akyürek et al., 2019) and Transformer (see Kodner et al. 2022) based models.

3 Materials and methods

The materials used for this paper come from the Lushootseed dictionary of Bates et al., 1994 and language learning binders by Zalmai Zahir and Peggy k^{w}iʔalq Ahvakana (Book 1 d^{z}ix^w First, Book 2 dəg^{w}i You, Book 3 s.ʔəɬəd Food, Book 4 ʔalʔal House) as well as a binder of transcriptions to recordings from the University of Washington archives received in 2003 on the Muckleshoot Reservation.

The method involves a mnemonic descriptive approach, implemented for a decidely deterministic machine and human-friendly solution – if there is such a thing. To this end, we adhere to a three-phoneme segment approach to Lushootseed description and simply start with the labeling 123. Here ‹1› indicates the first consonant of the radical (root), ‹2› the vowel (which seems to be absent/latent in at least a few roots), and ‹3› the second consonant. We then introduce a series of five ordered place holders to precede the root.

The insertion of place holders is convenient in this finite-state description if they come before the root. Although there are numerous segments of regular morphology, inserting a series of five place holders immediately before the root can be seen as just another step in regular concatenation. Here it might be mentioned that theoretic distinctions between inflection and clitics do not come before consideration for orthographic practices (cf. Beck 2018).

The five place holder, numbering away from the first three letters of the root is set so the odd numbers correlate with the consonants and the even numbers with the vowels. Thus, {p3} correlates with k^w, {p2} with *a*, and {p1} with *t*

{p5} {p4} {p3} {p2} {p1} k^w a t

k^{w}atač: k^{w}atač 'climb'

s‹k^{w}atač: sk^{w}atač 'mountain'

s ‹ {p5}:0 {p4}:0 {p3}:k^w {p2}:a {p1}:0 k^w a t a č :

sk^{w}ak^{w}ətač 'mountains'

s ‹ {p5}:0 {p4}:0 {p3}:k^w {p2}:a {p1}:0 k^w a:0 t a č :

sk^{w}ak^{w}tač 'hill'

With this as a point of departure, we can then enumerate four predominant tendencies, one – total reduplication, one – partial to the left, two partial to the right. First, total reduplication is 123123, which is extremely regular and typically distributive in meaning. Second, comes the diminutive with extensive variation: 1213, 12123, 1i13, 1i123, 1iq13. Third, and less frequent in the materials are 123

4 FST models

The finite-state description of Lushootseed involves several layers of experience. It addresses issues involving orthography, morphophonology, concatenation and symmetric tagging for subsequent machine readability. The orthography, which is canonized by the language's reduplication patterns, uses lower-case letters with multiple diacritics, as no precomposed letters are available for nearly half of the alphabet. The concatenative morphology, which with the exception of the possessive person marking strategy, is symmetric but involves abbreviated or short-hand forms for some consecutive morphemes. The variation in multiple reduplication patterns appears to be partially monolectic or geographic in nature, but there is definitely also breathing room for variation in where individual derivations are used. In general, both preposed and postposed affixing is present, and, in particular, there is asymmetry in the possessive person marking strategy. For language-independent comparison, we use flag diacritics in our models, which allows us supersegmental concatenation and facilitates regular tagging practices for use in downstream language technology, even work with Python libraries.

4.1 Orthography

Although there are established keyboard layouts provided on official language-community sites [2], there are other keyboards, which may include nonstandard diactritic and letter combinations, that are visibly present on the net and in easily accessible language materials. This has meant the establishment of *spellrelax* files to allow for recognizing non-word internal single right quotation mark, instead of a combining comma above diacritic, for example, or even small letter L with middle tilde ‹U+026B› in place of small letter L with belt ‹U+026C›.

4.2 Concatenation and Tagging

Reduplication has been dealt with as a problematic feature in earlier descriptions of the languages where it is regarded as nonlinear (see Urbanczyk 1996). Our solution has been to introduce a segment of five place holders that facilitate copying values directly to predefined positions. As our concatenation in compilation reads right-to-left, memory retention is minimized to the three phonemes before the place holder series {p5}{p4}{p3}{p2}{p1}. If these place holders are to be used, the machine has already seen the reduplication trigger, which appears left of the word stem.

The relatively mnemonic triggers have been named according to relative position in the radical model C_1VC_2, i.e., 123. Thus, the distributive reduplication $C_1VC_2C_1VC_2$ is labeled distr_trigger_123123. Analogically, the diminutive reduplications $C_1VC_1C_2$, $C_1iC_1C_2$, $C_1iʔC_1C_2$, $C_1iʔC_1VC_2$ are represented by the triggers dim_trigger1213, dim_trigger1i13, dim_trigger1iq13, dim_trigger1iq123, respectively. OC reduplication (out of control, random) in $C_1VC_2VC_2$ is represented by OC_12323.

The reduplication *g*^{w}*aadg*^{w}*ad* in *lə =bə =lə cu–g*^{w}*aadg*^{w}*ad* (source Beck 2018: example 13) 'talking' could be illustrated as $C_1VVC_2C_1VC_2$, i.e., trigger_122123. The underlying use of our placeholders, however, would show the following transformation

{p5}:1 {p4}:2 {p3}:0 {p2}:2 {p1}:3 1 2 3
{p5}:g^{w} {p4}:a {p3}:0 {p2}:a {p1}:d g^{w} a d

Reduplication triggers are accompanied by diacritic flags, which make it possible to position tags in the output. Flag diacritics are also used to address the symmetrical tagging of prefixes after the lemma, on the one hand, and to disallow simultaneous tagging for two possessive markers, on the other.

5 Current state

Presently the lexicon is extremely small. It contains 110 verbs and 283 nouns, which might explain the low coverage rate of 70%, i.e., 1822 unrecognized tokens out of a total of 6186 tokens in the test corpus.

The two-level model has 31 rules governing reduplication copying patterns in the place holders and vowel loss or permutation in the root. The vowel system has be complemented by vowels with acute and grave accents, which might be useful in pedagogical use of the language model, and in work with language variation across the continuum of the language community.

[2]https://tulaliplushootseed.com/software-and-fonts/

source	target
ł u l ə č ' i č ' č ' i č ' ə l p y a q i d	N Pl Nom
a d d ə x ʷ t u b u ʔ q ʷ ə x ʷ	N Sg Nom RemPst Ptc PxSg2 Clt
b ə a d d ə x ʷ t u b u ʔ b u ʔ q ʷ	N Pl Nom Anew RemPst Ptc PxSg2

Table 1: Examples of the training data

tag	Anew	Clt	Hab	Irr	Pl	Ptc	PxPl1	PxPl2	PxSP3	PxSg1	PxSg2	RemPst	Sg
precision	0.77	0.96	1.00	0.98	0.94	0.91	0.90	0.89	0.80	0.83	0.92	0.81	0.87
recall	0.97	0.77	0.89	0.97	0.95	0.89	0.79	0.55	0.61	0.90	0.91	0.99	0.82
F1-score	0.86	0.86	0.94	0.98	0.94	0.90	0.84	0.68	0.69	0.87	0.91	0.89	0.84

Table 2: Per tag results of the neural model

The lexc continuation lexica number at 135. These continuation lexica provide coverage for regular nominal and verbal inflection, which utilizes a mutual set of morphology controlled partially with flag diacritics.

6 Neural Extension

No matter how extensive an FST transducer is, it still cannot cover the entire lexicon of a language. For this reason, we also experiment with training neural models to do morphological analysis based on the FST transducer described in this paper. The goal is not to replace the FST we have described in this paper, but to develop a neural "fallback" model that can be used when a word is not covered by the FST.

We follow the approach suggested by Hämäläinen et al. (2021), we use the code that has been made available in UralicNLP (Hämäläinen, 2019). This approach consists of querying the FST transducer for all the possible morphological forms for a given lemma. For a given input, the FST will thus produce all possible inflections and their morphological readings.

We limit our data to nouns only, and we use a list of 214 Lushootseed nouns to generate all the possible morphological forms for. This way, we produce a dataset consisting of around 756,000 inflectional form-morphological reading tuplets. This means that we have an average of 3536 inflectional forms for each lemma. We split this data into 70% training, 15% validation and 15% testing. The test data has words that are completely unseen to the model in the training data. This means that in the testing, the model needs to analyze based on lemmas and word forms it has not seen before even in a partial paradigm.

For the model itself, we use a Python library called OpenNMT (Klein et al., 2017) and use it to train an LSTM based recurrent neural network architecture with the default settings of the library. The task is defined as a character-level neural machine translation problem where each word form are split into characters separated by a white-space in the target side and the morphological readings produced by the FST are split into separate morphological tokens. Examples of the training data can be seen in Table 1.

The overall **accuracy of the model is 71.9%**. This is measured by counting how many full morphological readings the model predicted correctly for each word form in the test corpus. The results per morphological tag can be seen in Table 2. These results exclude the *N* (noun) tag and *Nom* (nominative) tag because all morphological forms had those tags in the dataset.

7 Discussion and Conclusions

In order to further test the accuracy of our Lushootseed description, more test data and descriptions of regular inflection will be needed. The challenge is to continue with the outline given for an inflectional complex (see Lonsdale 2001) and define what can actually be described as regular.

More time will be required to model more recent reanalyses of the morphological complexes. This means we may need to establish whether a six-placeholder segment is required to aptly describe Lushootseed reduplication and put our description in line with a hypothesis of antigemination.

The idea of describing morphological complexes as series of aligned clitics is very interesting (see Beck 2018). This will actually provide fuel for future work with syntax, since most of the semantic information is already present in the word roots where the clitics conglomerate.

Limitations

The FST does not yet have an extensive coverage of the Lushootseed vocabulary, so it does not work on all domains of text. Also, writing an FST takes a lot of time and requires special knowledge of the language. The neural model is limited to nouns only, but it can work on out-of-vocabulary words unlike the FST, however, we have only tested its accuracy using the words that are known to the FST, which means that words that follow very different inflection patterns will, most likely, not be analyzed correctly. Furthermore, the neural model was not trained on derivational morphology, which means that word derivations might also result in erroneous predictions.

Ethics statement

When dealing with an endangered language it is important to make sure that the research also contributes to the language community. This is the reason why we open-source our FST and neural model. We also work on data that has been given to us by speakers of Lushootseed with the intention of us working on building morphological descriptons and tools for the language. This means that we are not conducting our research with no regard to the language community.

Acknowledgments

This research is supported by FIN-CLARIN and Academy of Finland (grant 345610 *Kielivarojen ja kieliteknologian tutkimusinfrastruktuuri*).

References

Ekin Akyürek, Erenay Dayanık, and Deniz Yuret. 2019. Morphological analysis using a sequence decoder. *Transactions of the Association for Computational Linguistics*, 7:567–579.

Cyril Allauzen, Michael Riley, Johan Schalkwyk, Wojciech Skut, and Mehryar Mohri. 2007. Openfst: A general and efficient weighted finite-state transducer library: (extended abstract of an invited talk). In *Implementation and Application of Automata: 12th International Conference, CIAA 2007, Praque, Czech Republic, July 16-18, 2007, Revised Selected Papers 12*, pages 11–23. Springer.

Antti Arppe, Marie-Odile Junker, and Delasie Torkornoo. 2017. Converting a comprehensive lexical database into a computational model: The case of East Cree verb inflection. In *Proceedings of the 2nd Workshop on the Use of Computational Methods in the Study of Endangered Languages*, pages 52–56, Honolulu. Association for Computational Linguistics.

Dawn Bates. 1986. An analysis of lushootseed diminutive reduplication. *Proceedings of the Twelfth Annual Meeting of the Berkeley Linguistics Society (1986), pp. 1–13.*

Dawn Bates, Thom Hess, and Vi Hilbert. 1994. *Lushootseed Dictionary*. University of Washington Press. Seattle and London. Bates, Dawn (ed.).

D. Beck. 1999. Words and prosodic phrasing in lushootseed narrative. *In Hall, T. A. and Kleinhenz, U., editors, Studies on the Phonological Word, pages 23–46.*

David Beck. 2018. Aspectual affixation in lushootseed: A minor reanalysis. In *Wa7 xweysás i nqwal'utteníha i ucwalmícwa: He loves the people's languages. Essays in honour of Henry Davis*. UBC Occasional Papers in Linguistics.

Dustin Bowers, Antti Arppe, Jordan Lachler, Sjur Moshagen, and Trond Trosterud. 2017. A morphological parser for odawa. In *Proceedings of the 2nd Workshop on the Use of Computational Methods in the Study of Endangered Languages*, pages 1–9, Honolulu. Association for Computational Linguistics.

Ellen Broselow. 1983. Salish double reduplications: Subjacency in morphology. *Natural Language Linguistic Theory 1(3).*

Joshua Crowgey. 2019. *Braiding Language (by Computer): Lushootseed Grammar Engineering*. University of Washington. A dissertation submitted in partial fulfillment of the requirements for the degree of Doctor of Philosophy,.

Mika Hämäläinen. 2019. Uralicnlp: An nlp library for uralic languages. *Journal of open source software.*

Mika Hämäläinen. 2021. Endangered languages are not low-resourced! *Multilingual Facilitation.*

Mika Hämäläinen, Niko Partanen, Jack Rueter, and Khalid Alnajjar. 2021. Neural morphology dataset and models for multiple languages, from the large to the endangered. In *Proceedings of the 23rd Nordic Conference on Computational Linguistics (NoDaLiDa)*, pages 166–177, Reykjavik, Iceland (Online). Linköping University Electronic Press, Sweden.

Thom. Hess. 1967. *Snohomish Grammatical Structure*. Unpublished Ph.D. dissertation. University of Washington.

Mans Hulden. 2009. Foma: a finite-state compiler and library. In *Proceedings of the Demonstrations Session at EACL 2009*, pages 29–32, Athens, Greece. Association for Computational Linguistics.

Sardana Ivanova, Jonathan Washington, and Francis Tyers. 2022. A free/open-source morphological analyser and generator for sakha. In *Proceedings of the Thirteenth Language Resources and Evaluation Conference*, pages 5137–5142, Marseille, France. European Language Resources Association.

Guillaume Klein, Yoon Kim, Yuntian Deng, Jean Senellart, and Alexander Rush. 2017. OpenNMT: Open-source toolkit for neural machine translation. In *Proceedings of ACL 2017, System Demonstrations*, pages 67–72, Vancouver, Canada. Association for Computational Linguistics.

Jordan Kodner, Salam Khalifa, Khuyagbaatar Batsuren, Hossep Dolatian, Ryan Cotterell, Faruk Akkus, Antonios Anastasopoulos, Taras Andrushko, Aryaman Arora, Nona Atanalov, Gábor Bella, Elena Budianskaya, Yustinus Ghanggo Ate, Omer Goldman, David Guriel, Simon Guriel, Silvia Guriel-Agiashvili, Witold Kieraś, Andrew Krizhanovsky, Natalia Krizhanovsky, Igor Marchenko, Magdalena Markowska, Polina Mashkovtseva, Maria Nepomniashchaya, Daria Rodionova, Karina Scheifer, Alexandra Sorova, Anastasia Yemelina, Jeremiah Young, and Ekaterina Vylomova. 2022. SIGMORPHON–UniMorph 2022 shared task 0: Generalization and typologically diverse morphological inflection. In *Proceedings of the 19th SIGMORPHON Workshop on Computational Research in Phonetics, Phonology, and Morphology*, pages 176–203, Seattle, Washington. Association for Computational Linguistics.

Arun Kumar, V Dhanalakshmi, RU Rekha, KP Soman, S Rajendran, et al. 2009. Morphological analyzer for agglutinative languages using machine learning approaches. In *2009 International Conference on Advances in Recent Technologies in Communication and Computing*, pages 433–435. IEEE.

Krister Lindén, Erik Axelson, Senka Drobac, Sam Hardwick, Juha Kuokkala, Jyrki Niemi, Tommi A Pirinen, and Miikka Silfverberg. 2013. Hfst—a system for creating nlp tools. In *Systems and Frameworks for Computational Morphology: Third International Workshop, SFCM 2013, Berlin, Germany, September 6, 2013 Proceedings 3*, pages 53–71. Springer.

Deryle. Lonsdale. 2001. A two-level implementation for lushootseed morphology. *Papers for ICSNL 36 (Bar-el, L., L. Watt, and I. Wilson, eds.). UBCWPL 6:203– 214.*

Andrew Matteson, Chanhee Lee, Youngbum Kim, and Heuiseok Lim. 2018. Rich character-level information for Korean morphological analysis and part-of-speech tagging. In *Proceedings of the 27th International Conference on Computational Linguistics*, pages 2482–2492, Santa Fe, New Mexico, USA. Association for Computational Linguistics.

Arya D. McCarthy, Christo Kirov, Matteo Grella, Amrit Nidhi, Patrick Xia, Kyle Gorman, Ekaterina Vylomova, Sabrina J. Mielke, Garrett Nicolai, Miikka Silfverberg, Timofey Arkhangelskiy, Nataly Krizhanovsky, Andrew Krizhanovsky, Elena Klyachko, Alexey Sorokin, John Mansfield, Valts Ernštreits, Yuval Pinter, Cassandra L. Jacobs, Ryan Cotterell, Mans Hulden, and David Yarowsky. 2020. UniMorph 3.0: Universal Morphology. In *Proceedings of the Twelfth Language Resources and Evaluation Conference*, pages 3922–3931, Marseille, France. European Language Resources Association.

Eric Raimy. 2000. *The phonology and morphology of reduplication*. de Gruyter.

Jack Rueter and Mika Hämäläinen. 2020. FST morphology for the endangered Skolt Sami language. In *Proceedings of the 1st Joint Workshop on Spoken Language Technologies for Under-resourced languages (SLTU) and Collaboration and Computing for Under-Resourced Languages (CCURL)*, pages 250–257, Marseille, France. European Language Resources association.

Jack Rueter, Mika Hämäläinen, and Niko Partanen. 2020. Open-source morphology for endangered mordvinic languages. In *Proceedings of Second Workshop for NLP Open Source Software (NLP-OSS)*, pages 94–100, Online. Association for Computational Linguistics.

Jack Rueter, Niko Partanen, Mika Hämäläinen, and Trond Trosterud. 2021. Overview of open-source morphology development for the Komi-Zyrian language: Past and future. In *Proceedings of the Seventh International Workshop on Computational Linguistics of Uralic Languages*, pages 29–39, Syktyvkar, Russia (Online). Association for Computational Linguistics.

Aleksi Sahala, Miikka Silfverberg, Antti Arppe, and Krister Lindén. 2020. BabyFST - towards a finite-state based computational model of ancient babylonian. In *Proceedings of the Twelfth Language Resources and Evaluation Conference*, pages 3886–3894, Marseille, France. European Language Resources Association.

Khaled Shaalan and Mohammed Attia. 2012. Handling unknown words in Arabic FST morphology. In *Proceedings of the 10th International Workshop on Finite State Methods and Natural Language Processing*, pages 20–24, Donostia–San Sebastián. Association for Computational Linguistics.

Conor Snoek, Dorothy Thunder, Kaidi Lõo, Antti Arppe, Jordan Lachler, Sjur Moshagen, and Trond Trosterud. 2014. Modeling the noun morphology of Plains Cree. In *Proceedings of the 2014 Workshop on the Use of Computational Methods in the Study of Endangered Languages*, pages 34–42, Baltimore, Maryland, USA. Association for Computational Linguistics.

Warren Snyder. 1968. *Southern Puget Sound Salish Texts, Place Names, and Dictionary*, volume 9. Sacramento; Sacramento Anthropological Society.

Xuri Tang. 2006. English morphological analysis with machine-learned rules. In *Proceedings of the 20th Pacific Asia Conference on Language, Information and*

Computation, pages 35–41, Huazhong Normal University, Wuhan, China. Tsinghua University Press.

Francis M. Tyers and Samuel Herrera Castro. 2023. Towards a finite-state morphological analyser for san mateo huave. In *Proceedings of the Sixth Workshop on the Use of Computational Methods in the Study of Endangered Languages*, pages 30–37, Remote. Association for Computational Linguistics.

Suzanne Urbanczyk. 1994. Double reduplication in parallel. *Proceedings of the June 1994 Prosodic Morphology Workshop. Utrecht.*

Suzanne Urbanczyk. 1996. Morphological templates in reduplication. *University of Massachusetts/University of British Columbia.*

Fine-tuning Sentence-RoBERTa to Construct Word Embeddings for Low-resource Languages from Bilingual Dictionaries

Diego Bear
University of New Brunswick
Faculty of Computer Science
diego.bear@unb.ca

Paul Cook
University of New Brunswick
Faculty of Computer Science
paul.cook@unb.ca

Abstract

Conventional approaches to learning word embeddings (Mikolov et al., 2013; Pennington et al., 2014) are limited to relatively few languages with sufficiently large training corpora. To address this limitation, we propose an alternative approach to deriving word embeddings for Wolastoqey and Mi'kmaq that leverages definitions from a bilingual dictionary. More specifically, following Bear and Cook (2022), we experiment with encoding English definitions of Wolastoqey and Mi'kmaq words into vector representations using English sequence representation models. For this, we consider using and fine-tuning sentence-RoBERTa models (Reimers and Gurevych, 2019). We evaluate our word embeddings using a similar methodology to that of Bear and Cook using evaluations based on word classification, clustering and reverse dictionary search. We additionally construct word embeddings for higher-resource languages — English, German and Spanish — using our methods and evaluate our embeddings on existing word-similarity datasets. Our findings indicate that our word embedding methods can be used to produce meaningful vector representations for low-resource languages such as Wolastoqey and Mi'kmaq and for higher-resource languages.

1 Introduction

Word embeddings (Mikolov et al., 2013; Pennington et al., 2014) are real-numbered vector representations of the meanings of words and are a fundamental component of many natural language processing (NLP) systems. Although word embeddings can often be learnt while training NLP systems end-to-end, pretrained word embeddings have been shown to bolster the performance of NLP systems in tasks such as machine translation (Qi et al., 2018) and information retrieval (Roy et al., 2018). Despite their utility, quality word embeddings can be difficult to obtain as they generally require large corpora of running text to train. This represents a significant limitation of conventional word embedding methods as, due to these data requirements, quality word embeddings can only be learnt for relatively few languages. Today, a majority of languages spoken around the world are low-resource (Arppe et al., 2016), and thus lack the text resources required to train high quality word embeddings. As this is the case, an alternative embedding approach is desirable to make better use of what data exists for low-resource languages.

In the case of Wolastoqey (also referred to as Passamaquoddy-Maliseet) and Mi'kmaq, there simply isn't enough data available in these languages to train quality word embeddings using conventional methods. Wolastoqey and Mi'kmaq are both low-resource Eastern Algonquin languages. There are currently approximately 300 remaining first language speakers of Wolastoqey and $7k$ speakers of Mi'kmaq (Statistics Canada, 2017) in Canada. Due to the low-resource state of these languages, developing language technologies for Wolastoqey and Mi'kmaq is challenging because there are no large corpora or annotated datasets available in these languages to train NLP systems. Despite not having large corpora or datasets available, both a bilingual Wolastoqey–English dictionary, known as the Passamaquoddy-Maliseet Dictionary (Francis and Leavitt, 2008), and a bilingual Mi'kmaq-English dictionary, known as the Mi'gmaq/Mi'kmaq Online Dictionary (Haberlin et al., 1997), are available. These dictionaries contain English definitions for Wolastoqey and Mi'kmaq headwords and consist of a total of $18.6k$ and $6.5k$ entries, respectively. In our work, we experiment with using these dictionaries to construct word embeddings for Wolastoqey and Mi'kmaq.

Previous work has demonstrated that bilingual lexicons and monolingual corpora can be leveraged to train cross-lingual word embeddings for low-resource languages. For example, Adams et al. (2017) showed that, by combining a large English

Proceedings of the Workshop on Natural Language Processing for Indigenous Languages of the Americas (AmericasNLP), pages 47–57
July 14, 2023

corpus with a small Yongning Na corpus, and by replacing words with their translations using a small bilingual lexicon, a pseudo-bilingual corpus can be created which can be used to train cross-lingual word embeddings. We do not consider this approach in our work because Wolastoqey and Mi'kmaq are polysynthetic languages, and as such, many tokens that occur in a corpus would not be expected to be found as dictionary headwords, which limits the applicability of this approach.

Instead, we look towards approaches based on sequence representation. Prior work has demonstrated that, by leveraging bilingual dictionaries, useful vector representations can be constructed for Nêhiyawêwin (Plains Cree) words. By averaging word embeddings corresponding to words that appear in English definitions of Nêhiyawêwin words, embeddings can be obtained which can be used to effectively cluster Nêhiyawêwin words (Harrigan and Arppe, 2021) and map them to preconstructed ontologies (Dacanay et al., 2021).

Bear and Cook (2022) extended the methodology of Harrigan and Arppe (2021) and Dacanay et al. (2021) to construct word embeddings for Wolastoqey. They used the average of word2vec embeddings to represent words from their dictionary definitions, as well as RoBERTa, and sentence-RoBERTa models to encode definitions into vector representations. These embeddings were then evaluated based on word classification tasks focused on predicting part-of speech, animacy, and transitivity; semantic clustering; and reverse dictionary search. In each evaluation, it was found that approaches using these embeddings outperformed task-specific baselines, indicating that sentence-transformer models can outperform approaches based on word embeddings for this purpose.

As this approach has been shown to perform relatively well, in this paper, we build upon the work of Bear and Cook (2022) by fine-tuning sequence representation models for this task. More specifically, we propose fine-tuning sentence-RoBERTa models on monolingual dictionary definitions to determine if doing so could improve the overall quality of the representations. Using these fine-tuned models, we construct word embeddings for Wolastoqey and Mi'kmaq from English definitions in the Passamaquoddy-Maliseet Dictionary and Mi'gmaq/Mi'kmaq Online Dictionary.

Following Bear and Cook (2022), we evaluate our Wolastoqey and Mi'kmaq word embeddings on word classification tasks focused on predicting part-of speech, animacy, and transitivity as well as semantic clustering and reverse dictionary search. We compare our word embeddings against task-specific baselines and embeddings produced using the techniques of Bear and Cook. To assess if this technique is viable for other higher-resource languages, we also construct word embeddings for English, Spanish and German, and evaluate the performance of our models on word similiarity datasets, comparing against previously reported results.

2 Methodology

To obtain embeddings for Wolastoqey and Mi'kmaq words, we experiment with encoding English definitions of Wolastoqey words in the Passamaquoddy-Maliseet Dictionary, and Mi'kmaq words in the Mi'gmaq/Mi'kmaq Online Dictionary, into vector representations. To construct vector representations from English definitions, we consider fine-tuning and using sentence-transformer models, masked language models specifically trained for sequence representation. More specifically, we consider fine-tuning sentence-RoBERTa models using three training regimens from Reimers and Gurevych (2019). We compare our embeddings constructed with this approach to those created using the methodology of Bear and Cook (2022).

In our work, we fine-tune our sentence-RoBERTa models on the dataset of Hill et al. (2016). This dataset consists of word–definition pairs collected from several English dictionaries and WordNet (Miller, 1995). In our experiments, we use the training and development splits from Zheng et al. (2020). This gives us a training set consisting of a total of 667.5k word–definition pairs corresponding to 45k unique types and a development set consisting of 75.8k definitions corresponding to 5k unique types. However, due to the data requirements of our fine-tuning regimens, we filter out any definitions corresponding to words with only one unique definition and filter out duplicate definitions from both our training and development sets. This reduces our effective training corpus size to 664.7k definitions corresponding to 42.5k unique types, and our development set to 75.6k definitions corresponding to 4.7k unique types. We use our development set to ensure overfitting does not occur and to monitor training performance.

To fine-tune our sentence-RoBERTa models,

we continue training from the nli-roberta-base-v2 model available in the sentence transformer 2.1.0 library.[1] This model represents a checkpoint that has been pretrained on a large natural language inference dataset, constructed by combining the Stanford NLI corpus (Bowman et al., 2015) and the multi-genre NLI corpus (Williams et al., 2018). We consider fine-tuning three models using the softmax, cosine, and triplet loss training objectives outlined in Reimers and Gurevych (2019). Each of these training objectives requires the model to be trained in a Siamese configuration in which two or more examples are passed through the network independently before being compared to compute training loss at a given time-step.

The softmax training objective is based on classification. In our work, the classification task we fine-tune our model on is determining if two definitions correspond to the same word. To construct training pairs for this fine-tuning regimen, we pair each definition in our training set with another definition to form either a positive or negative training example. We assign half of our definitions another definition corresponding to the same word, forming a positive pair, and we assign the other half definitions that do not correspond to the same word, forming negative pairs. This gives us $664.7k$ training examples, equal to the number of definitions in our training corpus.

The cosine training objective is based on regression. More specifically, in this fine-tuning regimen, we attempt to match the cosine similarity between two output vectors to some ground truth label. To obtain examples, we form training pairs similarly to how we did for the softmax fine-tuning regimen. However, instead of assigning a binary label to pairs, we assign a ground truth cosine similarity. For positive pairs, this is simply equal to 1.0. However, for negative pairs, to obtain ground-truth cosine similarities, we use the cosine similarities computed from vectors in a word2vec model. For this purpose, we use a word embedding model that has been trained on a Google News corpus consisting of roughly 100 billion words.[2] We obtain these embeddings using gensim 3.8.3 (Řehůřek and Sojka, 2010). For each negative sample, the ground-truth cosine similarity used for training is set to the cosine similarity calculated using the embeddings for the words each definition corresponds to. In this training configuration, loss is calculated as the mean squared error between the cosine similarity of the two input vectors and the ground truth reference.

Finally, triplet loss considers three inputs, in our case definitions, at a given timestep. More specifically, this training scheme requires an anchor, as well as two additional inputs that act as positive and negative instances. When fine-tuning with this training objective, we attempt to learn weights such that the representations produced for each anchor are closer to their corresponding positive than negative instance. As this is the case, to form training examples, we treat each definition in our training set as an anchor and assign each an accompanying positive instance — a definition corresponding to the same word — and a negative instance — a definition corresponding to a different word. Like before, this gives us a total of $664.7k$ training examples to fine-tune our model with.

For each training technique considered, we fine-tune our models using the default training parameters of the sentence-transformers library. We fine-tune our models for a single epoch, as, training for three epochs appeared to degrade performance on our word classification tasks in early testing. After fine-tuning, we are left with three models, each fine-tuned using a different training regimen.

To construct word embeddings using these models, we first preprocess our input definitions using the same preprocessing steps as Bear and Cook (2022). Namely, we consider removing bracketed content from our input definitions, as, in the dictionaries we use in our work, this typically consists of topical information that does not contribute to the core meaning of definitions. We then pass our preprocessed input definitions to our sentence-RoBERTa models to obtain a vector representation based on the mean output vectors of our sentence-RoBERTa models.

3 Word Classification

Following Bear and Cook (2022), we evaluate our word embeddings on word classification tasks to determine if they are capable of capturing information about the syntactic properties of words. We consider three word classification tasks focused on predicting, 1.) part-of-speech, 2.) noun animacy and 3.) verb type. For each task, we train logistic regression classifiers to predict the syntactic labels of words from their embeddings.

[1] https://www.sbert.net/

[2] https://code.google.com/archive/p/word2vec/

3.1 Experimental Setup

To construct datasets for these evaluations, we use gold-standard labels from the Passamaquoddy-Maliseet Dictionary and Mi'gmaq/Mi'kmaq Online Dictionary. For our part-of-speech classification tasks, we consider a total of $18k$ entries from the Passamaquoddy-Maliseet Dictionary, consisting of 53 pronouns, 231 preverbs, 570 particles, $13.7k$ verbs and $3.3k$ nouns, for Wolastoqey and $6.4k$ entries from the Mi'gmaq/Mi'kmaq Online Dictionary, consisting of 16 pronouns, 119 particles, $4.6k$ verbs and $1.6k$ nouns, for Mi'kmaq. For our noun animacy classification tasks, we remove any entries corresponding to words that can occur as both animate and inanimate. In total, we use $1.7k$ animate, and $1.3k$ inanimate nouns for Wolastoqey and 756 animate, and 806 inanimate, nouns for Mi'kmaq.

In both Wolastoqey and Mi'kmaq, verbs are categorized into four distinct groups based on their combination of animacy and transitivity. More specifically, Wolastoqey and Mi'kmaq verbs can be, animate intransitive, inanimate intransitive, transitive animate, or transitive inanimate. We remove any entries that correspond to more than one of these categories. This gives a total of $5.3k$ animate intransitive, $2.1k$ inanimate intransitive, $3k$ transitive animate, and $2.7k$ transitive inanimate Wolastoqey verbs, and $2k$ animate intransitive, 753 inanimate intransitive, $1k$ transitive animate and 847 transitive inanimate Mi'kmaq verbs, for our verb type classification tasks.

To conduct this evaluation, we first construct embeddings for each Wolastoqey and Mi'kmaq word using our proposed methodology. We then train logistic regression classifiers for each task and method. For this evaluation, we implement our logistic regression classifiers using scikit-learn 0.24.2. We use the default training parameters of this library, except max-iterations, which we set to 6000, so that all models finish converging. We train and evaluate in a 10-fold cross validation setup. We use macro-averaged accuracy, precision, recall, and F1-score as our evaluation metrics and compare our models to a most-frequent class baseline as well as the pretrained sentence-RoBERTa based approach proposed by Bear and Cook (2022) as it has been shown to achieve strong performance in this task.

Method	Accuracy	P	R	F1
Part of Speech				
Most Freq.	0.767	0.153	0.200	0.174
sRoBERTa	0.974	0.828	0.801	0.809
Cosine	0.976	0.858	**0.829**	**0.839**
Softmax	0.976	0.855	**0.829**	0.838
Triplet	**0.979**	**0.862**	0.823	0.837
Noun Animacy				
Most Freq.	0.552	0.276	0.500	0.355
sRoBERTa	0.801	0.800	0.798	0.798
Cosine	0.804	0.804	0.804	0.803
Softmax	0.789	0.791	0.787	0.787
Triplet	**0.806**	**0.805**	**0.805**	**0.804**
Verb Type				
Most Freq.	0.406	0.101	0.250	0.144
sRoBERTa	**0.951**	**0.953**	**0.953**	**0.953**
Cosine	0.921	0.926	0.925	0.925
Softmax	0.932	0.936	0.934	0.935
Triplet	0.947	0.950	0.950	0.950

Table 1: Results for each Wolastoqey word classification task using each embedding method, and a most-frequent class baseline. The best result for each task and metric is shown in boldface.

Method	Accuracy	P	R	F1
Part of Speech				
Most Freq.	0.730	0.182	0.250	0.211
sRoBERTa	0.973	0.823	0.795	0.800
Cosine	0.973	0.847	0.839	0.834
Softmax	0.976	0.844	0.819	0.823
Triplet	**0.977**	**0.861**	**0.841**	**0.841**
Noun Animacy				
Most Freq.	0.516	0.258	0.500	0.340
sRoBERTa	0.764	0.766	0.764	0.763
Cosine	0.783	**0.786**	0.782	0.782
Softmax	0.777	0.777	0.776	0.776
Triplet	**0.784**	0.785	**0.784**	**0.783**
Verb Type				
Most Freq.	0.439	0.110	0.250	0.152
sRoBERTa	0.865	0.861	0.860	0.860
Cosine	0.845	0.843	0.840	0.840
Softmax	0.850	0.849	0.845	0.846
Triplet	**0.872**	**0.868**	**0.868**	**0.867**

Table 2: Results for each Mi'kmaq word classification task using each embedding method, and a most-frequent class baseline. The best result for each evaluation metric and task is shown in boldface.

3.2 Results

Results are shown in Table 1 for Wolastoqey and Table 2 for Mi'kmaq. We observe that, for all tasks and evaluation metrics, all of our models outperform a most-frequent class baseline. This indicates that these approaches to representing Wolastoqey and Mi'kmaq words capture information about these syntactic properties.

We observe fine-tuning sentence-RoBERTa on English dictionary definitions leads to improved performance on classification tasks involving Wolastoqey nouns, however, it decreases performance on our Wolastoqey verb classification task. Of our fine-tuned sentence-RoBERTa models, the model trained with the triplet training objective performs the best on each Wolastoqey task except part-of-speech classification.

For Mi'kmaq, we again see that fine-tuning sentence-RoBERTa with our cosine and softmax training objectives results in a decrease in performance on verb classification but increases performance on part-of-speech and noun animacy classification. However, here we observe that our sentence-RoBERTa model fine-tuned with triplet loss outperforms all other models considered in all classification tasks in terms of accuracy and F1 score. From these results, and the results from our Wolastoqey evaluation, of our fine-tuned models, the model trained with our triplet loss is best able to represent Wolastoqey and Mi'kmaq words from their definitions.

4 Clustering

Here we explore using our embedding models to semantically cluster Wolastoqey and Mi'kmaq words. For this experiment, we largely follow the evaluation procedures of Bear and Cook (2022). For Wolastoqey, we reproduce the experiments of Bear and Cook for the purpose of comparison.

4.1 Experimental Setup

To perform our clustering evaluations, we require ground-truth labels to compare our results to. In the case of Wolastoqey, we consider using the same dataset as Bear and Cook (2022) for this purpose. More specifically, we consider obtaining categorical labels from Wolastoqewatu,[3] a website designed to help teach Wolastoqey, and Wolastoqey Latuwewakon,[4] a mobile application designed to teach Wolastoqey vocabulary. For Wolastoqewatu, we use the glossary categories as labels, while for Wolastoqey Latuwewakon, we use the top-level categories from the categories tab. We filter out words that appear in multiple categories and cross-reference the remaining words with the Passamaquoddy-Maliseet Dictionary to obtain word–category pairs. In total, using this approach, we are left with 1154 entries from Wolastoqewatu that correspond to 20 unique categories and 78 entries from Wolastoqey Latuwewakon that correspond to 6 unique categories.

To obtain gold-standard labels for our Mi'kmaq clustering evaluation, we use categories from the Mi'gmaq/Mi'kmaq Online Dictionary, which contains a glossary consisting of words grouped into topically-organized categories. We use these categories as ground truth references for our clustering evaluation. Using these labels, we create an evaluation set consisting of 6465 items corresponding to 237 classes. However, unlike our aforementioned Wolastoqey datasets, words in this evaluation set frequently correspond to more than one class. As this is the case, we do not remove these words from the evaluation set.

To cluster the words in each dataset, we use K-means, setting the number of clusters to the number of classes in each dataset (i.e., 20 for Wolastoqewatu, 6 for Wolastoqey Latuwewakon, and 237 for the Mi'kmaq dictionary dataset). For this, we use the default parameters of the scikit-learn 0.24.2 implementation of K-means. We evaluate the clustering using BCubed precision, recall, and F1-score. We compare our proposed methods to the pretrained sentence-RoBERTa approach of Bear and Cook (2022) to determine if our fine-tuning proceedures improve over pretrained sentence-RoBERTa models for this task.

4.2 Results

Results are shown in Table 3. We observe that additionally fine-tuning sentence-RoBERTa on monolingual dictionary definitions results in mixed improvements. On the Wolastoqewatu dataset, the only model that substantially outperforms our pretrained sentence-RoBERTa model across metrics is the softmax model. However, this does not hold true for the Wolastoqey Latuwewakon dataset, where all models fine-tuned using monolingual dictionary definitions outperform the pretrained sentence-RoBERTa model in terms of BCubed F1 score.

We observe different trends on our Mi'kmaq evaluation. Here, we observe that our pretrained

[3]https://wolastoqewatu.ca
[4]https://wolastoqey-latuwewakon.web.app/

Wolastoqewatu			
Method	BCubed P	BCubed R	BCubed F1
s-RoBERTa	0.371	0.324	0.346
Cosine	0.348	0.296	0.320
Softmax	0.392	**0.334**	**0.360**
Triplet	**0.391**	0.316	0.349
Wolastoqey Latuwewakon			
Method	BCubed P	BCubed R	BCubed F1
s-RoBERTa	0.668	0.496	0.569
Cosine	0.706	0.546	0.615
Softmax	**0.732**	**0.553**	**0.630**
Triplet	0.722	0.515	0.601
Mi'gmaq/Mi'kmaq Online Dictionary			
Method	BCubed P	BCubed R	BCubed F1
s-RoBERTa	**0.347**	**0.122**	**0.181**
Cosine	0.259	0.080	0.122
Softmax	0.329	0.108	0.162
Triplet	0.343	0.113	0.170

Table 3: Clustering evaluation results for each embedding method on each dataset. The best result for each evaluation metric and dataset is shown in boldface.

sentence-RoBERTa model substantially outperforms all other models in each evaluation metric, and that fine-tuning sentence-RoBERTa results in worse performance on all metrics.

Unlike the Wolastoqewatu and Wolastoqey Latuwewakon datasets, which consist mostly of nouns, the Mi'kmaq dataset is primarily composed of verbs. This could be why we see different trends in the results on this dataset. The finding that pretrained sentence-RoBERTa outperforms our fine-tuned models on our Mi'kmaq evaluation is consistent with the findings from 3.2 that our fine-tuned cosine and softmax models generally performed better than pretrained sentence-RoBERTa on Mi'kmaq classification tasks involving nouns, but, worse than pretrained sentence-RoBERTa on our verb classification task (Table 2). The findings for our triplet model, which performed slightly better on Mi'kmaq verb classification experiments than our pretrained sentence-RoBERTa model, are, however, not consistent with this.

5 Reverse Dictionary

Here we use our Wolastoqey and Mi'kmaq word representations to create reverse dictionary search systems. Such systems could potentially help Wolastoqey and Mi'kmaq learners to more-easily access language resources.

5.1 Datasets

We build datasets for our reverse dictionary search evaluations based on the principle that the English definition for a Wolastoqey word in the Passamaquoddy-Maliseet Dictionary, or a Mi'kmaq word in the Mi'gmaq/Mi'kmaq Online Dictionary, is expected to be similar to an alternative English definition for that word from another dictionary. In this evaluation, we use alternative English definitions for Wolastoqey and Mi'kmaq words as simulated queries, which we compare against search spaces composed of reference definitions from the Passamaquoddy-Maliseet Dictionary and Mi'gmaq/Mi'kmaq Online Dictionary.

As there are relatively few data sources containing English definitions for Wolastoqey and Mi'kmaq words, we use a similar approach to Bear and Cook (2022) to obtain alternative definitions for the Wolastoqey and Mi'kmaq words in our search spaces. We leverage the fact that many definitions in the Passamaquoddy-Maliseet Dictionary and Mi'gmaq/Mi'kmaq Online Dictionary are composed of a single-word. More specifically, we use an English dictionary, namely WordNet (Miller, 1995), to find alternative definitions for each Wolastoqey and Mi'kmaq word corresponding to a single-word definition in the Passamaquoddy-Maliseet Dictionary and Mi'gmaq/Mi'kmaq Online Dictionary. For each single-word definition in the Passamaquoddy-Maliseet Dictionary and Mi'gmaq/Mi'kmaq Online Dictionary that also occurs as a lemma in WordNet, we use the definition for the first WordNet synset associated with that lemma as a simulated query for this evaluation. Using the Wolastoqey word *amalhihpuwakon*, defined as 'dessert' in the Passamaquoddy-Maliseet Dictionary, as an example, we would use the WordNet definition 'a dish served as the last course of a meal' as an alternative definition for this word.

To expand the number of simulated queries available for our evaluations, we also use this approach to obtain alternative definitions for words that correspond to definitions that become single-words after certain words are removed. As dependent nouns and verbs are given in a third person form in the Passamaquoddy-Maliseet Dictionary and the Mi'gmaq/Mi'kmaq Online Dictionary, to obtain alternative definitions for these words, when identifying single word definitions, we remove the words *s/he* and *h/* (abbreviations for *she/he* and *her/his*, respectively) as well as *it* from definitions in the Passamaquoddy-Maliseet Dictionary and all instances of *he/she*, *him/her*, *it*, and *him/her/it* from definitions in the Mi'gmaq/Mi'kmaq Online Dictionary.

As both dictionaries contain definitions for a number of names, we remove all dictionary head-words corresponding to English names from both the pool of single-word definitions, as well as our search spaces, using a list of English names obtained from NLTK (Bird et al., 2009). In total, our approach gives 1091 Wolastoqey words and 1424 words from the Mi'gmaq/Mi'kmaq Online Dictionary, with alternative English definitions available in WordNet. We compare these alternative definitions to search spaces consisting of $17.9k$ Wolastoqey words and $6.4k$ Mi'kmaq words obtained from the Passamaquoddy-Maliseet Dictionary and the Mi'gmaq/Mi'kmaq Online Dictionary respectively.

5.2 Experimental Setup

To perform our reverse dictionary search evaluations, we construct vector representations for both the definitions in our search spaces and our simulated queries using our proposed embedding approaches. Using these vector representations, we calculate the cosine distances between each simulated query and each definition in its corresponding search space. We then use the resulting rank of the word corresponding to the simulated queries to calculate our evaluation metrics. Specifically, we consider median rank, mean reciprocal rank (MRR), and accuracy@k, for $k = 1, 5, 10, 20, 50, 100$.

5.3 Results

Results are shown in Table 4. Of our fine-tuned models, we observe that the model trained with the triplet loss training objective performs best, substantially improving over both the cosine and softmax models in terms of median rank and MRR for both languages. This model also outperforms pretrained sentence-RoBERTa for each evaluation metric and language, except for median rank on Mi'kmaq.

Despite all models outperforming the random baseline, the findings for our best model, the sentence-RoBERTa model fine-tuned using triplet loss, do not suggest that this could yet be used as a practical reverse dictionary search system. For example, the accuracy@100 of 0.544 for Wolastoqey indicates that only roughly half the time is this approach able to rank the correct word among the top-100. The disparity in length and complexity between our query definitions from WordNet and the single-word definitions from the Passamaquoddy-Maliseet Dictionary, and the Mi'gmaq/Mi'kmaq Online Dictionary, used in this evaluation could contribute towards making this experimental setup a particularly challenging task.

6 Word Similarity

Although our primary interest is methods for learning Wolastoqey and Mi'kmaq word representations, here we consider whether the proposed approach to encoding dictionary definitions can also be applied to represent words in higher-resource languages. Word similarity datasets are available for many languages and are commonly used to evaluate how well word embedding models are able to capture the similarity or relatedness between words. Here we consider constructing word embeddings for English, German and Spanish using our proposed methodologies and evaluating on word similarity datasets. As these datasets are frequently used in other works, where available, we compare against previously reported results for word2vec baselines.

6.1 Experimental Setup

In our experiments, we choose to use one Spanish, one German and two English word similarity datasets. For English, we consider SimLex-999 (Hill et al., 2015) as well as the MEN dataset (Bruni et al., 2014). We use these datasets, as SimLex-999 reflects word similarity, whereas the MEN dataset reflects relatedness. For the MEN dataset, we consider using the full 3000 word pair version of this dataset in our evaluation. For Spanish, we consider using a translation of WordSim-353 (ES-WS353, Finkelstein et al., 2002; Hassan and Mihalcea, 2009) and we use GUR350 (Gurevych, 2005) for German.

We construct embeddings for the words in these datasets using the same approach used to obtain word embeddings for Wolastoqey and Mi'kmaq in our prior evaluations. However, here we do not remove bracketed text from definitions, a pre-processing step motivated specifically based on common patterns in definitions of the Passamaquoddy-Maliseet Dictionary. To construct our English word embeddings, we consider using dictionary definitions from WordNet. As our method requires English definitions for non-English words, for words in the Spanish and German evaluation sets, we construct embeddings using web-scraped definitions from the Collins Spanish–English and German–English online dictionaries (HarperCollins, 2011).

Wolastoqey Search Space								
Method	Median	MRR	Acc@1	Acc@5	Acc@10	Acc@20	Acc@50	Acc@100
Random	9164	0.000	0.000	0.000	0.000	0.000	0.002	0.005
Bear and Cook (2022)	107	0.081	0.027	0.128	0.183	0.260	0.397	0.495
Cosine	311	0.056	0.025	0.072	0.118	0.170	0.269	0.350
Softmax	87	0.098	0.044	0.140	0.213	0.302	0.412	0.518
Triplet	**70**	**0.109**	**0.050**	**0.155**	**0.239**	**0.332**	**0.448**	**0.544**
Mi'kmaq Search Space								
Method	Median	MRR	Acc@1	Acc@5	Acc@10	Acc@20	Acc@50	Acc@100
Random	3300	0.001	0.000	0.000	0.000	0.002	0.006	0.015
Bear and Cook (2022)	**27**	0.174	0.086	0.263	0.364	0.464	0.568	0.634
Cosine	108	0.111	0.060	0.148	0.215	0.301	0.409	0.493
Softmax	37	0.181	0.099	0.261	0.343	0.435	0.545	0.633
Triplet	28	**0.198**	**0.107**	**0.296**	**0.386**	**0.466**	**0.581**	**0.667**

Table 4: Median rank, MRR, and accuracy@k for each threshold considered, for reverse dictionary experiments using each approach to representing Wolastoqey and Mi'kmaq words and a random baseline.

As it is expected that a number of words will not have definitions in the dictionaries we use, we set the embedding of any word without a definition to a vector of zeroes.

To evaluate how well our embeddings perform, we calculate cosine similarities for word pairs in each dataset using our embedding models. We then calculate the Spearman correlation between the predicted cosine similarities and the human annotated similarity scores for each dataset.

To establish a baseline, for SimLex-999, ES-WS353, and GUR350, we compare our models to previously reported results. More specifically, for SimLex-999, we compare our models to the word2vec results published by (Hill et al., 2015). For ES-WS353 and GUR350, we compare our models to the skipgram results reported in Bojanowski et al. (2017). For the MEN dataset, we calculate a baseline for comparison directly using a word2vec model. Here we use the same Google-News word2vec embeddings as in Section 2. As many words in the MEN dataset use British English spelling, and this word2vec model uses primarily American English spelling, we convert any British English word-forms not found in this embedding model to their American English equivalent.

6.2 Results

Results are shown in Table 5. We observe that on all datasets, except SimLex-999, our proposed embedding approaches do not outperform the chosen word2vec baselines. Despite this, all our models, achieve statistically significant correlation on all word similarity datasets considered. We observe that pretrained sentence-RoBERTa outperforms a word2vec baseline on SimLex-999, but fails to do so on the MEN dataset. This could indicate that

Method	Simlex-999	MEN	ES-WS353	GUR350
Baseline	0.414	**0.78**	**0.57**	**0.61**
sRoBERTa	**0.423**	0.568	0.297	0.538
Cosine	0.374	0.524	0.313	0.494
Softmax	0.416	0.560	0.334	0.579
Triplet	0.420	0.560	0.303	0.506

Table 5: Spearman correlations between cosine similarities and human-annotated similarity scores for each method on each dataset. The best correlation for each dataset is shown in boldface.

these embeddings better capture word similarity than relatedness.

Further fine-tuning sentence-RoBERTa does not improve performance on either English dataset. Despite this, all fine-tuned models outperform pretrained sentence-RoBERTa on ES-WS353 and our softmax model outperforms pretrained sentence-RoBERTa model on GUR350. Definition length may be a factor here, as the pre-trained sentence-RoBERTa model performs best on our English datasets, in which words have an average definition length of 11 tokens, whereas words in our Spanish and German datasets have an average definition length of 1 and 2 tokens, respectively. This would be consistent with the findings from Table 2, in which our fine-tuned models performed better in terms of F1-score on Mi'kmaq classification tasks involving nouns, which have comparatively short definitions, and worse on tasks involving verbs which tend to have longer definitions. However, definition length alone isn't enough to explain the disparity in model rankings, as, in contrast to the results observed for Mi'kmaq, the softmax model failed to outperform pretrained sentence-RoBERTa in Wolastoqey noun animacy classification. As this is the case, the best model configuration seems to be dependant on the language and task being considered.

7 Conclusions

In this paper, we considered approaches to forming word embeddings for Wolastoqey and Mi'kmaq based on their English definitions in bilingual dictionaries. Specifically we considered approaches to fine-tuning sentence-RoBERTa for this. Our findings indicate that our proposed approaches can be used to construct embeddings for Wolastoqey and Mi'kmaq words that capture syntactic and semantic information, and that fine-tuning often gives improvements over pre-trained sentence-RoBERTa, although this improvement is not consistent across languages, tasks, and approaches to fine-tuning. Our results from reverse dictionary evaluations indicate that these embeddings cannot yet be used to build a practical reverse dictionary search system. We further showed that these approaches can be applied to form embeddings for higher-resource languages. Although here these embeddings achieved significant correlations on word similarity and relatedness evaluations, they did not improve over conventional word2vec embeddings.

In future work, we intend to explore ways to improve the embeddings. Although we observed that fine-tuning sentence-RoBERTa did not give consistent improvements across tasks, we hypothesize that an alternative approach could give improvements. Definitions for verbs in the Passamaquoddy-Maliseet Dictionary in particular tend to be longer, while definitions for nouns are typically quite short and often composed of only a single word. This disparity in definition complexity could hinder the effectiveness of our proposed word embedding techniques. We therefore intend to explore the use of ULR-BERT (Li and Zhao, 2021), which is capable of representing words, phrases and sentences proficiently, for forming improved embeddings for Wolastoqey and Mi'kmaq words from their English definitions in bilingual dictionaries.

In addition to using ULR-BERT, we also intend to fine-tune sentence-transformer models that make use of different network architectures and pretraining regimens. In our work, we use a single RoBERTa checkpoint, pretrained on natural language inference, as a uniform starting point for fine-tuning. However, since the release of the original work on sentence transformers, other models have been made available through the sentence-BERT library, for example models based on MPNet (Song et al., 2020), which have been shown to outperform sentence-RoBERTa on sentence embedding benchmarks. As this is the case, the use of these models in-place of sentence-RoBERTa could potentially improve the quality of word embeddings produced using our methodology.

In our work, we demonstrated that we can construct meaningful word embeddings for Wolastoqey and Mi'kmaq dictionary headwords. In future work we will consider evaluating the impact of these embeddings on down-stream applications.

Limitations

Although improving the performance of our embedding methods is desirable, the most apparent limitation of our work is not the overall quality of representations produced, but rather the range of words our methodologies can be applied to. Currently, our methodology can only be used to construct word embeddings for dictionary headwords. This represents a considerable limitation, as Wolastoqey and Mi'kmaq are both polysyntheic languages, in which speakers often build new words by creatively combining roots. As this is the case, no dictionary is expected to contain definitions for all word-forms of these languages. Because of this, future work is required to extend our approach to construct embeddings for words that do not appear in a bilingual dictionary.

References

Oliver Adams, Adam Makarucha, Graham Neubig, Steven Bird, and Trevor Cohn. 2017. Cross-lingual word embeddings for low-resource language modeling. In *Proceedings of the 15th Conference of the European Chapter of the Association for Computational Linguistics: Volume 1, Long Papers*, pages 937–947, Valencia, Spain. Association for Computational Linguistics.

Antti Arppe, Jordan Lachler, Trond Trosterud, Lene Antonsen, and Sjur N Moshagen. 2016. Basic language resource kits for endangered languages: A case study of plains cree. In *Proceedings of the 2nd Workshop on Collaboration and Computing for Under-Resourced Languages Workshop (CCURL 2016), Portorož, Slovenia*, pages 1–8.

Diego Bear and Paul Cook. 2022. Leveraging a bilingual dictionary to learn wolastoqey word representations. In *Proceedings of the Thirteenth Language Resources and Evaluation Conference*, pages 1159–1166, Marseille, France. European Language Resources Association.

Steven Bird, Edward Loper, and Ewan Klein. 2009. *Natural Language Processing with Python.* O'Reilly Media Inc.

Piotr Bojanowski, Edouard Grave, Armand Joulin, and Tomas Mikolov. 2017. Enriching word vectors with subword information. *Transactions of the Association for Computational Linguistics*, 5:135–146.

Samuel R. Bowman, Gabor Angeli, Christopher Potts, and Christopher D. Manning. 2015. A large annotated corpus for learning natural language inference. In *Proceedings of the 2015 Conference on Empirical Methods in Natural Language Processing*, pages 632–642, Lisbon, Portugal. Association for Computational Linguistics.

Elia Bruni, Nam Khanh Tran, and Marco Baroni. 2014. Multimodal distributional semantics. *J. Artif. Int. Res.*, 49(1):1–47.

Daniel Dacanay, Atticus Harrigan, Arok Wolvengrey, and Antti Arppe. 2021. The more detail, the better? – investigating the effects of semantic ontology specificity on vector semantic classification with a Plains Cree / nêhiyawêwin dictionary. In *Proceedings of the First Workshop on Natural Language Processing for Indigenous Languages of the Americas*, pages 143–152, Online. Association for Computational Linguistics.

Lev Finkelstein, Evgeniy Gabrilovich, Y. Matias, Ehud Rivlin, Zach Solan, Gadi Wolfman, and Eytan Ruppin. 2002. Placing search in context: the concept revisited. *ACM Trans. Inf. Syst.*, 20:116–131.

David A. Francis and Robert M. Leavitt. 2008. A passamaquoddy-maliseet dictionary.

Iryna Gurevych. 2005. Using the structure of a conceptual network in computing semantic relatedness. In *Natural Language Processing – IJCNLP 2005*, pages 767–778.

Sean Haberlin, Eunice Metallic, Diane Mitchell, Watson Williams, Joe Wilmot, and Dave Ziegler. 1997. [link].

HarperCollins. 2011. Collins english dictionary | free online dictionary, thesaurus and reference materials. Released December 31, 2011. `https://www.collinsdictionary.com/`.

Atticus Harrigan and Antti Arppe. 2021. Leveraging English word embeddings for semi-automatic semantic classification in nêhiyawêwin (Plains Cree). In *Proceedings of the First Workshop on Natural Language Processing for Indigenous Languages of the Americas*, pages 113–121, Online. Association for Computational Linguistics.

Samer Hassan and Rada Mihalcea. 2009. Cross-lingual semantic relatedness using encyclopedic knowledge. In *Proceedings of the 2009 Conference on Empirical Methods in Natural Language Processing*, pages 1192–1201, Singapore. Association for Computational Linguistics.

Felix Hill, Kyunghyun Cho, Anna Korhonen, and Yoshua Bengio. 2016. Learning to Understand Phrases by Embedding the Dictionary. *Transactions of the Association for Computational Linguistics*, 4:17–30.

Felix Hill, Roi Reichart, and Anna Korhonen. 2015. SimLex-999: Evaluating semantic models with (genuine) similarity estimation. *Computational Linguistics*, 41(4):665–695.

Yian Li and Hai Zhao. 2021. Pre-training universal language representation. In *Proceedings of the 59th Annual Meeting of the Association for Computational Linguistics and the 11th International Joint Conference on Natural Language Processing (Volume 1: Long Papers)*, pages 5122–5133, Online. Association for Computational Linguistics.

Tomás Mikolov, Kai Chen, Greg Corrado, and Jeffrey Dean. 2013. Efficient estimation of word representations in vector space. In *1st International Conference on Learning Representations, ICLR 2013, Scottsdale, Arizona, USA, May 2-4, 2013, Workshop Track Proceedings*.

George A. Miller. 1995. WordNet: A lexical database for English. *Commun. ACM*, 38(11):39–41.

Jeffrey Pennington, Richard Socher, and Christopher Manning. 2014. GloVe: Global vectors for word representation. In *Proceedings of the 2014 Conference on Empirical Methods in Natural Language Processing (EMNLP)*, pages 1532–1543, Doha, Qatar. Association for Computational Linguistics.

Ye Qi, Devendra Sachan, Matthieu Felix, Sarguna Padmanabhan, and Graham Neubig. 2018. When and why are pre-trained word embeddings useful for neural machine translation? In *Proceedings of the 2018 Conference of the North American Chapter of the Association for Computational Linguistics: Human Language Technologies, Volume 2 (Short Papers)*, pages 529–535, New Orleans, Louisiana. Association for Computational Linguistics.

Radim Řehůřek and Petr Sojka. 2010. Software Framework for Topic Modelling with Large Corpora. In *Proceedings of the LREC 2010 Workshop on New Challenges for NLP Frameworks*, pages 45–50, Valletta, Malta. ELRA. `http://is.muni.cz/publication/884893/en`.

Nils Reimers and Iryna Gurevych. 2019. Sentence-BERT: Sentence embeddings using Siamese BERT-networks. In *Proceedings of the 2019 Conference on Empirical Methods in Natural Language Processing and the 9th International Joint Conference on Natural Language Processing (EMNLP-IJCNLP)*, pages 3982–3992, Hong Kong, China. Association for Computational Linguistics.

Dwaipayan Roy, Debasis Ganguly, Sumit Bhatia, Srikanta Bedathur, and Mandar Mitra. 2018. Using word embeddings for information retrieval: How collection and term normalization choices affect performance. In *Proceedings of the 27th ACM International Conference on Information and Knowledge Management*, CIKM '18, page 1835–1838, New York, NY, USA. Association for Computing Machinery.

Kaitao Song, Xu Tan, Tao Qin, Jianfeng Lu, and Tie-Yan Liu. 2020. Mpnet: Masked and permuted pre-training for language understanding. In *Proceedings of the 34th International Conference on Neural Information Processing Systems*, NIPS'20, Red Hook, NY, USA. Curran Associates Inc.

Statistics Canada. 2017. *Canada [Country] and Canada [Country] (table). Census Profile.* 2016 Census. Statistics Canada Catalogue no. 98-316-X2016001. Ottawa. Released November 29, 2017. `https://www12.statcan.gc.ca/census-recensement/2016/dp-pd/prof/index.cfm?Lang=E` (accessed August 13, 2021).

Adina Williams, Nikita Nangia, and Samuel Bowman. 2018. A broad-coverage challenge corpus for sentence understanding through inference. In *Proceedings of the 2018 Conference of the North American Chapter of the Association for Computational Linguistics: Human Language Technologies, Volume 1 (Long Papers)*, pages 1112–1122. Association for Computational Linguistics.

Lei Zheng, Fanchao Qi, Zhiyuan Liu, Yasheng Wang, Qun Liu, and Maosong Sun. 2020. Multi-channel reverse dictionary model. *Proceedings of the AAAI Conference on Artificial Intelligence*, 34:312–319.

Identification of Dialect for Eastern and Southwestern Ojibwe Words Using a Small Corpus

Kalvin Hartwig,
Independent Researcher
Bayfield, Wisconsin, USA
kalvin.hartwig@aya.yale.edu

Evan Lucas and **Timothy C. Havens**
Michigan Technological University
Houghton, Michigan, USA
{eglucas, thavens}@mtu.edu

Abstract

The Ojibwe language has several dialects that vary to some degree in both spoken and written form. We present a method of using support vector machines to classify two different dialects (Eastern and Southwestern Ojibwe) using a very small corpus of text. Classification accuracy at the sentence level is 90% across a five-fold cross validation and 72% when the sentence-trained model is applied to a data set of individual words. Our code and the word level data set are released openly at https://github.com/evanperson/OjibweDialect.

1 Introduction

The Ojibwe language is an Indigenous language of the Great Lakes region of Turtle Island (North America) and is also known by many other names such as Chippewa, Ojibwemowin, Anishinaabe, and Anishinaabemowin. Anishinaabemowin can also refer to the closely related tongues Potawatomi, Algonquin and Odawa. An Algonquian language, Ojibwe and its many sub-dialects can be mapped geographically. Though traditionally understood to be a prestigious language spoken by several Peoples trading or living with/near the Ojibwe, currently, Ojibwe is mostly spoken by Ojibwe people. While many Ojibwe live on reservations and reserves of sovereign Ojibwe Tribes/First Nations across *Anishinaabewaki*, Anishinaabe country, many also live in towns and cities outside of reservations and reserves.

The number of native-level fluent speakers is unfortunately fast dwindling. It is estimated that there are around 50 native-level fluent speakers living today south of the Medicine Line (the American-Canadian border), virtually all of whom are Elders (Burnette, 2023). Most of these 50 older speakers are living on two reservations. There are at least 10,000 fluent speakers north of the Medicine Line, many of whom are also older (Pangowish, 2023). The approximate distribution of current Anishinaabemowin speakers is shown in Figure 1. According to the U.S. Census Bureau (2011) and Canadian Encyclopedia (Bishop, 2019), there are about 330,000 Ojibwe living in *Anishinaabewaki*, conservatively making around 3% of the Ojibwe population fluent speakers.

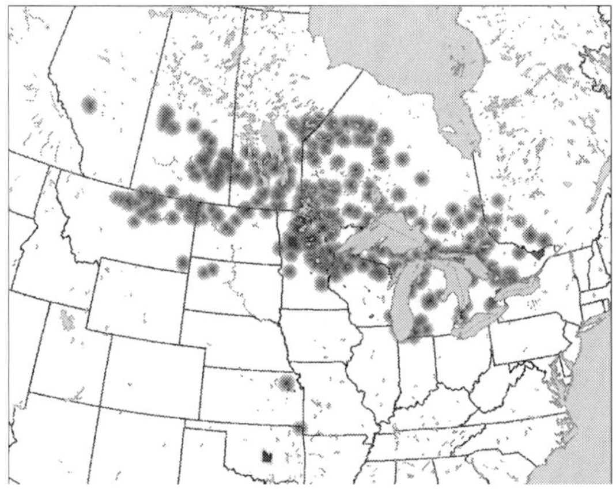

Figure 1: 2007 distribution of Anishinaabemowin speakers on Turtle Island, including Ojibwe and sister languages such as Potawatomi and Algonquin. From Lippert (2007)

There are many efforts in place to try and stem Ojibwe's decline. Passing along the knowledge and practice of speaking the Ojibwe language is an important part of maintaining Ojibwe culture; language is identified as one of the four pillars of Indigenous Peoplehood by Holm et al. (2003) along with ceremonies, land, and sacred history. Some say Ojibwe identity itself is at risk if the language is no longer spoken (Hartwig, 2012; McInnes, 2014) and therefore Ojibwemowin revitalization is one of the highest priorities for many language warriors. Language courses, as well as immersion and spending time with Elders, have been traditional tools of revitalizing Anishinaabemowin (Pitawanakwat, 2018). Over the past couple decades, there have also been efforts to use more media technology as

Proceedings of the Workshop on Natural Language Processing for Indigenous Languages of the Americas (AmericasNLP), pages 58–66
July 14, 2023

a tool for revitalizing the language (Hermes and King, 2013). Our work builds on this history.

The rest of this paper is organized as follows. Section 2 is split into three sub-sections: author and paper backgrounds are briefly reviewed in Section 2.1, a brief overview of Ojibwe dialects is covered in Section 2.2, and a review of related work is presented in Section 2.3. Methodology used and discussion of the written corpus used is presented in Section 3. A discussion of results is included in Section 4. We summarize our work in Section 5. We discuss the limitations of this work in the Limitations section and share some of the ethical concerns raised by this work in the Ethical Statement. Finally, we recognize and give thanks to the people who made this work possible in the Acknowledgements.

2 Background

2.1 Positionality

This work was performed as a collaboration between two of the authors (Hartwig and Lucas) as an exploratory work looking at ways that *Natural Language Processing* (NLP) tools could be used to aid Ojibwe language learners. The first discussions held between authors tried to address connections between the needs and interests of people working in Ojibwe language education and capabilities of NLP methods that work with limited text and varied dialects. To help capture background of the authors, we have included the following positionality statements:

- Mishkwaa-desi Kalvin Hartwig is a Member of the Sault Sainte Marie Tribe of Chippewa Indians. He serves as an independent filmmaker as well as the Anishinaabemowin gikinoo'amaagewin weninang / Anishinaabe language-culture coordinator for the Red Cliff Band of Lake Superior Chippewa Indians. He is not fluent in Ojibwe, but has been actively learning it.

- Evan Lucas is a White American who works as a graduate student studying NLP.

- Timothy Havens is a White American professor of computer science with research interests in challenging AI problems.

2.2 Ojibwe dialects

Across the geographic range shown in Figure 1, there are several dialects found (Valentine, 1994; Rhodes, 2006). Teachers and speakers of other dialects often consider Eastern Ojibwe and Odawa to be either one in the same or at least very similar. For this paper, we use "Eastern" to refer to Eastern Ojibwe, Odawa, or both. We decided to compare Eastern to the dialect of Southwestern Ojibwe; each having differences in spelling, some grammar rules, and sometimes morphological word construction (Nichols, 1980; Valentine, 2001a). A reader with familiarity in one dialect, but not another, may be unfamiliar with some of the word forms used in a different dialect. Having a tool to help identify dialects may be helpful to a language learner who may be reading a work in a different dialect, want to understand relationships between different dialects, and/or want to use spelling and grammar styles more aligned with a given dialect. Hartwig has witnessed learners of one dialect unwittingly use resources from another dialect, which may lead to confusion around spelling and grammar, but with the right guidance such confusion may be alleviated. Research with Indigenous Peoples should be a part of a reciprocal relationship, where work is done to benefit the People providing information by answering questions and exploring topics highlighted by the given Indigenous People (Smith, 2021).

Ojibwe is an oral language, but multiple writing systems have been developed to transcribe it (Treuer, 2010). Ojibwe have used pictographs and similar symbols to write out stories for an unknown period of time. As missionaries and others came to *Anishinaabewaki*, however, such newcomers decided to develop writing systems for the Ojibwe language. Various writing systems were created, including ones based on syllabics and others with Latin script. Roman character-based writing systems are most commonly used today, with the Fiero / double vowel / long vowel orthography being the most popularly used by Ojibwe language educators (Ningewance, 1999). For this reason, this paper will use examples written using the long vowel system.

2.3 Related work

Much of the computational language work that has been performed with Indigenous languages is rule-based (Mager et al., 2018), which often requires expert knowledge. Despite this, there have been attempts to use unsupervised learning methods to learn morphology of Indigenous languages with some success (Johnson and Martin, 2003). One notable example of a rule-based system that is designed for an Anishinaabe dialect is the construction of a morphological parser for Odawa (Bowers et al., 2017).

El Mekki et al. (2020) performs fusion between an n-gram based *support vector machine* (SVM) (Cortes and Vapnik, 1995) and a BERT (Devlin et al., 2019) model trained on Arabic to determine dialect across many countries and regions. The n-grams are computed at the word and character level and are normalized using *term-frequency inverse document frequency* (TF-IDF) before being used in the SVM.

Hämäläinen et al. (2021) also performs fusion between dialect classification models; however, their approach uses both text and audio as inputs and is focused on classifying 23 separate dialects of Finnish. A BERT model trained on Finnish is used to handle the text inputs, which are split at the sentence level.

Salameh et al. (2018) looks at the problem of Arabic dialect identification, introducing a commissioned data set that contains common phrases in dialects from different cities. They find that using character n-grams as well as individual words is a preferred method of featurizing inputs for sentence-level dialect determination with a Multinomial Naive Bayes classifier.

A deep learning approach utilizing pre-trained models was not considered for this work, due to the relatively small amount of text collected and the difficulty in transferring a deep learning model trained in one language to another. It has been noted by Singh et al. (2019) that tokenizers trained on one language do not necessarily transfer to another language efficiently. Another work (Maronikolakis et al., 2021) found that when transferring language models between languages, unless the tokenizer was re-trained, it was less efficient on the new language and required far more tokens to represent the same length of text.

3 Method

3.1 Text used

Several stories in Manitoulin Island varieties of Eastern Anishinaabemowin (Corbiere and Jones, 2012) and several stories from Volume 8 of the *Oshkaabewis Native Journal* (Treuer et al., 2012) for Southwestern Ojibwe were used for this work. Permission to use each of the works was granted from the respective editors. Additionally, dictionaries (Child and Nichols, 2012; Naokwegijig-Corbiere and Valentine, 2015) for each of the dialects were used to create a word list of common words that could also be used to evaluate the dialect classification model.

The amount of text used is quite small—611 sentences of Southwestern Ojibwe and 434 sentences of Eastern—which limits the use of deep learning methods that require large bodies of text from which to learn. For this reason, SVM's were chosen as a method appropriate for classifying small bodies of text, which are sometimes referred to as *low-resource* use-cases. Some sample statistics from both sets of text are included in Appendix B.

3.2 Text processing and model selection

Following the work of Hämäläinen et al. (2021) and El Mekki et al. (2020), the problem is formulated as a dialect prediction for an arbitrary number of sentences. Based on these works, an SVM using character n-grams is utilized with n-gram features combined between the relevant sentences. Stochastic gradient descent was used to train the model, minimizing hinge loss. The SVM implementation written by Pedregosa et al. (2011) was used for this work. N-grams were generated by splitting each word into all possible sets of n characters and were combined for varying numbers of sentences. For example, the word *aaniin* contains the unigrams of *a, n* and *i*; the bigrams of *aa, an, ni, ii* and *in*; and so on for three and four character combinations. Since each sentence could not possibly contain all of the n-grams in the entire text, and because SVM's require a consistent input feature set, all possible n-grams were found from the two combined sets of text and an n-gram dictionary with zero values for all n-grams was used to initialize each sentence set.

These n-grams were counted for each set of sentences and analyzed with the SVM. The two sets of text were randomly split into five parts, maintaining an equal proportion of each dialect in each split, and cross validation was performed; the model was trained on four folds of the data and the unseen fifth was used to validate the model.

Table 1: Model performance as a function of number of sentences used to infer dialect

Number of grouped sentences	Accuracy
1	0.90
2	0.95
3	0.98
4	0.98
5	0.97

4 Results

4.1 Sentence level model training and evaluation

The number of correct and incorrect predictions were summed across all five validation folds and the resulting average accuracy, weighted by class membership, is presented in Table 1. The computation and counting of n-grams was performed using single sentences up to groupings of five sentences. By grouping more sentences together, a wider sample of word parts is captured and allows the model to more easily predict which dialect is present, which is indicated by our results. In our tests, we were able to achieve nearly zero errors with five sentences being used to compute each set of n-grams.

4.2 Interpretability of model

One advantage of using an SVM is that the model weights—i.e., the support vector weights—can be used to understand which features are most influential. In the case of our problem, we are able to associate the n-grams with the highest weights to those that are (based on the training data) most associated with a given dialect. The presence of a given n-gram does not indicate dialect alone, but indicates that a word or sentence containing that n-gram is more likely to belong to a given dialect. The n-grams most associated with each dialect are given in Table 2 and are drawn from the full data set averaged across five folds, and considering all n-grams from single characters up to 4-grams.

Eastern began to reduce unstressed vowels in the early part of the twentieth century (Bloomfield, 1957), and Eastern speakers are often playfully joked about as being vowel droppers. Many vowelless n-grams, such as *bn* picked up by our model for Eastern, would be rarer to find in Southwestern Ojibwe. Several examples of vowel dropping can be found in the word list included in Appendix C such as the word for *otter* being *ngig* in Eastern and *nigig* in Southwestern.

Table 2: Top ten n-grams most associated with each dialect

N-grams most associated with Eastern Ojibwe	N-grams most associated with Southwestern Ojibwe
bn	ay
bm	aye
wi	in
oo	izhi
gd	iz
iinw	izh
gs	gay
booz	gaye
boo	ye
hoo	ina

It is possible that we are observing aspects other than dialect in our analysis, such as the language preferences of the authors of our given texts. For example, the discourse marker *izhi*, meaning *'and so'*, is noted by Fairbanks (2016) as being more frequently used by first language speakers of Ojibwe than second language speakers (among other discourse markers). However, it is also possible that *izhi* has, much like certain vowels, fallen out of common use in Eastern; determining the answer to this question is outside of the scope of our work and is something that could be explored in future collaborations with Anishinaabe language keepers. To address whether our model is overfitting to language preferences rather than aspects of dialect, using writings from a wider range of authors could be used.

4.3 Applying sentence level model to individual words

To further evaluate the model developed, a small dictionary of 50 common words that differ in spelling between Eastern and Southwestern Ojibwe was compiled. Applying the model from the sentence level training to evaluation on word level inputs is an interesting experiment in model transfer and has practical value; as many language learners will encounter unknown words and may want to determine what dialect they are originating from. Each individual word from this dictionary was evaluated using the model trained on groups of five sentences. The model was found to be 72% accu-

Actual \ Predicted	E	SW
E	37	13
SW	14	33

Figure 2: Confusion matrix of individual word predictions using sentence-trained SVM

rate. A confusion matrix of the word predictions is presented in Figure 2, which shows that the model does not favor either dialect. Due to multiple common words being used in Eastern for some of the selected words, three words of Southwestern are repeated and not included in the confusion matrix. The full results of this study, including each word used and its predicted dialect, can be found in Appendix C. We considered repeating the sentence level experiment with the individual words, but found that our dictionary was insufficiently small.

5 Conclusions

In this work, we have proposed and evaluated a method for identifying dialects in Ojibwe given a small set of labeled examples. We showed that our method is 90% accurate at the single-sentence level and higher still at the multi-sentence scale. We also achieved a 72% accuracy when the sentence-level model was applied to a selected set of individual words. The model proposed also offers insight into how dialects are classified by the model, demonstrated by explaining the significance of some of the n-grams found to be most significant in determining dialect. This aspect of interpretability could offer language learners insight into features differentiating written dialects as well as providing a tool to help determine the dialect of unfamiliar text.

Limitations

This work focuses on using computational tools to determine dialect based on a small quantity of writings of a spoken language, using a writing system that was adapted recently, rather than one that evolved alongside the language for thousands of years. This limitation in orthography leads to differences in character usage, frequently between dialects (which is helpful for this problem), but there is also variation also within dialects depending on the author. For example, different writers will use different methods of transcribing a nasal sound; Eastern tends to use *nh* for nasal sounds in the middle of a word, although some writers will use a capital *N*. Southwestern Anishinaabemowin tends to use *ny, ns* or *nz* for these same nasal sounds within words. As noted by Valentine (2001b), there are variations in language within dialects, including age-stratified language proficiency, where older speakers tend to be more fluent than younger ones, largely due to differences in opportunities to learn the language. These differences might be detected and interpreted as dialect differences if the diversity in writers is not comparable between the two sets of texts being compared. Additionally, an individual's word choice may change depending on their gender or occupation (Valentine, 2001b), and having only a small sample of writings does not allow us to capture these differences well. To test how much our model is learning author preferences over dialects, using some writings from authors not included in the training data would provide some insight. Future work could do a better job of tracking authorship between cross validation folds as well as sourcing from a wider set of writers. Only small quantities of text were used for each dialect, which was limiting in terms of methods that could be used. The methods utilized in this paper could be easily applied to minority languages that do not have large quantities of written text available, of course, with permission from and in collaboration with Indigenous language keepers. Our future work could involve the collection of larger quantities of text, which would allow the use of a wider range of language analysis.

Ethical Statement

Some of the texts used for our samples were transcribed *aadizookaanan*, a type of traditional story highly revered by Ojibwe. These particular stories are not to be spoken out loud during non-winter months without snow on the ground. There are particular spiritual reasons for this, and unfortunate things can happen to individuals telling or hearing these stories when there is no nearby snow. Therefore, we will not write out the stories here and we strongly encourage citation followers to heed precaution. For more information, bring your tobacco and questions to a trusted Anishinaabe knowledge keeper.

Indigenous Peoples have experienced a long history of colonialism, including by well-meaning researchers. Please remember that Indigenous Peoples must maintain sovereignty over their languages, traditional stories, and other knowledge. All research involving Indigenous knowledge, including that for the development of generative AI, should be done ethically in reciprocal relationships with Indigenous Peoples. The research should also meet their needs and wants, as described by the given Indigenous Peoples (Smith, 2021).

Acknowledgements

Miigwech / thank you, Dr. Waagosh Anton Treuer, Dr. Ojiig Alan Corbiere, Dr. Migizi Michael Sullivan, Nswi Aanddegook Isadore Toulouse, Ninaatig Staats Pangowish, Gimiwan Dustin Burnette, Jared Blanche, Aandeg Muldrew, and everyone else who has supported us with the writing of this article.

References

Charles A Bishop. 2019. Ojibwa.

Leonard Bloomfield. 1957. *Eastern Ojibwa: Grammatical sketch, texts, and word list*. University of Michigan Press.

Dustin Bowers, Antti Arppe, Jordan Lachler, Sjur Moshagen, and Trond Trosterud. 2017. A morphological parser for odawa. In *Proceedings of the 2nd Workshop on the Use of Computational Methods in the Study of Endangered Languages*, pages 1–9.

Gimiwan Dustin Burnette. 2023. Personal communication.

Brenda J Child and John Nichols. 2012. The ojibwe people's dictionary.

Alan Corbiere and Alana Jones. 2012. Baadwewdangig. University of Toronto Linguistics Department course Language Revitalization (LIN458) Project.

Corinna Cortes and Vladimir Vapnik. 1995. Support-vector networks. *Machine learning*, 20:273–297.

Jacob Devlin, Ming-Wei Chang, Kenton Lee, and Kristina Toutanova. 2019. Bert: Pre-training of deep bidirectional transformers for language understanding. In *Proceedings of the 2019 Conference of the North American Chapter of the Association for Computational Linguistics: Human Language Technologies, Volume 1 (Long and Short Papers)*, pages 4171–4186.

Abdellah El Mekki, Ahmed Alami, Hamza Alami, Ahmed Khoumsi, and Ismail Berrada. 2020. Weighted combination of bert and n-gram features for nuanced arabic dialect identification. In *Proceedings of the Fifth Arabic Natural Language Processing Workshop*, pages 268–274.

Brendan Fairbanks. 2016. *Ojibwe discourse markers*. U of Nebraska Press.

Mika Hämäläinen, Khalid Alnajjar, Niko Partanen, and Jack Rueter. 2021. Finnish dialect identification: The effect of audio and text. In *Proceedings of the 2021 Conference on Empirical Methods in Natural Language Processing*, pages 8777–8783.

Kalvin Hartwig. 2012. *Language as an Aspect of Identity and Indigeneity*. Masters major paper, Yale University.

Mary Hermes and Kendall A King. 2013. Ojibwe language revitalization, multimedia technology, and family language learning.

Tom Holm, J Diane Pearson, and Ben Chavis. 2003. Peoplehood: A model for the extension of sovereignty in american indian studies. *Wicazo Sa Review*, 18(1):7–24.

Howard Johnson and Joel Martin. 2003. Unsupervised learning of morphology for english and inuktitut. In *Companion volume of the proceedings of HLT-NAACL 2003-short papers*, pages 43–45.

C J Lippert. 2007. Location of all anishinaabe reservations/reserves in north america, with diffusion rings about communities speaking an anishinaabe language. cities with anishinaabe population also shown.

Manuel Mager, Ximena Gutierrez-Vasques, Gerardo Sierra, and Ivan Meza. 2018. Challenges of language technologies for the indigenous languages of the americas. In *Proceedings of the 27th International Conference on Computational Linguistics*, pages 55–69.

Antonis Maronikolakis, Philipp Dufter, and Hinrich Schütze. 2021. Wine is not v i n. on the compatibility of tokenizations across languages. In *Findings of the Association for Computational Linguistics: EMNLP 2021*, pages 2382–2399.

Brian D McInnes. 2014. Teaching and learning ojibwe as a second language: Considerations for a sustainable future. *Journal of Language Teaching and Research*, 5(4):751.

Mary Ann Naokwegijig-Corbiere and Rand Valentine. 2015. Nishnaabemwin web dictionary.

John David Nichols. 1980. *Ojibwe morphology: a thesis*. Ph.D. thesis, Harvard University.

Pat Ningewance. 1999. *Naasaab Izhi-anishinaabebii'igeng Conference Report: A Conference to Find a Common Anishinaabemowin Writing System*. Ministry of Education & Training, Workplace Preparation Branch, Literacy ....

Ninaatig Staats Pangowish. 2023. Naadimaadizang mi-inwaa naadimaading, helping one's self and help one another. Anishinaabemowin Teg.

F. Pedregosa, G. Varoquaux, A. Gramfort, V. Michel, B. Thirion, O. Grisel, M. Blondel, P. Prettenhofer, R. Weiss, V. Dubourg, J. Vanderplas, A. Passos, D. Cournapeau, M. Brucher, M. Perrot, and E. Duchesnay. 2011. Scikit-learn: Machine learning in Python. *Journal of Machine Learning Research*, 12:2825–2830.

Brock Pitawanakwat. 2018. Strategies and methods for anishinaabemowin revitalization. *Canadian Modern Language Review*, 74(3):460–482.

Richard A Rhodes. 2006. Ojibwe language shift: 1600-present. *Historical Linguistics and Hunter-Gatherer Populations in Global Perspective, MPI-EVA Leipzig*.

Mohammad Salameh, Houda Bouamor, and Nizar Habash. 2018. Fine-grained arabic dialect identification. In *Proceedings of the 27th international conference on computational linguistics*, pages 1332–1344.

Jasdeep Singh, Bryan McCann, Richard Socher, and Caiming Xiong. 2019. Bert is not an interlingua and the bias of tokenization. In *Proceedings of the 2nd Workshop on Deep Learning Approaches for Low-Resource NLP (DeepLo 2019)*, pages 47–55.

Linda Tuhiwai Smith. 2021. *Decolonizing methodologies: Research and indigenous peoples*. Bloomsbury Publishing.

Anton Treuer. 2010. *Living our language: Ojibwe tales and oral histories*. Minnesota Historical Society Press.

Anton Treuer, Joe Chosa, David Treuer, James Clark, William Jones, Diane Amour, Edward Benton-Banai, Jessie Clark, Alex Decoteau, Michelle DeFoe, George Fairbanks, Rick Gresczyk, Charles Grolla, Jason Jones, Jeremy Kingsbury, Earl Otchingwanigan, and Vernon Whitefeather. 2012. *Oshkaabewis Native Journal (Vol. 8, No. 1)*. Lulu.com.

U.S. Census Bureau. 2011. 2010 census. U.S. Department of Commerce.

J Randolph Valentine. 2001a. Being and becoming in ojibwe. *Anthropological linguistics*, pages 431–470.

Jerry Randolph Valentine. 1994. *Ojibwe dialect relationships*. The University of Texas at Austin.

Randy Valentine. 2001b. *Nishnaabemwin reference grammar*. University of Toronto Press.

A Appendix A: Feature Scale Study

To understand the number of features being created and used by the model, a simple scale study was performed. Model features were counted for various numbers of n-grams used and model performance as a function of limited n-grams was computed. To understand how many of the most common n-grams are shared between dialects, the n-gram dictionaries for each dialect were sorted and compared for overlapping n-grams. The results of this are presented in Table 3, where it can be seen that the relative overlap in n-grams decreases with increasing dictionary sizes. Intuitively, this makes sense, as a common language would share the most common features between dialects and differences should become more apparent with larger feature sets. To quantify the performance of our proposed model with a very limited feature set, the smallest truncated dictionary was used to repeat the analysis and is presented in Table 4. Performance with n-grams derived from single sentences is substantially lower than when using the full n-gram dictionary, which shows how important the less common character combinations are to identifying the dialect present. Interestingly, when n-grams from four sentences are combined, performance between models is comparable.

Table 3: Overlap in top n-grams

Number of most common n-grams used	**Number of overlapping n-grams**	**Combined dictionary size**
100	82	118
500	348	652
1000	650	1350
All	2217	6259

Table 4: Model performance as a function of number of sentences used per example, using truncated n-gram dictionary with 118 n-grams.

Number of grouped sentences	**Accuracy**
1	0.64
2	0.73
3	0.82
4	0.98
5	0.97

B Appendix B: Text Statistics

To help illustrate the corpus used for this work, some statistics are shared in Table 3.1. To help keep the data set sizes similar, not all of the stories from Treuer et al. (2012) were used in this work.

Table 5: Information about texts used

Text	Number of sentences	Average number of words per sentence
Southwestern	611	6.7
Eastern	434	7.6

C Appendix C: Full Results of Individual Word Classification

The full table of word pairs between Eastern and Southwestern Ojibwe is presented in Table 6. Fifty word pairs, along with their approximate English translation, were selected by choosing words that a language learner might learn at an early stage in their learning process. When multiple words are commonly used for a similar meaning in one dialect but not another (for example *makwa, mkwa* and *mko*), the table repeats the word for the dialect without multiple common words found in the appropriate dictionary. This is done for visual clarity for the reader. Multliple words were not included in the statistics computed in Figure 2.

Table 6: Fifty common words that vary between Eastern and Southwestern Ojibwe and our model's classification

Ojibwe SW dictionary form	Classified by our model as	Ojibwe E/Odawa dictionary form	Classified by our model as	English (approximate)
aaniin	E	aanii	E	hello (pc interj)
daga	E	bna	E	please (pc disc)
niin	E	niinii	E	me (n)
niin	E	nii	E	me (n)
giin	E	gii	SW	you (n)
enyanh'	E	ehenh	E	yes (pc disc)
en'	E	enh	E	yes (pc disc)
gaawiin	SW	gaa	E	no (pc disc)
gaawiin	SW	kaa	E	no (pc disc)
wiindan	SW	waawiindaan	E	name (vti)
izhinikaazowin	SW	zhnikaazwin	E	name (n)
minawaanigozi	SW	mnowaan'gozi	E	is happy (vai)
izhinaagozi	SW	zhinaagzi	E	look a certain way (vta)
izhinaagwad	SW	zhinaagot	SW	look a certain way (vti)
ojiim	SW	jiimaa	SW	kiss (vta)
ojiindan	SW	jiindaan	SW	kiss (vti)
wiiisini	SW	wiisni	E	eat (vai)
amo	E	mwaa	E	eat (vta)
minikwe	SW	mnikwe	E	drink(vai)
aabitoojiin	SW	aabtoojiinaa	E	hug around middle (vta)
giziibiiga'an	SW	gziibiignaan	E	wash something (vti)
opin	SW	pin	SW	potato (n)
manoomin	SW	mnoomin	E	wild rice (n)
mishiimin	SW	mshiimin	E	apple (n)
odaabaan	SW	daabaan	SW	car (n)
makwa	SW	mkwa	E	bear(n)
makwa	SW	mko	E	bear (n)
ma'iingan	SW	m'iingan	SW	wolf (n)
nigig	SW	ngig	SW	otter (n)
mooz	E	moos	E	moose (n)
waawaashkeshi	E	waawaashkesh	E	white-tailed deer (n)
giingoo	E	giigoonh	E	fish (n)
ogaa	SW	gawaak	SW	walleye / pickerel (n)
adikameg	SW	dikmek	E	whitefish (n)
mitig	SW	mtik	E	tree (n)
nagamo	E	n'gamo	E	sing (vai)
giiwese	SW	giiwse	E	hunt (vai)
baashkigizige	SW	baashkzige	E	shoot (vai)
agindaaso	SW	n'gidaaso	SW	read (vai)
babaamose	SW	bbaamse	E	walk about (vai)
bikwaakwad	SW	bkwaakwat	E	ball (n)
gimiwan	SW	gmiwan	SW	rain (n)
waabooz	E	waaboos	E	rabbit (n)
bakwezhigan	SW	bkwezhgan	E	bread (n)
waasechigan	SW	waasechgan	SW	window (n)
wewebizo	SW	wewebza	E	swing (vai)
akwaandawe	SW	kwaandw	E	climb (vai)
bagizo	SW	bgiza	SW	swim (vai)

Enriching Wayúunaiki–Spanish Neural Machine Translation with Linguistic Information

Nora Graichen,[1] Josef van Genabith,[1,2] Cristina España-Bonet[2]
[1]Saarland University, Saarland Informatics Campus, Germany
[2]German Research Center for Artificial Intelligence (DFKI GmbH)
graichen@coli.uni-saarland.de
{cristinae, Josef.Van_Genabith}@dfki.de

Abstract

We present the first neural machine translation system for the low-resource language pair Wayúunaiki–Spanish and explore strategies to inject linguistic knowledge into the model to improve translation quality. We explore a wide range of methods and combine complementary approaches. Results indicate that incorporating linguistic information through linguistically motivated subword segmentation, factored models, and pretrained embeddings helps the system to generate improved translations, with the segmentation contributing most. In order to evaluate translation quality in a general domain and go beyond the available religious domain data, we gather and make publicly available a new test set and supplementary material. Although translation quality as measured with automatic metrics is low, we hope these resources will facilitate and support further research on Wayúunaiki.

1 Introduction

Due to a lack of data (text or speech data), languages are digitally divided between high and low-resourced (LRL) (Bender, 2019). Actually, the low-resource scenario has been identified as one of the main challenges in the field of Natural Language Processing (NLP) (Koehn and Knowles, 2017). At the same time, research conducted and presented at major conferences often focuses on a few highly resourced languages, languages with similar characteristics, or a handful of well-studied languages (Joshi et al., 2020). Fortunately, research in low-resource settings and with LRLs is slowely becoming quite popular in the NLP community, with a steadily growing body of work for the low-resource scenario (Wang et al., 2021). This does not imply that the division between low- and high-resourced NLP scenarios has been overcome. In fact, there are many open challenges for research on and with LRLs.

The majority of the world's 7000 languages are understudied and underresourced (Joshi et al., 2020), due to the lack of research and resources. LRLs face a lack of data quality and quantity, NLP tools, and engagement with native speakers of that language, which, if overcome, can support the conservation and preservation of those languages and their culture, preserving cultural and linguistic diversity.

In this work, we aim at fostering research for Wayúunaiki by providing data and pretrained Neural Machine Translation (NMT) models. We present the first Wayúunaiki–Spanish NMT system, and explore different approaches to inject linguistic knowledge to improve translation quality. We aim at assisting the Wayúu community, whose language is emerging from an endangered situation according to Ethnologue.[1] Even though the Wayúu people are the most numerous indigenous people in Colombia (Departamento Administrativo Nacional de Estadística, 2021), Wayúunaiki is vulnerable, i.e. the language is spoken by children but only in certain, restricted domains, for instance at home. Our research hypothesis in this work is that the injection of linguistic knowledge will increase the translation quality for the language pair Wayúunaki–Spanish. We enrich the data to represent implicit linguistic information (e.g., linguistically motivated subword segmentation, annotating POS tag factors, and pretrained embeddings) as, if insufficient amounts of training data is available, linguistic information may help the model identify patterns present in the text, which may alleviate the data sparsity problem. We build on and extend previous work on NMT for LRLs by Sennrich and Haddow (2016) and Chen and Fazio (2021). We combine complementary approaches to maximize improvements. We find that while linguistically motivated subword segmentation helps, factored models and pretrained embeddings lead

[1]https://www.ethnologue.com/language/guc/

Proceedings of the Workshop on Natural Language Processing for Indigenous Languages of the Americas (AmericasNLP), pages 67–83
July 14, 2023

to a performance degradation due to data sparsity and low quality annotations. While the results of this work do not provide good quality translation models yet, we expect to contribute to the development of NMT systems for LRLs and to inspire further research. We integrate our best-performing system for Wayúunaiki to Spanish into the document translation interface *TransIns*[2] (Steffen and van Genabith, 2021) for public use. Our collected supplementary material, the new general domain test data set, as well as code are also publicly available.[3]

2 Related Work

Various ways of incorporating linguistic knowledge into NMT systems have been explored. These include the addition of (linguistic) factors (e.g., Sennrich and Haddow (2016), España-Bonet and van Genabith (2018), Manzanares, 2020), or using different subword segmentation techniques (e.g., Sennrich et al. (2016), Kudo and Richardson (2018) Grönroos et al., 2014) with the aim of improving translation quality. Improvements are possible, especially in LRL scenarios (e.g., Sennrich and Zhang, 2019), morphologically rich languages (e.g., Ortega et al., 2020), and for out-of-domain texts (e.g., Chen and Fazio, 2021).

Subword segmentation is essential in NMT since it eases the out-of-vocabulary (OOV) problem and allows training smaller models (Mielke et al., 2021). Subword units offer a representation, that builds a bridge between word and character-level, based on the statistical properties of the text. A good choice of subword units will offer a good balance between the vocabulary size, the size of the model and therefore the decoding efficiency.

Data-driven, unsupervised subword segmentation is a statistically-informed process that incorporates implicit linguistic knowledge present in the text, like statistical patterns that present regularities of encountered word forms. This approach is limited to the data used during training the segmentation model, such that text variations (e.g., inconsistent orthography or out-of domain context) might result in segmentation variations and over-segmentation (Amrhein and Sennrich, 2021).

The *Byte-Pair-Encoding* (BPE) algorithm (Gage, 1994) is a widely used, unsupervised approach for subword segmentation. BPE merges the most frequent pairs of characters in a corpus to create a new subunit, and repeats the process until the desired number of merge operations are performed. With BPE, common words form a single unit while rare words are split into subunits. The first application in MT by Sennrich et al. (2016) lead to a strong improvement in performance. Further approaches include SentencePiece (Kudo and Richardson, 2018), a tokeniser that implements both BPE and *unigram language model* (LM) (Kudo, 2018). In Kudo (2018) subword segmentation is combined with a regularization method, offering a robust alternative to the deterministic BPE. For the segmentation technique by Kudo (2018), an initial subword set is pruned, according to the contribution of each subword to the unigram LM (Mielke et al., 2021). Another alternative for creating more segmentation variety in the training data is the regularization method particularly for BPE called BPE-dropout (Provilkov et al., 2020).

Semi-supervised segmentation techniques incorporate and exploit linguistically labeled training data to guide the segmentation process. Linguistic annotation can help to learn the correct segmentation rules, especially in low quantity and quality data scenarios (Chen and Fazio, 2021).

The semi-supervised segmentation technique, *Prefix-Root-Postfix-Encoding* (PRPE) by Zuters et al. (2018) is a morphologically guided algorithm, that incorporates linguistic knowledge without requiring any morphological rules. Nonetheless, a list of affixes is essential during the construction of the segmenter. In comparison to the BPE algorithm, subwords that include positional information of a word are extracted in form of prefixes, roots, and postfixes. This subword segmentation algorithm has been shown to improve translation quality, measured with BLEU, in comparison to other systems, in which unsupervised algorithms were applied (Chen and Fazio, 2021). The algorithm is not thought to be used as a morphological segmentation tool, even though it produces text that resembles morphologically segmented text. Moreover, it avoids over-segmentation by sometimes only partially performing the morphological splitting with the motivation that too many subwords would reduce the translation quality (Zuters et al., 2018).

FlatCat (Grönroos et al., 2014) is a variant of the toolkit Morfessor (Smit et al., 2014) for statistical morphological segmentation which can be

[2] https://transins.dfki.de

[3] https://github.com/norgrai/wayuunaiki

applied in an unsupervised or semi-supervised manner. The system consists of a category-based hidden Markov model (HMM) and a flat lexicon structure for morphological segmentation. The states of the HMM are the morph categories (prefix, stem, suffix, and non-morphs, with the last category catching subwords that are not proper morphemes but segments of a longer morph). Morfessor FlatCat is best suited for semi-supervised training where some morphological splitting guidelines are given; in fully unsupervised training with no annotations over-segmentation or under-segmentation will probably occur (Grönroos et al., 2014). Zuters et al. (2018), in their comparison between PRPE and Morfessor FlatCat, acknowledge previous, small improvements using Morfessor for inflected languages in statistical MT, but these improvements are not reproduced in their experiments.

Sennrich and Haddow (2016) were one of the first to introduce **linguistic factors** like lemmas, part-of-speech (POS) tags, dependency labels, and morphological features as factors into an NMT model.[4] The additional linguistic information is coupled with each subword by concatenating or averaging the embeddings. As their main objective was reducing data sparsity, they tested the factored architecture on high and LRL pairs, obtaining significant translation improvements in BLEU for the model with all factors included, for both high and low resource scenarios. In their experiments, the best results with only one factor were achieved with a POS tag or lemma factor in a RNN encoder–decoder architecture with attention for English to German translation. Similar performance for lemma factors was observed by Armengol-Estapé et al. (2021) with the Transformer architecture (Vaswani et al., 2017). By adding a lemma factor to the subwords, different inflections of a words are linked to the same representation. By introducing POS tags, it is possible to discriminate between different word categories, that share the same surface word.

Word embeddings capture both semantic knowledge (Mikolov et al., 2013; Brunila and LaViolette, 2022) and, to a lower extent, syntactic knowledge (Mikolov et al., 2013; Andreas and Klein, 2014). Syntax is more evident in embeddings when the training data is scarce (Andreas and Klein, 2014). Qi et al. (2018) showed that leveraging pretrained word embeddings can lead to significant improvements for certain LRL pairs. However, Qi et al. (2018) use of pretrained embeddings by Bojanowski et al. (2017) limits the scope of the comparison, since only a few Indigenous languages, such as Quechua, have access to such rich representations or have sufficient data available for training them.

According to Fernandez et al. (2013), there were very few projects that involve the development of a translator for Indigenous languages in Colombia such as Wayúunaiki. At the same time Llerena García (2013) presented the reasons and need for a "Software traductor de español a lengua wayuu" (*Spanish to Wayúu language translator software*). Unfortunately, to the best of our knowledge, even now, 10 years after Fernandez et al. (2013) and Llerena García (2013), there still exists no publicly accessible translation system, that supports the Wayúu community.

3 Language Description

Wayúunaiki is the native language spoken by a minority (compared to Spanish) in the Wayúu community, located in the Caribbean region, connecting Colombia and Venezuela. More than half a million people of this bi-national community speak this LRL. The Wayúu community is the most numerous indigenous community in Colombia (Departamento Administrativo Nacional de Estadística, 2021). There are 380,460 Wayúus in Colombia[5] and about 415,500 Wayúus in Venezuela (INE, 2012).

Wayúunaiki belongs linguistically to the Arawak languages. This language family flourished among ancient, indigenous nations in South America and consists of polysynthetic, mainly head-marking languages with different degrees of agglutination (Méndez-Rivera, 2020). Spanish, the high-resourced language spoken in the same countries, is a fusional, inflected language with a flexible syntactic order. The preferred pattern is subject + verb + object (SVO), while Wayúunaiki has a VSO order. Both languages have their own phonological system and do not share the same alphabet: Spanish has 22 consonants and 5 vowels in its phonological repertoire, while Wayúunaiki has 16 consonant and

[4]Linguistic information was earlier introduced by Alexandrescu and Kirchhoff (2006) in a neural NLP model.

[5]According to the latest census information: the *Censo Nacional de Población y Vivienda* (CNPV) was conducted in 2018 by the National Administrative Department of Statistics (DANE).

data set	# of samples	tokens		TTR	
		esp	guc	esp	guc
train	41499	776k	591k	0.029	0.048
development	1001	18.7k	14.0k	0.175	0.220
in-domain test set	1001	18.7k	14.2k	0.181	0.219
Total	43501	814k	620k	0.028	0.047
additional data:					
out-of-domain test	1107	15.1k	10.6k	0.203	0.360

Table 1: Description of the bitext data sets: number of samples, words, and type-token-ratio (TTR) for the Wayúunaiki (guc) and Spanish (esp) data set from the Tatoeba MT Challenge with our partitions, and the additional, manually collected data.

source	# of samples	parallel sentences
Lozano R. and Mejía V. (2007)	402	yes & aligned text
Álvarez (2016)	211	yes
Álvarez (2011)	425 69	yes aligned text
Total:	1107	

Table 2: Description of out-of-domain data set, collected bitext for Spanish–Wayúunaiki.

source	language	# of samples, tokens		language unit
de Saint-Exupéry et al. (2016)	guc	1933	19.5k	sentence
David M. Captain (2005)	guc	3177	3.2k	word
Total:	5.1k units			
WikiDump (Wikipedia, 2020)	esp	29.02M	597M	sentence

Table 3: Description of monolingual data in Wayúunaiki (guc) and Spanish (esp).

12 vowel phonemes —6 vowel pairs of long and short ones (Viloria Rodríguez et al., 2022). An inconsistent writing system for the Wayúu language, due to the two main "official" orthographic systems, in combination with a very small amount of written material in Wayúunaiki, make the orthographic situation challenging (Álvarez, 2017).[6]

4 Data Collection and Preprocessing

Parallel corpora. We use the only online parallel corpus for Wayúunaiki and Spanish available in the Tatoeba MT Challenge, version v2021-08-07 (Tiedemann, 2020). The bitext is a subpart of the no longer available JW300, a parallel corpus from Agić and Vulić (2019) with religious-themed data, addressing a wider range of topics including bible psalms.[7] The Wayúunaiki part of the bitext follows the official writing norm ALIV (Alfabeto de Lenguas Indígenas de Venezuela, *alphabet of indigenous languages of Venezuela*). The corpus consists of ~43k sentence pairs, which we divided into a train, development, and test set. Table 1 gives a summary of the parallel corpora utilized.

The usage of highly domain-specific (here religious) data limits the translation quality in other domains and when used for other domains introduces a strong ideological, and gender-related bias, given the biblical content: gender pronouns and person names do not appear in the data with a balanced frequency,[8] nor do they share a similar word context, regarding activities or occupations (Storks et al., 2019). Furthermore, we asked two native Wayúunaiki speakers to perform a revision of random Wayúu sentences in the Tatoeba corpora. The revision showed the low quality of the resource. Some sentences are not direct translations and miss important information. In the example below, the personal name (Margaret) is absent in the Wayúunaiki sentence (a), but given in the official translation (b). According to bilingual Spanish and Wayúunaiki speakers, the correct translation would be (c).

(a) Sü'lakajaaka pireewa sümaa saatsa aainjuushi süka keesü nayaalu'u na süikeyuukana süka shiain nekaajüin ma'in.

(b) Margaret trajo la comida y la puso en el centro de la mesa, donde estaban todos sentados.
Margaret brought the food and put it in the center of the table, where everyone was sitting.

(c) Nos cocinaron fideos en salsa con queso porque es la comida que comen ellos.
They cooked us noodles in sauce with cheese because that's the food they eat.

In order to create a general domain parallel data set and assess the generalizability of the translation systems, we collected data from Spanish–Wayúunaiki dictionaries and illustrative grammar booklets for non-Wayúunaiki speakers to learn the language. Table 2 shows the number of samples and sources we used to build the general domain test set.

Monolingual corpora Table 3 lists the details of the monolingual data we collected. We extracted Wayúunaiki text from the translation[9] of

[6]Since 1984, the official *Alfabeto de Lenguas Indígenas de Venezuela*, the alphabet of indigenous languages of Venezuela has been the norm in Colombia and Venezuela, but the system of Miguel Ángel Jusayú is being utilized alongside.

[7]The web-crawled data stems from the website jw.org of a religious society, covering many low-resource languages. Aside from the Bible, the Jehovah's Witnesses provide magazines, books, and other multi-media content.

[8]For instance, the female pronoun *ella* occurs less than one-fourth of the times the male pronoun *él* occurs.

[9]https://www.academia.edu/37583043/Pürinsipechonkai

the book *The Little Prince* by Antoine de Saint-Exupery. This corpus is used as monolingual data, since it does not align at sentence level with the Spanish version. We also extract from a bilingual Spanish–Wayúunaiki dictionary (David M. Captain, 2005) entries in Wayúunaiki, which we used, one token per line, as additional data. The Wayúu data follows the the official writing norm ALIV. For Spanish, we use a subset of 10M sentences from the Spanish Wikipedia dump from May 2020 (Wikipedia, 2020) extracted with *WikiTailor* (España-Bonet et al., 2023). Notice the data asymmetry between Wayúunaiki and Spanish. While we obtain 5000 sentences in Wayúunaiki, the Spanish Wikipedia alone has almost 30M sentences. This reflects the typical data imbalance between high- and low-resourced languages.

The monolingual corpus is used in our work combined with the monolingual parts of the parallel corpus to train word embeddings.

Supplementary Material Some of our experiments require supplementary information in the form of linguistic annotations, or dictionaries. We extracted morphological analyses of verb conjugations in Wayúunaiki from the work of Álvarez (2017) to guide the semi-supervised training of the segmentation models (Prefix-Root-Postfix-Encoding and FlatCat). For this, the morph categories prefix, stem, and suffix were manually annotated. An example file is listed in Appendix A and we make all files available online.[10] We perform a similar morphological annotation with Spanish samples taken from lecture slides from Doctor Lluís Simarro Lacabra (2014), an educational institution.

Preprocessing We split the monolingual text into sentences and tokens using the *nltk* tokenizer. Since there is no tokenizer for Wayúunaiki, we use regular expressions (RE). The character ' in Wayúunaiki, which in the Latin alphabet represents the glottal stop consonant [ʔ] known as "saltillo", *little skip*, had to be stripped from additional white spaces. For simplification, all possible saltillos (‘ ′ ’ ´) were mapped to the ' character in the parallel data sets. Likewise, quotations (» « “ ”) were normalized to ". Bible verses number references were detected with REs and removed. Enumerations with brackets, numbers with punctuation at the beginning of the sentence, and URLs were also removed. We train a truecaser with Moses scripts (Koehn et al., 2007) for each language on the parallel data and applied them to all data sets accordingly.

5 NMT Systems

All our models are based on a transformer architecture (Vaswani et al., 2017) and developed with Marian v1.11.0 (Junczys-Dowmunt et al., 2018).

5.1 Baseline System

We perform a wide hyperparameter search on a transformer following van Biljon et al. (2020) (see Appendix B for the parameters, the ranges we explore and the best configuration). With the gained insights from the random search, we chose the configuration of the most promising model, a small transformer model with 3 encoder, 3 decoder layers, 4 heads and hidden layers with a size of 1024, and use it in all systems.

We train a baseline system on unsegmented data without (**BASE**) and with (**BASE+EMB**) pretrained embeddings. The embeddings for each language are trained independently with *fastText* (Bojanowski et al., 2017) on the preprocessed, unsegmented monolingual text, using the continuous skip-gram model (Mikolov et al., 2010). In our experiments, the model achieved the best results with embeddings that have a dimension of 256.

5.2 Subword Segmentation Techniques

We investigate different subword segmentation algorithms and apply them separately for each language: BPE without (**SUBW-bpe**) and with applied dropout (**SUBW-dp**), a unigram LM (**SUBW-uni**) for segmentation, PRPE (**SUBW-prpe**), and Morfessor FlatCat (**SUBW-fc**).

For SUBW-bpe, we explore both the impact of separate and joint vocabulary, and of different vocabulary sizes, using the *subword-nmt* toolkit (Sennrich et al., 2016). The chosen merge operations range from 100 to 15000 merges. According to the results (detailed numbers in Appendix C), we use for SUBW-bpe with 4k merge operations with separate vocabularies if not stated otherwise.

Reported models with pretrained embeddings (SUBW-bpe+EMB) are trained with *fastText* like the ones for the baseline but with segmented monolingual text.

[10] `https://github.com/norgrai/wayuunaiki`

5.3 Factored Models

We investigate factored models, where POS tag information is injected. Since an NLP tool for POS tagging or lemmatization in Wayúunaiki is not available, we adapt Spanish–Wayúunaiki dictionaries into linguistic knowledge-based vocabularies: Wayúu vocabulary entries were annotated with the Spanish translation and POS tag to represent implicit linguistic information. We use a bilingual dictionary from the Apertium (Forcada et al., 2011) GitHub[11] and an illustrated dictionary from David M. Captain (2005). We match their different POS tag annotations for Wayúu with the POS tag categories of the *FreeLing* analyzer (Padró and Stanilovsky, 2012) for Spanish.[12]

Approximately 40% of the Wayúu training data could be annotated in this way, mostly due to annotation of the closed class "punctuation" with makes up about 15% of the tokens. The high number of unclassified words is mainly due to the lack of a lemmatizer: only dictionary entries can be looked up automatically, so most tokens with inflectional and derivational variation cannot be matched with their corresponding POS tag. This stands in stark contrast to the annotation with *FreeLing* for Spanish, where much more fine-grained classes were used and every word is assigned a POS tag.

5.4 Evaluation

For the automatic evaluation, we use SacreBLEU (Post, 2018) to calculate BLEU[13] (Papineni et al., 2002) and chrF2++[14] (Popović, 2015). As semantic metric we use BLEURT[15] (Sellam et al., 2020) and for all cases, we estimate 95% confidence intervals via bootstrap resampling (Koehn et al., 2003) with 1000 samples.

Since the surface-based n-gram scoring methods can strongly restrict the expressiveness of agglutinative languages like Wayúunaiki, we also include example model translations for a qualitative manual comparison.

[11] https://github.com/apertium/apertium-guc-spa

[12] See the detailed resulting alignments among languages and the percentage of categories in our training data in Appendix A.

[13] BLEU|nrefs:1|bs:1000|seed:12345|case:mixed|eff:no|tok:13a|smooth:exp|version:2.3.1

[14] chrF2++|nrefs:1|bs:1000|seed:12345|case:mixed|eff:yes|nc:6|nw:0|space:no|version:2.3.1

[15] BLEURT v0.0.2 using checkpoint BLEURT-20

6 Results and Discussion

We report the translation scores for Wayúunaiki to Spanish in Tables 4 (religious domain) and 5 (general domain) for each method with the best system per metric boldfaced. In Table 6 we report translation results for Spanish to Wayúunaiki for the most representative systems (the best segmentation approach together with a factored and a pretrained embeddings model).

Model Architecture. van Biljon et al. (2020) demonstrated improvements for translating English text into agglutinative LRLs with a transformer by halving the model's depth to 3 encoder and 3 decoder layers. We obtain the same conclusion from the hyperparameter search for translating from and into Wayúunaiki. Our BASE model is also a small transformer with 3 encoder and 3 decoder layers but Wayúunaiki–Spanish turns out to be a challenging language pair with baseline translation quality close to zero.

Pretrained embeddings alone do not significantly improve the results (BASE+EMB, SUBW-bpe+EMB), although they have been shown to provide a better representation of less frequent concepts in LRLs (Haddow et al., 2022). Qi et al. (2018) showed that pretrained embeddings seem to be effective for not-too-distant translation pairs. This may well be the reason for our lack of improvement, Wayúunaiki and Spanish are very distant, but we conjecture that the most important problem we face is the lack of sufficient data to train Wayúu embeddings: the monolingual Wayúu corpus we use is almost equivalent to the size of the parallel corpus. Still the results of Qi et al. (2018) indicate that pretrained embeddings seem to introduce semantic and syntactic information of words improving translations even for distant translation pairs: systems are able to capture overall basic language characteristics and generate more grammatically well-formed sentences. Qi et al. (2018) indicate that for very little but sufficient training data, that allows training the system, using pretrained word embeddings from (Bojanowski et al., 2017) are most effective. Their usage of pretrained embeddings by Bojanowski et al. (2017) make comparison with our results very difficult, as such embeddings are trained on billions of tokens.

Notice that our BASE systems trained on unsegmented data are well below any subword segmentation we apply. This contradicts the conclusions for Quechua-Spanish in Chen and Fazio (2021):

model guc-esp	BLEU	chrF2	BLEURT
BASE	0.5 ± 0.2	6.0 ± 0.3	0.17 ± 0.01
BASE+EMB	0.7 ± 0.2	11.8 ± 0.4	0.094 ± 0.007
SUBW-bpe	4.2 ± 0.7	20.5 ± 0.8	0.21 ± 0.01
SUBW-dp	3.1 ± 0.5	16.7 ± 0.8	**0.22 ± 0.01**
SUBW-uni	3.3 ± 0.6	**22.0 ± 0.7**	0.20 ± 0.01
SUBW-prpe	1.0 ± 0.3	7.0 ± 0.3	0.15 ± 0.01
SUBW-fc	**4.5 ± 0.8**	21.0 ± 0.8	0.21 ± 0.01
SUBW-bpe+			
+FACT	1.0 ± 0.2	8.9 ± 0.4	0.127 ± 0.006
+EMB	0.6 ± 0.2	7.9 ± 0.3	0.090 ± 0.005
+FACT+EMB	0.8 ± 0.2	13.6 ± 0.4	0.115 ± 0.007

Table 4: Automatic evaluation scores of the **Wayúunaiki to Spanish** translations with the religious **in-domain** test set.

model guc-esp	BLEU	chrF2	BLEURT
BASE	0.08 ± 0.04	4.8 ± 0.3	0.106 ± 0.006
BASE+EMB	0.06 ± 0.03	8.8 ± 0.6	0.048 ± 0.004
SUBW-bpe	**0.20 ± 0.10**	13.2 ± 0.9	0.075 ± 0.006
SUBW-dp	0.14 ± 0.08	8.8 ± 0.7	**0.132 ± 0.006**
SUBW-uni	0.16 ± 0.08	13.8 ± 0.9	0.070 ± 0.005
SUBW-prpe	0.11 ± 0.08	4.5 ± 0.3	0.104 ± 0.006
SUBW-fc	0.12 ± 0.03	**14.0 ± 0.8**	0.067 ± 0.005
SUBW-bpe+			
+FACT	0.07 ± 0.02	6.5 ± 0.5	0.082 ± 0.004
+EMB	0.07 ± 0.03	6.8 ± 0.6	0.067 ± 0.004
+FACT+EMB	0.03 ± 0.01	9.6 ± 0.6	0.059 ± 0.005

Table 5: Automatic evaluation scores of the **Wayúunaiki to Spanish** translations with the **general domain** test set.

in an out-of-domain evaluation their model outperformed all of their systems trained with different segmentation methods (e.g., BPE, unigram LM, PRPE).

Segmentation technique. Although all segmentation methods yield a statistically significant improvement over the baseline, the scores both on the general and in-domain test set emphasize that models do not provide good or even reasonable quality translation yet. Notice also that no single model outperforms other models in all automatic evaluation metrics.

While the results show some potential of Morfessor Flatcat to be used as a segmentation technique,[16] the need to tune additional parameters (perplexity threshold and weight) make the approach more complex and provide no statistically significant improvements with respect to the most straightforward SUBW-bpe. We therefore use SUBW-bpe in our factored models.

The unigram LM subword segmentation method of SentencePiece, used in many NLP systems (Mielke et al., 2021), offers a non-deterministic alternative, though with the SUBW-uni model for the first time in our experiments we observe subwords that are ungrammatical. For instance, the verbs gobernar (Eng: rule) in the reference (2) and the translation (4), which has an incorrect duplication of the character "r":

(1) mapa, kettaapa tü miit juya Nuluwataainjachikalü o'u, nüle'ejireerü tü aluwataayakat nümüin chi nüshikai .

(2) después de gobernar como rey por mil años , le devolverá el reino a su padre .
and after ruling as king for a thousand years, he will return the kingdom to his father

(3) finalmente , cuando llegue el día de su vida , comenzó a gobernarrse con él .
finally, when the day of his life came, he began to govern himself with it .

Observed word repetitions and hallucinations in SUBW-uni or SUBW-dp suggest that the training is still not optimized. The following examples are common translation outputs (they appear several times with diffent and unrelated source sentences) for general domain inputs unrelated to the Bible:

(a) la biblia dice : " el nombre de Jehová
the bible says : " the name of Jehovah

(b) Jesús dijo : " tú , tú , tú ,
Jesus said: " you, you, you,

Fu et al. (2020) argue that the repetition problem is the expression of human language itself: words that produce high probabilities tend to be chosen as the subsequent word again, constructing prediction loops, which result in repetitions. We observe single-word repetitions; however, word pair repetitions are more common, exemplified with "tú" and "," in (b).

Similar to the findings of Raunak et al. (2021), we encounter fluent but "detached", and non-grammatical translation outputs with repetitive structure of hallucinations. The investigation of Lee et al. (2018) on hallucinations with a medium-sized corpus (4.5M training sentences) let them conclude that the noisy and finite characteristics of the data sets are the source for the phenomenon. They propose data augmentation as the

[16]Zuters et al. (2018) introduced a method of segmentation post-processing to control the effective vocabulary size and support an open vocabulary: they performed the Morfessor subword segmentation in an unsupervised fashion on the data on which they applied additionally the BPE algorithm. We tried out this approach but could not achieve comparable results to the reported SUBW-fc.

model esp-guc	BLEU	chrF2	BLEURT
religious domain:			
SUBW-bpe+	1.2 ± 0.3	13.9 ± 0.4	0.239 ± 0.007
+FACT	0.7 ± 0.2	10.7 ± 0.4	0.240 ± 0.008
+EMB	0.5 ± 0.1	17.1 ± 0.6	0.255 ± 0.008
+FACT+EMB	0.7 ± 0.2	19.3 ± 0.6	0.252 ± 0.008
general domain:			
SUBW-bpe+	0.10 ± 0.06	11.3 ± 0.5	0.205 ± 0.007
+FACT	0.06 ± 0.01	9.9 ± 0.5	0.212 ± 0.007
+EMB	0.01 ± 0.01	9.3 ± 0.7	0.232 ± 0.007
+FACT+EMB	0.02 ± 0.00	13.0 ± 0.8	0.228 ± 0.005

Table 6: Automatic evaluation scores of the **Spanish to Wayúunaiki** translations with the religious **in-domain test** set (top rows) and the **general domain** test set (bottom rows).

most promising approach for preventing hallucinations. Still, their techniques require knowledge of hallucinations and exhaustive filtering of the training data. Similar conclusions are made by Raunak et al. (2021); furthermore, they emphasize that invalid or misaligned sentence pairs that do not provide accurate translations should be removed.

Although the overall scores are very low, we find that introduced linguistic knowledge in the shape of linguistically inspired morphs helps the system to better accomplish the translation task. Yet, the segmentation has to be carried out invariably: one possible explanation for the qualitatively lower translations of the models with applied BPE Dropout or the SentencePiece unigram LM is the statistical noise introduced in the segmentation process, being both non-deterministic segmentations contrary to the BPE algorithm.

Linguistic Factors and Embeddings. The performance of the +FACT methods is worse than the original SUBW-bpe. The same happens when adding pretrained word embeddings (+EMB). The introduced linguistic information in the shape of POS tags, pretrained embeddings, and the combination of both does not help to overcome the difficulties of this LRL translation pair. The main reason is the low coverage for Wayúunaiki, both in the amount of data to train the embeddings and therefore their quality, and in POS annotations as explained in Section 5.3.

It is generally acknowledged that introducing linguistic factors coupled with a word or its subwords improves translation quality only to a modest extent (Sennrich and Haddow, 2016). Hence, for language pairs in a high resource setting, it is not advisable to invest time and effort in a factored NMT approach (Casas et al., 2021). Still, in an LRL setting that possibly involves morphologically rich languages, the data sparsity problem can be eased by converting the plain parallel text into a factored representation on the source side.

Translation quality should not be evaluated only automatically though, as low scores are difficult to compare and different metrics show different trends (see their correlations in Appendix C). No single model outperforms all of the others in Table 4 measured across all three metrics. Although none of the proposed models achieved a higher BLEU score than SUBW-bpe for translating into Wayúunaiki in Table 6, the chrF2 score indicates improvements (± 3.2), which we verified by manually examining example translations, e.g., (2) and (3).

(1) **input**: hablémosle sin prisas .
let's talk to him without haste .

(2) **SUBW-bpe+EMB**: püküja **nümüin** tü alatakat **nümüin** . . .] .] *tell those who cut for him . . .] .]*

(3) **SUBW-bpe**: shia süka tü kee'ireekat paa'in .
this is what you want .

(4) **reference**:
nnojoishii ashapajaainjanain waya waashajaapa **nümaa** .

7 Conclusion and Future Work

In this work we applied various unsupervised and semisupervised subword segmentation methods to enrich the data used to train a transformer-based NMT model with linguistic information. Additionally, we extended the architecture of the standard SUBW-bpe model by adding linguistic information in the form of POS tag factors and/or supplying the system with pretrained embeddings. In line with previous research on Indigenous LRL pairs that include Spanish, we observed that the addition of subword information is crucial to improve translation quality (e.g., Ortega et al. (2020), Mager et al. (2021), Chen and Fazio, 2021). In particular, the Indigenous languages of America, which are mostly characterized by a rich morphology, and part of agglutinative and polysynthetic languages, benefit from approaches that consider the LRL's morphology and apply subword segmentation techniques that are suitable for the language pair. In contrast, we did not achieve any improvement with factors and pretrained embeddings. The lack of resources, in terms of data and annotation coverage, is the likely cause for the low performance of these models.

Our next steps are focused on investigating the effectiveness of injecting linguistic knowledge for the Wayúu language by exploring datasets without repetitive sequences and less sparse and noisy annotations. To do this, more sophisticated approaches to obtain implicit linguistic knowledge from LRL text, such as introducing linguistic information also on the target side in the form of POS-tag or lemma factors are possible.

Problems related to the lack of resources for factored training could in principle be overcome by applying a linguistically inspired subword segmentation technique, for instance, Morfessor's FlatCat. By splitting a word into its subwords, chances of determining the stem are higher, if the segmentation into subwords representing stems and suffixes is both accurate and consistent. Given the stem, the word can be annotated with its POS tag from the linguistic knowledge-based vocabulary. We note that this is limited to languages without infixation and would work only for words without assimilatory processes between affixes and stem. Still, it presents a possible approach to obtain labeled data.

Besides enriching the data with linguistic information, our observations on word repetitions and hallucinations indicate that additional cleaning, filtering of unaligned source and target translations, and orthographic normalization could significantly enhance data quality and hence translation performance.

We believe that injecting linguistic information, especially for LRL pairs can alleviate the data sparsity problem and aid the models with the annotation of implicit linguistic knowledge present in the data. By enriching the data to represent such information present in the text (e.g., annotating POS tags), a model can better identify patterns inherent in the data. Still, choosing between the different approaches and techniques requires taking into account the nature of the LRL pair and the available resources, particularly supported NMT tools and data sets.

Limitations

In this work we explored transfer learning approaches only by using pretrained word embeddings. Transfer learning should be explored further. Some of the segmentation methods have their own hyperparameters which are usually obtained for high-resourced languages and might be suboptimal in our case. These hyperparameters should be systematically explored. Finally, token-free pretrained models fine-tuned on our data should be investigated.

It is costly and difficult to acquire human translations, due to the limited number of speakers and exclusive LRL communities; moreover, the fact that we are not Wayúunaiki speakers limited our qualitative assessment.

Acknowledgements

Thanks to two supportive natives of the Wayúu community, we were able to analyze our translation results beyond automatic evaluation scores. Both bilingual speakers are non-professional interpreters and translators that helped voluntarily. Adolfo y señora Gladys: ¡Muchas gracias por su ayuda con las traducciones, interés y confianza en el proyecto! We thank Jörg Steffen for the integration of the Wayúunaiki–Spanish system in TransIns.

References

Željko Agić and Ivan Vulić. 2019. JW300: A wide-coverage parallel corpus for low-resource languages. In *Proceedings of the 57th Annual Meeting of the Association for Computational Linguistics*, pages 3204–3210, Florence, Italy. Association for Computational Linguistics.

Andrei Alexandrescu and Katrin Kirchhoff. 2006. Factored neural language models. In *Proceedings of the Human Language Technology Conference of the NAACL, Companion Volume: Short Papers*, pages 1–4, New York City, USA. Association for Computational Linguistics.

Chantal Amrhein and Rico Sennrich. 2021. How suitable are subword segmentation strategies for translating non-concatenative morphology? In *Findings of the Association for Computational Linguistics: EMNLP 2021*, pages 689–705, Punta Cana, Dominican Republic. Association for Computational Linguistics.

Jacob Andreas and Dan Klein. 2014. How much do word embeddings encode about syntax? In *Proceedings of the 52nd Annual Meeting of the Association for Computational Linguistics (Volume 2: Short Papers)*, pages 822–827, Baltimore, Maryland. Association for Computational Linguistics.

Jordi Armengol-Estapé, Marta R. Costa-jussà, and Carlos Escolano. 2021. Enriching the transformer with linguistic factors for low-resource machine translation. In *Proceedings of the International Conference on Recent Advances in Natural Language Processing (RANLP 2021)*, pages 73–78, Held Online. INCOMA Ltd.

Emily Bender. 2019. The #benderrule: On naming the languages we study and why it matters. *The Gradient*.

Piotr Bojanowski, Edouard Grave, Armand Joulin, and Tomas Mikolov. 2017. Enriching Word Vectors with Subword Information. volume 5, pages 135–146.

Mikael Brunila and Jack LaViolette. 2022. What company do words keep? revisiting the distributional semantics of J.R. firth & zellig Harris. In *Proceedings of the 2022 Conference of the North American Chapter of the Association for Computational Linguistics: Human Language Technologies*, pages 4403–4417, Seattle, United States. Association for Computational Linguistics.

Noe Casas, Jose A. R. Fonollosa, and Marta R. Costa-jussà. 2021. Sparsely factored neural machine translation. *CoRR*, abs/2102.08934.

William Chen and Brett Fazio. 2021. Morphologically-guided segmentation for translation of agglutinative low-resource languages. In *Proceedings of the 4th Workshop on Technologies for MT of Low Resource Languages (LoResMT2021)*, pages 20–31, Virtual. Association for Machine Translation in the Americas.

Linda B. Captain David M. Captain. 2005. *Diccionario Básico Ilustrado, wayuunaiki-español español-wayuunaiki*. Editorial Fundación para el Desarrollo de los Pueblos Marginados, Editorial Buena Semilla.

A. de Saint-Exupéry, José Álvarez, and Jean-Marc Probst Foundation. 2016. *The Little Prince*. The Jean-Marc Probst Foundation.

DANE Departamento Administrativo Nacional de Estadística. 2021. *Información sociodemográfica del pueblo Wayúu*. Number 2805-6345 in Informes de Estadística Sociodemográfica Aplicada. DANE Colombia.

Shuoyang Ding, Adithya Renduchintala, and Kevin Duh. 2019. A call for prudent choice of subword merge operations in neural machine translation. In *Proceedings of Machine Translation Summit XVII: Research Track*, pages 204–213, Dublin, Ireland. European Association for Machine Translation.

L'Institut d'Educació Secundària Doctor Lluís Simarro Lacabra. 2014. Análisis morfológico de la palabra. lengua castellana y literatura. Lecture slides http://Análisis-morfológico-de-la-palabra.pdf.

Cristina España-Bonet, Alberto Barrón-Cedeño, and Lluís Màrquez. 2023. Tailoring and Evaluating the Wikipedia for in-Domain Comparable Corpora Extraction. *Knowledge and Information Systems*, pages 1365–1397.

Cristina España-Bonet and Josef van Genabith. 2018. Multilingual Semantic Networks for Data-driven Interlingua Seq2Seq Systems. In *Proceedings of the LREC 2018 MLP-MomenT Workshop*, pages 8–13, Miyazaki, Japan.

Dayana Fernandez, Jose Atencia, Ornela Gamboa, and Óscar Bedoya. 2013. Design and implementation of an "Web API" for the automatic translation Colombia's language pairs: Spanish-Wayuunaiki case. pages 1–9.

Mikel L. Forcada, Mireia Ginestí-Rosell, Jacob Nordfalk, Jimmy O'Regan, Sergio Ortiz Rojas, Juan Antonio Pérez-Ortiz, Felipe Sánchez-Martínez, Gema Ramírez-Sánchez, and Francis M. Tyers. 2011. Apertium: a free/open-source platform for rule-based machine translation. *Machine Translation*, 25:127–144.

Zihao Fu, Wai Lam, Anthony Man-Cho So, and Bei Shi. 2020. A theoretical analysis of the repetition problem in text generation. In *AAAI Conference on Artificial Intelligence*.

Philip Gage. 1994. A new algorithm for data compression. *The C Users Journal archive*, 12:23–38.

Stig-Arne Grönroos, Sami Virpioja, Peter Smit, and Mikko Kurimo. 2014. Morfessor FlatCat: An HMM-based method for unsupervised and semi-supervised learning of morphology. In *Proceedings of COLING 2014, the 25th International Conference on Computational Linguistics: Technical Papers*, pages 1177–1185, Dublin, Ireland. Dublin City University and Association for Computational Linguistics.

Barry Haddow, Rachel Bawden, Antonio Valerio Miceli Barone, Jindřich Helcl, and Alexandra Birch. 2022. Survey of low-resource machine translation. volume 48, pages 673–732, Cambridge, MA. MIT Press.

Pratik Joshi, Sebastin Santy, Amar Budhiraja, Kalika Bali, and Monojit Choudhury. 2020. The state and fate of linguistic diversity and inclusion in the NLP world. In *Proceedings of the 58th Annual Meeting of the Association for Computational Linguistics*, pages 6282–6293, Online. Association for Computational Linguistics.

Marcin Junczys-Dowmunt, Roman Grundkiewicz, Tomasz Dwojak, Hieu Hoang, Kenneth Heafield, Tom Neckermann, Frank Seide, Ulrich Germann, Alham Fikri Aji, Nikolay Bogoychev, André F. T. Martins, and Alexandra Birch. 2018. Marian: Fast neural machine translation in C++. In *Proceedings of ACL 2018, System Demonstrations*, pages 116–121, Melbourne, Australia. Association for Computational Linguistics.

Philipp Koehn, Hieu Hoang, Alexandra Birch, Chris Callison-Burch, Marcello Federico, Nicola Bertoldi, Brooke Cowan, Wade Shen, Christine Moran, Richard Zens, Chris Dyer, Ondřej Bojar, Alexandra Constantin, and Evan Herbst. 2007. Moses: Open source toolkit for statistical machine translation. In *Proceedings of the 45th Annual Meeting of the Association for Computational Linguistics Companion Volume Proceedings of the Demo and Poster Sessions*, pages 177–180, Prague, Czech Republic. Association for Computational Linguistics.

Philipp Koehn and Rebecca Knowles. 2017. Six challenges for neural machine translation. In *Proceedings of the First Workshop on Neural Machine Translation*, pages 28–39, Vancouver. Association for Computational Linguistics.

Philipp Koehn, Franz J. Och, and Daniel Marcu. 2003. Statistical phrase-based translation. In *Proceedings of the 2003 Human Language Technology Conference of the North American Chapter of the Association for Computational Linguistics*, pages 127–133.

Taku Kudo. 2018. Subword regularization: Improving neural network translation models with multiple subword candidates. In *Proceedings of the 56th Annual Meeting of the Association for Computational Linguistics (Volume 1: Long Papers)*, pages 66–75, Melbourne, Australia. Association for Computational Linguistics.

Taku Kudo and John Richardson. 2018. SentencePiece: A simple and language independent subword tokenizer and detokenizer for neural text processing. In *Proceedings of the 2018 Conference on Empirical Methods in Natural Language Processing: System Demonstrations*, pages 66–71, Brussels, Belgium. Association for Computational Linguistics.

Katherine Lee, Orhan Firat, Ashish Agarwal, Clara Fannjiang, and David Sussillo. 2018. Hallucinations in neural machine translation. In *Interpretability and Robustness in Audio, Speech, and Language (IRASL) Workshop, Conference on Neural Information Processing Systems (NeurIPS)*, Montreal, Canada.

Ernesto Llerena García. 2013. Software traductor de español a lengua wayuu. pages 353–356.

Jorge Lozano R. and Julián David' Mejía V. 2007. Wayuunkeera - cartilla trilingüe & cuaderno de actividades, wayuunaiki español english. Universidad Libre.

Manuel Mager, Arturo Oncevay, Abteen Ebrahimi, John Ortega, Annette Rios, Angela Fan, Ximena Gutierrez-Vasques, Luis Chiruzzo, Gustavo Giménez-Lugo, Ricardo Ramos, Ivan Vladimir Meza Ruiz, Rolando Coto-Solano, Alexis Palmer, Elisabeth Mager-Hois, Vishrav Chaudhary, Graham Neubig, Ngoc Thang Vu, and Katharina Kann. 2021. Findings of the AmericasNLP 2021 shared task on open machine translation for indigenous languages of the Americas. In *Proceedings of the First Workshop on Natural Language Processing for Indigenous Languages of the Americas*, pages 202–217, Online. Association for Computational Linguistics.

Noé Casas Manzanares. 2020. *Injection of linguistic knowledge into neural text generation models*. Ph.D. thesis, Universitat Politècnica de Catalunya.

Sabrina Mielke, Zaid Alyafeai, Elizabeth Salesky, Colin Raffel, Manan Dey, Matthias Gallé, Arun Raja, Chenglei Si, Wilson Lee, Benoît Sagot, and Samson Tan. 2021. Between words and characters: A Brief History of Open-Vocabulary Modeling and Tokenization in NLP. *CoRR*, abs/2112.10508.

Tomas Mikolov, Kai Chen, Greg Corrado, and Jeffrey Dean. 2013. Efficient estimation of word representations in vector space. arXiv.

Tomas Mikolov, Martin Karafiát, Lukas Burget, Jan Cernockỳ, and Sanjeev Khudanpur. 2010. Recurrent neural network based language model. In *Interspeech*, volume 2, pages 1045–1048. Makuhari.

Nelson J. Méndez-Rivera. 2020. *Linguistic outcomes of the Wayuunaiki-Spanish Language contact situation*. Ph.D. thesis, University of Ottawa.

John E. Ortega, Richard Castro Mamani, and Kyunghyun Cho. 2020. Neural machine translation with a polysynthetic low resource language. *Machine Translation*, 34(4):325–346.

Lluís Padró and Evgeny Stanilovsky. 2012. FreeLing 3.0: Towards wider multilinguality. In *Proceedings of the Eighth International Conference on Language Resources and Evaluation (LREC'12)*, pages 2473–2479, Istanbul, Turkey. European Language Resources Association (ELRA).

Kishore Papineni, Salim Roukos, Todd Ward, and Wei-Jing Zhu. 2002. Bleu: A method for automatic evaluation of machine translation. In *Proceedings of the 40th Annual Meeting on Association for Computational Linguistics*, ACL '02, page 311–318, USA. Association for Computational Linguistics.

Maja Popović. 2015. chrF: character n-gram F-score for automatic MT evaluation. In *Proceedings of the Tenth Workshop on Statistical Machine Translation*, pages 392–395, Lisbon, Portugal. Association for Computational Linguistics.

Matt Post. 2018. A call for clarity in reporting BLEU scores. In *Proceedings of the Third Conference on Machine Translation: Research Papers*, pages 186–191, Brussels, Belgium. Association for Computational Linguistics.

Ivan Provilkov, Dmitrii Emelianenko, and Elena Voita. 2020. BPE-dropout: Simple and effective subword regularization. In *Proceedings of the 58th Annual Meeting of the Association for Computational Linguistics*, pages 1882–1892, Online. Association for Computational Linguistics.

Ye Qi, Devendra Sachan, Matthieu Felix, Sarguna Padmanabhan, and Graham Neubig. 2018. When and why are pre-trained word embeddings useful for neural machine translation? In *Proceedings of the 2018 Conference of the North American Chapter of the Association for Computational Linguistics: Human Language Technologies, Volume 2 (Short Papers)*, pages 529–535, New Orleans, Louisiana. Association for Computational Linguistics.

Vikas Raunak, Arul Menezes, and Marcin Junczys-Dowmunt. 2021. The curious case of hallucinations in neural machine translation. In *Proceedings of the 2021 Conference of the North American Chapter of the Association for Computational Linguistics: Human Language Technologies*, pages 1172–1183, Online. Association for Computational Linguistics.

Thibault Sellam, Dipanjan Das, and Ankur Parikh. 2020. BLEURT: Learning robust metrics for text generation. In *Proceedings of the 58th Annual Meeting of the Association for Computational Linguistics*, pages 7881–7892, Online. Association for Computational Linguistics.

Rico Sennrich and Barry Haddow. 2016. Linguistic input features improve neural machine translation. In *Proceedings of the First Conference on Machine Translation: Volume 1, Research Papers*, pages 83–91, Berlin, Germany. Association for Computational Linguistics.

Rico Sennrich, Barry Haddow, and Alexandra Birch. 2016. Neural machine translation of rare words with subword units. In *Proceedings of the 54th Annual Meeting of the Association for Computational Linguistics (Volume 1: Long Papers)*, pages 1715–1725, Berlin, Germany. Association for Computational Linguistics.

Rico Sennrich and Biao Zhang. 2019. Revisiting low-resource neural machine translation: A case study. In *Proceedings of the 57th Annual Meeting of the Association for Computational Linguistics*, pages 211–221, Florence, Italy. Association for Computational Linguistics.

Peter Smit, Sami Virpioja, Stig-Arne Grönroos, and Mikko Kurimo. 2014. Morfessor 2.0: Toolkit for statistical morphological segmentation. Technical report, Gothenburg, Sweden.

Jörg Steffen and Josef van Genabith. 2021. TransIns: Document translation with markup reinsertion. In *Proceedings of the 2021 Conference on Empirical Methods in Natural Language Processing: System Demonstrations*, pages 28–34, Online and Punta Cana, Dominican Republic. Association for Computational Linguistics.

Shane Storks, Qiaozi Gao, and Joyce Yue Chai. 2019. Recent Advances in Natural Language Inference: A Survey of Benchmarks, Resources, and Approaches. *CoRR*, abs/1904.01172.

Jörg Tiedemann. 2020. The tatoeba translation challenge – realistic data sets for low resource and multilingual MT. In *Proceedings of the Fifth Conference on Machine Translation*, pages 1174–1182, Online. Association for Computational Linguistics.

Elan van Biljon, Arnu Pretorius, and Julia Kreutzer. 2020. On optimal transformer depth for low-resource language translation. *CoRR*, abs/2004.04418.

Ashish Vaswani, Noam Shazeer, Niki Parmar, Jakob Uszkoreit, Llion Jones, Aidan N Gomez, Ł ukasz Kaiser, and Illia Polosukhin. 2017. Attention is all you need. In *Advances in Neural Information Processing Systems*, volume 30. Curran Associates, Inc.

Leonel Viloria Rodríguez, Johan Yacomelo, Rudecindo González, and Daniela Segura. 2022. Pronombres en wayuunaiki y español; una mirada contrastiva. *Íkala, Revista de Lenguaje y Cultura*, 27.

Rui Wang, Xu Tan, Renqian Luo, Tao Qin, and Tie-Yan Liu. 2021. A survey on low-resource neural machine translation. pages 4636–4643.

Inc. Wikimedia Foundation Wikipedia. 2020. In *Wikimedia downloads.* [link].

Jānis Zuters, Gus Strazds, and Kārlis Immers. 2018. *Semi-automatic Quasi-morphological Word Segmentation for Neural Machine Translation: 13th International Baltic Conference, DBIS 2018, Trakai, Lithuania, July 1-4, 2018, Proceedings*, pages 289–301.

José Álvarez. 2011. Pütchimaajatü komputatoorachiki wayuunaikiru'usu. Diccionario de computación en wayuunaiki. Microsoft Venezuela.

José Álvarez. 2016. La conjugación del verbo en la lengua wayuu. Instituto Caro Y Cuervo.

José Álvarez. 2017. *Manual de la lengua wayuu, Karalouta atüjaaya saa'u wayuunaikikuwa'ipa*. Organización Indígena de La Guajira Yanama.

A Supplementary Material Annotation

A.1 Morph Categories

We manually annotate the morph categories prefix, stem, and suffix of 26 words in Wayúunaiki and 91 in Spanish for the Morfessor Flatcat approach. To perform Prefix-Root-Postfix-Encoding, we created two heuristics that contain the common suffixes, prefixes and endings for the Wayúu and Spanish languages. The example below shows 10 words annotated for Wayúunaiki.

Listing 1 Example annotations for Wayúunaiki used for semi-supervision in the Morfessor Flatcat (Grönroos et al., 2014) system. Morph categories are indicated by PRE (prefix), STM (stem), and SUF (suffix).

```
aya'lajaa a/PRE ya'laja/STM a/SUF
aya'lajeewaa a/PRE ya'laja/STM ee/SUF a/SUF
aya'lajiraa a/PRE ya'laja/STM ira/SUF a/SUF
aya'lajünaa a/PRE ya'laja/STM na/SUF a/SUF
apütüshi a/PRE pütü/STM shi/SUF
apütüichi a/PRE pütü/STM i/SUF chi/SUF
apütüeechi a/PRE pütü/STM ee/SUF chi/SUF
apütüinjachi a/PRE pütü/STM inja/SUF chi/SUF
apütüshijachi a/PRE pütü/STM shi/SUF ja/SUF chi/SUF
apütüichipa a/PRE pütü/STM i/SUF chi/SUF pa/SUF
```

A.2 POS Tagset Alignment

We summarize our alignment between the POS tags of the different sources in Wayúunaiki and the POS tag categories of the *FreeLing* analyzer for Spanish in Table 7. Due to different categorizations of some determiners, we replaced entries that were referring to the determiners as either adverb or pronoun in David M. Captain (2005) and mapped them uniformly to the POS tag D. About 80 references to another surface form of the same word were looked up and matched with their corresponding POS tag.

Spanish		Wayúunaiki	
class	abbr.	class	abbr.
adjective	**A**	(1)(2) adjetivo	adj.
conjunction	**C**	(1) conjunción	conj.
determiner	**D**	(3) determinante	det
punctuation	**F**	puntuación	punct.
pronoun	**P**	(1) pronombre	pron.
adverb	**R**	(1) adverbio	adv.
adposition	**S**	(1) posposición	posp.
		(2) Postposición	post.
verb	**V**	(1) verbo transitivo	v.t.
		(1) verbo intransitivo	v.i.
		(2) verbos	vblex
noun	**N**	(1) nombre	n
		(2) Alineable	ali.
		(2) Inalineable	ina.
interjection	**I**	(1) interjección	interj.
		(2) Interjeccion	ij

Table 7: Description of Tagset for Spanish (left): POS classes with the category and the abbreviation used. Alignment with the Wayúunaiki data (right): (1) refers to the dictionary in David M. Captain (2005), (2) Forcada et al. (2011), and (3) the manually extracted, closed classes in Lozano R. and Mejía V. (2007).

A.3 POS Tags Distribution

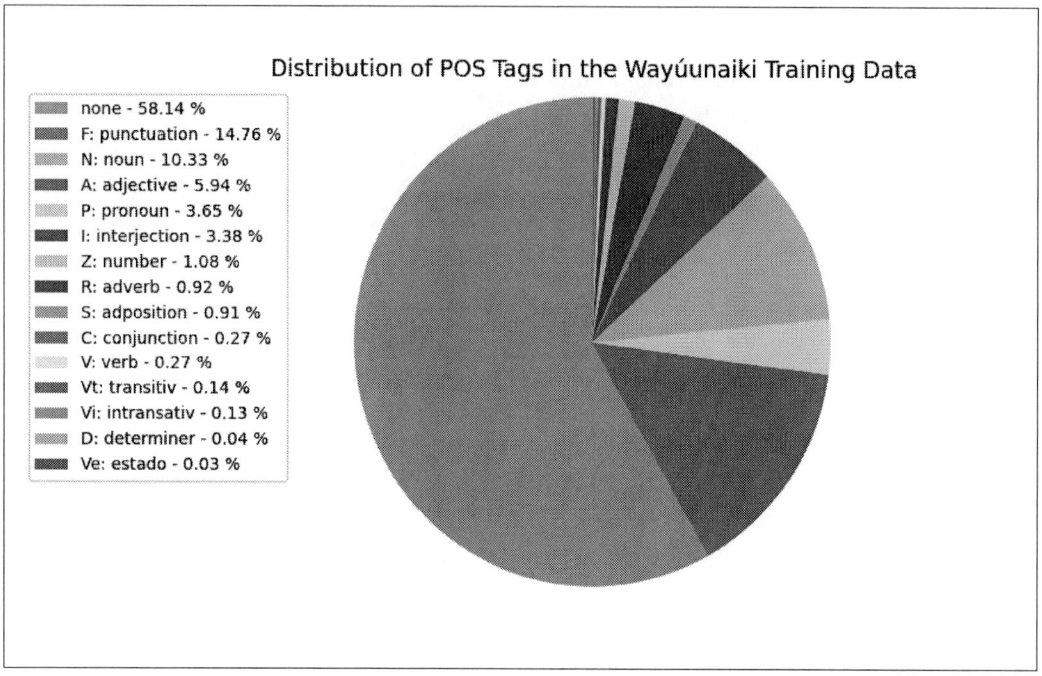

Figure 1: POS tags of the Wayúu training data, which we annotated based on linguistic knowledge-based vocabularies.

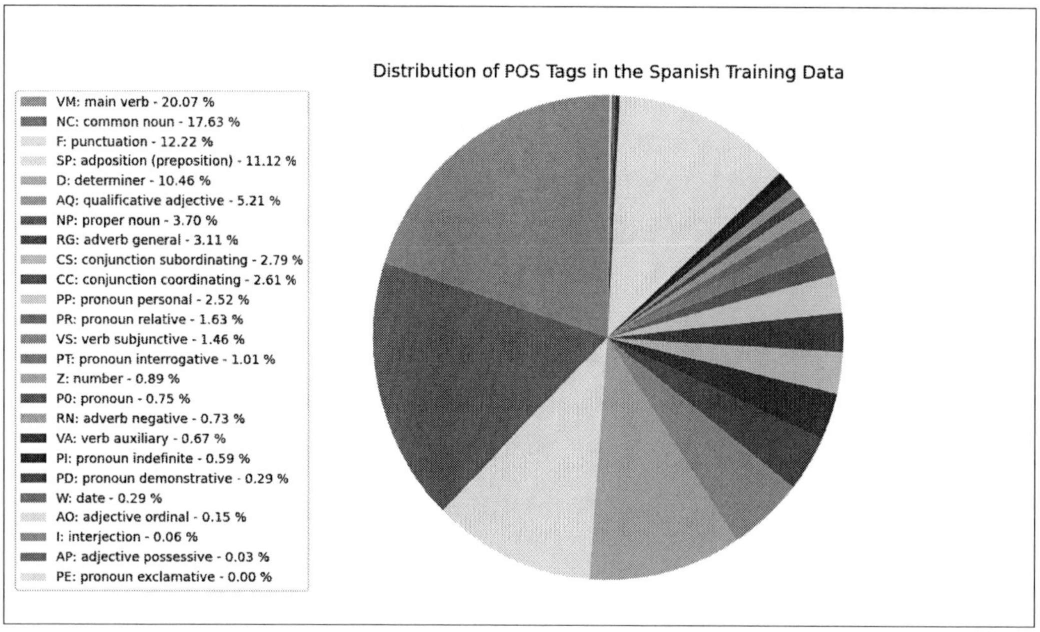

Figure 2: POS tags of the Spanish training data, annotated with *FreeLing* (Padró and Stanilovsky, 2012). We summarized the subclasses of determiner (D), numbers (Z), and punctuation (F) for representation purposes only.

B NMT Hyperparameter Exploration

Building upon findings from van Biljon et al. (2020), we explore different hyperparameters which are specially relevant in the LR scenario. Table 8 summarizes the hyperparameter space explored. Table 9 shows the best configuration that is used for the baseline system (BASE). Finally, we show the segmentation-related hyperparameters used for the segmented-based models (SUBW-*) in Table 10.

Hyperparameter	Values
# attention heads:	2, 4, 8
# of encoder/decoder layers:	2, 3, 4
embedding size:	256, 512, 1024
tied embeddings:	True, False
learning-rate:	1e-3, 1e-4 3e-4, 5e-4
warm-up steps:	1000, 4000
adam optimizer beta:	0.98, 0.999
label-smoothing:	0, 0.1, 0.2
layer-normalization:	True, False
train-position-embeddings:	True, False
exponential-smoothing:	0, 0.0001
clip-norm:	0, 1, 5
seeds:	0, 42, 1111

Table 8: Hyperparameters explored (as required by Marian software) with the corresponding values considered.

```
type: transformer
hidden layer size: 1024
embedding size: 256
tied embeddings: False
decoder depth: 3
encoder depth: 3
transformer heads: 4
transformer-dim-ffn: 1024
transformer-postprocess: da
transformer-preprocess: n
dropout - transformer: 0.3
        - ffn: 0.25
        - attention: 0
clip-norm: False
exponential-smoothing: 0
layer normalization: False
label smoothing: 0.1
learning-rate (lr): 3e-4
    lr-warmup: 1000
    lr-decay-inv-sqrt: 4000
optimizer (betas): adam (0.9, 0.999,1e-9)
seed: 42
early stopping patience: 15
beam size: 5
mini-batch-words: 1000
max-sentence length: 100
```

Table 9: Network configuration for the baseline **BASE**. Operation: d=dropout, a=add, n=normalize. As in Table 8, the parameters are those used by Marian.

```
(0) subword_nmt/learn_bpe.py
    bpe_operations: 4000
    separate vocabulary setting

(1) subword_nmt/apply_bpe.py
    dropout: 0.05

(2) sentencepiece-options:
    vocab size: 4000
    character coverage: 0.9998
    sentencepiece-alphas: 0 0

(3) segmentation:
    prefix rate: 32
    suffix rate: 500
    postfix rate (esp): 180
    postfix rate (guc): 500
    vocab size: 5000
    model training:
    dim-vocabs 4000 4000

(4) segmentation:
    perplexity (esp): 200
    perplexity (guc): 15
    α: 0.1
    β: 1.0
```

Table 10: Additional configuration for (0) **SUBW-bpe**, (1) **SUBW-dp**, (2) **SUBW-uni**, (3) **SUBW-prpe**, (4) **SUBW-fc**.

C Systems Evaluation

C.1 Translation Quality vs Vocabulary Size

The size of the vocabulary is very important in low resourced settings. We therefore perform a deep exploration of the merge operations in our SUBW-bpe system. Figure 3 shows translation quality with the three metrics (BLEU, chrF and BLEURT) varying the merge operations between 100 and 15000 per language.

Similarly to Ding et al. (2019), we find performance drops with increasing merge operations, confirming made findings, that in low-resource settings fewer merge operations, hence smaller vocabulary sizes seem to be appropriate (Mielke et al., 2021). Interestingly, we note a strong decline in performance for merge operations greater than 2k and smaller than 4k merges, Figure 3. Since the merge-depending vocabulary size influences the final amount of parameters, we suppose that for 2k or 4k, an optimal setting for the SUBW-bpe architecture is encountered.

1

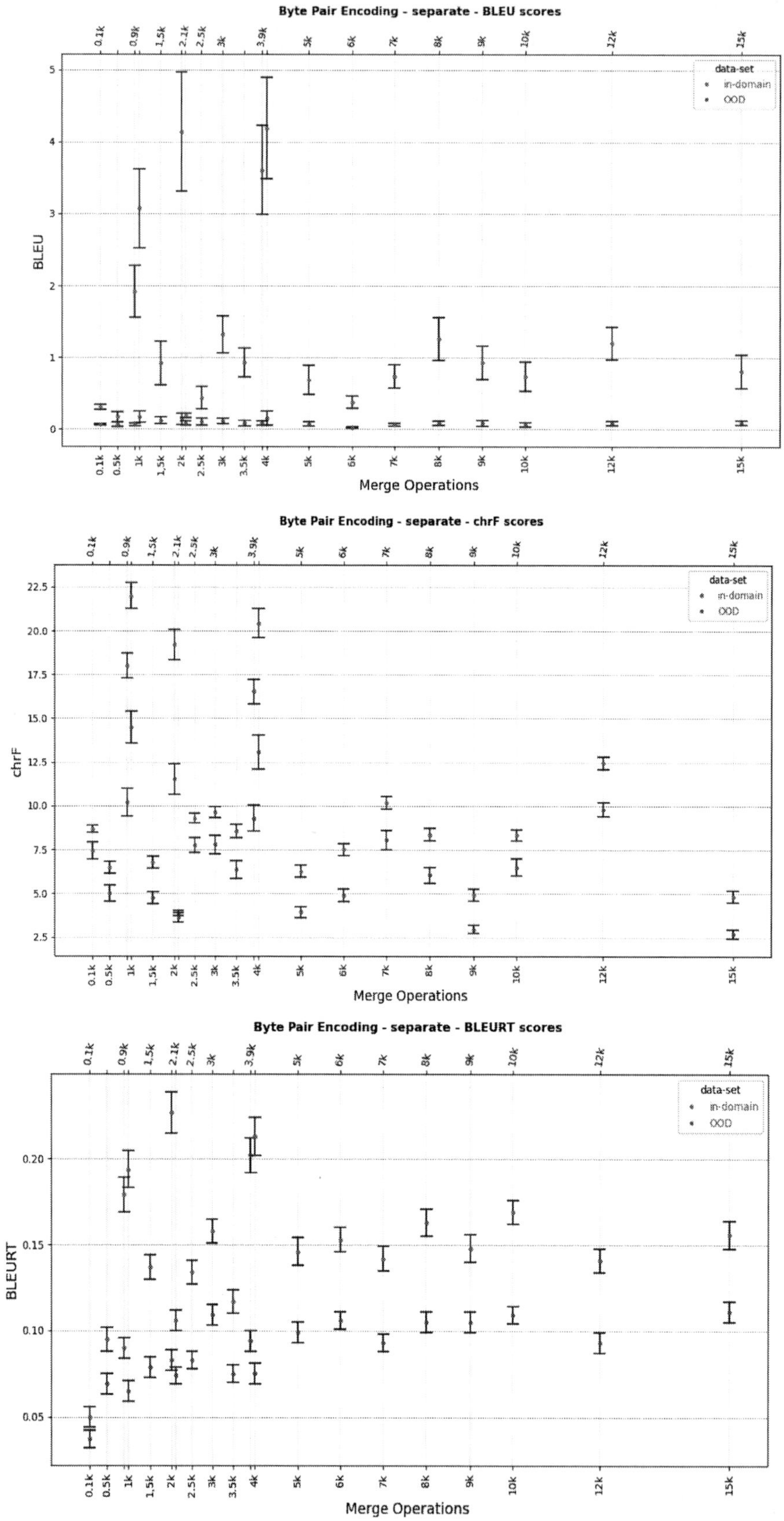

Figure 3: Automatic evaluation scores of the translations with the religious, in-domain and below the OOD-test set of the Transformer **SUBW-bpe** system trained with different BPE merge operations in a seperate vocabulary setting. The confidence intervals were obtained via bootstrap resampling

C.2 The Use of Automatic Metrics

Results in Section 6 show very low scores for the automatic metrics. Notice, that even if improvements with respect to the baselines are statistically significant, different metrics point to different rankings of the systems. This problem appears generally with low scores and with small differences between systems, both issues we encounter in Wayúunaiki–Spanish translation. As result, metrics do not correlate well with each other. The Pearson correlation among pairs of metrics (BLEU, chrF, BLEURT) is $r < 0.6$, being far from linearity. We show in Table 4 the scores of all our systems projected into the 2D spaces for BLEU-chrF (black crosses, $r = 0.534$, $\rho = 0.451$), BLEU-BLEURT (red stars, $r = 0.571$, $\rho = 0.720$) and chrF-BLEURT (green dots, $r = 0.498$, $\rho = 0.377$).

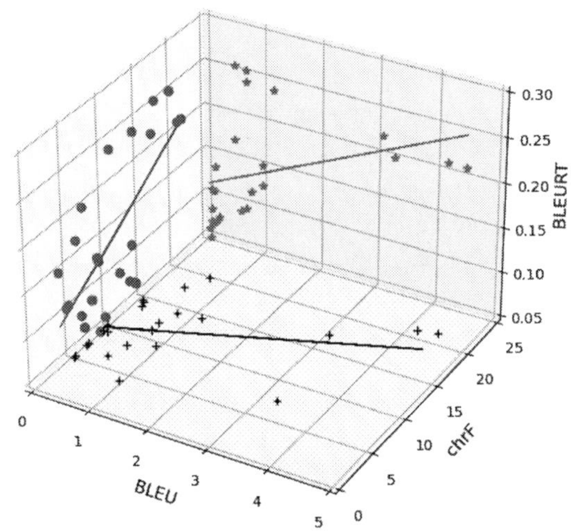

Figure 4: Correlation between the metrics used in the automatic evaluation. We include all of the model scores reported in Tables 4, 5 and 6.

Towards the First Named Entity Recognition of Inuktitut for an Improved Machine Translation

Ngoc Tan Le and **Ikram Kasdi** and **Fatiha Sadat**
Université du Québec à Montréal
le.ngoc_tan@uqam.ca and ikramkasdi@gmail.com and sadat.fatiha@uqam.ca

Abstract

Named Entity Recognition is a crucial step to ensure good quality performance of several Natural Language Processing applications and tools, including machine translation and information retrieval. Moreover, it is considered as a fundamental module of many Natural Language Understanding tasks such as question-answering systems. This paper presents a first study on NER for an under-represented Indigenous Inuit language of Canada, Inuktitut, which lacks linguistic resources and large labeled data. Our proposed NER model for Inuktitut is built by transferring linguistic characteristics from English to Inuktitut, based on either rules or bilingual word embeddings. We provide an empirical study based on a comparison with the state of the art models and as well as intrinsic and extrinsic evaluations. In terms of Recall, Precision and F-score, the obtained results show the effectiveness of the proposed NER methods. Furthermore, it improved the performance of Inuktitut-English Neural Machine Translation.

1 Introduction

In recent years, Artificial Intelligence has recently gained much attention in research and development, particularly when applied to the field of Natural Language Processing (NLP) and Human Language Technologies. This paper focuses on Named Entities Recognition (NER), one of the crucial tasks in several NLP applications and resources. The latter consists in identifying and classifying the names of the specified categories according to predefined semantic types, such as, the names of people, the place, the organization and the numerical expressions, in particular, the currency, the date and the percentage (Nadeau and Sekine, 2007). NER being among the most important tasks of NLP; however, the success of such models is highly dependent on the amount of available annotated data, which is scarce and difficult to obtain. Furthermore, because of the unavailability of annotated data, it is more difficult to apply these NLP methods to low resourced languages and domains, such as Inuktitut, one of the main Indigenous languages in North America and the Canadian Arctic, and part of a larger Inuit language family, stretching from Alaska to Greenland[1].

According to UNESCO, 75% of Indigenous languages are threatened with extinction, and language loss is currently occurring at an accelerating rate due to globalization. Therefore, the revitalization of endangered languages has become an important task for the preservation of cultural diversity on our planet (Bird, 2020).

In our research, we are interested in Inuktitut. Our main objective in this framework is to address the linguistic challenges and to detect named entities for this language through the following contributions:

- Explore the NER task for the Inuktitut language. To our knowledge, works on this task in related with Indigenous languages such as Inuktitut are rare, or non-existent. Therefore, our study will be the first to be carried out for this task.

- Perform a comparative study between two methods, using: (i) rule-based projection based on a morphological analyzer and a word aligner; and (ii) bilingual word embeddings based on semantic similarity in a bilingual vector space.

- Build an annotated corpus in Inuktitut for the NER task. This corpus will contribute to future work for various subfields of NLP, namely information retrieval, neural machine translation, and conversational agents (chatbots).

[1] https://www.thecanadianencyclopedia.ca/en/article/inuktitut

Proceedings of the Workshop on Natural Language Processing for Indigenous Languages of the Americas (AmericasNLP), pages 84–93
July 14, 2023

Also, this work would contribute to the preservation and revitalization of the Inuktitut as well as other (related) Indigenous languages.

- Improve the performance of a Neural Machine Translation (NMT) system by including a NER module.

The current paper is organised as follows: Section 2 introduces Indigenous knowledge including research on several domains such as language, culture, and identity, as well as the relevant works in NER domain. Section 3 presents our methodology via several methods to deal with NER task, and an empirical case study of the Machine Translation task including the NER. Experiments and evaluations are presented in Sections 4 and 5. Finally, Section 6 gives some conclusions and future research directions.

2 A dive into Indigenous Research and NLP

Since 2020, new directions for Indigenous research were put in place by Canada research coordinating committee[2], to help Indigenous peoples and communities partner with research fields, to support and to encourage them to conduct their own research[3]. As with any culture, language is an essential part of Indigenous knowledge, it is also one of the important disciplines of Indigenous research in Canada.

Indigenous languages in Canada have changed and evolved over time and over generations. Like all languages, they carry literary, cultural, traditional, but also historical values (Dorais, 1995). One of the particularities of the Indigenous languages of Canada is that, for some, they are not spoken elsewhere in the world and are specific to Canada[4]. As a result, these languages must be preserved because they represent one of the linguistic and therefore cultural riches of Canada. It is mentioned in the Canadian statistics[5], that the 2016 census recorded more than 70 Indigenous languages divided into 12 language families. The Inuit languages are considered the second Indigenous language family with the largest number of speakers after the Algonquian languages. The most used language in this linguistic family is Inuktitut, mainly spoken in Nunavut and Quebec. In our research, we are particularly interested in this language, rich and at the same time morphologicall complex, as presented in the following section.

2.1 Linguistic challenges in Inuktitut

Indigenous languages in Canada are considered as endangered languages, that reflect the richness of cultures, the history of a people and the diversity of knowledge. Inuktitut is one of the four major sets of dialects of Inuit languages in Canada, from Alaska to Greenland. Mainly spoken in Nunavut and Quebec, it is also spoken in areas of Newfoundland and Labrador as well as in the Northwest Territories. In 2016, the census counted 39,770 speakers, with 65% living in Nunavut and 30.8% living in Quebec.

The preservation of Inuit languages is valued by Indigenous peoples because they are languages that are not spoken elsewhere in the world and their transmission to future generations is not easy. Indeed, Statistics Canada reports that in 2006, 21.4% of the Indigenous population reported being able to carry on a conversation in an Indigenous language. Nevertheless, this percentage decreased to 15.6% in 2016.

Inuktitut is written with a syllabic system, that said, it also has an orthography of the Roman alphabet and the orientation of the writing of the sentences is done, as for French or English, from left to right. The Inuktitut syllabary has differences between dialects. This is because certain sounds exist in one dialect and not in the other. This feature is also found in the spelling system or the spelling of the Roman alphabet of the Inuktitut language, these differences are represented by additional symbols.

The Inuktitut spelling, based on the letters of the Roman alphabet, aims to be more faithful to the pronunciations and specificities of the language in order to be standardized and made more systematic (Compton, 2021).

The Inuktitut language has a particular grammar and fairly complex word compositions that differ-

[2]Canada Research Coordinating Committee: https://www.canada.ca/fr/comite-coordination-recherche/priorites/recherche-autochtone/plan-strategique-2019-2022.html

[3]Indigenous Peoples and Communities: https://www.rcaanc-cirnac.gc.ca/fra/1100100013785/1529102490303

[4]Indigenous languages of First Nations, Métis and Inuit: https://www12.statcan.gc.ca/census-recensement/2016/as-sa/98-200-x/2016022/98-200-x2016022-fra.cfm

[5]Census record: https://www12.statcan.gc.ca/census-recensement/2016/as-sa/98-200-x/2016022/98-200-x2016022-eng.cfm

entiate it from other languages.

Example[6] :

Tusaatsiarunnanngittualuujunga, that means *I don't hear very well*

That sentence word could be segmented as follows: The root Tusaa- (to hear) is followed by 5 suffixes: tsiag- (well), -junnag- (to be able), -nngit- (negation), -tualuu- (much), -junga (first person singular and present tesnse).

2.2 NER for Indigenous languages

In the NER task for Indigenous languages, we classify mainly two types of methods: (1) the one based on rules, and (2) the other ones based on transfer learning, a method that uses the knowledge acquired from one task to be transferred to a second task, recently relying heavily on deep learning. In the first category, sets of rules are manually made for each entity type based on context and morphological features (Fong et al., 2011). In the second category, the transfer approach, such as in the NER model, from rich-resource languages, is an attractive achievement, due to the large amounts of annotated data available (Collobert et al., 2011; Huang et al., 2015; Peters et al., 2018). In this research, we propose methods that use parallel corpora or word embeddings to project the annotation across languages.

Recently, the state of the art of NER for low-resource languages relies on multi-parallel corpora or word embeddings as proposed by Ehrmann et al. (2011), with a goal to annotate corpora in several languages such as French, Spanish, and German. In their research, they used the IBM model to extract word-for-word alignments and therefore aligned entities that represented a group of words.

Other methods used Machine Translation (MT) to project the annotation between languages. Tiedemann et al. (2014) aimed to rule out noisy annotation as to the source language of a parallel corpus. They relied on manual annotation through the UD tree bank (Universal Dependencies) combined with MT. This combination made it possible to train a fully lexicalized analyzer. On the other hand, Mayhew et al. (2017) performed word-to-word or sentence-to-sentence translation using lexicons to translate available annotated data in rich-resource languages.

Stengel-Eskin et al. (2019) introduced an alignment model based on an encoder-decoder architecture, which was integrated into a MT model based on Transformers. They evaluated the performance of their system on the projection of NER data from English to Chinese and outperformed the fast-align based model in terms of F-measure.

Jain et al. (2019) proposed a system that improved through three methods of entity projection: (a) to exploit machine translation systems twice: first, sentence translation; next, entity translation; (b) to match entities based on spelling and phonetic similarity; and (c) to identify matches based on distributional statistics drawn from the parallel data set. Their approach achieved improvements on the cross-lingual NER task and achieved state-of-the-art F1 score for the Armenian language.

In addition, more relevant research to the NER task on Nordic languages, are presented as under-represented or Indigenous languages, such as Icelandic (Ingólfsdóttir et al., 2019), Finnish (Hou et al., 2019; Luoma et al., 2021), Nynorsk (Johansen, 2019), Danish(Plank, 2019).

Other works, such as Azmat et al. (2020), introduced a named entity annotation transfer method also based on NMT. Their approach consists in pre-training an NMT system, from a parallel Uyghur-Chinese corpus. Then, the boundary information that marks the named entities is added to the source language sentences to re-train the previously trained model so that it can learn to align the named entities. The results show that their system obtains a considerable improvement over the base model in terms of F_measure.

Hatami et al. (2021) used the fast-align tool to extract word matchings. Then, two heuristics were applied to obtain alignments in both directions for parallel English-Brazilian Portuguese data. The latter being a low-resource language.

Xie et al. (2018) proposed a method which trains the monolingual word embeddings, projects the two spaces of embeddings of the words of the two languages in the same space, translates each word into the source language by finding the nearest neighbor, uses MT to translate named entities.

Adelani et al. (2020, 2022) considered that the incorporation of word embeddings represents a key element for NER. First, they used a rule-based method to identify named entities in addition to entity lists obtained from dictionaries. Second, they used a noise elimination technique based on the (Hedderich and Klakow, 2018) method in order to clean the annotated corpora automatically by the

[6]https://www.mustgo.com/worldlanguages/inuit/

rule-based method. The performances shown that their method was successful for the two Indigenous languages of Africa: Hausa and Yoruba.

Among the methods that deal with low-resource languages, Yohannes and Amagasa (2022) introduced TigRoBERTa which was trained on corpora in Tigrinya, an Ethiopian Semitic language. Then they performed fine-tuning on downstream tasks such as NER.

3 Methodology

A promising solution for NER task in low-resource languages, without annotated data, is from rich-resource languages using unsupervised transfer models. Given the unavailable annotated data for the Inuktitut and the availability of the latter in English, the main idea of our approach is to transfer the linguistic features of English to Inuktitut. However, the main challenge of this method is the mapping of lexical items between languages. Indeed, this is due to differences in words and word order across languages.

We present, here, two approaches. The first approach consists of transferring the NER annotation from English to Inuktitut by combining rules using a morphological analyzer with word alignment; while the second approach is based on the bilingual word embeddings using a bilingual dictionary (English-Inuktitut) that we built.

3.1 Rules-based approach

In this approach, we used word alignment information with a morphological rule set. The main steps consist of:

- Extracting named entities from the English corpus. For instance, *Ms. Perkison, first Legislative Assembly of Nunavut.*

- Performing a morphological analysis of Inuktitut sentences. Example: the morphological analysis of the word *Titiraqsimaningit* which means in English *First* is:
{titiraq:titiraq/1v}{sima:sima/1vv}
{ni:niq/2vn}{ngit:ngit/**tn**-nom-p-4s}. The word ending is a tn, which means it's a noun ending.

- Identifying nominal groups of Inuktitut text. For instance, in Inuktitut text, *mis puukisan, sivulliqpaami nunavuup maligaliurvinganni.*

- Filtering out nominal groups that do not represent named entities, by using word alignment.

- Building a dictionary of bilingual named entities (English-Inuktitut). For instance:
  - Ms. Perkison - mis puukisan - PER
  - Legislative Assembly of Nunavut - nunavuup maligaliurvinganni - ORG
  - Assembly - maligaliurviup - ORG

- Building a knowledge base in the Indigenous language (Inuktitut), which will help in carrying out NLP tasks downstream and in preserving Indigenous culture.

Figure 1 illustrates the pipeline of our rule-based method.

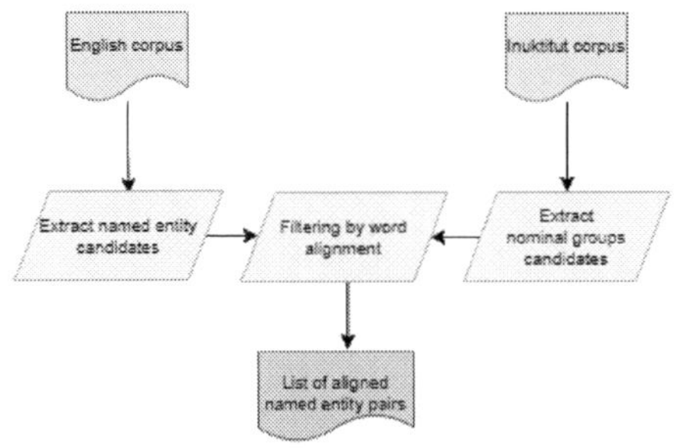

Figure 1: Architecture of our framework: rule-based approach.

3.2 Bilingual word embedding-based approach

Cross-lingual named entities is the transfer of knowledge from a rich-resource language supporting many named entity tags to a low-resource language (Ehrmann et al., 2011). In this approach, we adopt the unsupervised transfer method based on the bilingual word embeddings. This approach addresses the two major challenges: how to solve the word order problem between the languages and effectively to perform the lexical mapping between the two languages. The main steps consist of:

- Building a bilingual English-Inuktitut dictionary.

- Recognizing named entity in English source.

- Training monolingual word embedding on each corpus (English and Inuktitut).

- Translingual projection by performing a linear mapping between the two monolingual word embeddings in the same space and using a bilingual dictionary.

- Calculating the distance between vectors of bilingual named entities.
- Selecting the nearest neighbor as the translation entity.

Figure 2 shows the pipeline of our word embeddings-based approach.

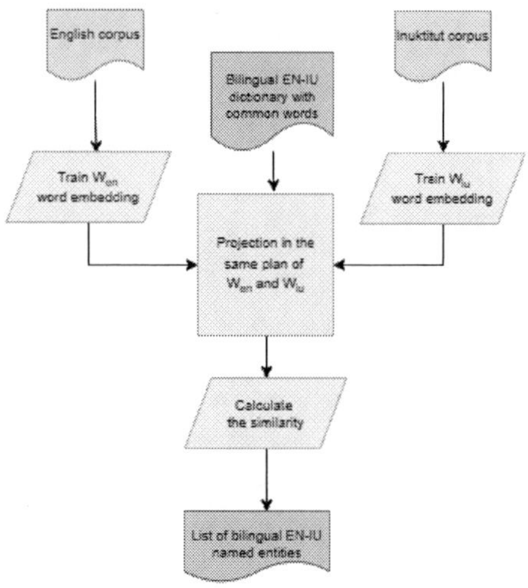

Figure 2: Architecture of our framework: word embedding-based approach.

3.3 Machine Translation Downstream Task

Inspired by (Font and Costa-Jussa, 2019), we built an NMT framework (English-Inuktitut) by taking advantage of pretrained word embeddings, and also source-target alignment information as additional feature.

First, the pretrained word embeddings are used to initialize the embedding layers of the NMT model, both in the encoder and the decoder. We deal with the morphology complexity by applying the morpheme segmentation for Inuktitut (Le and Sadat, 2020).

Second, source-target alignment information is incorporated in the training step. We apply an unsupervised word aligner (Dyer et al., 2013) to generate symmetrical source-target alignments.

Third, we inject, in the decoding, the source-target morphological information, such as bilingual lexicon. We apply a lexicon extractor from Moses (Koehn et al., 2007) to prepare a bilingual lexical shortlist which is passed to the decoder.

4 Experiments

4.1 Data preparation

This corpus includes the proceedings of the 687 days of debates with 8,068,977 words in Inuktitut and 17,330,271 words in English, which gives approximately 1,3 million sentence pairs. This corpus has been used in several research works, particularly in the shared task. The Nunavut Hansard Inuktitut–English Parallel Corpus 3.0 (Joanis et al., 2020) is used to train and to evaluate our proposed models (Table 1).

Dictionary

Using the UQAILAUT[7] project database, we were able to build a bilingual dictionary of 1,560 words. This constitutes root word meanings as well as suffix meanings. We used the Microsoft Bing translator[8] to translate the most frequent English words in the parallel corpora into Inuktitut.

Dataset	Train set	Dev set	Test set
Inuktitut (iu)	1,293,348	5,433	6,139
English (en)	1,293,348	5,433	6,139

Table 1: Statistics of Nunavut Hansard for Inuktitut-English (Joanis et al., 2020).

4.2 Settings for embeddings pretraining

We setup an experimental environment in Table 2. To pretrain word embeddings, the hyper-parameters are configured in Table 2. The *fastText* toolkit (Bojanowski et al., 2017) is used to pretrain them.

Hyper-parameters
Epochs = *50*
Dimension size = *300*
Window size = *2*
Alpha value = *0.03*
Loss function = *softmax*

Table 2: Settings of the hyper-parameters for embedding pretraining.

4.3 Settings for Neural Machine Translation

Regarding the NMT task, we used the *fairseq* tool (Ott et al., 2019) to train the Transformer-based models with the parameters mentioned in Table

[7]UQAILAUT project database: https://www.inuktitutcomputing.ca/Uqailaut/

[8]Bing translator: https://www.bing.com/translator (accessed: March 2023)

3. As pre-processing, we used Moses tool (Koehn et al., 2007) to tokenize. Additionally, we applied Byte-Pair Encoding (BPE) subword segmentation with *subword-nmt* tool (Sennrich et al., 2015) to create a 20k vocabulary. In this paper, we performed only two specific experimental models as follows:

- Baseline: standard Transformer-based model
- Model 1: Transformer-based model with word alignment information
- Model 2: Transformer-based model with bilingual word embedding information

The relevant hyperparameters of NMT models are shown in Table 3.

Hyper-parameter	**Value**
Maximum sentence length	128
Batch size	32
Dropout rate	0.3
Transformer layers	12
Transformer hidden layers	768
Learning rate	0.0005
Epoch	40
Optimizer	adam

Table 3: Settings of hyper-parameters for NMT models

5 Evaluations

To evaluate our proposed method, we used automatic evaluation metrics such as, Recall, Precision, F1, alignment error rate (AER), BLEU score for BiLingual Evaluation Understudy (Papineni et al., 2002) with SacreBLEU (Post, 2018), chrF++ (Popović, 2015) for calculating character n-gram F-score, and translation error rate (TER).

5.1 Evaluations on word alignment

Table 4 represents the word alignment results of words tested using several alignment tools. We also compare our results with those of the Shared Task (Koehn et al., 2005) obtained by (Langlais et al., 2005) namely NUKTI and JAPA in the Table 5.

The word alignment tools were trained on the Nunavut Hansard Inuktitut–English parallel corpora (Joanis et al., 2020), as our same training dataset, and were evaluated on a gold alignment set used in the Shared Task. The performances obtained with the *Eflomal* tool (HMM + fertility) shown a significant improvement in the alignment error rate compared to the others. This is explained by the iteration sampling method that this model uses.

	AER	**P**	**R**	**F1**
Fast align	0.643	0.25	0.623	0.25
GIZA	0.669	0.32	0.33	0.33
Eflomal (ours)	0.474	0.367	0.930	0.367
Eflomal (IBM + HMM)	0.499	0.351	0.874	0.351
Eflomal (IBM1)	0.596	0.281	0.721	0.281

Table 4: Performance of the word alignment tools.

The word alignment results obtained a higher alignment error rate compared to the shared task aligners. Our results are close to the results obtained by the NUKTI model combined with the JAPA model but still remain less efficient than the NUKTI model.

5.2 Evaluations on rule-based method

In order to evaluate the named entities projection performance, we built a small annotated dataset of named entities in Inuktitut. This dataset contains 4 types of named entities: 45 LOC (location) entities, 38 ORG (organization) entities, 111 PER (person) entities and 11 MISC (miscellaneous) entities which do not belong to any type. Table 6 presents the evaluation results of our rule-based method.

The results of this approach could be interesting, especially for the PER entity in proportion to all named entities. Due to the morphology of Inuktitut which is very different from that of English, the word alignment tool could be misled.

Unlike languages admitting the same morphological typology, the alignment error rate is much lower. Moreover, the parts of the text which represent a PER entity consisting of n words generally admit a translation of n words (word-for-word translation). For instance, the translation of the

	AER	**P**	**R**	**F1**
Eflomal (ours)	0.474	0.367	0.930	0.367
NUKTI	0.306	0.631	0.659	0.645
NUKTI+JAPA	0.465	0.513	0.536	0.524
JAPA	0.713	0.262	0.745	0.387

Table 5: Comparison about performance of several word aligners.

	P	R	F1
PER	0.84	0.73	0.78
ORG	0.81	0.54	0.65
LOC	0.95	0.59	0.73
MISC	0.90	0.20	0.33

Table 6: Performance of our proposed rule-based NER model, with 4 classes such as Person, Organization, Location and Miscellaneous.

en2iu	BLEU	ChrF++	TER
Baseline	31.31	42.02	53.83
Model 1	**32.84**	**44.07**	**56.46**
Model 2	31.70	42.54	54.49

Table 8: Performances on NMT in terms of lowercase word BLEU score in the direction English to Inuktitut. BLEU signature: "nrefs:1| case:mixed| eff:no| tok:13a| smooth:exp| version:2.0.0".

PER entity "Glenn McLean" is "gilin maklain". On the other hand, the translation of the LOC entity "Whale Cove" is "tikirarjuaq".

5.3 Evaluations on bilingual word embedding-based method

In order to evaluate the translation performance in the common word embedding space, we constructed a bilingual evaluation dictionary consisting of 30 word pairs.

The evaluation was done by calculating the accuracy of the translation of the words in the neighborhood of k = 1, 5, 10. We took into account the similarity between the word to be translated and the neighboring words.

k	Precision
1	0.367
5	0.400
10	0.433

Table 7: Results of the word-to-word translation by our proposed bilingual word embedding-based method, in terms of precision.

We notice that the performance for the neighborhood of k = 10 is the best, with 0.433 in terms of precision (Table 7). This is explained by the fact that the probability of finding the correct word translation is high when the number of neighbors is large.

5.4 Results on Neural Machine Translation downstream task

For the NMT downstream task, we observed a gain in the performance. The model 1 obtained the best performance than the baseline and the model 2 in terms of BLEU, ChrF++ and TER. The reason is that model 1 succeeds in aligning the entities in the parallel corpus despite the alignment error rate.

Contrary to the model 2 which performed the translation of named entities word by word in the space of bilingual word embeddings by selecting the nearest neighbor. This sometimes distorts the translation of named entities, particularly Inuktitut words representing sentences.

5.5 Error analysis and discussion

Regarding the method based on rules and word alignment, the performance is higher for PER(son) and LOC(ation) entities. This is explained by the morphology complexity. However, proper nouns are usually translated verbatim, while other entities such as ORG(anization) and MISC(ellaneous) represent sentences whose the translation in Inuktitut is just a single word.

Example: the translation of the PER entity "Hunter Tootoo" is "Hanta tutu", the translation of the ORG entity "Legislative Assembly" is "Maligaliurvik".

The morphological difference between the two languages caused misalignments of words, which resulted in the erroneous projection of named entities.

The evaluation results of the three models show that the model 1 which is based on the words alignment is the most efficient, then the model 2 which is based on the bilingual word embeddings. The reason is that the model 1, apart from alignment errors, is still able to align named entities in both languages.

On the other hand, the model 2 performed word-to-word entity translations. However, as previously explained, the Inuktitut language, being a polysynthetic language, a sentence can be represented by a single word.

We noticed the main error types as follows:

(1) *Projection errors due to word alignment errors*, as illustrated with the following examples:

(iu) Uqausiksait jain sutuuatmut, maligaliuqti, inulirijituqakkunnut ministarijaujuq.

(en) Presentation by the Hon. Jane Stewart, MP, Minister of Indian Affairs and Northern Development.

Here, the PER entity "Jane Stewart" is aligned with "sutuuatmut", instead of "jain sutuuatmut".

(2) *Errors in the identification of nominal groups.* Sometimes, a noun, that follows or precedes an entity named in Inuktitut, is considered part of the entity, since sequences of names have been considered named entities, as illustrated in these examples:

(iu) Nuqqausirutigilugu, uqausirikkannirumavakka katimajiuqatima ukausirisimajangit taivit alakannuap, sinnattuumajunnaiqpugut.

(en) In closing, I would like to echo comments by my colleague Ovide Alakannuark, we are no longer dreaming.

The PER entity Ovide Alakannuark has been aligned with the whole nominal group ukausirisimajangit taivit alakannuap instead of taivit alakannuap.

(3) *Translation errors due to out-of-vocabulary words and restricted data domain.*

This is due to the data source which concerns the legislative assembly. Unlike the dictionary built from the UQAILAUT project database, the word pairs come from the general domain, as well as the out-of-vocabulary words. Examples:

(en) Legislative Assembly Of Nunavut.

(iu) maligaliurvia Ralaa Jumaar Nunavut, instead of nunavut maligaliurvia.

(en) South Baffin

(iu) Nginni baffin, instead of qikiqtaaluup niggiani.

Through the conducted error analysis, we found shortcomings in our models. However, we have found that the method based on word embeddings is less efficient than the method based on rules because of the change it brings to the translation of named entities.

It is interesting to carry out a hybridization involving the two methods based on rules and word embeddings.

6 Conclusion and perspective

In this paper, we have built a named entity recognition system for Inuktitut, an Inuit language of Canada. Counted among the four major dialectal groups of Inuit languages, Inuktitut is written using the Native Canadian syllabary. Indeed, it is a low-resource Indigenous language that has no labeled data for NER; which presents a great challenge to the construction of the first NER system. Also, the Inuktitut language, being a polysynthetic language, has a particular grammar and fairly complex word compositions that differentiate it from other languages. To overcome these problems, the main idea of our approach is to use English, given that it is a language rich in resources and that has labeled data for NER and a parallel Inuktitut-English corpus is available. Thus, in this paper, we built a model capable of detecting named entities in Inuktitut, by transferring linguistic characteristics from English to Inuktitut.

In addition to being the first research on named entities recognition for Inuktitut Indigenous language, this project contributes to the preservation of this language and its culture. Furthermore, by building a knowledge base in the Inuktitut language involving named entities, this will contribute to the realization of future works that affects other NLP sub-tasks , such as Information Retrieval, Machine Translation or question0answering systems.

As a future research, we aim to integrate knowledge bases such as those related to toponymy and data from Indigenous knowledge in training word embeddings and improving the performance of our systems (NER and NMT). In addition, we aim to emphasize a differentiation between named entities of Inuktitut origin (such as the names of people and places) and those borrowed. All with the aim of pursuing collaborations with an Indigenous community in Nunavut whose mother tongue is Inuktitut.

References

David Adelani, Graham Neubig, Sebastian Ruder, Tatiana Moteu, Dietrich Klakow, and et al. 2022. MasakhaNER 2.0: Africa-centric transfer learning for named entity recognition. In *Proceedings of the 2022 Conference on Empirical Methods in Natural Language Processing*, pages 4488–4508, Abu Dhabi, United Arab Emirates. Association for Computational Linguistics.

David Ifeoluwa Adelani, Michael A. Hedderich, Dawei Zhu, Esther van den Berg, and Dietrich Klakow. 2020. Distant supervision and noisy label learning for low resource named entity recognition: A study on hausa and yorùbá.

Anwar Azmat, Li Xiao, Yang Yating, Dong Rui, and Osman Turghun. 2020. Constructing Uyghur name entity recognition system using neural machine translation tag projection. In *Proceedings of the 19th Chinese National Conference on Computational Linguistics*, pages 1006–1016, Haikou, China. Chinese Information Processing Society of China.

Steven Bird. 2020. Decolonising speech and language technology. In *Proceedings of the 28th International Conference on Computational Linguistics*, pages 3504–3519, Barcelona, Spain (Online). International Committee on Computational Linguistics.

Piotr Bojanowski, Edouard Grave, Armand Joulin, and Tomas Mikolov. 2017. Enriching word vectors with subword information. *Transactions of the Association for Computational Linguistics*, 5:135–146.

Ronan Collobert, Jason Weston, Leon Bottou, Michael Karlen, Koray Kavukcuoglu, and Pavel Kuksa. 2011. Natural language processing (almost) from scratch.

Richard Compton. 2021. Inuktitut. In *The canadian encyclopedia*.

Louis-Jacques Dorais. 1995. Language, culture and identity: Some inuit examples. *Canadian Journal of Native Studies*, 15(2):293–308.

Chris Dyer, Victor Chahuneau, and Noah A Smith. 2013. A simple, fast, and effective reparameterization of ibm model 2. In *Proceedings of the 2013 Conference of the North American Chapter of the Association for Computational Linguistics: Human Language Technologies*, pages 644–648.

Maud Ehrmann, Marco Turchi, and Ralf Steinberger. 2011. Building a multilingual named entity-annotated corpus using annotation projection. pages 118–124.

Yong Soo Fong, Bali Ranaivo-Malançon, and Alvin W. Yeo. 2011. Nersil - the named-entity recognition system for iban language. In *PACLIC*.

Joel Escudé Font and Marta R Costa-Jussa. 2019. Equalizing gender biases in neural machine translation with word embeddings techniques. *arXiv preprint arXiv:1901.03116*.

Ali Hatami, Ruslan Mitkov, and Gloria Corpas Pastor. 2021. Cross-lingual named entity recognition via FastAlign: a case study. In *Proceedings of the Translation and Interpreting Technology Online Conference*, pages 85–92, Held Online. INCOMA Ltd.

Michael A. Hedderich and Dietrich Klakow. 2018. Training a neural network in a low-resource setting on automatically annotated noisy data.

Jue Hou, Maximilian Koppatz, José María Hoya Quecedo, and Roman Yangarber. 2019. Projecting named entity recognizers without annotated or parallel corpora. In *Proceedings of the 22nd Nordic Conference on Computational Linguistics*, pages 232–241, Turku, Finland. Linköping University Electronic Press.

Zhiheng Huang, Wei Xu, and Kai Yu. 2015. Bidirectional lstm-crf models for sequence tagging.

Svanhvít Lilja Ingólfsdóttir, Sigurjón Þorsteinsson, and Hrafn Loftsson. 2019. Towards high accuracy named entity recognition for Icelandic. In *Proceedings of the 22nd Nordic Conference on Computational Linguistics*, pages 363–369, Turku, Finland. Linköping University Electronic Press.

Alankar Jain, Bhargavi Paranjape, and Zachary C. Lipton. 2019. Entity projection via machine translation for cross-lingual ner.

Eric Joanis, Rebecca Knowles, Roland Kuhn, Samuel Larkin, Patrick Littell, Chi-kiu Lo, Darlene Stewart, and Jeffrey Micher. 2020. The Nunavut Hansard Inuktitut–English parallel corpus 3.0 with preliminary machine translation results. In *Proceedings of the Twelfth Language Resources and Evaluation Conference*, pages 2562–2572, Marseille, France. European Language Resources Association.

Bjarte Johansen. 2019. Named-entity recognition for Norwegian. In *Proceedings of the 22nd Nordic Conference on Computational Linguistics*, pages 222–231, Turku, Finland. Linköping University Electronic Press.

Philipp Koehn, Hieu Hoang, Alexandra Birch, Chris Callison-Burch, Marcello Federico, Nicola Bertoldi, Brooke Cowan, Wade Shen, Christine Moran, Richard Zens, Chris Dyer, Ondřej Bojar, Alexandra Constantin, and Evan Herbst. 2007. Moses: Open source toolkit for statistical machine translation. In *Proceedings of the 45th Annual Meeting of the Association for Computational Linguistics Companion Volume Proceedings of the Demo and Poster Sessions*, pages 177–180, Prague, Czech Republic. Association for Computational Linguistics.

Philipp Koehn, Joel Martin, Rada Mihalcea, Christof Monz, and Ted Pedersen, editors. 2005. *Proceedings of the ACL Workshop on Building and Using Parallel Texts*. Association for Computational Linguistics, Ann Arbor, Michigan.

Philippe Langlais, Fabrizio Gotti, and Guihong Cao. 2005. NUKTI: English-Inuktitut word alignment system description. In *Proceedings of the ACL Workshop on Building and Using Parallel Texts*, pages 75–78, Ann Arbor, Michigan. Association for Computational Linguistics.

Tan Ngoc Le and Fatiha Sadat. 2020. Revitalization of indigenous languages through pre-processing and neural machine translation: The case of Inuktitut. In *Proceedings of the 28th International Conference on Computational Linguistics*, pages 4661–4666, Barcelona, Spain (Online). International Committee on Computational Linguistics (COLING 2020).

Jouni Luoma, Li-Hsin Chang, Filip Ginter, and Sampo Pyysalo. 2021. Fine-grained named entity annotation for Finnish. In *Proceedings of the 23rd Nordic Conference on Computational Linguistics (NoDaLiDa)*, pages 135–144, Reykjavik, Iceland (Online). Linköping University Electronic Press, Sweden.

Stephen Mayhew, Chen-Tse Tsai, and Dan Roth. 2017. Cheap translation for cross-lingual named entity recognition. In *Proceedings of the 2017 Conference on Empirical Methods in Natural Language Processing*, pages 2536–2545, Copenhagen, Denmark. Association for Computational Linguistics.

David Nadeau and Satoshi Sekine. 2007. A survey of named entity recognition and classification. *Lingvisticae Investigationes*, 30.

Myle Ott, Sergey Edunov, Alexei Baevski, Angela Fan, Sam Gross, Nathan Ng, David Grangier, and Michael Auli. 2019. fairseq: A fast, extensible toolkit for sequence modeling.

Kishore Papineni, Salim Roukos, Todd Ward, and Wei-Jing Zhu. 2002. Bleu: a method for automatic evaluation of machine translation. In *Proceedings of the 40th annual meeting on association for computational linguistics*, pages 311–318. Association for Computational Linguistics.

Matthew E. Peters, Mark Neumann, Mohit Iyyer, Matt Gardner, Christopher Clark, Kenton Lee, and Luke Zettlemoyer. 2018. Deep contextualized word representations.

Barbara Plank. 2019. Neural cross-lingual transfer and limited annotated data for named entity recognition in Danish. In *Proceedings of the 22nd Nordic Conference on Computational Linguistics*, pages 370–375, Turku, Finland. Linköping University Electronic Press.

Maja Popović. 2015. chrf: character n-gram f-score for automatic mt evaluation. In *Proceedings of the Tenth Workshop on Statistical Machine Translation*, pages 392–395.

Matt Post. 2018. A call for clarity in reporting BLEU scores. In *Proceedings of the Third Conference on Machine Translation: Research Papers*, pages 186–191, Brussels, Belgium. Association for Computational Linguistics.

Rico Sennrich, Barry Haddow, and Alexandra Birch. 2015. Neural machine translation of rare words with subword units.

Elias Stengel-Eskin, Tzu-Ray Su, Matt Post, and Benjamin Van Durme. 2019. A discriminative neural model for cross-lingual word alignment.

Jörg Tiedemann, Željko Agić, and Joakim Nivre. 2014. Treebank translation for cross-lingual parser induction. In *Proceedings of the Eighteenth Conference on Computational Natural Language Learning*, pages 130–140, Ann Arbor, Michigan. Association for Computational Linguistics.

Jiateng Xie, Zhilin Yang, Graham Neubig, Noah A. Smith, and Jaime Carbonell. 2018. Neural cross-lingual named entity recognition with minimal resources.

Hailemariam Mehari Yohannes and Toshiyuki Amagasa. 2022. Named-entity recognition for a low-resource language using pre-trained language model. In *Proceedings of the 37th ACM/SIGAPP Symposium on Applied Computing*, SAC '22, page 837–844, New York, NY, USA. Association for Computing Machinery.

Parallel Corpus for Indigenous Language Translation: Spanish-Mazatec and Spanish-Mixtec

Atnafu Lambebo Tonja[1], **Christian Maldonado-Sifuentes**[2], **David Alejandro Mendoza Castillo**[2], **Olga Kolesnikova**[1], **Noé Castro-Sánchez**[3], **Grigori Sidorov**[1], **Alexander Gelbukh**[1]

[1]Instituto Politécnico Nacional (IPN), Centro de Investigación en Computación (CIC), Mexico,

[2]Transdisciplinary Research for Augmented Innovation - Laboratory (TRAI-L), Mexico,

[3]Departamento de Ciencias Computacionales Tecnológico Nacional de México, Mexico

Abstract

In this paper, we present a parallel Spanish-Mazatec and Spanish-Mixtec corpus for machine translation (MT) tasks, where Mazatec and Mixtec are two indigenous Mexican languages. We evaluated the usability of the collected corpus using three different approaches: transformer, transfer learning, and fine-tuning pre-trained multilingual MT models. Fine-tuning the Facebook M2M100-48 model outperformed the other approaches, with BLEU scores of 12.09 and 22.25 for Mazatec-Spanish and Spanish-Mazatec translations, respectively, and 16.75 and 22.15 for Mixtec-Spanish and Spanish-Mixtec translations, respectively. The findings show that the dataset size (9,799 sentences in Mazatec and 13,235 sentences in Mixtec) affects translation performance and that indigenous languages work better when used as target languages. The findings emphasize the importance of creating parallel corpora for indigenous languages and fine-tuning models for low-resource translation tasks. Future research will investigate zero-shot and few-shot learning approaches to further improve translation performance in low-resource settings. The dataset and scripts are available at `https://github.com/atnafuatx/Machine-Translation-Resources`.

1 Introduction

Natural Language Processing (NLP), a sub-field of Artificial Intelligence (AI), has been attracting a lot of attention in terms of research and development as a result of the surge in the number of applications it has in a variety of different industries (Kalyanathaya et al., 2019). Machine Translation (MT), Sentiment or Opinion Analysis, POS Tagging, Question Classification (QC) and Answering (QA), Chunking, Named Entity Recognition (NER), Emotion Detection, and Semantic Role Labeling are currently highly researched areas in various high-resource languages (Tonja et al., 2023a).

The domain of machine translation (MT) is advancing at a rapid pace due to the growing prevalence of computational tasks and the expanding global reach of the Internet, which caters to diverse, multilingual communities (Kenny, 2018). MT systems have demonstrated remarkable translation outcomes for language pairs that possess abundant resources, such as English-Spanish, English-French, English-Russian, and English-Portuguese. However, in scenarios with limited or no resources, MT systems encounter difficulties due to the primary obstacle of inadequate training data for certain languages (Mager et al., 2018; Tonja et al., 2021, 2022, 2023b).

Low-resource languages have been suffering from a lack of new language technology designs. When the resources are limited and only a small amount of unlabeled data is available, it is very hard to reach a true breakthrough in creating powerful novel methods for language applications (Tonja et al., 2022), the problem becomes worse if there is no parallel dataset for certain languages.

Mexico is a multicultural and multilingual country with 68 officially recognized indigenous languages, 238 variants, and Spanish, a widely used language spoken by 90 percent of the population (Mager et al., 2021). Few language technologies have been developed for indigenous languages spoken in Northern and Southern America; moreover, many indigenous languages spoken in the Americas face a risk of extinction (Mager et al., 2018).

Indigenous language speakers often experience feelings of shame or reluctance to use their native languages, primarily due to limited opportunities for application in the presence of pervasive, dominant majority languages (Hornberger, 2008; Skutnabb-Kangas, 2000). This phenomenon can be attributed to social and cultural pressures that prioritize the use of majority languages over minority languages, thereby marginalizing indigenous linguistic communities and undermining the value

Proceedings of the Workshop on Natural Language Processing for Indigenous Languages of the Americas (AmericasNLP), pages 94–102
July 14, 2023

of their linguistic heritage (Hinton, 2011).

In this paper, we introduce the first parallel corpus for machine translation tasks for two indigenous languages that are spoken in Mexico and benchmark experimental results. The contributions of our work are the following:

- We introduce the first parallel corpus for machine translation for Mazatec and Mixtec languages.
- We evaluate the performance of the collected corpus and present benchmark results by using transformers, transfer learning, and fine-tuning approaches.
- We open-source the parallel corpus and the scripts used in this paper.

The rest of the paper is organized as follows: Section 2 describes previous research related to this study, Section 3 describes the properties of Mazatec and Mixtec languages, Section 4 describes the statistics of the collected dataset, Section 5 describes models used for baseline experiments and their results, and Section 6 describes the conclusion of the paper.

2 Related works

Due to an increase in the enormous amount of data for different languages, machine translation is currently one of the most researched areas in NLP and has shown promising results in high-resource languages (Tonja et al., 2022). There are different MT approaches that have been used by different researchers, neural machine translation (NMT)is one of the current state-of-the-art approaches trained on huge datasets containing sentences in a source language and their equivalent target language translations (Belay et al., 2022). Basically, NMT takes advantage of huge translation memories with hundreds of thousands or even millions of translation units (Forcada, 2017). However, NMT for low-resource languages still under-performs due to the scarcity of parallel datasets (Tonja et al., 2022, 2023b).

Many researchers explored different approaches to solving low-resource machine translation problems. Zoph et al. (2016) proposed a transfer learning method to improve the MT performance of low-resource languages. The authors first train a high-resource language pair (the parent model), then transfer some of the learned parameters to the low-resource pair (the child model) to initialize and constrain training. The data augmentation approach proposed by Fadaee et al. (2017), targets low-frequency words by generating new sentence pairs containing rare words in new, synthetically created contexts. Pourdamghani and Knight (2019) proposed using high-resource language resources to improve MT performance for low-resource languages without requiring any parallel data. Copying monolingual data of the target language is proposed by Currey et al. (2017) to improve the performance of low-resource MT. Tonja et al. (2023b) proposed the use of source-side monolingual data as another way of improving low-resource MT performance. Transfer learning method, where one first trains a "parent" model for a high-resource language pair and then continues training on a low-resource pair only by replacing the training corpus was proposed by Kocmi and Bojar (2018). Mixing low-resource language resources during training, as proposed by Tonja et al. (2022) showed an improvement in MT performance for low-resource languages.

There have been promising research works done for indigenous languages; Feldman and Coto-Solano (2020) presented an NMT model and a dataset for the Bribri Chibchan language for Bribri-Spanish translation. Kann et al. (2022) compiled AmericasNLI, a natural language inference dataset covering 10 indigenous languages of the Americas. They conducted experiments with pre-trained models, exploring zero-shot learning in combination with model adaptation. Oncevay (2021) proposed the first multilingual translation models for four languages spoken in Peru: Aymara, Ashaninka, Quechua, and Shipibo-Konibo, providing both many-to-Spanish and Spanish-to-many models, outperformed pairwise baselines. Zheng et al. (2021) presented a low-resource MT system that improves translation accuracy using cross-lingual language model pre-training. The authors used an mBART implementation of fairseq to pre-train on a large set of monolingual data from a diverse set of high-resource languages before fine-tuning on 10 low-resource indigenous American languages: Aymara, Bribri, Asháninka, Guaraní, Wixarika, Náhuatl, Hñähñu, Quechua, Shipibo-Konibo, and Rarámuri. On average, their proposed system achieved BLEU scores that were 1.64 higher and chrF scores that were 0.0749 higher than the baseline. Nagoudi et al. (2021) introduced

IndT5, the first Transformer language model for 10 Indigenous American languages: Aymara, Bribri, Asháninka, Guaraní, Wixarika, Náhuatl, Hñähñu, Quechua, Shipibo-Konibo, and Rarámuri. To train IndT5, they built IndCorpus–a new dataset for ten indigenous languages and Spanish.

3 Languages

3.1 Mazatec

The Mazatec language comprises a collection of closely related indigenous languages spoken primarily in the Northern region of Oaxaca, with smaller populations in the adjacent states of Puebla and Veracruz in Mexico. Approximately 200,000 individuals speak Mazatec; however, this number may fluctuate depending on which particular dialects or linguistic variations are taken into account (Léonard et al., 2019).

Mazatec belongs to the Oto-Manguean language family, a large family of indigenous Mesoamerican languages which also includes Mixtec, Zapotec, Otomi, among others (Vielma Hernández, 2017). Linguistic characteristics of Mazatec include tonal distinctions (Garellek and Keating, 2011), complex consonant clusters, and a rich morphology (Léonard et al., 2012). The Mazatec languages are known for their agglutinative structure, where words are formed by combining multiple morphemes, each with a distinct meaning (Vielma Hernández, 2017).

3.1.1 Writing system

Vowels - Mixtec has five basic vowels, similar to those in Spanish:

- a (as in "car"),
- e (as in "bet"),
- i (as in "bit"),
- o (as in "bore"),
- u (as in "boot").

These vowels can also appear nasalized, indicated by a tilde ($\tilde{a}$, $\tilde{e}$, $\tilde{i}$, $\tilde{o}$, $\tilde{u}$), and long, indicated by a colon ($a :, e :, i :, o :, u :$). Tones can be associated with vowels, too.

Consonants - The Mazatec consonant inventory includes the following sounds:

- Stops: p, t, k, b, d, g,
- Affricates: ts, tʃ, dz, dʒ,
- Fricatives: s, ʃ, h, z, ʒ,
- Nasals: m, n, ng,
- Approximants: w, j (pronounced as "y" in "yes"),
- Lateral approximant: l,
- Rhotics: r.

Numerals/Numbers - Mazatec uses a vesimal numeral system (base-20). Here are the numbers 1 to 10 in Mazatec: (1) - kia̲, (2) - chjɨ, (3) - tsi, (4)- sti, (5) - nka̲, (6) - tsjɨ, (7) - kja, (8) - chjɨn, (9) - tsi̲, (10) - sti̲.

Word order - Typically, Mazatec exhibits a VSO (Verb-Subject-Object) word order; however, alternative structures such as SVO can also occur depending on the sentence, the focus of the statement, and the context.

Example sentence:

Kitsaara kji xi makjíñeni kua apana (I gave a pill for the headache to my father) - VSO order

3.2 Mixtec

The Mixtec language comprises a group of closely related indigenous languages predominantly spoken in the region known as La Mixteca, which spans the states of Oaxaca, Puebla, and Guerrero in Southern Mexico. Estimates indicate that there are approximately 500,000 speakers of Mixtec; however, this number may fluctuate depending on the specific dialects or language varieties considered (Josserand, 1983).

As Mazatec, Mixtec is a member of the Oto-Manguean language family (Rensch, 1977; Pike and Cowan, 1961; Hollenbach, 2000) possessing the characteristic mentioned in Section 3.1. It also shares the phonemic system with Mixtec (see vowels and consonants inventory in Section 3.1.1) as well as the word order features and the base-20 number system. Here are numbers from 1 to 10 in Mixtec: (1)- in, (2) - ña'a, (3) - ta'a , (4) - na'a, (5) - ma'a, (6) - chiko, (7) - chikue, (8) - chikuiin, (9) - chikunña'a, (10) - ndo'o.

And here are a couple of examples sentences:

- Ka'nu ña'a nuu ntaa (Sitting on the plain) - VSO order
- Ña'a nuu ntaa ka'nu (On the plain, sitting) - SVO order

Note that the Mixtec language has many dialects, so the phonetic inventory, numerals, word order, and example sentences provided here may vary across different Mixtec-speaking communities. The examples given here are intended to provide a general overview of the language's features

4 Parallel Dataset

Data is one of the crucial building blocks of any NLP application (Belay et al., 2022; Tonja et al., 2023a), and a parallel corpus is essential to the success of any machine translation task. For Mazatec and Mixtec, we were unable to find publicly available datasets for the MT task. We collected datasets for these two indigenous Mexican languages from two main domains: *religious* and *constitution*. We also collected additional resources for the Mixtec language from different *textbooks* which have a similar translation to Spanish. Table 1 shows the statistics of the collected parallel corpus for Mazatec and Mixtec.

Text Alignment - We took a base directory path where text files were stored as input. Then we read and merged the content of all text files in the directory, and obtained a list of lists containing the content of each file. We proceeded to iterate through each file in the directory and read their contents line by line. Each line was normalized using the Unicode Normalization Form KC (NFKC) before being appended to the resulting list. We added a function that takes a language code `lang` as input, which determines the filename of the text file to be read from a predefined folder. The function read the file line by line, normalized each line using NFKC, and concatenated the lines into a single string. The result was returned as an array.

With another function, we added the two lists as input: one containing the content of the files to be aligned, and the other containing the filenames for the output files. We then iterated through the content list and aligned the text by iterating through the chapters and paragraphs of each translation. The aligned text was written to the corresponding output file as tab-separated values (TSV). Then we defined the root path where the input files were located, initialized the name and content arrays, and called the function that populated the content array with the pre-processed text. Finally, the function that writes the file was called to align and write the output files.

Pre-processing - After aligning the texts of two indigenous languages with their equivalent translations in Spanish, we pre-processed the corpus before splitting it for our experiments. The pre-processing steps included removing the numbers and special character symbols such as ;,",?, etc. For the baseline experiment, we split the pre-processed corpus into training, development, and test sets in the ratio of 70:10:20, respectively. Table 2 shows the split of the dataset used for our experiments.

5 Baseline Experiment and Discussion

In this section, we discuss the models used for the baseline experiment, the hyper-parameter used, the benchmark results, and the discussion. We used three approaches to evaluate the usability of the collected corpus. These are :-

- **Transformer** - is a type of neural network architecture first introduced in the paper *Attention Is All You Need* (Vaswani et al., 2017). The key innovation of the Transformer architecture is the attention mechanism, which allows the network to selectively focus on different parts of the input sequence when making predictions. This is in contrast to traditional recurrent neural networks (RNNs), which process input sequentially and are prone to the vanishing gradient problem.

  In the transformer architecture, the input sequence is processed in parallel by multiple layers of self-attention and feed-forward neural networks. Each layer can be thought of as a "block" that takes the output of the previous layer as input and applies its own set of transformations to it. The self-attention mechanism allows the network to weigh the importance of each element in the input sequence when making predictions, while the feed-forward networks help to capture non-linear relationships between the elements.

  Currently, transformers are state-of-the-art approaches and are widely used in NLP tasks such as MT, text summarization, sentiment analysis, etc. We used the base transformer configuration as described in (Vaswani et al., 2017) work.

- **Transfer learning**- refers to the process of leveraging pre-trained language models to improve the performance of downstream NLP tasks. Specifically, transfer learning involves

Source	Mazatec (maq) - Spanish (spa)			Mixtec (xtn) - Spanish (spa)		
	#sentences	#tokens (maq)	#tokens (spa)	#sentences	#tokens (xtn)	#tokens (spa)
Religion	8,203	269,753	187,773	8,208	278,874	183,050
Constitution	1,596	138,504	68,392	1,185	104,497	68,393
Others	-	-	-	3,842	71,628	70,080
Total	9,799	408,257	256,165	13,235	454,999	321,523

Table 1: Parallel dataset distribution of Mazatec-Spanish and Mixtec-Spanish

Language pairs	Number of Sentences		
	Train	Dev	Test
Mazatec - Spanish	7,056	784	1,959
Mixtec - Spanish	9,529	1,059	2,647

Table 2: Dataset split used in baseline experiments

using a pre-trained model to initialize the parameters of an MT system and then fine-tuning the system on a smaller dataset specific to the target language pair or domain.

Transfer learning can be especially useful in MT because training a high-quality MT system from scratch requires a large amount of data and computational resources, which may not be available for all language pairs or domains. By leveraging pre-trained models, transfer learning allows MT systems to achieve high performance with fewer data and fewer resources. For our baseline experiments, we used English-Spanish as parent model with two (**opus-mt-es-en**[1] and **opus-mt-tc-big-en-es** [2]) pre-trained models available from Hugging Face[3] trained for English-Spanish on the OPUS dataset (Tiedemann and Thottingal, 2020) by *Helsinki-NLP group*.

- **Fine tuning** - is the process of taking a pre-trained MT model and adapting it to a specific translation task, such as translating between a particular language pair or in a specific domain. The process of fine-tuning involves taking the pre-trained model, which has already learned representations of words and phrases from a large corpus of text, and training it on a smaller dataset of specific task examples. This involves updating the parameters of the pre-trained model to better capture the patterns and structures present in the target translation task.

  Fine-tuning can be useful in MT because it allows the pre-trained model to quickly adapt to a new task without having to train a new model from scratch. This is especially beneficial when working with limited data or when there is a need to quickly adapt to changing translation requirements. We used two commonly known pre-trained multilingual MT models:

  - **M2M100-48** - is a multilingual encoder-decoder (seq-to-seq) model trained for many-to-many multilingual translation (Fan et al., 2020). We used a model with 48M parameters due to computing resource limitations.
  - **mBART50** - is a multilingual sequence-to-sequence model pre-trained using the *Multilingual Denoising pre-training* objective (Tang et al., 2020).

Hyper-parameters - For the transformer approach we tokenized the source and target parallel sentences into subword tokens using Byte Pair Encoding (BPE) (Gage, 1994). The BPE representation was chosen in order to remove vocabulary overlap during dataset combinations. For other approaches we applied the tokenizer of each model, Table 3 shows hyper-parameters used in our baseline experiments.

5.1 Results

Table 4 and Figure 1 shows the benchmark experimental results for bi-directional neural machine translation for Mazatec(maq) - Spanish(spa) and Mixtec(xtn) - Spanish(spa). In our baseline experiments, we observed that employing a transformer model for low-resource languages shows sub-optimal results compared to transfer learning and fine-tuning methodologies. As demonstrated in Table 4 and Figure 1, the performance of the **transformer** was inferior to alternative approaches utilized in the study. This finding substantiates the hypothesis that the efficacy of transformer models is heavily reliant on the availability of exten-

[1] https://huggingface.co/Helsinki-NLP/opus-mt-es-en

[2] https://huggingface.co/Helsinki-NLP/opus-mt-tc-big-en-es

[3] https://huggingface.co/

Approaches	Models	Parameters
Transformer	transformer	- enc_layers: 6 - dec_layers: 6 - heads: 8 - hidden_size: 512 - optimizer: adam - warmup_steps: 4000 - training_steps: 30000 - learning _rate: 5e-2
Transfer learning	opus-mt-es-en	- max_seq_length: 128
	opus-mt-tc-big-en-es	- num_train_epochs: 3
Fine-tuning	mBART50	- per_device_batch_size: 4
	M2M100-48	- num_beams: 5

Table 3: Hyper-parameters used for baseline experiments

Models	xx-spa BLEU score		spa-xx BLEU score	
	maq-spa	xtn-spa	spa-maq	spa-xtn
M1	5.89	6.23	11.41	12.62
M2	6.91	10.47	14.49	13.73
M3	8.45	12.44	19.61	17.27
M4	10.45	15.66	21.2	16.93
M5	**12.09**	**16.75**	**22.5**	**22.15**

Table 4: Benchmark experimental result for bi-directional Mazatec(maq)-Spanish(spa) and Mixtec(xtn)-Spanish(spa) neural machine translation, M1, M2, M3, M4, and M5 represents transformer, opus-mt-es-en, opus-mt-tc-big-en-es,mBART50, and M2M100-48 models respectively.

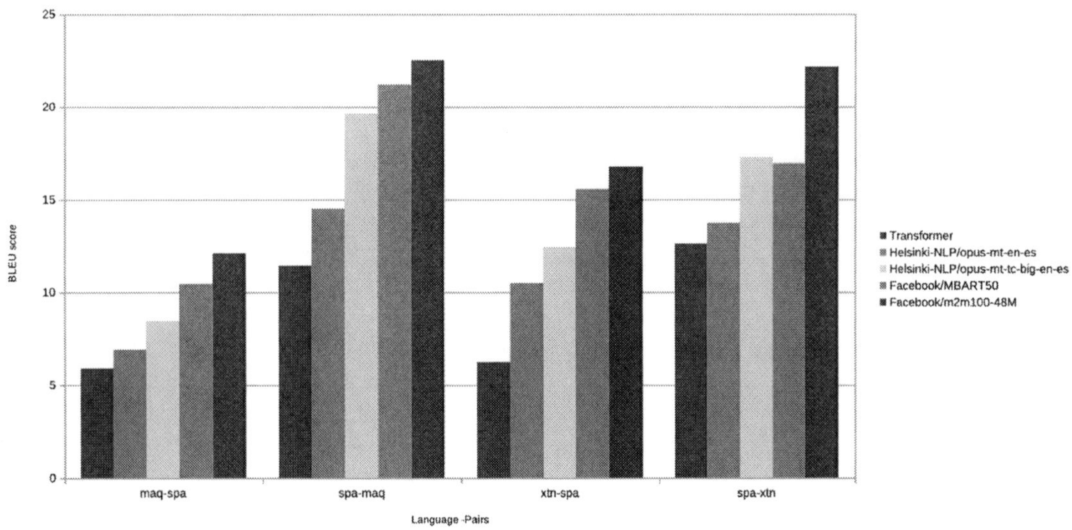

Figure 1: Benchmark results of selected approaches

sive parallel corpora for machine translation tasks. Upon further examination of language pair performance, we discovered that utilizing indigenous languages as the target language surpasses the performance achieved when using Spanish as the target language. This observation indicates that translating from Spanish to indigenous languages is a less complex task for the model as opposed to translating indigenous languages to Spanish.

Transfer learning approach showed more

promising results for the indigenous low-resource languages than the transformer approach. Out of the two models used in the transfer learning experiment, the model with *transformer-big* configuration outperformed the model with *transformer-base* configuration. This shows that the transfer learning approach depends on the size of the model parameter. Similarly, when using the transfer learning approach for indigenous low-resource languages by utilizing models trained on high-resource languages, better results were obtained when Spanish was used as the source language than when Spanish was used as the target language.

Fine-tuning approach outperformed the rest of the approaches used in our baseline experiment in both translation directions. This shows that using a multilingual pre-trained translation model for fine-tuning low-resource languages outperforms other models. From the two multilingual models used in the experiment, the **M2M100-48** model outperformed the **mBART50** multilingual model. The M2M100-48 model showed 4.7 and 5.5 BLEU scores on average for Mazatec (maq)-Spanish (spa) and Spanish (spa)-Mazatec (maq) translation. For Mixtec (xtn)-Spanish (spa) and Mixtec (xtn)-Spanish (spa), the M2M100-48 model showed a 10.2 and 7.5 BLEU score improvement on average when compared to the other models used in the experiments. When comparing the results of the two languages in all the approaches used, Mixtec (xtn)-Spanish (spa) translation showed better performance than Mazatec (maq)-Spanish (spa) translation when using Spanish as the target language, This shows that the availability of the parallel corpora for the language pairs has a high impact on the performance of the translation models. The overall results show that using multilingual MT models for fine-tuning in our selected indigenous low-resource languages gives promising results.

5.2 Discussion

In our analysis, we conducted an error analysis to identify the strengths and weaknesses of the three approaches: transformer, transfer learning, and fine-tuning. We found that the transformer approach, which relies on large parallel corpora, yielded sub-optimal results for low-resource languages. It struggled to capture the linguistic patterns and structures specific to indigenous languages. This limitation indicates that the transformer model's performance is highly dependent on the availability of extensive parallel corpora for effective machine translation.

On the other hand, the transfer learning approach showed more promising results for low-resource indigenous languages. We observed that models pre-trained on high-resource languages, such as Spanish, and fine-tuned on the indigenous languages improved translation quality. However, even with transfer learning, the performance was not satisfactory, and there were errors that persisted across all three approaches.

The general error that all three approaches failed to address adequately was the translation of domain-specific and culturally specific terms in Mazatec and Mixtec. These languages have unique vocabulary and cultural nuances that require a deeper understanding and context to ensure accurate translation. The limited availability of domain-specific parallel corpora for these languages hampered the models' ability to capture and translate such terms effectively.

6 Conclusion

In this paper, we presented a parallel corpus for two indigenous Mexican languages (Mazatec (maq) and Mixtec (xtn)) for machine translation tasks and evaluate the usability of the collected corpus using three different approaches. From the approaches, fine-tuning multilingual pre-trained MT models outperformed the rest of the experiments; Facebook's M2M100-48 outperformed all other models with BLEU scores of 12.09 and 22.25 for maq-spa and spa-maq, respectively, and 16.75 and 22.15 for xtn-spa and spa-xtn, respectively. We noticed from the experimental results that the dataset size has less impact when using indigenous languages as a target than the source. This observation highlights the potential benefits of focusing on developing and fine-tuning models specifically designed for translation tasks involving low-resource languages. Moreover, it underscores the value of creating and employing parallel corpora tailored to indigenous languages, as these resources can significantly improve machine translation performance, particularly when used in conjunction with advanced multilingual pre-trained models.

Our BLEU results for Mizatec and Miztec to Spanish translation were very low on the best configuration to have any usability in real-life applications, but the translation in the opposite direction demonstrated BLEU scores above 22 facilitating uses, for example in government apps to present hints to Mixtec and Mazatec native speakers who have a low level of Spanish comprehension, in the government web pages. This could significantly improve the usefulness of the native language of the speakers, thus promoting communication of the language and its preservation.

In future research, we plan to investigate the efficacy of advanced techniques, including zero-shot and few-shot learning, for low-resource languages in the context of limited parallel datasets. These methodologies hold promise for effectively leveraging sparse data available in low-resource settings, as they capitalize on pre-existing knowledge from related tasks or languages without requiring extensive fine-tuning or additional annotated data. By exploring these approaches, we aim to uncover potential benefits and improvements in the machine translation performance of low-resource languages, thus contributing to developing more robust and accurate translation systems for underrepresented linguistic communities.

Acknowledgements

The work was done with partial support from the Mexican Government through the grant A1S-47854 of CONACYT, Mexico, grants 20220852, 20220859, and 20221627 of the Secretaría de Investigación y Posgrado of the Instituto Politécnico Nacional, Mexico. The authors thank the CONACYT for the computing resources brought to them through the Plataforma de Aprendizaje Profundo para Tecnologías del Lenguaje of the Laboratorio de Supercómputo of the INAOE, Mexico, and acknowledge the support of Microsoft through the Microsoft Latin America PhD Award.

References

Tadesse Destaw Belay, Atnafu Lambebo Tonja, Olga Kolesnikova, Seid Muhie Yimam, Abinew Ali Ayele, Silesh Bogale Haile, Grigori Sidorov, and Alexander Gelbukh. 2022. The effect of normalization for bi-directional amharic-english neural machine translation. In *2022 International Conference on Information and Communication Technology for Development for Africa (ICT4DA)*, pages 84–89. IEEE.

Anna Currey, Antonio Valerio Miceli-Barone, and Kenneth Heafield. 2017. Copied monolingual data improves low-resource neural machine translation. In *Proceedings of the second conference on machine translation*, pages 148–156.

Marzieh Fadaee, Arianna Bisazza, and Christof Monz. 2017. Data augmentation for low-resource neural machine translation. *arXiv preprint arXiv:1705.00440*.

Angela Fan, Shruti Bhosale, Holger Schwenk, Zhiyi Ma, Ahmed El-Kishky, Siddharth Goyal, Mandeep Baines, Onur Celebi, Guillaume Wenzek, Vishrav Chaudhary, Naman Goyal, Tom Birch, Vitaliy Liptchinsky, Sergey Edunov, Edouard Grave, Michael Auli, and Armand Joulin. 2020. Beyond english-centric multilingual machine translation.

Isaac Feldman and Rolando Coto-Solano. 2020. Neural machine translation models with back-translation for the extremely low-resource indigenous language bribri. In *Proceedings of the 28th International Conference on Computational Linguistics*, pages 3965–3976.

Mikel L Forcada. 2017. Making sense of neural machine translation. translation spaces, 6 (2), 291-309.

Philip Gage. 1994. A new algorithm for data compression. *C Users Journal*, 12(2):23–38.

Marc Garellek and Patricia Keating. 2011. The acoustic consequences of phonation and tone interactions in jalapa mazatec. *Journal of the International Phonetic Association*, 41(2):185–205.

Leanne Hinton. 2011. Language revitalization and language pedagogy: New teaching and learning strategies. *Language and Education*, 25(4):307–318.

Barbara E. Hollenbach. 2000. Mixtec - a new look at an old problem. *International Journal of American Linguistics*, 66(1):62–82.

Nancy H Hornberger. 2008. *Can schools save indigenous languages? Policy and practice on four continents*. Springer.

J. Kathryn Josserand. 1983. *Mixtec Dialectology: A Survey*. Tulane University.

Krishna Prakash Kalyanathaya, D Akila, and P Rajesh. 2019. Advances in natural language processing–a survey of current research trends, development tools and industry applications. *International Journal of Recent Technology and Engineering*, 7(5C):199–202.

Katharina Kann, Abteen Ebrahimi, Manuel Mager, Arturo Oncevay, John E Ortega, Annette Rios, Angela Fan, Ximena Gutierrez-Vasques, Luis Chiruzzo, Gustavo A Giménez-Lugo, et al. 2022. Americasnli: Machine translation and natural language inference systems for indigenous languages of the americas. *Frontiers in Artificial Intelligence*, 5:266.

Dorothy Kenny. 2018. Machine translation. In *The Routledge handbook of translation and philosophy*, pages 428–445. Routledge.

Tom Kocmi and Ondřej Bojar. 2018. Trivial transfer learning for low-resource neural machine translation. *arXiv preprint arXiv:1809.00357*.

Jean Léo Léonard, Vittorio Dell'Aquila, and Antonella Gaillard-Corvaglia. 2012. The almaz (atlas lingüístico mazateco): From geolinguistic data processing to typological traits. *STUF-Language Typology and Universals*, 65(1):78–94.

Jean Léo Léonard, Marco Patriarca, Els Heinsalu, Kiran Sharma, and Anirban Chakraborti. 2019. *Patterns of Linguistic Diffusion in Space and Time: The Case of Mazatec*, pages 139–170. Springer International Publishing, Cham.

Manuel Mager, Ximena Gutierrez-Vasques, Gerardo Sierra, and Ivan Meza. 2018. Challenges of language technologies for the indigenous languages of the americas. *arXiv preprint arXiv:1806.04291*.

Manuel Mager, Alejandro Oncevay, Ali Ebrahimi, Juan Ortega, Alexander R Gonzales, Angela Fan, and Katharina Kann. 2021. Findings of the americasnlp 2021 shared task on open machine translation for indigenous languages of the americas. In *Proceedings of the First Workshop on Natural Language Processing for Indigenous Languages of the Americas*, pages 202–217.

El Moatez Billah Nagoudi, Wei-Rui Chen, Muhammad Abdul-Mageed, and Hasan Cavusogl. 2021. Indt5: a text-to-text transformer for 10 indigenous languages. *arXiv preprint arXiv:2104.07483*.

Arturo Oncevay. 2021. Peru is multilingual, its machine translation should be too? In *Proceedings of the First Workshop on Natural Language Processing for Indigenous Languages of the Americas*, pages 194–201.

Kenneth L. Pike and Charles F. Cowan. 1961. *Language in Relation to a Unified Theory of the Structure of Human Behavior*. Mouton.

Nima Pourdamghani and Kevin Knight. 2019. Neighbors helping the poor: improving low-resource machine translation using related languages. *Machine Translation*, 33(3):239–258.

Calvin R. Rensch. 1977. *Oto-Manguean, Overview*. Summer Institute of Linguistics.

Tove Skutnabb-Kangas. 2000. *Linguistic genocide in education-or worldwide diversity and human rights?* Lawrence Erlbaum Associates Publishers.

Yuqing Tang, Chau Tran, Xian Li, Peng-Jen Chen, Naman Goyal, Vishrav Chaudhary, Jiatao Gu, and Angela Fan. 2020. Multilingual translation with extensible multilingual pretraining and finetuning. *arXiv e-prints*, pages arXiv–2008.

Jörg Tiedemann and Santhosh Thottingal. 2020. OPUS-MT – building open translation services for the world. In *Proceedings of the 22nd Annual Conference of the European Association for Machine Translation*, pages 479–480, Lisboa, Portugal. European Association for Machine Translation.

Atnafu Lambebo Tonja, Tadesse Destaw Belay, Israel Abebe Azime, Abinew Ali Ayele, Moges Ahmed Mehamed, Olga Kolesnikova, and Seid Muhie Yimam. 2023a. Natural language processing in ethiopian languages: Current state, challenges, and opportunities. *arXiv preprint arXiv:2303.14406*.

Atnafu Lambebo Tonja, Olga Kolesnikova, Muhammad Arif, Alexander Gelbukh, and Grigori Sidorov. 2022. Improving neural machine translation for low resource languages using mixed training: The case of ethiopian languages. In *Advances in Computational Intelligence: 21st Mexican International Conference on Artificial Intelligence, MICAI 2022, Monterrey, Mexico, October 24–29, 2022, Proceedings, Part II*, pages 30–40. Springer.

Atnafu Lambebo Tonja, Olga Kolesnikova, Alexander Gelbukh, and Grigori Sidorov. 2023b. Low-resource neural machine translation improvement using source-side monolingual data. *Applied Sciences*, 13(2):1201.

Atnafu Lambebo Tonja, Michael Melese Woldeyohannis, and Mesay Gemeda Yigezu. 2021. A parallel corpora for bi-directional neural machine translation for low resourced ethiopian languages. In *2021 International Conference on Information and Communication Technology for Development for Africa (ICT4DA)*, pages 71–76. IEEE.

Ashish Vaswani, Noam Shazeer, Niki Parmar, Jakob Uszkoreit, Llion Jones, Aidan N Gomez, Łukasz Kaiser, and Illia Polosukhin. 2017. Attention is all you need. *Advances in neural information processing systems*, 30.

Jonathan Daniel Vielma Hernández. 2017. Panorama de los estudios lingüísticos sobre el mazateco. *Cuadernos de Lingüística de El Colegio de México*, 4(1):211–272.

Francis Zheng, Machel Reid, Edison Marrese-Taylor, and Yutaka Matsuo. 2021. Low-resource machine translation using cross-lingual language model pretraining. In *Proceedings of the First Workshop on Natural Language Processing for Indigenous Languages of the Americas*, pages 234–240.

Barret Zoph, Deniz Yuret, Jonathan May, and Kevin Knight. 2016. Transfer learning for low-resource neural machine translation. *arXiv preprint arXiv:1604.02201*.

A finite-state morphological analyser for Highland Puebla Nahuatl

Francis M. Tyers
Department of Linguistics
Indiana University
Bloomington, IN 47401
ftyers@iu.edu

Robert Pugh
Department of Linguistics
Indiana University
Bloomington, IN 47401
pughrob@iu.edu

Abstract

This paper describes the development of a free/open-source finite-state morphological transducer for Highland Puebla Nahuatl, a Uto-Aztecan language spoken in the state of Puebla in Mexico.[1] The finite-state toolkit used for the work is the Helsinki Finite-State Toolkit (HFST); we use the `lexc` formalism for modelling the morphotactics and `twol` formalism for modelling morphophonological alternations. An evaluation is presented which shows that the transducer has a reasonable coverage—around 90%—on freely-available corpora of the language, and high precision—over 95%—on a manually verified test set.

1 Introduction

This paper describes a new morphological analyser for Highland Puebla Nahuatl, an endangered language spoken in the state of Puebla in Mexico (see Figure 1[2]). The analyser is based on finite-state technology, which means that it can be used for both the analysis and the generation of forms — a finite-state morphological transducer maps between surface forms and lexical forms (lemmas and morphosyntactic tags).

An analyser of this sort has a wide variety of uses, including for automating the process of corpus annotation for linguistic research as well as for creating proofing tools (such as spellcheckers) and for lemmatising for electronic dictionary lookup for language learners — in a language with heavy prefixing and suffixing morphology, determining the stem is not a simple matter.

Our approach is based on the Helsinki Finite-State Toolkit (HFST, Lindén et al. (2011)).

[1] `https://github.com/apertium/apertium-azz`

[2] Figure 1 is based on work by users TUBS (`https://commons.wikimedia.org/wiki/File:Puebla_in_Mexico_(location_map_scheme).svg`) and Battroid (`https://commons.wikimedia.org/wiki/File:Mexico_Puebla_Puebla_location_map.svg`)

2 Prior art

Finite state transducers (FST) for modeling morphology has a long history within the field of computational linguistics (Kornai, 1996; Beesley and Karttunen, 2003).

Work on morphological analysers for Nahuatl languages includes an effort, inspired by literate programming, to use the code for the transducer as a descriptive grammar of a Nahuatl variety spoken in the state of Guerrero (Maxwell, 2015), and morphological analysers specifically targeting colonial-era Nahuatl, either for the exploration of colonial texts (Thouvenot, 2009), or as a means to evaluate similarity between written Nahuatl varieties (Farfan, 2019). One drawback of these projects is that they are not to our knowledge freely-available or easily-accessible.

Nicolai et al. (2020) describe the development of morphological analysers and generators for more than one thousand languages using the Johns Hopkins University Bible Corpus (McCarthy et al., 2020), including some variants of Nahuatl (however, not Highland Puebla Nahuatl).

Pugh et al. (2021) presents the first open-source morphological analyser for the Western Sierra Puebla Nahuatl variant group. Tona et al. (2023) expand on that system, extending it to support Huasteca Nahuatl. This latter work, however, has not been released.

3 Highland Puebla Nahuatl

Nahuatl (or Nahuat, Nahual) is a polysynthetic, agglutinating Uto-Aztecan language continuum spoken throughout Mexico and Mesoamerica. The Mexican Government's *Instituto Nacional de Lenguas Indígenas* (INALI) recognizes 30 distinct variants (INALI, 2009).

Highland Puebla Nahuatl, (or *Sierra Puebla Nahuatl*, also referred to by INALI as *Náhuatl del noreste central*, `ISO-639-3` *azz*) is a Nahuatl vari-

Proceedings of the Workshop on Natural Language Processing for Indigenous Languages of the Americas (AmericasNLP), pages 103–108
July 14, 2023

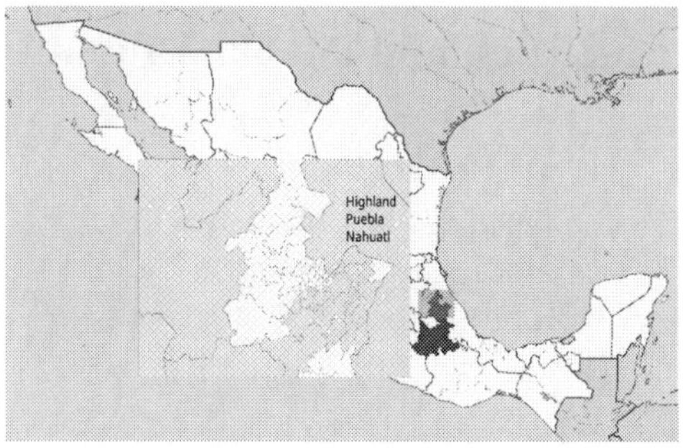

Figure 1: A map highlighting where Highland Puebla Nahuatl (salmon colour) is spoken in Mexico.

ant group spoken in the Northeastern Sierra region of the state of Puebla, Mexico, mainly in the municipalities of Tetela de Ocampo, Zacapoaxtla, and Cuetzalan. According to Ethnologue's 2007 estimate, it is spoken by an estimated 70,000 speakers.

This particular Nahuatl variant has been the subject of a number of descriptive works (Key, 1960; Robinson, 1970; Key and Key, 1953) and dictionaries (Key and Richie de Key, 1953; Cortez Ocotlán, 2017).

4 Data

The source data used to develop the FST comes from three sources: (1) A dataset of transcribed recordings of interviews and conversations, mainly about plants (Amith et al.), (2) a subset of texts in the *azz* variant from the multi-variant parallel corpus Axolotl (Gutierrez-Vasques et al., 2016), and (3) technical publications by the Sociedad Mexicana de Física[3], which consist of translations of various scientific texts. The breakdown of volume for each of these sources is presented in Table 1.

5 Orthography

Writing practices in Nahuatl vary and are characterized by multiple competing views (de la Cruz Cruz, 2014). The most well-known and widely-disseminated orthographic standards for Nahuatl are ACK, a colonial-inspired orthography named after scholars Anderson, Campbell, and Karttunen, who popularized it in their work, the standard from the *Instituto Nacional de Lenguas Indígenas* (INALI) (INALI, 2018), and that used by the Secretaría de Educación Pública (SEP). In practice, Nahuatl writing contains a great deal of orthographic variation, often even within the writing of a single author.

The orthography used for building the analyser follows what was taught in the Nahuatl course for adult learners given in the municipality of Tetela de Ocampo, Puebla in the summer of 2022 (TO). This broadly follows the SEP, but with the addition of the letter *h* which is used before *u* for /w/ after vowels or at the beginning of words. For example SEP *ueueyi*, TO *huehueyi* 'big', SEP *mochiua*, TO *mochihua* "it is made".

We maintain a separate finite-state transducer to account for orthographic and spelling variation. This includes rules for orthographic changes like *ts* (SEP, INALI) → *tz* (ACK) (e.g. *tejuatsin* 'you-HON' → *tehhuatzin*), spelling changes, such as *w$* → *j$* and abbreviations that are found in the transcriptions from the spoken corpora, such as *^t'* → *^tik*.

6 Methodology

In this section, we outline some of the implementation details of the analyzer, including a description of relevant linguistic features.

6.1 Lexicon

The lexicon consists of around 5,000 lexemes which were added in frequency order (calculated using the corpora described in §4) and with reference to the two available dictionaries (Key and Richie de Key, 1953; Cortez Ocotlán, 2017) for part-of-speech classification. The lexicon was created in the `lexc` formalism, which is standard in HFST.

Closed categories (pronouns, conjunctions, etc.) were added manually based on class notes and on existing grammatical descriptions (Key, 1960; Robinson, 1970; Cortez Ocotlán, 2017).

6.2 Tagset

The tagset is based on the tagset of the Apertium project (Forcada et al., 2011), each tag is encased in greater than '<' and less than '>' symbols. The tag names are mnemonic, some of them coming from other analysers in the Apertium project and being based on English, Spanish, or Catalan terms, and some are based on Nahuatl terms. We include a conversion from this Apertium-based tagset to one based on Universal Dependencies (Nivre et al., 2020).

[3]`https://site.inali.gob.mx/SMF/Libros2.0/nhtl/index.html`

Corpus	Genre	Ortho.	Tokens	Types	Coverage	
					Tokens	*Types*
Puebla-Nahuatl (Amith et al.)	spoken	INALI	353,006	23,174	93.02	44.33
Axolotl (Gutierrez-Vasques et al., 2016)	non-fiction	SEP	18,338	3,492	84.78	48.0
Sociedad Mexicana de Física	non-fiction	SEP	1,649	599	92.05	84.47

Table 1: A breakdown of the three data sources used for developing the analyser, with information about the genre (following Müller-Eberstein et al. (2021)), orthography used, data volume, and analyser coverage. Note that the Puebla-Nahuatl dataset's orthography differs slightly from the INALI norms in that it explicitly represents vowel-length with the colon ':'.

Category	Stems	Category	Stems
Verbs	2,937	Other	116
Nouns	1,284	Numerals	42
Adverbs	222	Pronouns	33
Adjectives	202	Conjunctions	27
Proper nouns	160	Determiners	20
Total:			5,043

Table 2: Composition of the stem lexicon in the `lexc` file.

6.3 Morphotactics

The morphotactics of Highland Sierra Nahuatl is very similar to that of other Nahuatl varieties. It is characterised by a concatenative affixing morphology with a large number of inflectional and derivational morphemes. It also features long-distance dependencies between prefixes and suffixes.

6.3.1 Nouns

Nouns inflect for number and possession. They also have very productive derived forms, such as the reverential *-tsin* (1) and less productive derivations, such as *-k(o)* for locative, and can appear as predicates with the addition of subject prefixes. We implement the morphotactics for inflection and for the most frequent subset of the derived forms. Nouns are therefore split into separate continuation classes for their different combinatorial possibilities.

(1) *kikouaj* *in*
ki-koua-j in
O.SG3-buy-S.PL the
tokniuantsitsin
to-kni-uan-tsi~tsin
POSS.PL1-person-PL-PL.HON
"People buy it." (lit. "Our brethren buy it")

In (1), the noun *(i)kni* 'sibling' appears with the first person plural possessive prefix *to-*, the possessed plural marker *-uan*, and the reverential marker *tsi~tsin*, where plurality is further marked with partial reduplication of the *-tsin* morpheme.

Relational nouns: There is also a subcategory of nouns, called "relational nouns," used for expressing spatial and temporal relations, as well as other non-core semantic roles. Unlike common nouns, these nouns have obligatory possession.

(2) *In mochiua* *kuoujtaj,* *in eua*
In mo-chiua kuoujtaj, in eua
O.REFL-make mountains, born
talixko, *amo itech*
tal-ix-ko, amo i-tech
ground-RELN-LOC, NEG POSS.SG3-on
kuapalak.
kuapalak.
tree.trunks
"It grows in the mountains, it comes up from the ground, it doesn't grow in tree trunks."

In (2) we see two methods in which relational nouns can be used. The first is *talixko* where the the relational noun *-ixko* 'in front of / on the surface of' is compounded with the noun *tali* 'ground/earth'. This relational noun itself is composed of *ix* 'face' and *ko* a locative morpheme.

The second method is using a free-standing relational noun with a complement, *itech kuapalak* 'in rotten tree trunks', is composed of a possessive form of the relational noun *-tech* 'on' and the noun compliment *kuapalak* 'tree trunk'.

These relational nouns can also appear separated from their complement, as in (3, where the complement of *iuan* 'with' is *emol* 'beans', but it appears to the right of the verbal complex *se kikua* "it is eaten".

(3) *uan iuan* *se* *kikua* *emol*
uan i-uan se ki-kua emol
and POSS.SG3-with one O.SG3-eat beans
"... and it is eaten with beans"

They can also receive reverential morphology as in one of the typical ways of expressing goodbye, *mohuantsin* 'with you' (4).

(4) *mohuantsin*
mo-huan-tsin
POSS.2SG-with-HON
"with you"

Locatives: In addition to compounding with relational nouns there is also a locative derivational suffix *-k(o)* which forms locative nouns from places. For example *ima* 'her hand', *imako* 'in her hands'.[4]

6.3.2 Verbs

Verbs inflect for number and person of subject and object(s), and for tense, aspect and mood. They also can be compounded with auxiliary verbs and can have incorporated adverbial items for both direction of movement and for manner of action. Additionally there is reverential agreement for the second person.

(5) *Xe ma nimitsonchiya huan*
Xe ma ni-mits-on-chiya huan
QST OPT S.SG1-O.SG2-HON-wait and
tisentakuaskej?
ti-sen-ta-kua-s-kej
S.PL1-TOGETHER-O.NN3-eat-FUT-S.PL
"Shall I wait for you and we'll eat together?"

In (5) we see examples of incorporated adverbials, *tisentakuaskej* "we will eat **together**", affixal agreement, *ti-*[...]*-kej* for the first person plural subject and *ta-* for the indefinite object and the future tense suffix *-s*. The verb *nimitsonchiya* has the *on-* prefix, indicating reverentiality towards the addressee.

(6) *se mokouilia komo se*
se mo-kou-ilia komo se
one O.REF-buy-APP if one
kikuasneki.
ki-kua-s-neki
O.SG3-eat-FUT-want
"One goes and buys it if one wants to eat it."

[4] Although the name is the same, these locatives are unlike those found in other languages as inflection because: (1) not every word can take a locative suffix, (2) they are not selected for by argument structure, (3) the resulting meaning can be idiosyncratic. For this reason we categorise them as derivation as opposed to inflection.

```
^Ixua/<s_sg3>ixua<v><iv><pres>$
^uan/huan<cnjcoo>$
^moskaltia/<s_sg3>moskaltia<v><iv><pres>$
^,/,<cm>$
^ijuak/ijhuak<cnjsub>$
^motamiti/<s_sg3>motami<v><iv><and>$
^peua/<s_sg3>pehua<v><iv><pres>$
^xochiyoua/<s_sg3>xochiyohua<v><iv><pres>$
^./.<sent>$
```

Figure 2: Example output of the analyser for the sentence *Ixua uan moskaltia, ijuak motamiti peua xochiyoua* "It sprouts, grows and later starts to flower".

(7) *se kiualkui*
se ki-ual-kui
one O.3SG-VEN-bring
"It is brought." (lit. One brings it (here))

6.4 Morphophonology

Phonological processes are implemented via `twol` rules. There are relatively few of these, and they include degemination (/kk/ →[k]) and nasal assimilation (/n/ →[m] // m).

7 Results

To evaluate the analyzer, we calculate the naïve coverage for both tokens and types. The naïve coverage is reported for each data source in Table 1. Naïve coverage is the percentage of surface forms in a given corpus that receive at least one morphological analysis. Forms counted by this measure may have other analyses which are not delivered by the transducer.

7.1 Evaluation

Since we don't have a large, annotated dataset for evaluation, we performed a manual inspection of two random samples of data to get a sense of the the system's precision and to understand the reasons for any missed words.

First, we sampled 100 random analyses from the corpora and identified any mistakes. The precision on this sample was 95%. Next, in order to find out where the most work remains to be done with respect to coverage, we randomly sampled 100 types that are currently not recognised by the system. These words were categorised by part of speech, and in addition we marked each with one or more of the following seven error categories: (1) missing morphotactics, (2) missing orthographic normalisation, (3) missing compound word, (4) reduplication, (5) loan word / code-switching, (6) tokenisation error, and (7) missing lexicon entry.

Over half of all unknown words were verb forms. Of these, five were caused by missing orthographic normalisation rules, for example *t'titipitstoti* is an abbreviated form of *tiktitipitstoti* 'you will be blowing the fire', and 10 were due to missing stems in the lexicon.

Around ten percent of the sampled unknown words were caused by errors in tokenisation. The speech corpus contains false starts, for example *amo nike..., amo nikmati* "I don't kn..., I don't know", and these do not currently receive any analysis.

8 Concluding remarks

We have described a robust finite-state morphological analyser for Highland Puebla Nahuatl. This work contributes to the recent increased focus in language technologies for Nahuatl, and may play an important role in supporting further Nahuatl language technology in the future.

In future work we would like to expand the lexicon to include more stems, to increase the coverage of all of the corpora, and to obtain new corpora for testing. We intend to include support for compounding and incorporation and for weighting the transducer. We already have 10,000 tokens manually disambiguated and will use these to weight more probable analyses.

Acknowledgements

We would like to thank Patricia Aguilar Romero, don Pedro Rivera, and Mitsuya Sasaki for their help with the work described in this manuscript. In addition we would like to thank the anonymous reviewers for their helpful comments.

References

Jonathan D. Amith, Amelia Dominguez Alcántara, Hermelindo Salazar Osollo, Ceferino Salgado Castañeda, and Eleuterio Gorostiza Salazar. Audio corpus of Sierra Nororiental and Sierra Norte de Puebla Nahuat(l) with accompanying time-code transcriptions in ELAN.

Kenneth R Beesley and Lauri Karttunen. 2003. Finite-state morphology: Xerox tools and techniques. *CSLI, Stanford.*

Pedro Cortez Ocotlán. 2017. *Diccionario Nahuat–Español de la Sierra Nororiental del Estado de Puebla*. Tetsijtsilin, Tzinacapan, Cuetzalan.

Victoriano de la Cruz Cruz. 2014. La escritura náhuatl y los procesos de su revitalización. *Contribution in New World Archaeology*, 7:187–197.

J.I.E. Farfan. 2019. *Nahuatl Contemporary Writing: Studying Convergence in the Absence of a Written Norm*. University of Sheffield.

Mikel L. Forcada, María Ginestí-Rosell, Jacob Nordfalk, Jim O'Regan, Sergio Ortiz-Rojas, Juan Antonio Pérez-Ortiz, Felipe Sánchez-Martínez, Gema Ramírez-Sánchez, and Francis M. Tyers. 2011. Apertium: a free/open-source platform for rule-based machine translation. *Machine Translation*, 25(2):127–144.

Ximena Gutierrez-Vasques, Gerardo Sierra, and Isaac Hernandez Pompa. 2016. Axolotl: a web accessible parallel corpus for spanish-nahuatl. In *Proceedings of the Tenth International Conference on Language Resources and Evaluation (LREC'16)*, pages 4210–4214.

INALI. 2009. *Catálogo de las lenguas indígenas nacionales: Variantes lingüísticas de México con sus autodenominaciones y referencias geoestadísticas*. Instituto Nacional de Lenguas Indígenas, México, D.F.

INALI. 2018. Breviario: Norma ortográfica del idioma náhuatl, méxico. (conforme al avance preliminar de la norma de escritura de la lengua náhuatl a nivel nacional).

Harold Key. 1960. Stem construction and affixation of Sierra Nahuat verbs. *International Journal of American Linguistics*, 28(2):130–145.

Harold Key and Mary Richie de Key. 1953. *Vocabulario Mejicano de la Sierra de Zacapoaxtla, Puebla*. Instituto Lingüístico de Verano, México, D.F.

Mary Key and Harold Key. 1953. The phonemes of sierra nahuat. *International Journal of American Linguistics*, 19(1):53–56.

András Kornai. 1996. Extended finite state models of language. *Natural Language Engineering*, 2(4):287–290.

Krister Lindén, Erik Axelson, Sam Hardwick, Tommi Pirinen, and Miikka Silfverberg. 2011. HFST—framework for compiling and applying morphologies. *Communications in Computer and Information Science*, 100:67–85.

Michael Maxwell. 2015. Grammar debugging. In *Systems and Frameworks for Computational Morphology: Fourth International Workshop, SFCM 2015, Stuttgart, Germany, September 17-18, 2015. Proceedings 4*, pages 166–183. Springer.

Arya D. McCarthy, Rachel Wicks, Dylan Lewis, Aaron Mueller, Winston Wu, Oliver Adams, Garrett Nicolai, Matt Post, and David Yarowsky. 2020. The Johns Hopkins University Bible corpus: 1600+ tongues for typological exploration. In *Proceedings of the Twelfth Language Resources and Evaluation Conference*, pages 2884–2892, Marseille, France. European Language Resources Association.

Max Müller-Eberstein, Rob van der Goot, and Barbara Plank. 2021. Genre as weak supervision for cross-lingual dependency parsing. In *Proceedings of the 2021 Conference on Empirical Methods in Natural Language Processing*, pages 4786–4802, Online and Punta Cana, Dominican Republic. Association for Computational Linguistics.

Garrett Nicolai, Dylan Lewis, Arya D. McCarthy, Aaron Mueller, Winston Wu, and David Yarowsky. 2020. Fine-grained morphosyntactic analysis and generation tools for more than one thousand languages. In *Proceedings of the Twelfth Language Resources and Evaluation Conference*, pages 3963–3972, Marseille, France. European Language Resources Association.

Joakim Nivre, Marie-Catherine de Marneffe, Filip Ginter, Jan Hajič, Christopher D. Manning, Samppo Pyysalo, Sebastian Schuster, Francis Tyers, and Dan Zeman. 2020. Universal Dependencies v2: An evergrowing multilingual treebank collection. In *Proceedings of the 12th Conference on Language Resources and Evaluation (LREC 2020)*, pages 4027–4036.

Robert Pugh, Marivel Huerta Mendez, and Francis M. Tyers. 2021. Towards an open source finite-state morphological analyzer for Zacatlán-Ahuacatlán-Tepetzintla Nahuatl. In *Proceedings of the 4th Workshop on the Use of Computational Methods in the Study of Endangered Languages*.

Dow F. Robinson. 1970. *Aztec studies 2: Sierra Nahuat word structure*. Summer Institute of Linguistics.

Marc Thouvenot. 2009. *CEN juntamente : compendio enciclopédico del Náhuatl*. Instituto Nacional de Antropología e Historia, México, D.F.

Ana Tona, Guillaume Thomas, and Ewan Dunbar. 2023. A morphological analyzer for Huasteca Nahuatl. In *Proceedings of the Sixth Workshop on the Use of Computational Methods in the Study of Endangered Languages*, pages 112–116.

Neural Machine Translation for the Indigenous Languages of the Americas: An Introduction

Manuel Mager[♡*] **Rajat Bhatnagar**[♠] **Graham Neubig**[♯]
Ngoc Thang Vu[◊] **Katharina Kann**[♠]
[♡]AWS AI Labs [♯]Carnegie Mellon University
[♠]University of Colorado Boulder [◊]University of Stuttgart

Abstract

Neural models have drastically advanced state of the art for machine translation (MT) between high-resource languages. Traditionally, these models rely on large amounts of training data, but many language pairs lack these resources. However, an important part of the languages in the world do not have this amount of data. Most languages from the Americas are among them, having a limited amount of parallel and monolingual data, if any. Here, we present an introduction to the interested reader to the basic challenges, concepts, and techniques that involve the creation of MT systems for these languages. Finally, we discuss the recent advances and findings and open questions, product of an increased interest of the NLP community in these languages.

1 Introduction

More than 7 billion people on Earth communicate in nearly 7000 different languages (Pereltsvaig, 2020). Of these, approximately 900 languages are native of the American continent (Campbell, 2000). Most of these indigenous languages of the Americas (ILA) are endangered at some degree (Thomason, 2015). This huge variety in languages is simultaneously a rich treasure for humanity and also a barrier to communication among people from different backgrounds. Human translators have been important in overcoming language barriers. However, trained translators are not accessible to everyone on Earth and even scarcer for endangered and minority languages. The need for translations is even written in the constitutions of several countries like Mexico, Peru, Paraguay, Venezuela, and Bolivia (Zajícová, 2017) to allow native speakers to have equal language rights regarding law.

This is why developing MT is crucial: it helps humanity overcome language barriers while simultaneously allowing people to continue using their native tongue. However, the challenges to achieving these problems are not trivial. It is not only the amount of available data (a common thesis among the NLP community) but also a set of challenging issues (dialectical and orthographic variations, noisy texts, complex morphology, etc.) that must be addressed.

MT has always been an important task within the larger area of natural language processing (NLP). In 1954, the Georgetown–IBM experiment (Hutchins, 2004) was the first that showed at least some effectiveness of MT. Further research resulted in rule-based systems and statistical models. In 2023, neural models define state of the art for MT if training data is plentiful – i.e., for so-called high-resource languages (HRLs) – and have also achieved impressive results for low-resource languages (LRLs). MT is also the most studied NLP task for the ILA (Mager et al., 2018b; Littell et al., 2018). The common issue among these languages is the extreme low-resource conditions they are confronted with. The research interest for these languages has increased in the last years, including the recent AmericasNLP 2021 shared task (Mager et al., 2021) on 10 indigenous languages to Spanish, and the WMT (Conference on Machine Translation) shared task for Inuktitut–English (Barrault et al., 2020).

In this work we aim to provide a comprehensive introduction to the challenges that involve creating MT systems for ILA, and the current status of the existing work. We organize this work as follows: We start by introducing state-of-the-art NMT models (§2). Then, we discuss the current challenges for these languages (§3); and we introduce the key concepts related to low-resource NMT and the implications for endangered languages of the Americas(§3). This is followed by a discussion of available data (§4). Afterwards, we introduce the important concepts for LRL and endangered languages (§5); then we introduce the main strategies

*Work done while at the University of Stuttgart.

Proceedings of the Workshop on Natural Language Processing for Indigenous Languages of the Americas (AmericasNLP), pages 109–133
July 14, 2023 ©2023 Association for Computational Linguistics

aimed at improving NMT with limited training data (§6); and finally we give an overview of the work done for ILA on MT (§7). In doing so, we provide insights into the following questions: Which systems define the state of the art on low-resource NMT applied to the ILA? What is the route that ahead to improve the translations of the ILA?

2 Background and Definitions

Formally, the task of MT consists of converting text X in a source language L_x into text Y in a target language L_y that conveys the same meaning.[1] Translating text $X \in L_x$ into $Y \in L_y$ can be described as a function (Neubig, 2017):

$$Y = \texttt{MT}(X). \tag{1}$$

X and Y can be of variable length, such as phrases, sentences, or even documents.

If other languages are used during the translation process, e.g., as pivots, we denote them as $L_1, \ldots, L_n$. We refer to a corpus of monolingual sentences in language L_i as $M^{L_i} = S_1, ..., S_n$.

Probabilistic Modeling and Data When using probabilistic MT models, the goal is to find $Y \in L_y$ with the highest conditional probability, given $X \in L_x$. Under the supervised machine learning paradigm, a parallel corpus $C_{parallel} = (X_1, Y_1), ..., (X_n, Y_n)$ is used to learn a set of parameters θ, which define a probability distribution over possible translations. Given $C_{parallel}$, the training objective of an NMT model is generally to maximize the log-likelihood $\mathcal{L}$ with respect to θ:

$$\mathcal{L}_\theta = \sum_{(X_i, Y_i) \in C_{parallel}} \log p(Y_i | X_i; \theta). \tag{2}$$

Within this overall framework, there are a number of design decisions one has to make, such as which model architecture to use, how to generate translations, and how to evaluate.

Decoding Decoding refers to the generation of output $\hat{Y}$, given the parameters θ and an input X. Often, decoding is done by approximately solving the following maximization problem:

$$\text{argmax}_{\hat{Y}} p(\hat{Y} | X; \theta) \tag{3}$$

[1]This is an approximation, since it is in general not possible to map the meaning of text exactly into another language (Nida, 1945; Sechrest et al., 1972; Baker, 2018).

Most NMT systems factorize the probability of $\hat{Y} = \hat{y_1}, ..., \hat{y_T}$ in a left-to-right fashion:

$$p(\hat{Y}) = \prod_{t=1}^{T} p(\hat{y}_t | \hat{y}_{<t}, X, \theta) \tag{4}$$

Thus, the probability of token $\hat{y}_t$ at time step t is computed using the previously generated tokens $\hat{y}_{<t}$, the source sentence X and the model parameters θ. Common algorithms for finding a high-probability translation are greedy decoding, i.e., picking the token with the highest probability at each time step, and beam search (Lowerre, 1976).

2.1 Input Representations

The texts X and Y are input into an NMT system as sequences of continuous vectors. However, defining which units should be represented as such vectors is non-trivial. The classic way is to represent each *word* within X and Y as a vector (or embedding). However, in a low-resource setting, often not all vocabulary items appear in the training data (Jean et al., 2015; Luong et al., 2015). This issue especially effects languages with a rich inflectional morphology (Sennrich et al., 2016c): as many word forms can represent the same lemma, the vocabulary coverage decreases drastically. Furthermore, for many LRLs, boundaries between words or morphemes are not easy to obtain or not well defined in the case of languages without a standard orthography. Alternative input units have been explored, such as characters (Ling et al., 2015), byte pair encoding (BPE; Sennrich et al., 2016a), morphological representations (Vania and Lopez, 2017; Ataman and Federico, 2018), syllables (Zhang et al., 2019), or, recently, a visual representation of rendered text (Salesky et al., 2021). No clear advantage has been discovered for using morphological segmentations over BPEs when testing them on LRLs (Saleva and Lignos, 2021).

Input representations can be pretrained. The two most common options are: i) word embeddings, where each type is represented by a vector, e.g., Word2Vec (Mikolov et al., 2013), Glove (Pennington et al., 2014), or Fasttext (Bojanowski et al., 2017)) embeddings, and ii) contextualized word representations, where entire sentences are being encoded at a time, e.g., ELMo (Peters et al., 2018) or BERT (Devlin et al., 2019). However, training of these methods requires large monolingual training corpora, which may not be readily available for LRLs. As most ILA have rich morphology, this topic has gathered special interest. The discussion about the usage of morpholigical segmented input for NMT models is recurrent. (Mager et al., 2022) show that the unsupervised morphologically inspired models outperform BPE pre-processing (experimented on 4 language pares). Similar experiments done on Quechua–Spanish and Inuktitut–Enlgish (Schwartz et al., 2020), comparing BPEs against Morfessor (Smit et al., 2014). Also (Ortega et al., 2020a) improves the SOTA (state-of-the-art) for Quechua–Spanish MT using a morphological guided BPE algorithm.

2.2 Architectures

NMT models typically are sequence-to-sequence models. They encode a variable-length sequence into a vector or matrix representation, which they then decode back into a variable-length sequence (Cho et al., 2014). The two most frequent architectures are: i) recurrent neural networks (RNN), such as LSTMs (Hochreiter and Schmidhuber, 1997) or GRUs (Cho et al., 2014), and ii) transformers (Vaswani et al., 2017), which define the current state of the art in the high-resource setting.

As for most neural network models, training an NMT system on a limited number of instances is challenging (Fernández-Delgado et al., 2014). There are common problems that arise from limited data in the training set. One major advantage of neural models is their ability to learn representations from raw data, in contrast to manually engineered features (Barron, 1993). However, problems arise when not enough data is provided to enable effective learning of features. Another strength of neural networks is their generalization capacity (Kawaguchi et al., 2017). However, training a neural network on a small dataset easily leads to overfitting (Rolnick et al., 2017). Recent studies, however, show empirically that this does not necessarily happen if the network is tuned correctly (Olson et al., 2018).

2.3 Evaluation

Accurately judging translation quality is difficult and, thus, often still done manually: bilingual speakers assign scores according to provided criteria such as fluency and adequacy (*Does the output have the same meaning as the input?*). However, manual evaluation is expensive and slow. Moreover, in the case of endangered languages, bilingual speakers can be hard or impossible to find.

Automatic metrics provide an alternative.[2] These metrics assign a score to system output, given one or more ground truth reference translations. The most widely used metric is BLEU (Papineni et al., 2002), which relies on token-level n-gram matches between the translation to be rated and one or more gold-standard translations. For morphologically rich languages, character-level metrics, such as chrF (Popović, 2017), are often more suitable, as they allow for more flexibility. In the AmericasNLP ST (Mager et al., 2021) this metric was used over BLEU, as it fits better to the rich morphology of many ILA.

To have a concrete example, lets have the following Wixarika phrase with an English translation:

yu-huta-me	ne-p+-we-'iwa
an-two-ns	1sg:s-asi-2pl:o-brother

I have two brothers

As discussed in (Mager et al., 2018c) it is difficult to translate back from Spanish (or other Fusional language) the morpheme *p+* as it has not equivalent in these languages. So if we would ignore these morpheme at all, BLEU would penalize the entire word *nep+we'iwa*. In contrast, chrF would give credit to the translation, even if the *p+* is missing.

One shortcoming of these evaluation metrics is that the evaluation is very dependent on the surface forms and not on the ultimate goal of semantic similarity and fluency. Recent work uses pretrained models to evaluate semantic similarity between translations and the gold standard (Zhang et al., 2020d), but these methods are limited to languages for which such models are available. This is not possible for the ILA, as the amount of monolingual data is not enough to train a reliable pretrained language model[3].

3 Challenges and open questions

In an overview of the datasets and recent studies of MT for the ILA, we found the following main issues to be handled.

Extreme low-resource parallel datasets Even with the recent advances, the resources available to train MT systems are extremely scarce, having

[2]For a detailed overview of automatic metrics for MT we refer the interested reader to specialized reviews (Han, 2016; Celikyilmaz et al., 2020; Chatzikoumi, 2020).

[3]One exception to this is Quechua, that has a large enough monolingual dataset to train a BERT like model (Zevallos et al., 2022)

training set between 4k and 20k sentences (see §4), with notable exceptions for Inuktitut, Guarani and Quechua (Joanis et al., 2020; Ortega et al., 2020a).

Lack of monolingual data Most of these languages are mostly used in spoken form. In recent years, with the advancement and democratization of mobile technologies, indigenous languages have seen a slight increase in massaging systems and private spheres (Rosales et al.). However, the usage of these languages on the internet is rather limited. Even Wikipedia has a limited amount of these languages (Mager et al., 2018b).

Low domain diversity . As most parallel datasets are scarce, they are restricted to a small number of domains, making it challenging to adapt it, or try to aim for general translation models. This has been recognized as a major problem during the AmericasNLP ST (Mager et al., 2021).

Rich morphology An important number of these languages are morphological highly rich. In many cases, we find polysynthetic, with or highly agglutinative languages (Kann et al., 2018) or even fusional phenomenon (Mager et al., 2020).

Distant paired language The most common languages that we find that ILA is translated into are Spanish, English, and Portuguese. However, these languages are distantly related to the ILA, and have completely different linguistically phenomenons (Campbell, 2000; Romero et al., 2016).

Noisy text environments Monolingual texts, if exist, are found in social media that often use a non-canonical witting (Rosales et al.).

Code-Swithing This phenomenon is strongly present in ILA, as all of these languages are minority languages in their own countries. The bilingualism among their communities is strong (and CS is a common phenomenon in this setup (Çetinoğlu, 2017)). The final result of this phenomenon is the inclusion of code-switching on a common base (Mager et al., 2019) in their language.

Lack of orthographic normalization The usage of ILA faces the problem of having a unified orthographic standard. This is not always possible, as the suggestions of linguists and official entities do not always match the day-by-day writing of the speakers. Moreover, in some cases, special symbols present in the orthographic standards are not accessible in English or Spanish keyboard and need to be replaced with other symbols. The winner of the AmericasNLP ST got important improvements using orthographic normalizers developed specifically for each American language (Vázquez et al., 2021).

Dialectal variety The indigenous languages have a strong dialectal variety, making it hard for native speakers to understand even speakers from neighboring villages. The linguistic richness of entire regions is so diverse that even a single state like the Mexican Oaxaca could correspond to the diversity in the whole Europe (McQuown, 1955).

4 Available MT datasets for ILA

The parallel datasets available for MT have been increasing during the last years. At this moment, we can show in two folds the development of these resources: as shown in table 2 work on specific language has emerged; but also broader datasets have started to cover the ILA (see table 1).

Language-specific corpus collection work has been done for many languages, where parallel corpus has been the main component. In recent time we have seen Cherokee–English (OPUS) (Zhang et al., 2020c), Wixarika–Spanish (Mager et al., 2018a), Shipio–Konibo (Feldman and Coto-Solano, 2020), and others (see table 2). The most prominent of these datasets has been the Inuktitut–English parallel data. The last version of this dataset corpora (Joanis et al., 2020) is has medium size with 1,450,094 sentences. Previous versions of this corpus are (Martin et al., 2003). This data set was used for the WMT 2020 Shared Task on Unsupervised, and Low Resourced MT (Barrault et al., 2020).

For wide-spoken languages like Guarani, it is even possible to collect a web crawled dataset, including news articles and social media parallel aligned data (Chiruzzo et al., 2020; Góngora et al., 2021) This dataset also includes monolingual data. This is possible as Guaraní is one of the most spoken indigenous languages of the continent.

In contrast to the language-specific datasets, we find broader approaches (see table 1). The broadest multilingual dataset, which contains the Bible's New Testament, includes about 1600 languages (Mayer and Cysouw, 2014; McCarthy et al., 2020) of the 2,508 that have been collected by the Summer Institute of Linguistic (SIL) (Anderson and Anderson, 2012). Another remarkable effort to obtain broad language coverage is the PanLex project (Kamholz et al., 2014), which has gathered lexical

Dataset	Paired-languages	Authors
AmericasNLI	Aymara, Asháninka, Bribri, Guaraní, Nahuatl, Otomí, Quechua, Rarámuri, Shipibo-Konibo, Wixarika	(Ebrahimi et al., 2022)
CPML	Ch'ol, Maya, Mazatec, Mixtec, Nahuatl and Otomi	(Sierra Martínez et al., 2020)
OPUS	*	(Tiedemann, 2016)
New testament Bible	*	(McCarthy et al., 2020)

Table 1: Parallel dataset collections that contain one or more indigenous languages of the Americas

Language	Paried-language	ISO	Family	Sentences	Domain	Authors
Asháninka	Spanish	cni	Arawak	3883		(Ortega et al., 2020b)
Bribri	Spanish	bzd	Chibchan	5923		(Feldman and Coto-Solano, 2020)
Guarani	Spanish	gn	Tupi-Guarani		News, Blogs	(Abdelali et al., 2006)
Guarani	Spanish	gn	Tupi-Guarani	14,531	News, Blogs	(Chiruzzo et al., 2020)
Guarani	Spanish	gn	Tupi-Guarani	14,792	News, Social Media	(Góngora et al., 2021)
Guarani	Spanish	gn	Tupi-Guarani	30855	8 Domains	(Chiruzzo et al., 2022)
Nahuatl	Spanish	nah	Uto-Aztecan	16145	Diverse Books	(Gutierrez-Vasques et al., 2016)
Otomí	Spanish	oto	Oto-Manguean	4889	Diverse Books	`https://tsunkua.elotl.mx`
Rarámuri	Spanish	tar	Uto-Aztecan	14721	Dictionary Examples	(Mager et al., 2022)
Shipibo-Konibo	Spanish	shp	Panoan	14592	Educational, Religious	(Galarreta et al., 2017)
Wixarika	Spanish	hch	Uto-Aztecan	8966	Literature	(Mager et al., 2018a)
Cherokee	English	chr	Uto-Aztecan		OPUS	(Zhang et al., 2020c)
Inuktitut	English	iku	Eskimo–Aleut	1,450,094	Legislative	(Joanis et al., 2020)
Ayuuk	Spanish	mir	Mixe–Zoque	7553	Diverse	(Zacarías Márquez and Meza Ruiz, 2021)
Mazatec	Spanish	Many	Oto-Manguean	9799	Diverse	(Tonja et al., 2023)
Mixtec	Spanish	Many	Oto-Manguean	13235	Diverse	(Tonja et al., 2023)

Table 2: Parallel datasets that have been released focusing on one indigenous language

translation dictionaries for over 5,700 languages. However, for most languages, PanLex contains only a few dozen words. Duan et al. (2020) show that such dictionaries can be used to create an NMT system, making bilingual dictionaries relevant for further studies.

Recently community-driven research groups have started the creation of own parallel datasets, such as Masakhane (Orife et al., 2020; Nekoto et al., 2020) for African languages, and AmericasNLP for indigenous languages of the Americas (Ebrahimi et al., 2021; Mager et al., 2021). The AmericasNLI dataset is an important effort to have a common evaluation benchmark for the 10 indigenous languages of the Americas for the MT and NLI tasks.

Given the constitutional rights of indigenous languages in many countries of the Americas, it is possible to access this data. Vázquez et al. (2021) made available this resource during their shared task system development.

Finally, it is important to mention that many of the languages spoken in the Americas have Wikipedia's set of articles available[4].

Collection of New Data A common way to create parallel data with the help of bilingual speakers is via elicitation (translating the foreign text into another language). It has the disadvantage of biasing the created text to forms and topics, culture, and even grammatical forms towards the source language (Lörscher, 2005). A method that avoids this problem is language documentation, which consists of storing and annotating commonly used speech or text (Himmelmann, 2008). However, it is

[4]The available languages in wikipedia can be consulted at: `https://es.wikipedia.org/wiki/Portal:Lenguas_indígenas_de_América`. Until the publication of this article, there were only entries in Nahuatl, Navajo, Guarani, Aymara, Klaalisut, Esquimal, Inukitut, Cherokee, and Cree.

costly and requires specialists. In this process, involving the community members that are bilingual speakers is important (Bird, 2020).

5 Low-resource MT

For the purpose of this paper we define LRLs as languages for which standard techniques are unable to create well performing systems, which makes it necessary to resort to other techniques (cf. Figure 1) such as transfer learning. For MT, the amount of available resources differs widely across language pairs: some have less than 10k parallel sentences, while other have more than 500k, with some exceptions in the orders of several million.

Emulating a low-resource scenario by downsampling available data for high-resource languages is common and helps understanding a model's performance across different settings. However, further evaluating methods on a diverse set of low-resource languages is crucial, since many languages exhibit particular linguistic phenomena (Mager et al., 2020), that perturb the final results, especially since most large datasets are from the Indo-European language family, to which only 6.16% of the world's languages belong (Lewis, 2009).

Importantly, there is no strong correlation between the number of resources available per language and the number of speakers: Javanese with 95 million speakers and Kannada with 44 million are considered LRLs, while French, with only 64 million native speakers, is among the most widely studied languages. Improving models to handle LRLs will extend access to information online as well as human language technology to all monolingual speakers of those languages. In the case of ILA, most languages are endangered at some degree, but most of them have the same issue: they are low resourced for parallel and monolingual data.

Endangered Languages Krauss (1992) estimates that 50% of all languages are doomed or dying, and that in this century we will see either the death or the doom of 90% of all human languages. The current proportion of languages that are already extinct or moribund ranges from 31% down to 8% depending on the region, with the most severe cases in the Americas and Australia (Simons and Lewis, 2013). To determine how endangered a language is, Lewis and Simons (2010) proposes a classification scale called EGIDS with 13 levels. The higher the number on this scale, the greater the level of disruption of the language's inter-generational transmission.[5] MT for endangered LRLs has the potential to help with documentation, promotion and revitalization efforts (Galla, 2016; Mager et al., 2018b). However, as these languages are commonly spoken by small communities, or indigenous people, researchers should aim for a direct involvement of those communities (Bird, 2020).

What is polysynthesis? A polysynthetic language is defined by the following linguistic features: the verb in a polysynthetic language must have an agreement with the subject, objects and indirect objects (Baker, 1996); nouns can be incorporated into the complex verb morphology (Mithun, 1986); and, therefore, polysynthetic languages have agreement morphemes, pronominal affixes and incorporated roots in the verb (Baker, 1996), and also encode their relations and characterizations into that verb. The most common word orders present in these languages are SOV, VSO, SVO and free order. It is important to notice that a polysynthtic language can have a aggutinative [6] or can have also fusional characteristics, like Totonaco or Tepehua (Mager et al., 2020).

6 Low-resource MT paradigms

Most languages of the Americas do not have high amount of data for MT. Therefore, we introduce the most important paradigms to improve low-resourced machine translation. Figure 1 shows a general overview of the methods and options to improve LRL MT. For a more detailed understanding of this techniques we refer the reader to specialized low-resource MT surveys (Haddow et al., 2022; Wang et al., 2021; Ranathunga et al., 2021).

6.1 Multilingual Supervised Training

With a multilingual set of parallel data $D_{parallel}$ between different language pairs $\{(L_1, L_2), \ldots, (L_m, L_n)\}$ we can train a model that is able to map a sentence from any source language L_x into any target language L_y that is contained in $D_{parallel}$ (see 2). These multilingual NMT models have seen a growth in popularity and efficiency in recent years. We will now cover the different training algorithms for these models: 1) many source languages and one target

[5] The complete EGIDS scale can be found at `https://www.ethnologue.com/about/language-status`

[6] Agglutination refers to a concatenation of morphemes, with minimal changes to the surface form.

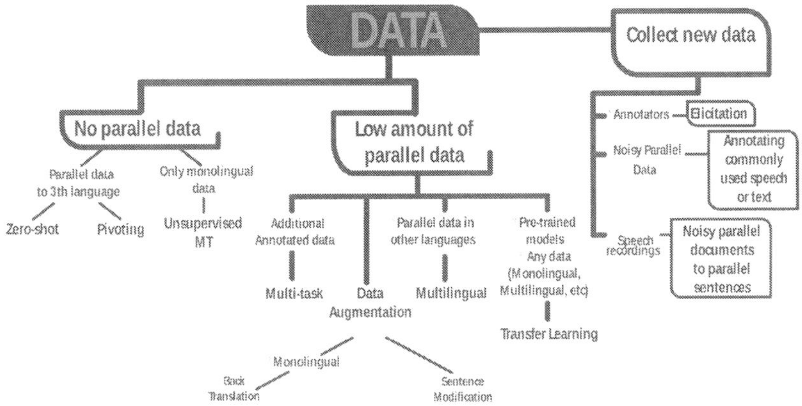

Figure 1: What to do when we have low o no data to train our machine translation models? This diagram shows basic scenarios, solutions, and common requirements for each method, with the section describing the method.

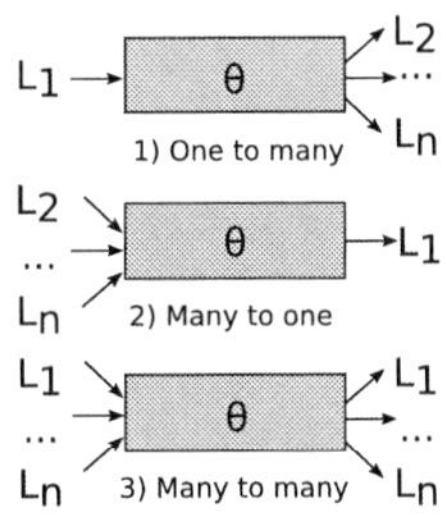

Figure 2: An overview of different multilingual setups.

language (*many-to-one*), 2) one source and many target languages (*one-to-many*), and 3) many source languages and many target languages (*many-to-many*). For a general overview of multilingual MT, we refer the reader to surveys dedicated to this topic (Tan et al., 2019; Dabre et al., 2019). Johnson et al. (2017) are the first to introduce a multilingual NMT model, trained on translating from a large number of languages to English as well as in the opposite direction. The authors show that these models improve over single-language pair models for LRLs.

6.2 Multi-task Training

Multi-task training (Caruana, 1997) aims to improve the performance of the main task – MT in our case – by adding one or more auxiliary tasks to the training. The easiest way is to share all parameters of the network, using the ideas already explored in multilingual NMT (§6.1). This can be done with a special flag in the input that specifies the current task. It is also possible to share only the encoder and have two separate decoders for each task.

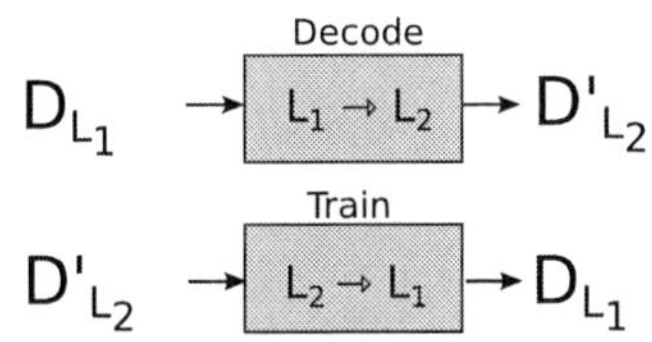

Figure 3: Backtranslation

Multilingual Modeling In order to handle multilinguality it is also possible to adapt modify the NMT models. The main proposals to do so has been: sharing all parameter except the attention mechanism of a RNN NMT model (Blackwood et al., 2018); parameter sharing in the transformer architecture Sachan and Neubig (2018);

6.3 Data Augmentation

Back-Translation A straightforward way to leverage monolingual data for low-resource MT is to generate a meaningful signal with the help of an already initialized MT model (see Figure 3). This method is called back-translation (BT; Sennrich et al., 2016b): With monolingual data M^{L_x} in source language L_x and a trained model that is able to translate from L_x into a target language L_y we can generate a translation M'^{L_y}. This pseudo parallel data (M^{L_x}, M'^{L_y}) is then used to train a new model in the opposite direction. This process can be applied iteratively to improve the translation (Hoang et al., 2018).

Sentence Modification Other methods to generate more parallel sentences are based on lexical substitution. Fadaee et al. (2017) explores replacing frequent words with low-frequency ones in both source and target to improve the translation of rare words. This is done using language models (LMs) and automatic alignment.

Pivoting If no parallel corpus between languages L_x and L_y is available, but both of them have parallel corpora with a third language L_p, pivoting is an option. The basic idea is to train two MT systems: one that translates $L_x \to L_p$ and another for $L_p \to L_y$. Pivoting has first been introduced for SMT (Wu and Wang, 2007; Cohn and Lapata, 2007; Utiyama and Isahara, 2007).

6.4 Semi-supervised and Unsupervised MT

Transfer Learning via Pretraining Transfer learning refers to using knowledge learned from one task to improve performance on a related task (Weiss et al., 2016). In recent years this approach has gained popularity with big multilingual models such as Conneau and Lample (2019) that proposes training the encoder and the decoder separately in order to get cross-language representations (XLM). This idea has further been extended by Song et al. (2019, MASS) to masking a *sequence* of tokens from the input (multilingual MASS (Siddhant et al., 2020)). Another approach is to train the entire transformer model as a denoising autoencoder (BART; Lewis et al., 2019) (multilingual BART (mBART) (Liu et al., 2020)). It is also possible to pretrain a transformer in a multi-task, text-to-text fashion, where one of the tasks is MT (T5; Raffel et al., 2020) (multilingual version (Xue et al., 2021)).

Unsupervised MT UMT covers approaches that do *not* require any parallel text, relying only on monolingual data. This differs from zero-shot translation, which uses parallel data for other language pairs. Early approaches tackled the problem with an auto-encoder with adversarial training (Lample et al., 2017) or with auto-encoders with a shared encoding space as well as separate decoders for each target language (Artetxe et al., 2018). The main problem for these approches is the need of a big monolingual dataset, that is not available for most ILA.

7 Advances in MT for the indigenous languages of the Americas

In recent years the interest in MT for indigenous languages of the Americas has increased. The task is not easy. The first usage of NMT systems has not been successful (Mager and Meza, 2021). However, with the use of LRL MT methods, we have witnessed great improvements.

The Cherokee–English (Zhang et al., 2020c) language pair has been explored using a pre-trained BERT (Devlin et al., 2019) for the English side. A system demonstration of this approach is also accessible (Zhang et al., 2021). The back translation strategy for Bribri–Spanish NMT transformers has also been explored (Feldman and Coto-Solano, 2020) and by (Oncevay, 2021) (for four Peruvian languages to Spanish) with good results. The scarce indigenous language monolingual text can be replaced to some extent with Spanish text or extracted from PDFs, and other sources (Bustamante et al., 2020).

One of the main challenges for the complex morphological languages in the area has been the prepossessing step. Schwartz et al. (2020) show that even if morphological segmentation has less perplexity a the language modeling time, it is still under-performing or equivalent against BPEs for MT (for Inuktitut-–English, Yupik—English Data, Guaraní—Spanish Data). A more comprehensive (on the segmentation modeling side) was done by (Mager et al., 2022) exploring a wide array of segmentation models.The latter study showed that supervised morphological segmentation underperform unsupervised. However, unsupervised morphological segmentation like LMVR (Ataman et al., 2017) and FlatCat (Grönroos et al., 2014) perform better than BPEs. (Ngoc Le and Sadat, 2020) studied how better to perform word segmentation for the Inuktitut–English pair. They found that for this language pair, a morphological segmentation, or a combination of BPEs and morphological segmentation, works better than just applying vanilla BPEs. Also, training word embeddings for Guarani–Spanish translation is an excellent opportunity to increase the MT performance of these languages (Góngora et al., 2022).

The usage of transfer learning from multilingual systems has been tried, with limited results (Nagoudi et al., 2021) (training an own T5 model for indigenous languages) and (Zheng et al., 2021). However, pertaining a Spanish–English model together with ILA, and then fine-tuning it (together with a careful prepossessing and filtering step) has been the most successful strategy (Vázquez et al., 2021).

The quality of MT systems of ILA has been a constant debate. However, Ebrahimi et al. (2021) shows that the quality of MT for these languages is enough to improve other tasks like natural language inference (NLI).

Inuktitut–Enlgish ST The WMT 2020 news translation task included Inuktitut–English translation (Barrault et al., 2020). The participating systems explored the difficulties of working with a polysynthetic language in a medium resource scenario. Participating teams in this competition were: (Kocmi, 2020; Hernandez and Nguyen, 2020; Scherrer et al., 2020; Roest et al., 2020; Lo, 2020; Knowles et al., 2020; Zhang et al., 2020e; Krubiński et al., 2020).

AmericasNLP 2021 and 2023 ST In 2021, the AmericasNLP community organized a workshop on Machine Translation for 10 indigenous languages of the Americas in 2021 (Mager et al., 2021) and 2023 (Ebrahimi et al., 2023) with an additional indigenous language (Chatino). The AmericasNLP shared task winner was (Vázquez et al., 2021) in 2021, and a more mixed result in 2023[7]. Other participants in this shared task are (Nagoudi et al., 2021; Bollmann et al., 2021; Zheng et al., 2021; Knowles et al., 2021; Parida et al., 2021; Nagoudi et al., 2021). It is important to point at the importance of clean datata. For Quechua, (Moreno, 2021) got the best results generating an additional amount of clean data.

AmericasNLP 2022 Competition is a competition on Speech-to-Text translation is organized and is targeting the following language pairs: Bribri–Spanish, Guaraní–Spanish, Kotiria–Portuguese, Wa'ikhana–Portuguese, and Quechua–Spanish (Ebrahim et al., 2023)[8].

8 Ethical aspects

When working with ILAs are also interacting with communities and nations that speak these languages. In most cases, these speakers have been exposed to a colonial past, or to a local oppression, by the majority language and culture. It is important to point to best practices and recommendations when performing our research. Bird (2020) and Liu et al. (2022) advocate to include community members as co-authors (Liu et al., 2022) as well as considering data and technology sovereignty. This is also aligned with the community building aimed at by Zhang et al. (2022). Mager et al. (2023) summarizes the main aspects that should be considered as follows: i) *Consultation, Negotiation and Mutual Understanding*. It is important to inform the community about the planned research, negotiating a possible outcome, and reaching a mutual agreement on the directions and details of the project should happen in all cases. ii) *Respect of the local culture and involvement*. As each community has its own culture and view of the world, researchers should be familiar with the history and traditions of the community. Also, it should be recommended that local researchers, speakers, or internal governments should be involved in the project. iii) *Sharing and distribution of data and research*. The product of the research should be available for use by the community, so they can take advantage of the generated materials, like papers, books, or data.

9 Conclusion

Machine translation for ILA has gained interest in the NLP community over the last few years. Here, we provide an exhaustive overview of the basic MT concepts and the particular challenges for MT for ILA (in the context of low-resource scenarios and its relation to endangered languages). We additionally survey the current advances of MT for these languages.

Limitations

This paper's aim is to give an introduction to researchers, students, of interested community indigenous community members to the topic of Machine Translation for Indigenous languages of the Americas. Therefore, this paper is not an in-depth survey of the literature on indigenous languages nor a more technical survey of low-resource machine translation. We would point the reader to more specific surveys on these aspects (Haddow et al., 2022; Mager et al., 2018b).

Ethical statement

We could not find any specific Ethical issue for this paper or potential danger. Nevertheless, we want to point to the reader that working with indigenous languages (in this case, MT) implies a set of ethical questions that are important to handle. For a deeper understanding of the matter, we suggest specialized literature to the reader (Mager et al., 2023; Bird, 2020; Schwartz, 2022).

[7] Up to this moment, no official desciption papers for the 2023 are published.

[8] `http://turing.iimas.unam.mx/americasnlp/st.html`

References

Ahmed Abdelali, James Cowie, Steve Helmreich, Wanying Jin, Maria Pilar Milagros, Bill Ogden, Mansouri Rad, and Ron Zacharski. 2006. Guarani: A case study in resource development for quick ramp-up MT. In *Proceedings of the 7th Conference of the Association for Machine Translation in the Americas: Technical Papers*, pages 1–9, Cambridge, Massachusetts, USA. Association for Machine Translation in the Americas.

Idris Abdulmumin, Bashir Shehu Galadanci, and Aliyu Garba. 2019. Tag-less back-translation. *arXiv preprint arXiv:1912.10514*.

Roee Aharoni, Melvin Johnson, and Orhan Firat. 2019. Massively multilingual neural machine translation. In *Proceedings of the 2019 Conference of the North American Chapter of the Association for Computational Linguistics: Human Language Technologies, Volume 1 (Long and Short Papers)*, pages 3874–3884.

Benyamin Ahmadnia and Bonnie J Dorr. 2019. Augmenting neural machine translation through round-trip training approach. *Open Computer Science*, 9(1):268–278.

Antonios Anastasopoulos and David Chiang. 2018. Tied multitask learning for neural speech translation. In *Proceedings of the 2018 Conference of the North American Chapter of the Association for Computational Linguistics: Human Language Technologies, Volume 1 (Long Papers)*, pages 82–91, New Orleans, Louisiana. Association for Computational Linguistics.

Stephen R Anderson and Stephen Anderson. 2012. *Languages: A very short introduction*, volume 320. Oxford University Press.

Naveen Arivazhagan, Ankur Bapna, Orhan Firat, Roee Aharoni, Melvin Johnson, and Wolfgang Macherey. 2019a. The missing ingredient in zero-shot neural machine translation. *arXiv preprint arXiv:1903.07091*.

Naveen Arivazhagan, Ankur Bapna, Orhan Firat, Dmitry Lepikhin, Melvin Johnson, Maxim Krikun, Mia Xu Chen, Yuan Cao, George Foster, Colin Cherry, et al. 2019b. Massively multilingual neural machine translation in the wild: Findings and challenges. *arXiv preprint arXiv:1907.05019*.

Mikel Artetxe, Gorka Labaka, Eneko Agirre, and Kyunghyun Cho. 2018. Unsupervised neural machine translation. In *6th International Conference on Learning Representations, ICLR 2018*.

Mikel Artetxe and Holger Schwenk. 2019. Massively multilingual sentence embeddings for zero-shot cross-lingual transfer and beyond. *Transactions of the Association for Computational Linguistics*, 7:597–610.

Duygu Ataman and Marcello Federico. 2018. Compositional representation of morphologically-rich input for neural machine translation. In *Proceedings of the 56th Annual Meeting of the Association for Computational Linguistics (Volume 2: Short Papers)*, pages 305–311.

Duygu Ataman, Matteo Negri, Marco Turchi, and Marcello Federico. 2017. Linguistically motivated vocabulary reduction for neural machine translation from turkish to english.

Jimmy Lei Ba, Jamie Ryan Kiros, and Geoffrey E Hinton. 2016. Layer normalization. *stat*, 1050:21.

Mark C Baker. 1996. *The polysynthesis parameter*. Oxford University Press.

Mona Baker. 2018. *In other words: A coursebook on translation*. Routledge.

Loïc Barrault, Magdalena Biesialska, Ondřej Bojar, Marta R. Costa-jussà, Christian Federmann, Yvette Graham, Roman Grundkiewicz, Barry Haddow, Matthias Huck, Eric Joanis, Tom Kocmi, Philipp Koehn, Chi-kiu Lo, Nikola Ljubešić, Christof Monz, Makoto Morishita, Masaaki Nagata, Toshiaki Nakazawa, Santanu Pal, Matt Post, and Marcos Zampieri. 2020. Findings of the 2020 conference on machine translation (WMT20). In *Proceedings of the Fifth Conference on Machine Translation*, pages 1–55, Online. Association for Computational Linguistics.

Andrew R Barron. 1993. Universal approximation bounds for superpositions of a sigmoidal function. *IEEE Transactions on Information theory*, 39(3):930–945.

Christos Baziotis, Barry Haddow, and Alexandra Birch. 2020. Language model prior for low-resource neural machine translation. *arXiv preprint arXiv:2004.14928*.

Yonatan Belinkov and Yonatan Bisk. 2018. Synthetic and natural noise both break neural machine translation. In *International Conference on Learning Representations*.

Steven Bird. 2020. Decolonising speech and language technology. In *Proceedings of the 28th International Conference on Computational Linguistics*, pages 3504–3519, Barcelona, Spain (Online). International Committee on Computational Linguistics.

Graeme Blackwood, Miguel Ballesteros, and Todd Ward. 2018. Multilingual neural machine translation with task-specific attention. In *Proceedings of the 27th International Conference on Computational Linguistics*, pages 3112–3122.

Piotr Bojanowski, Edouard Grave, Armand Joulin, and Tomas Mikolov. 2017. Enriching word vectors with subword information. *Transactions of the Association for Computational Linguistics*, 5:135–146.

Marcel Bollmann, Rahul Aralikatte, Héctor Murrieta Bello, Daniel Hershcovich, Miryam de Lhoneux, and Anders Søgaard. 2021. Moses and the character-based random babbling baseline: CoAStaL at AmericasNLP 2021 shared task. In *Proceedings of the First Workshop on Natural Language Processing for Indigenous Languages of the Americas*, pages 248–254, Online. Association for Computational Linguistics.

Tom B. Brown, Benjamin Mann, Nick Ryder, Melanie Subbiah, Jared Kaplan, Prafulla Dhariwal, Arvind Neelakantan, Pranav Shyam, Girish Sastry, Amanda Askell, Sandhini Agarwal, Ariel Herbert-Voss, Gretchen Krueger, Tom Henighan, Rewon Child, Aditya Ramesh, Daniel M. Ziegler, Jeffrey Wu, Clemens Winter, Christopher Hesse, Mark Chen, Eric Sigler, Mateusz Litwin, Scott Gray, Benjamin Chess, Jack Clark, Christopher Berner, Sam McCandlish, Alec Radford, Ilya Sutskever, and Dario Amodei. 2020. Language models are few-shot learners.

Gina Bustamante, Arturo Oncevay, and Roberto Zariquiey. 2020. No data to crawl? monolingual corpus creation from PDF files of truly low-resource languages in Peru. In *Proceedings of the 12th Language Resources and Evaluation Conference*, pages 2914–2923, Marseille, France. European Language Resources Association.

Lyle Campbell. 2000. *American Indian languages: the historical linguistics of Native America*, volume 4. Oxford University Press on Demand.

Rich Caruana. 1997. Multitask learning. *Machine learning*, 28(1):41–75.

Isaac Caswell, Ciprian Chelba, and David Grangier. 2019. Tagged back-translation. In *Proceedings of the Fourth Conference on Machine Translation (Volume 1: Research Papers)*, pages 53–63.

Asli Celikyilmaz, Elizabeth Clark, and Jianfeng Gao. 2020. Evaluation of text generation: A survey. *arXiv preprint arXiv:2006.14799*.

Özlem Çetinoğlu. 2017. A code-switching corpus of Turkish-German conversations. In *Proceedings of the 11th Linguistic Annotation Workshop*, pages 34–40, Valencia, Spain. Association for Computational Linguistics.

Bharathi Raja Chakravarthi, Ruba Priyadharshini, Shubhanker Banerjee, Richard Saldanha, John P. McCrae, Anand Kumar M, Parameswari Krishnamurthy, and Melvin Johnson. 2021. Findings of the shared task on machine translation in Dravidian languages. In *Proceedings of the First Workshop on Speech and Language Technologies for Dravidian Languages*, pages 119–125, Kyiv. Association for Computational Linguistics.

Eirini Chatzikoumi. 2020. How to evaluate machine translation: A review of automated and human metrics. *Natural Language Engineering*, 26(2):137–161.

Guanhua Chen, Shuming Ma, Yun Chen, Li Dong, Dongdong Zhang, Jia Pan, Wenping Wang, and Furu Wei. 2021. Zero-shot cross-lingual transfer of neural machine translation with multilingual pretrained encoders. In *Proceedings of the 2021 Conference on Empirical Methods in Natural Language Processing*, pages 15–26, Online and Punta Cana, Dominican Republic. Association for Computational Linguistics.

Yong Cheng. 2019. Joint training for pivot-based neural machine translation. In *Joint Training for Neural Machine Translation*, pages 41–54. Springer.

Yong Cheng, Lu Jiang, and Wolfgang Macherey. 2019. Robust neural machine translation with doubly adversarial inputs. In *Proceedings of the 57th Annual Meeting of the Association for Computational Linguistics*, pages 4324–4333.

Yong Cheng, Lu Jiang, Wolfgang Macherey, and Jacob Eisenstein. 2020. AdvAug: Robust adversarial augmentation for neural machine translation. In *Proceedings of the 58th Annual Meeting of the Association for Computational Linguistics*, pages 5961–5970, Online. Association for Computational Linguistics.

Yong Cheng, Zhaopeng Tu, Fandong Meng, Junjie Zhai, and Yang Liu. 2018. Towards robust neural machine translation. In *Proceedings of the 56th Annual Meeting of the Association for Computational Linguistics (Volume 1: Long Papers)*, pages 1756–1766.

Luis Chiruzzo, Pedro Amarilla, Adolfo Ríos, and Gustavo Giménez Lugo. 2020. Development of a Guarani - Spanish parallel corpus. In *Proceedings of the 12th Language Resources and Evaluation Conference*, pages 2629–2633, Marseille, France. European Language Resources Association.

Luis Chiruzzo, Santiago Góngora, Aldo Alvarez, Gustavo Giménez-Lugo, Marvin Agüero-Torales, and Yliana Rodríguez. 2022. Jojajovai: A parallel guarani-spanish corpus for mt benchmarking. In *Proceedings of the Thirteenth Language Resources and Evaluation Conference*, pages 2098–2107.

Kyunghyun Cho, Bart van Merriënboer, Caglar Gulcehre, Dzmitry Bahdanau, Fethi Bougares, Holger Schwenk, and Yoshua Bengio. 2014. Learning phrase representations using rnn encoder–decoder for statistical machine translation. In *Proceedings of the 2014 Conference on Empirical Methods in Natural Language Processing (EMNLP)*, pages 1724–1734.

Trevor Cohn and Mirella Lapata. 2007. Machine translation by triangulation: Making effective use of multi-parallel corpora. In *Proceedings of the 45th Annual Meeting of the Association of Computational Linguistics*, pages 728–735.

Alexis Conneau and Guillaume Lample. 2019. Cross-lingual language model pretraining. In *Advances in Neural Information Processing Systems*, pages 7057–7067.

Alexis Conneau, Guillaume Lample, Marc'Aurelio Ranzato, Ludovic Denoyer, and Hervé Jégou. 2017. Word translation without parallel data. *arXiv preprint arXiv:1710.04087*.

Raj Dabre, Chenhui Chu, and Anoop Kunchukuttan. 2019. A survey of multilingual neural machine translation. *arXiv preprint arXiv:1905.05395*.

Jacob Devlin, Ming-Wei Chang, Kenton Lee, and Kristina Toutanova. 2019. Bert: Pre-training of deep bidirectional transformers for language understanding. In *Proceedings of the 2019 Conference of the North American Chapter of the Association for Computational Linguistics: Human Language Technologies, Volume 1 (Long and Short Papers)*, pages 4171–4186.

Xiangyu Duan, Baijun Ji, Hao Jia, Min Tan, Min Zhang, Boxing Chen, Weihua Luo, and Yue Zhang. 2020. Bilingual dictionary based neural machine translation without using parallel sentences. In *Proceedings of the 58th Annual Meeting of the Association for Computational Linguistics*, pages 1570–1579.

Abteen Ebrahim, Manuel Mager, Pavel Oncevay Arturo Danni Liu Koneru Sai Ugan Enes Yavuz Wiemerslage, Adam Denisov, Zhaolin Li, Jan Niehues, Monica Romero, Ivan G Torre, Tanel Alumäe, Jiaming Kong, Sergey Polezhaev, Yury Belousov, Wei-Rui Chen, Peter Sullivan, Ife Adebara, Bashar Talafha, Inciarte Alcides Alcoba, Muhammad Abdul-Mageed, Luis Chiruzzo, Rolando Coto-Solano, Hilaria Cruz, Sofía Flores-Solórzano, Aldo Andrés Alvarez López, Ivan Meza-Ruiz, John E. Ortega, Alexis Palmer, Rodolfo Joel Zevallos Salazar, Kristine, Thang Vu Stenzel, and Katharina Kann. 2023. Findings of the second americasnlp competition on speech-to-text translation. *preprint*.

Abteen Ebrahimi, Manuel Mager, Arturo Oncevay, Vishrav Chaudhary, Luis Chiruzzo, Angela Fan, John Ortega, Ricardo Ramos, Annette Rios, Ivan Vladimir Meza Ruiz, Gustavo Giménez-Lugo, Elisabeth Mager, Graham Neubig, Alexis Palmer, Rolando Coto-Solano, Thang Vu, and Katharina Kann. 2022. AmericasNLI: Evaluating zero-shot natural language understanding of pretrained multilingual models in truly low-resource languages. In *Proceedings of the 60th Annual Meeting of the Association for Computational Linguistics (Volume 1: Long Papers)*, pages 6279–6299, Dublin, Ireland. Association for Computational Linguistics.

Abteen Ebrahimi, Manuel Mager, Arturo Oncevay, Vishrav Chaudhary, Luis Chiruzzo, Angela Fan, John Ortega, Ricardo Ramos, Annette Rios, Ivan Vladimir, Gustavo A. Giménez-Lugo, Elisabeth Mager, Graham Neubig, Alexis Palmer, Rolando A. Coto Solano, Ngoc Thang Vu, and Katharina Kann. 2021. Americasnli: Evaluating zero-shot natural language understanding of pretrained multilingual models in truly low-resource languages.

Abteen Ebrahimi, Manuel Mager, Arturo Oncevay, Enora Rice, Cynthia Montaño, John Ortega, Shruti Rijhwani, Alexis Palmer, Rolando Coto-Solano, Hilaria Cruz, and Katharina Kann. 2023. Findings of the AmericasNLP 2023 shared task on machine translation into indigenous languages. In *Proceedings of the Third Workshop on Natural Language Processing for Indigenous Languages of the Americas*. Association for Computational Linguistics.

Javid Ebrahimi, Daniel Lowd, and Dejing Dou. 2018. On adversarial examples for character-level neural machine translation. In *Proceedings of the 27th International Conference on Computational Linguistics*, pages 653–663, Santa Fe, New Mexico, USA. Association for Computational Linguistics.

Sergey Edunov, Alexei Baevski, and Michael Auli. 2019. Pre-trained language model representations for language generation. In *Proceedings of the 2019 Conference of the North American Chapter of the Association for Computational Linguistics: Human Language Technologies, Volume 1 (Long and Short Papers)*, pages 4052–4059.

Sergey Edunov, Myle Ott, Michael Auli, and David Grangier. 2018. Understanding back-translation at scale. In *Proceedings of the 2018 Conference on Empirical Methods in Natural Language Processing*, pages 489–500.

Marzieh Fadaee, Arianna Bisazza, and Christof Monz. 2017. Data augmentation for low-resource neural machine translation. In *Proceedings of the 55th Annual Meeting of the Association for Computational Linguistics (Volume 2: Short Papers)*, pages 567–573.

Isaac Feldman and Rolando Coto-Solano. 2020. Neural machine translation models with back-translation for the extremely low-resource indigenous language Bribri. In *Proceedings of the 28th International Conference on Computational Linguistics*, pages 3965–3976, Barcelona, Spain (Online). International Committee on Computational Linguistics.

Manuel Fernández-Delgado, Eva Cernadas, Senén Barro, and Dinani Amorim. 2014. Do we need hundreds of classifiers to solve real world classification problems? *The journal of machine learning research*, 15(1):3133–3181.

Alexander Fraser. 2020. Findings of the WMT 2020 shared tasks in unsupervised MT and very low resource supervised MT. In *Proceedings of the Fifth Conference on Machine Translation*, pages 765–771, Online. Association for Computational Linguistics.

Ana-Paula Galarreta, Andrés Melgar, and Arturo Oncevay. 2017. Corpus creation and initial SMT experiments between Spanish and Shipibo-konibo. In *Proceedings of the International Conference Recent Advances in Natural Language Processing, RANLP 2017*, pages 238–244, Varna, Bulgaria. INCOMA Ltd.

Candace Kaleimamoowahinekapu Galla. 2016. Indigenous language revitalization, promotion, and education: Function of digital technology. *Computer Assisted Language Learning*, 29(7):1137–1151.

Xavier Garcia, Pierre Foret, Thibault Sellam, and Ankur P Parikh. 2020. A multilingual view of unsupervised machine translation. *arXiv preprint arXiv:2002.02955*.

Mozhdeh Gheini, Xiang Ren, and Jonathan May. 2021. Cross-attention is all you need: Adapting pretrained Transformers for machine translation. In *Proceedings of the 2021 Conference on Empirical Methods in Natural Language Processing*, pages 1754–1765, Online and Punta Cana, Dominican Republic. Association for Computational Linguistics.

Santiago Góngora, Nicolás Giossa, and Luis Chiruzzo. 2021. Experiments on a Guarani corpus of news and social media. In *Proceedings of the First Workshop on Natural Language Processing for Indigenous Languages of the Americas*, pages 153–158, Online. Association for Computational Linguistics.

Santiago Góngora, Nicolás Giossa, and Luis Chiruzzo. 2022. Can we use word embeddings for enhancing Guarani-Spanish machine translation? In *Proceedings of the Fifth Workshop on the Use of Computational Methods in the Study of Endangered Languages*, pages 127–132, Dublin, Ireland. Association for Computational Linguistics.

Yvette Graham, Barry Haddow, and Philipp Koehn. 2020. Statistical power and translationese in machine translation evaluation. In *Proceedings of the 2020 Conference on Empirical Methods in Natural Language Processing (EMNLP)*, pages 72–81, Online. Association for Computational Linguistics.

Stig-Arne Grönroos, Sami Virpioja, Peter Smit, and Mikko Kurimo. 2014. Morfessor flatcat: An hmm-based method for unsupervised and semi-supervised learning of morphology. In *Proceedings of COLING 2014, the 25th International Conference on Computational Linguistics: Technical Papers*, pages 1177–1185.

Jiatao Gu, Yong Wang, Kyunghyun Cho, and Victor OK Li. 2019. Improved zero-shot neural machine translation via ignoring spurious correlations. In *Proceedings of the 57th Annual Meeting of the Association for Computational Linguistics*, pages 1258–1268.

Caglar Gulcehre, Orhan Firat, Kelvin Xu, Kyunghyun Cho, Loic Barrault, Huei-Chi Lin, Fethi Bougares, Holger Schwenk, and Yoshua Bengio. 2015. On using monolingual corpora in neural machine translation. *arXiv preprint arXiv:1503.03535*.

Ximena Gutierrez-Vasques, Gerardo Sierra, and Isaac Hernandez Pompa. 2016. Axolotl: a web accessible parallel corpus for Spanish-Nahuatl. In *Proceedings of the Tenth International Conference on Language Resources and Evaluation (LREC'16)*, pages 4210–4214, Portorož, Slovenia. European Language Resources Association (ELRA).

Barry Haddow, Rachel Bawden, Antonio Valerio Miceli Barone, Jindřich Helcl, and Alexandra Birch. 2022. Survey of low-resource machine translation. *Computational Linguistics*, pages 1–67.

Lifeng Han. 2016. Machine translation evaluation resources and methods: A survey. *arXiv preprint arXiv:1605.04515*.

François Hernandez and Vincent Nguyen. 2020. The ubiqus English-Inuktitut system for WMT20. In *Proceedings of the Fifth Conference on Machine Translation*, pages 213–217, Online. Association for Computational Linguistics.

Nikolaus P Himmelmann. 2008. Language documentation: What is it and what is it good for? In *Essentials of language documentation*, pages 1–30. De Gruyter Mouton.

Vu Cong Duy Hoang, Philipp Koehn, Gholamreza Haffari, and Trevor Cohn. 2018. Iterative back-translation for neural machine translation. In *Proceedings of the 2nd Workshop on Neural Machine Translation and Generation*, pages 18–24.

Sepp Hochreiter and Jürgen Schmidhuber. 1997. Long short-term memory. *Neural computation*, 9(8):1735–1780.

J Edward Hu, Huda Khayrallah, Ryan Culkin, Patrick Xia, Tongfei Chen, Matt Post, and Benjamin Van Durme. 2019. Improved lexically constrained decoding for translation and monolingual rewriting. In *Proceedings of the 2019 Conference of the North American Chapter of the Association for Computational Linguistics: Human Language Technologies, Volume 1 (Long and Short Papers)*, pages 839–850.

W John Hutchins. 2004. The georgetown-ibm experiment demonstrated in january 1954. In *Conference of the Association for Machine Translation in the Americas*, pages 102–114. Springer.

Sébastien Jean, Kyunghyun Cho, Roland Memisevic, and Yoshua Bengio. 2015. On using very large target vocabulary for neural machine translation. In *Proceedings of the 53rd Annual Meeting of the Association for Computational Linguistics and the 7th International Joint Conference on Natural Language Processing (Volume 1: Long Papers)*, pages 1–10, Beijing, China. Association for Computational Linguistics.

Eric Joanis, Rebecca Knowles, Roland Kuhn, Samuel Larkin, Patrick Littell, Chi-kiu Lo, Darlene Stewart, and Jeffrey Micher. 2020. The Nunavut Hansard Inuktitut–English parallel corpus 3.0 with preliminary machine translation results. In *Proceedings of the 12th Language Resources and Evaluation Conference*, pages 2562–2572, Marseille, France. European Language Resources Association.

Melvin Johnson, Mike Schuster, Quoc V Le, Maxim Krikun, Yonghui Wu, Zhifeng Chen, Nikhil Thorat, Fernanda Viégas, Martin Wattenberg, Greg Corrado, et al. 2017. Google's multilingual neural machine translation system: Enabling zero-shot translation. *Transactions of the Association for Computational Linguistics*, 5:339–351.

David Kamholz, Jonathan Pool, and Susan M Colowick. 2014. Panlex: Building a resource for panlingual lexical translation. In *LREC*, pages 3145–3150.

Katharina Kann, Jesus Manuel Mager Hois, Ivan Vladimir Meza-Ruiz, and Hinrich Schütze. 2018. Fortification of neural morphological segmentation models for polysynthetic minimal-resource languages. In *Proceedings of the 2018 Conference of the North American Chapter of the Association for Computational Linguistics: Human Language Technologies, Volume 1 (Long Papers)*, pages 47–57, New Orleans, Louisiana. Association for Computational Linguistics.

Kenji Kawaguchi, Leslie Pack Kaelbling, and Yoshua Bengio. 2017. Generalization in deep learning. *arXiv preprint arXiv:1710.05468*.

Huda Khayrallah, Brian Thompson, Matt Post, and Philipp Koehn. 2020. Simulated multiple reference training improves low-resource machine translation. *arXiv preprint arXiv:2004.14524*.

Rebecca Knowles, Darlene Stewart, Samuel Larkin, and Patrick Littell. 2020. NRC systems for the 2020 Inuktitut-English news translation task. In *Proceedings of the Fifth Conference on Machine Translation*, pages 156–170, Online. Association for Computational Linguistics.

Rebecca Knowles, Darlene Stewart, Samuel Larkin, and Patrick Littell. 2021. NRC-CNRC machine translation systems for the 2021 AmericasNLP shared task. In *Proceedings of the First Workshop on Natural Language Processing for Indigenous Languages of the Americas*, pages 224–233, Online. Association for Computational Linguistics.

Sosuke Kobayashi. 2018. Contextual augmentation: Data augmentation by words with paradigmatic relations. In *Proceedings of the 2018 Conference of the North American Chapter of the Association for Computational Linguistics: Human Language Technologies, Volume 2 (Short Papers)*, pages 452–457.

Tom Kocmi. 2020. CUNI submission for the Inuktitut language in WMT news 2020. In *Proceedings of the Fifth Conference on Machine Translation*, pages 171–174, Online. Association for Computational Linguistics.

Michael Krauss. 1992. The world's languages in crisis. *Language*, 68(1):4–10.

Mateusz Krubiński, Marcin Chochowski, Bartłomiej Boczek, Mikołaj Koszowski, Adam Dobrowolski, Marcin Szymański, and Paweł Przybysz. 2020. Samsung R&D institute Poland submission to WMT20 news translation task. In *Proceedings of the Fifth Conference on Machine Translation*, pages 181–190, Online. Association for Computational Linguistics.

Surafel M Lakew, Quintino F Lotito, Matteo Negri, Marco Turchi, and Marcello Federico. 2018. Improving zero-shot translation of low-resource languages. In *Proceedings of the 14h IWSLT*, pages 113–119.

Guillaume Lample, Alexis Conneau, Ludovic Denoyer, and Marc'Aurelio Ranzato. 2017. Unsupervised machine translation using monolingual corpora only. *arXiv preprint arXiv:1711.00043*.

Sahinur Rahman Laskar, Abdullah Faiz Ur Rahman Khilji, Partha Pakray, and Sivaji Bandyopadhyay. 2020. Zero-shot neural machine translation: Russian-Hindi @LoResMT 2020. In *Proceedings of the 3rd Workshop on Technologies for MT of Low Resource Languages*, pages 38–42, Suzhou, China. Association for Computational Linguistics.

Yichong Leng, Xu Tan, Tao Qin, Xiang-Yang Li, and Tie-Yan Liu. 2019. Unsupervised pivot translation for distant languages. In *Proceedings of the 57th Annual Meeting of the Association for Computational Linguistics*, pages 175–183.

M Paul Lewis. 2009. *Ethnologue: Languages of the world.* SIL international.

M Paul Lewis and Gary F Simons. 2010. Assessing endangerment: expanding fishman's gids. *Revue roumaine de linguistique*, 55(2):103–120.

Mike Lewis, Yinhan Liu, Naman Goyal, Marjan Ghazvininejad, Abdelrahman Mohamed, Omer Levy, Ves Stoyanov, and Luke Zettlemoyer. 2019. Bart: Denoising sequence-to-sequence pre-training for natural language generation, translation, and comprehension. *arXiv preprint arXiv:1910.13461*.

Zuchao Li, Rui Wang, Kehai Chen, Masso Utiyama, Eiichiro Sumita, Zhuosheng Zhang, and Hai Zhao. 2020. Data-dependent gaussian prior objective for language generation. In *International Conference on Learning Representations*.

Zehui Lin, Xiao Pan, Mingxuan Wang, Xipeng Qiu, Jiangtao Feng, Hao Zhou, and Lei Li. 2020. Pre-training multilingual neural machine translation by leveraging alignment information. In *Proceedings of the 2020 Conference on Empirical Methods in Natural Language Processing (EMNLP)*, pages

2649–2663, Online. Association for Computational Linguistics.

Wang Ling, Isabel Trancoso, Chris Dyer, and Alan W Black. 2015. Character-based neural machine translation. *arXiv preprint arXiv:1511.04586*.

Patrick Littell, Anna Kazantseva, Roland Kuhn, Aidan Pine, Antti Arppe, Christopher Cox, and Marie-Odile Junker. 2018. Indigenous language technologies in Canada: Assessment, challenges, and successes. In *Proceedings of the 27th International Conference on Computational Linguistics*, pages 2620–2632, Santa Fe, New Mexico, USA. Association for Computational Linguistics.

Yinhan Liu, Jiatao Gu, Naman Goyal, Xian Li, Sergey Edunov, Marjan Ghazvininejad, Mike Lewis, and Luke Zettlemoyer. 2020. Multilingual denoising pre-training for neural machine translation. *arXiv preprint arXiv:2001.08210*.

Zihan Liu, Yan Xu, Genta Indra Winata, and Pascale Fung. 2019. Incorporating word and subword units in unsupervised machine translation using language model rescoring. In *Proceedings of the Fourth Conference on Machine Translation (Volume 2: Shared Task Papers, Day 1)*, pages 275–282.

Zoey Liu, Crystal Richardson, Richard Hatcher Jr, and Emily Prud'hommeaux. 2022. Not always about you: Prioritizing community needs when developing endangered language technology. *arXiv preprint arXiv:2204.05541*.

Chi-kiu Lo. 2020. Extended study on using pretrained language models and YiSi-1 for machine translation evaluation. In *Proceedings of the Fifth Conference on Machine Translation*, pages 895–902, Online. Association for Computational Linguistics.

Wolfgang Lörscher. 2005. The translation process: Methods and problems of its investigation. *Meta: journal des traducteurs/Meta: Translators' Journal*, 50(2):597–608.

Bruce T Lowerre. 1976. The harpy speech recognition system. Technical report, CARNEGIE-MELLON UNIV PITTSBURGH PA DEPT OF COMPUTER SCIENCE.

Yichao Lu, Phillip Keung, Faisal Ladhak, Vikas Bhardwaj, Shaonan Zhang, and Jason Sun. 2018. A neural interlingua for multilingual machine translation. In *Proceedings of the Third Conference on Machine Translation: Research Papers*, pages 84–92.

Thang Luong, Ilya Sutskever, Quoc Le, Oriol Vinyals, and Wojciech Zaremba. 2015. Addressing the rare word problem in neural machine translation. In *Proceedings of the 53rd Annual Meeting of the Association for Computational Linguistics and the 7th International Joint Conference on Natural Language Processing (Volume 1: Long Papers)*, pages 11–19, Beijing, China. Association for Computational Linguistics.

Manuel Mager, Diónico Carrillo, and Ivan Meza. 2018a. Probabilistic finite-state morphological segmenter for wixarika (huichol) language. *Journal of Intelligent & Fuzzy Systems*, 34(5):3081–3087.

Manuel Mager, Özlem Çetinoğlu, and Katharina Kann. 2019. Subword-level language identification for intra-word code-switching. In *Proceedings of the 2019 Conference of the North American Chapter of the Association for Computational Linguistics: Human Language Technologies, Volume 1 (Long and Short Papers)*, pages 2005–2011, Minneapolis, Minnesota. Association for Computational Linguistics.

Manuel Mager, Özlem Çetinoğlu, and Katharina Kann. 2020. Tackling the low-resource challenge for canonical segmentation. *arXiv preprint arXiv:2010.02804*.

Manuel Mager, Ximena Gutierrez-Vasques, Gerardo Sierra, and Ivan Meza-Ruiz. 2018b. Challenges of language technologies for the indigenous languages of the Americas. In *Proceedings of the 27th International Conference on Computational Linguistics*, pages 55–69, Santa Fe, New Mexico, USA. Association for Computational Linguistics.

Manuel Mager, Elisabeth Mager, Katharina Kann, and Ngoc Thang Vu. 2023. Ethical considerations for machine translation of indigenous languages: Giving a voice to the speakers. *arXiv preprint arXiv:2305.19474*.

Manuel Mager, Elisabeth Mager, Alfonso Medina-Urrea, Ivan Vladimir Meza Ruiz, and Katharina Kann. 2018c. Lost in translation: Analysis of information loss during machine translation between polysynthetic and fusional languages. In *Proceedings of the Workshop on Computational Modeling of Polysynthetic Languages*, pages 73–83, Santa Fe, New Mexico, USA. Association for Computational Linguistics.

Manuel Mager and Ivan Meza. 2021. Retos en construcción de traductores automáticos para lenguas indígenas de México. *Digital Scholarship in the Humanities*, 36.

Manuel Mager, Arturo Oncevay, Abteen Ebrahimi, John Ortega, Annette Rios, Angela Fan, Ximena Gutierrez-Vasques, Luis Chiruzzo, Gustavo Giménez-Lugo, Ricardo Ramos, Anna Currey, Vishrav Chaudhary, Ivan Vladimir Meza Ruiz, Rolando Coto-Solano, Alexis Palmer, Elisabeth Mager, Ngoc Thang Vu, Graham Neubig, and Katharina Kann. 2021. Findings of the AmericasNLP 2021 Shared Task on Open Machine Translation for Indigenous Languages of the Americas. In *Proceedings of theThe First Workshop on NLP for Indigenous Languages of the Americas*, Online. Association for Computational Linguistics.

Manuel Mager, Arturo Oncevay, Elisabeth Mager, Katharina Kann, and Thang Vu. 2022. BPE vs. morphological segmentation: A case study on machine translation of four polysynthetic languages. In *Findings of the Association for Computational Linguistics: ACL 2022*, pages 961–971, Dublin, Ireland. Association for Computational Linguistics.

Chaitanya Malaviya, Graham Neubig, and Patrick Littell. 2017. Learning language representations for typology prediction. In *Proceedings of the 2017 Conference on Empirical Methods in Natural Language Processing*, pages 2529–2535.

Benjamin Marie, Raphael Rubino, and Atsushi Fujita. 2020. Tagged back-translation revisited: Why does it really work? In *Proceedings of the 58th Annual Meeting of the Association for Computational Linguistics*, pages 5990–5997, Online. Association for Computational Linguistics.

Joel Martin, Howard Johnson, Benoit Farley, and Anna Maclachlan. 2003. Aligning and using an english-inuktitut parallel corpus. In *Proceedings of the HLT-NAACL 2003 Workshop on Building and using parallel texts: data driven machine translation and beyond-Volume 3*, pages 115–118. Association for Computational Linguistics.

Thomas Mayer and Michael Cysouw. 2014. Creating a massively parallel bible corpus. *Oceania*, 135(273):40.

Arya D. McCarthy, Rachel Wicks, Dylan Lewis, Aaron Mueller, Winston Wu, Oliver Adams, Garrett Nicolai, Matt Post, and David Yarowsky. 2020. The johns hopkins university bible corpus: 1600+ tongues for typological exploration. In *Proceedings of The 12th Language Resources and Evaluation Conference*, pages 2884–2892, Marseille, France. European Language Resources Association.

Norman A McQuown. 1955. The indigenous languages of latin america. *American Anthropologist*, 57(3):501–570.

Antonio Valerio Miceli-Barone, Jindřich Helcl, Rico Sennrich, Barry Haddow, and Alexandra Birch. 2017. Deep architectures for neural machine translation. In *Proceedings of the Second Conference on Machine Translation*, pages 99–107.

Tomas Mikolov, Kai Chen, Greg Corrado, and Jeffrey Dean. 2013. Efficient estimation of word representations in vector space. *arXiv preprint arXiv:1301.3781*.

Marianne Mithun. 1986. On the nature of noun incorporation. *Language*, 62(1):32–37.

Oscar Moreno. 2021. The REPU CS' Spanish–Quechua submission to the AmericasNLP 2021 shared task on open machine translation. In *Proceedings of the First Workshop on Natural Language Processing for Indigenous Languages of the Americas*, pages 241–247, Online. Association for Computational Linguistics.

El Moatez Billah Nagoudi, Wei-Rui Chen, Muhammad Abdul-Mageed, and Hasan Cavusoglu. 2021. IndT5: A text-to-text transformer for 10 indigenous languages. In *Proceedings of the First Workshop on Natural Language Processing for Indigenous Languages of the Americas*, pages 265–271, Online. Association for Computational Linguistics.

Wilhelmina Nekoto, Vukosi Marivate, Tshinondiwa Matsila, Timi Fasubaa, Taiwo Fagbohungbe, Solomon Oluwole Akinola, Shamsuddeen Muhammad, Salomon Kabongo Kabenamualu, Salomey Osei, Freshia Sackey, Rubungo Andre Niyongabo, Ricky Macharm, Perez Ogayo, Orevaoghene Ahia, Musie Meressa Berhe, Mofetoluwa Adeyemi, Masabata Mokgesi-Selinga, Lawrence Okegbemi, Laura Martinus, Kolawole Tajudeen, Kevin Degila, Kelechi Ogueji, Kathleen Siminyu, Julia Kreutzer, Jason Webster, Jamiil Toure Ali, Jade Abbott, Iroro Orife, Ignatius Ezeani, Idris Abdulkadir Dangana, Herman Kamper, Hady Elsahar, Goodness Duru, Ghollah Kioko, Murhabazi Espoir, Elan van Biljon, Daniel Whitenack, Christopher Onyefuluchi, Chris Chinenye Emezue, Bonaventure F. P. Dossou, Blessing Sibanda, Blessing Bassey, Ayodele Olabiyi, Arshath Ramkilowan, Alp Öktem, Adewale Akinfaderin, and Abdallah Bashir. 2020. Participatory research for low-resourced machine translation: A case study in African languages. In *Findings of the Association for Computational Linguistics: EMNLP 2020*, pages 2144–2160, Online. Association for Computational Linguistics.

Graham Neubig. 2017. Neural machine translation and sequence-to-sequence models: A tutorial. *arXiv preprint arXiv:1703.01619*.

Graham Neubig and Junjie Hu. 2018. Rapid adaptation of neural machine translation to new languages. In *Proceedings of the 2018 Conference on Empirical Methods in Natural Language Processing*, pages 875–880.

Tan Ngoc Le and Fatiha Sadat. 2020. Revitalization of indigenous languages through pre-processing and neural machine translation: The case of Inuktitut. In *Proceedings of the 28th International Conference on Computational Linguistics*, pages 4661–4666, Barcelona, Spain (Online). International Committee on Computational Linguistics.

Dat Quoc Nguyen, Kairit Sirts, and Mark Johnson. 2015. Improving topic coherence with latent feature word representations in MAP estimation for topic modeling. In *Proceedings of the Australasian Language Technology Association Workshop 2015*, pages 116–121, Parramatta, Australia.

Toan Q Nguyen and David Chiang. 2017. Transfer learning across low-resource, related languages for neural machine translation. In *Proceedings of the Eighth International Joint Conference on Natural Language Processing (Volume 2: Short Papers)*, pages 296–301.

Eugene Nida. 1945. Linguistics and ethnology in translation-problems. *Word*, 1(2):194–208.

Jan Niehues and Eunah Cho. 2017. Exploiting linguistic resources for neural machine translation using multi-task learning. In *Proceedings of the Second Conference on Machine Translation*, pages 80–89, Copenhagen, Denmark. Association for Computational Linguistics.

Jan Niehues, Eunah Cho, Thanh-Le Ha, and Alex Waibel. 2016. Pre-translation for neural machine translation. In *Proceedings of COLING 2016, the 26th International Conference on Computational Linguistics: Technical Papers*, pages 1828–1836, Osaka, Japan. The COLING 2016 Organizing Committee.

Farhad Nooralahzadeh, Giannis Bekoulis, Johannes Bjerva, and Isabelle Augenstein. 2020. Zero-shot cross-lingual transfer with meta learning. *arXiv preprint arXiv:2003.02739*.

Atul Kr. Ojha, Valentin Malykh, Alina Karakanta, and Chao-Hong Liu. 2020. Findings of the LoResMT 2020 shared task on zero-shot for low-resource languages. In *Proceedings of the 3rd Workshop on Technologies for MT of Low Resource Languages*, pages 33–37, Suzhou, China. Association for Computational Linguistics.

Matthew Olson, Abraham Wyner, and Richard Berk. 2018. Modern neural networks generalize on small data sets. In *Advances in Neural Information Processing Systems*, pages 3619–3628.

Arturo Oncevay. 2021. Peru is multilingual, its machine translation should be too? In *Proceedings of the First Workshop on Natural Language Processing for Indigenous Languages of the Americas*, pages 194–201, Online. Association for Computational Linguistics.

Iroro Orife, Julia Kreutzer, Blessing Sibanda, Daniel Whitenack, Kathleen Siminyu, Laura Martinus, Jamiil Toure Ali, Jade Abbott, Vukosi Marivate, Salomon Kabongo, et al. 2020. Masakhane–machine translation for africa. *arXiv preprint arXiv:2003.11529*.

John E Ortega, Richard Castro Mamani, and Kyunghyun Cho. 2020a. Neural machine translation with a polysynthetic low resource language. *Machine Translation*, 34(4):325–346.

John E Ortega, Richard Alexander Castro-Mamani, and Jaime Rafael Montoya Samame. 2020b. Overcoming resistance: The normalization of an Amazonian tribal language. In *Proceedings of the 3rd Workshop on Technologies for MT of Low Resource Languages*, pages 1–13, Suzhou, China. Association for Computational Linguistics.

Yirong Pan, Xiao Li, Yating Yang, and Rui Dong. 2020. Multi-task neural model for agglutinative language translation. In *Proceedings of the 58th Annual Meeting of the Association for Computational Linguistics: Student Research Workshop*, pages 103–110, Online. Association for Computational Linguistics.

Kishore Papineni, Salim Roukos, Todd Ward, and Wei-Jing Zhu. 2002. Bleu: a method for automatic evaluation of machine translation. In *Proceedings of the 40th Annual Meeting of the Association for Computational Linguistics*, pages 311–318, Philadelphia, Pennsylvania, USA. Association for Computational Linguistics.

Shantipriya Parida, Subhadarshi Panda, Amulya Dash, Esau Villatoro-Tello, A. Seza Doğruöz, Rosa M. Ortega-Mendoza, Amadeo Hernández, Yashvardhan Sharma, and Petr Motlicek. 2021. Open machine translation for low resource South American languages (AmericasNLP 2021 shared task contribution). In *Proceedings of the First Workshop on Natural Language Processing for Indigenous Languages of the Americas*, pages 218–223, Online. Association for Computational Linguistics.

Jeffrey Pennington, Richard Socher, and Christopher Manning. 2014. GloVe: Global vectors for word representation. In *Proceedings of the 2014 Conference on Empirical Methods in Natural Language Processing (EMNLP)*, pages 1532–1543, Doha, Qatar. Association for Computational Linguistics.

Asya Pereltsvaig. 2020. *Languages of the World*. Cambridge University Press.

Matthew Peters, Mark Neumann, Mohit Iyyer, Matt Gardner, Christopher Clark, Kenton Lee, and Luke Zettlemoyer. 2018. Deep contextualized word representations. In *Proceedings of the 2018 Conference of the North American Chapter of the Association for Computational Linguistics: Human Language Technologies, Volume 1 (Long Papers)*, pages 2227–2237.

Alberto Poncelas, Maja Popović, Dimitar Shterionov, Gideon Maillette de Buy Wenniger, and Andy Way. 2019. Combining pbsmt and nmt back-translated data for efficient nmt. In *Proceedings of the International Conference on Recent Advances in Natural Language Processing (RANLP 2019)*, pages 922–931.

Maja Popović. 2017. chrf++: words helping character n-grams. In *Proceedings of the second conference on machine translation*, pages 612–618.

Nima Pourdamghani and Kevin Knight. 2019. Neighbors helping the poor: improving low-resource machine translation using related languages. *Machine Translation*, 33(3):239–258.

Ofir Press and Lior Wolf. 2017. Using the output embedding to improve language models. In *Proceedings of the 15th Conference of the European Chapter of the Association for Computational Linguistics: Volume 2, Short Papers*, pages 157–163.

Colin Raffel, Noam Shazeer, Adam Roberts, Katherine Lee, Sharan Narang, Michael Matena, Yanqi Zhou, Wei Li, and Peter J Liu. 2020. Exploring the limits of transfer learning with a unified text-to-text transformer. *Journal of Machine Learning Research*, 21:1–67.

Alessandro Raganato, Raúl Vázquez, Mathias Creutz, and Jörg Tiedemann. 2021. An empirical investigation of word alignment supervision for zero-shot multilingual neural machine translation. In *Proceedings of the 2021 Conference on Empirical Methods in Natural Language Processing*, pages 8449–8456, Online and Punta Cana, Dominican Republic. Association for Computational Linguistics.

Surangika Ranathunga, En-Shiun Annie Lee, Marjana Prifti Skenduli, Ravi Shekhar, Mehreen Alam, and Rishemjit Kaur. 2021. Neural machine translation for low-resource languages: A survey. *arXiv preprint arXiv:2106.15115*.

Shuo Ren, Yu Wu, Shujie Liu, Ming Zhou, and Shuai Ma. 2020. A retrieve-and-rewrite initialization method for unsupervised machine translation. In *Proceedings of the 58th Annual Meeting of the Association for Computational Linguistics*, pages 3498–3504, Online. Association for Computational Linguistics.

Parker Riley, Isaac Caswell, Markus Freitag, and David Grangier. 2020. Translationese as a language in "multilingual" NMT. In *Proceedings of the 58th Annual Meeting of the Association for Computational Linguistics*, pages 7737–7746, Online. Association for Computational Linguistics.

Christian Roest, Lukas Edman, Gosse Minnema, Kevin Kelly, Jennifer Spenader, and Antonio Toral. 2020. Machine translation for English–Inuktitut with segmentation, data acquisition and pre-training. In *Proceedings of the Fifth Conference on Machine Translation*, pages 274–281, Online. Association for Computational Linguistics.

David Rolnick, Andreas Veit, Serge Belongie, and Nir Shavit. 2017. Deep learning is robust to massive label noise. *arXiv preprint arXiv:1705.10694*.

Carlos Barron Romero, Jesús Manuel Mager Hois, and Fernando Reyes Avilés. 2016. Richard feynman, los alfabetos y los lenguajes. *Relingüística aplicada*, (19):2.

Mónica Jasso Rosales, Manuel Mager, and Ivan Vladimir Meza Ruız. Towards a twitter corpus of the indigenous languages of the americas.

Devendra Singh Sachan and Graham Neubig. 2018. Parameter sharing methods for multilingual self-attentional translation models. *arXiv preprint arXiv:1809.00252*.

Elizabeth Salesky, David Etter, and Matt Post. 2021. Robust open-vocabulary translation from visual text representations. *arXiv preprint arXiv:2104.08211*.

Jonne Saleva and Constantine Lignos. 2021. The effectiveness of morphology-aware segmentation in low-resource neural machine translation. In *Proceedings of the 16th Conference of the European Chapter of the Association for Computational Linguistics: Student Research Workshop*, pages 164–174, Online. Association for Computational Linguistics.

Motoki Sano, Jun Suzuki, and Shun Kiyono. 2019. Effective adversarial regularization for neural machine translation. In *Proceedings of the 57th Annual Meeting of the Association for Computational Linguistics*, pages 204–210.

Yves Scherrer, Stig-Arne Grönroos, and Sami Virpioja. 2020. The University of Helsinki and aalto university submissions to the WMT 2020 news and low-resource translation tasks. In *Proceedings of the Fifth Conference on Machine Translation*, pages 1129–1138, Online. Association for Computational Linguistics.

Lane Schwartz. 2022. Primum non nocere: Before working with indigenous data, the acl must confront ongoing colonialism. In *Proceedings of the 60th Annual Meeting of the Association for Computational Linguistics (Volume 2: Short Papers)*, pages 724–731.

Lane Schwartz, Francis Tyers, Lori Levin, Christo Kirov, Patrick Littell, Chi-kiu Lo, Emily Prud'hommeaux, Hyunji Hayley Park, Kenneth Steimel, Rebecca Knowles, et al. 2020. Neural polysynthetic language modelling. *arXiv preprint arXiv:2005.05477*.

Lee Sechrest, Todd L Fay, and SM Hafeez Zaidi. 1972. Problems of translation in cross-cultural research. *Journal of cross-cultural psychology*, 3(1):41–56.

Rico Sennrich, Barry Haddow, and Alexandra Birch. 2016a. Improving neural machine translation models with monolingual data. In *Proceedings of the 54th Annual Meeting of the Association for Computational Linguistics (Volume 1: Long Papers)*, pages 86–96, Berlin, Germany. Association for Computational Linguistics.

Rico Sennrich, Barry Haddow, and Alexandra Birch. 2016b. Improving neural machine translation models with monolingual data. In *Proceedings of the 54th Annual Meeting of the Association for Computational Linguistics (Volume 1: Long Papers)*, pages 86–96.

Rico Sennrich, Barry Haddow, and Alexandra Birch. 2016c. Neural machine translation of rare words with subword units. In *Proceedings of the 54th Annual Meeting of the Association for Computational Linguistics (Volume 1: Long Papers)*, pages 1715–1725, Berlin, Germany. Association for Computational Linguistics.

Joan Serra, Didac Suris, Marius Miron, and Alexandros Karatzoglou. 2018. Overcoming catastrophic forgetting with hard attention to the task. In *International*

Conference on Machine Learning, pages 4548–4557. PMLR.

Aditya Siddhant, Ankur Bapna, Yuan Cao, Orhan Firat, Mia Chen, Sneha Kudugunta, Naveen Arivazhagan, and Yonghui Wu. 2020. Leveraging monolingual data with self-supervision for multilingual neural machine translation. In *Proceedings of the 58th Annual Meeting of the Association for Computational Linguistics*, pages 2827–2835, Online. Association for Computational Linguistics.

Gerardo Sierra Martínez, Cynthia Montaño, Gemma Bel-Enguix, Diego Córdova, and Margarita Mota Montoya. 2020. CPLM, a parallel corpus for Mexican languages: Development and interface. In *Proceedings of the 12th Language Resources and Evaluation Conference*, pages 2947–2952, Marseille, France. European Language Resources Association.

Gary F Simons and M Paul Lewis. 2013. The world's languages in crisis. *Responses to language endangerment: In honor of Mickey Noonan. New directions in language documentation and language revitalization*, 3:20.

Peter Smit, Sami Virpioja, Stig-Arne Grönroos, Mikko Kurimo, et al. 2014. Morfessor 2.0: Toolkit for statistical morphological segmentation. In *The 14th Conference of the European Chapter of the Association for Computational Linguistics (EACL), Gothenburg, Sweden, April 26-30, 2014*. Aalto University.

Anders Søgaard, Sebastian Ruder, and Ivan Vulić. 2018. On the limitations of unsupervised bilingual dictionary induction. In *Proceedings of the 56th Annual Meeting of the Association for Computational Linguistics (Volume 1: Long Papers)*, pages 778–788.

Haiyue Song, Raj Dabre, Zhuoyuan Mao, Fei Cheng, Sadao Kurohashi, and Eiichiro Sumita. 2020. Pre-training via leveraging assisting languages and data selection for neural machine translation. *arXiv preprint arXiv:2001.08353*.

Kaitao Song, Xu Tan, Tao Qin, Jianfeng Lu, and Tie-Yan Liu. 2019. Mass: Masked sequence to sequence pre-training for language generation. In *International Conference on Machine Learning*, pages 5926–5936.

Xabier Soto, Dimitar Shterionov, Alberto Poncelas, and Andy Way. 2020. Selecting backtranslated data from multiple sources for improved neural machine translation. In *Proceedings of the 58th Annual Meeting of the Association for Computational Linguistics*, pages 3898–3908, Online. Association for Computational Linguistics.

Tejas Srinivasan, Ramon Sanabria, and Florian Metze. 2019. Multitask learning for different subword segmentations in neural machine translation. *arXiv preprint arXiv:1910.12368*.

Dario Stojanovski, Viktor Hangya, Matthias Huck, and Alexander Fraser. 2019. The lmu munich unsupervised machine translation system for wmt19. In *Proceedings of the Fourth Conference on Machine Translation (Volume 2: Shared Task Papers, Day 1)*, pages 393–399.

Haipeng Sun, Rui Wang, Kehai Chen, Masao Utiyama, Eiichiro Sumita, and Tiejun Zhao. 2020. Robust unsupervised neural machine translation with adversarial training. *arXiv preprint arXiv:2002.12549*.

Xu Tan, Yichong Leng, Jiale Chen, Yi Ren, Tao Qin, and Tie-Yan Liu. 2019. A study of multilingual neural machine translation. *arXiv preprint arXiv:1912.11625*.

Sarah G Thomason. 2015. *Endangered languages*. Cambridge University Press.

Jörg Tiedemann. 2016. Opus–parallel corpora for everyone. *Baltic Journal of Modern Computing*, page 384.

Jörg Tiedemann. 2018. Emerging language spaces learned from massively multilingual corpora. *arXiv preprint arXiv:1802.00273*.

Atnafu Lambebo Tonja, Christian Maldonado-Sifuentes, David Alejandro Mendoza Castillo, Olga Kolesnikova, Noé Castro-Sánchez, Grigori Sidorov, and Alexander Gelbukh. 2023. Parallel corpus for indigenous language translation: Spanish-mazatec and spanish-mixtec. *arXiv preprint arXiv:2305.17404*.

Antonio Toral, Sheila Castilho, Ke Hu, and Andy Way. 2018. Attaining the unattainable? reassessing claims of human parity in neural machine translation. In *Proceedings of the Third Conference on Machine Translation: Research Papers*, pages 113–123.

Hai-Long Trieu, Duc-Vu Tran, Ashwin Ittoo, and Le-Minh Nguyen. 2019. Leveraging additional resources for improving statistical machine translation on asian low-resource languages. *ACM Trans. Asian Low-Resour. Lang. Inf. Process.*, 18(3).

Masao Utiyama and Hitoshi Isahara. 2007. A comparison of pivot methods for phrase-based statistical machine translation. In *Human Language Technologies 2007: The Conference of the North American Chapter of the Association for Computational Linguistics; Proceedings of the Main Conference*, pages 484–491.

Clara Vania and Adam Lopez. 2017. From characters to words to in between: Do we capture morphology? In *Proceedings of the 55th Annual Meeting of the Association for Computational Linguistics (Volume 1: Long Papers)*, pages 2016–2027, Vancouver, Canada. Association for Computational Linguistics.

Ashish Vaswani, Noam Shazeer, Niki Parmar, Jakob Uszkoreit, Llion Jones, Aidan N Gomez, Łukasz Kaiser, and Illia Polosukhin. 2017. Attention is all you need. In *Advances in neural information processing systems*, pages 5998–6008.

Raúl Vázquez, Yves Scherrer, Sami Virpioja, and Jörg Tiedemann. 2021. The Helsinki submission to the AmericasNLP shared task. In *Proceedings of the First Workshop on Natural Language Processing for Indigenous Languages of the Americas*, pages 255–264, Online. Association for Computational Linguistics.

Ivan Vulić, Goran Glavaš, Roi Reichart, and Anna Korhonen. 2019. Do we really need fully unsupervised cross-lingual embeddings? In *Proceedings of the 2019 Conference on Empirical Methods in Natural Language Processing and the 9th International Joint Conference on Natural Language Processing (EMNLP-IJCNLP)*, pages 4407–4418, Hong Kong, China. Association for Computational Linguistics.

Ivan Vulić, Sebastian Ruder, and Anders Søgaard. 2020. Are all good word vector spaces isomorphic? *arXiv preprint arXiv:2004.04070*.

Liang Wang, Wei Zhao, Ruoyu Jia, Sujian Li, and Jingming Liu. 2019a. Denoising based sequence-to-sequence pre-training for text generation. In *Proceedings of the 2019 Conference on Empirical Methods in Natural Language Processing and the 9th International Joint Conference on Natural Language Processing (EMNLP-IJCNLP)*, pages 3994–4006.

Qiang Wang, Bei Li, Tong Xiao, Jingbo Zhu, Changliang Li, Derek F. Wong, and Lidia S. Chao. 2019b. Learning deep transformer models for machine translation. In *Proceedings of the 57th Annual Meeting of the Association for Computational Linguistics*, pages 1810–1822, Florence, Italy. Association for Computational Linguistics.

Rui Wang, Xu Tan, Renqian Luo, Tao Qin, and Tie-Yan Liu. 2021. A survey on low-resource neural machine translation. In *Proceedings of the Thirtieth International Joint Conference on Artificial Intelligence, IJCAI-21*, pages 4636–4643. International Joint Conferences on Artificial Intelligence Organization. Survey Track.

Xinyi Wang, Hieu Pham, Philip Arthur, and Graham Neubig. 2019c. Multilingual neural machine translation with soft decoupled encoding. In *International Conference on Learning Representations (ICLR)*, New Orleans, LA, USA.

Xinyi Wang, Yulia Tsvetkov, and Graham Neubig. 2020. Balancing training for multilingual neural machine translation. In *Proceedings of the 58th Annual Meeting of the Association for Computational Linguistics*, pages 8526–8537, Online. Association for Computational Linguistics.

Karl Weiss, Taghi M Khoshgoftaar, and DingDing Wang. 2016. A survey of transfer learning. *Journal of Big Data*, 3(1):9.

John Wieting, Taylor Berg-Kirkpatrick, Kevin Gimpel, and Graham Neubig. 2019. Beyond bleu: Training neural machine translation with semantic similarity. In *Proceedings of the 57th Annual Meeting of the Association for Computational Linguistics*, pages 4344–4355.

Hua Wu and Haifeng Wang. 2007. Pivot language approach for phrase-based statistical machine translation. *Machine Translation*, 21(3):165–181.

Xing Wu, Shangwen Lv, Liangjun Zang, Jizhong Han, and Songlin Hu. 2019. Conditional bert contextual augmentation. In *International Conference on Computational Science*, pages 84–95. Springer.

Haoran Xu, Benjamin Van Durme, and Kenton Murray. 2021. BERT, mBERT, or BiBERT? a study on contextualized embeddings for neural machine translation. In *Proceedings of the 2021 Conference on Empirical Methods in Natural Language Processing*, pages 6663–6675, Online and Punta Cana, Dominican Republic. Association for Computational Linguistics.

Linting Xue, Noah Constant, Adam Roberts, Mihir Kale, Rami Al-Rfou, Aditya Siddhant, Aditya Barua, and Colin Raffel. 2021. mt5: A massively multilingual pre-trained text-to-text transformer. In *Proceedings of the 2021 Conference of the North American Chapter of the Association for Computational Linguistics: Human Language Technologies*, pages 483–498.

Delfino Zacarías Márquez and Ivan Vladimir Meza Ruiz. 2021. Ayuuk-Spanish neural machine translator. In *Proceedings of the First Workshop on Natural Language Processing for Indigenous Languages of the Americas*, pages 168–172, Online. Association for Computational Linguistics.

Lenka Zajícová. 2017. Lenguas indígenas en la legislación de los países hispanoamericanos. *Onomázein*, (NE III):171–203.

Poorya Zaremoodi, Wray Buntine, and Gholamreza Haffari. 2018. Adaptive knowledge sharing in multi-task learning: Improving low-resource neural machine translation. In *Proceedings of the 56th Annual Meeting of the Association for Computational Linguistics (Volume 2: Short Papers)*, pages 656–661.

Rodolfo Zevallos, John Ortega, William Chen, Richard Castro, Núria Bel, Cesar Toshio, Renzo Venturas, Aradiel, and Hilario Nelsi Melgarejo. 2022. Introducing QuBERT: A large monolingual corpus and BERT model for Southern Quechua. In *Proceedings of the Third Workshop on Deep Learning for Low-Resource Natural Language Processing*, pages 1–13, Hybrid. Association for Computational Linguistics.

Biao Zhang, Philip Williams, Ivan Titov, and Rico Sennrich. 2020a. Improving massively multilingual neural machine translation and zero-shot translation. *arXiv preprint arXiv:2004.11867*.

Biao Zhang, Philip Williams, Ivan Titov, and Rico Sennrich. 2020b. Improving massively multilingual neural machine translation and zero-shot translation. In *Proceedings of the 58th Annual Meeting of the Association for Computational Linguistics*, pages 1628–1639, Online. Association for Computational Linguistics.

Shiyue Zhang, Ben Frey, and Mohit Bansal. 2022. How can nlp help revitalize endangered languages? a case study and roadmap for the cherokee language. *arXiv preprint arXiv:2204.11909*.

Shiyue Zhang, Benjamin Frey, and Mohit Bansal. 2020c. ChrEn: Cherokee-English machine translation for endangered language revitalization. In *Proceedings of the 2020 Conference on Empirical Methods in Natural Language Processing (EMNLP)*, pages 577–595, Online. Association for Computational Linguistics.

Shiyue Zhang, Benjamin Frey, and Mohit Bansal. 2021. ChrEnTranslate: Cherokee-English machine translation demo with quality estimation and corrective feedback. In *Proceedings of the 59th Annual Meeting of the Association for Computational Linguistics and the 11th International Joint Conference on Natural Language Processing: System Demonstrations*, pages 272–279, Online. Association for Computational Linguistics.

Tianyi Zhang, Varsha Kishore, Felix Wu, Kilian Q Weinberger, and Yoav Artzi. 2020d. Bertscore: Evaluating text generation with bert. In *ICLR*.

Yuhao Zhang, Ziyang Wang, Runzhe Cao, Binghao Wei, Weiqiao Shan, Shuhan Zhou, Abudurexiti Reheman, Tao Zhou, Xin Zeng, Laohu Wang, Yongyu Mu, Jingnan Zhang, Xiaoqian Liu, Xuanjun Zhou, Yinqiao Li, Bei Li, Tong Xiao, and Jingbo Zhu. 2020e. The NiuTrans machine translation systems for WMT20. In *Proceedings of the Fifth Conference on Machine Translation*, pages 338–345, Online. Association for Computational Linguistics.

Zhuosheng Zhang, Yafang Huang, and Hai Zhao. 2019. Open vocabulary learning for neural chinese pinyin ime. In *Proceedings of the 57th Annual Meeting of the Association for Computational Linguistics*, pages 1584–1594.

Francis Zheng, Machel Reid, Edison Marrese-Taylor, and Yutaka Matsuo. 2021. Low-resource machine translation using cross-lingual language model pretraining. In *Proceedings of the First Workshop on Natural Language Processing for Indigenous Languages of the Americas*, pages 234–240, Online. Association for Computational Linguistics.

Hao Zheng, Yong Cheng, and Yang Liu. 2017. Maximum expected likelihood estimation for zero-resource neural machine translation. In *IJCAI*, pages 4251–4257.

Shuyan Zhou, Xiangkai Zeng, Yingqi Zhou, Antonios Anastasopoulos, and Graham Neubig. 2019. Improving robustness of neural machine translation with multi-task learning. In *Proceedings of the Fourth Conference on Machine Translation (Volume 2: Shared Task Papers, Day 1)*, pages 565–571, Florence, Italy. Association for Computational Linguistics.

Changfeng Zhu, Heng Yu, Shanbo Cheng, and Weihua Luo. 2020a. Language-aware interlingua for multilingual neural machine translation. In *Proceedings of the 58th Annual Meeting of the Association for Computational Linguistics*, pages 1650–1655, Online. Association for Computational Linguistics.

Jinhua Zhu, Fei Gao, Lijun Wu, Yingce Xia, Tao Qin, Wengang Zhou, Xueqi Cheng, and Tie-Yan Liu. 2019. Soft contextual data augmentation for neural machine translation. *arXiv preprint arXiv:1905.10523*.

Jinhua Zhu, Yingce Xia, Lijun Wu, Di He, Tao Qin, Wengang Zhou, Houqiang Li, and Tie-Yan Liu. 2020b. Incorporating bert into neural machine translation. *arXiv preprint arXiv:2002.06823*.

Barret Zoph, Deniz Yuret, Jonathan May, and Kevin Knight. 2016. Transfer learning for low-resource neural machine translation. *arXiv preprint arXiv:1604.02201*.

A Appendix

In this appendix we expand the information regarding current work on MT for LRL.

A.1 Expanded LR work on Multilingual supervised training

Arivazhagan et al. (2019a) introduce a representational invariance training objective across languages that achieves comparable results with pivoting methods. Promising results of multilingual models have encouraged experiments with models trained on a massive amount of language pairs, resulting in large multilingual models: Aharoni et al. (2019) train a single model on 102 languages to and from English in contrast to the 58 languages used by Neubig and Hu (2018).

The negative aspect of this approach is the size of the network. Arivazhagan et al. (2019b) perform an extensive study on 102 language pairs to explore different settings and training setups and achieve good results for LRLs, while maintaining good performance for high-resource languages. Related massively multilingual NMT systems have been trained for analytic proposes (Tiedemann, 2018; Malaviya et al., 2017) and general zero-shot transfer learning (Artetxe and Schwenk, 2019). mRASP (Lin et al., 2020) use for pretraining of the multilingual model and add a randomly aligned substitution loss that aims to bring words and phrases closer in the cross-lingual space.

Zhang et al. (2020a) explores the main problems that arise for such models: multilingual NMT usually underperforms bilingual models (Arivazhagan et al., 2019b), the larger the number of languages gets the more the performance drops (Aharoni et al., 2019), languages in datasets used for multilingual training are unbalanced in size, and poor zero-shot performance compared to pivot models (cf. §6.3). Zhang et al. (2020a) addresses these problems with a language-aware input layer, a deep transformer architecture (Wang et al., 2019b), and an online back-translation approach. These modifications boost zero-shot translation performance for multilingual models.

To improve the problem of imbalanced and linguistically diverse training data, mostly heuristic methods have been proposed: Arivazhagan et al. (2019b) samples training data from different languages based on a data size scaled by temperature term. These heuristics have an impact on performance, and ignore other factors that are not size. Oversampling of data is used by Johnson et al. (2017); Neubig and Hu (2018); Conneau and Lample (2019). Wang et al. (2020) proposes a differentiable data selection method that automatically learns to weight training data, optimizing translation on all languages.

Multilingual modeling Sharing all parameters except for the attention mechanism shows improvements compared with sharing everything in an RNN NMT model (Blackwood et al., 2018). Sachan and Neubig (2018) explores parameter sharing in the transformer architecture for the decoder in the one-to-many translation setting and shows that transformers are more suitable than RNNs for this task. Also, parameter sharing in the decoder and embedding layer further improves performance. Lu et al. (2018) proposes a shared layer intended to capture the interlingua knowledge and an extension to the typical RNN network with multiple blocks along with a trainable routing network. The routing network enables adaptive collaboration by dynamic sharing of blocks conditioned on the task at hand, input, and model state (Zaremoodi et al., 2018). Zhang et al. (2020a) proposes a language-aware layer to improve such architectures further. With a similar idea, Zhu et al. (2020a) incorporates two special language embeddings into the self-attention mechanism. The first encodes the unique characteristics of each language, while the second captures common semantics across languages.

One problem in multilingual NMT systems is the translation into the wrong language. To address this problem, Zhang et al. (2020b) add a language-aware layer normalization and a linear transformation that is inserted between the encoder and the decoder to induce a language-specific translation. Raganato et al. (2021) explore to weight the target language label with jointly training one cross attention head with word alignments.

Other modifications of NMT model architectures to improve their performance on low-resource languages include: deep RNNs (Miceli-Barone et al., 2017), normalization layers (Ba et al., 2016), direct lexical connections (Nguyen et al., 2015), word embedding layers conducive to lexical sharing (Wang et al., 2019c).

A.2 Extended Multi-task training

Zhou et al. (2019) uses this approach, but extends it with a cascade architecture: the first decoder reads the encoder, and the second decoder reads the encoder and the first decoder (Niehues et al., 2016; Anastasopoulos and Chiang, 2018). The auxiliary task (first decoder) is a denoising decoder. With RNN NMT architectures, one can further decide if the attention mechanism should be shared among tasks (Niehues and Cho, 2017). The authors compare all architectures and find that they perform similarly, with only sharing the encoder being slightly better.

Using linguistic information as an auxiliary task has not yet been explored exhaustively. Niehues and Cho (2017) studies the usage of part-of-speech (POS) and named entity (NE) tags, finding that training on named entity recognition (NER), POS tagging and MT together improves performance the most. For agglutinative languages, morphological auxiliary tasks can be beneficial: Pan et al. (2020) uses stemming with fully shared parameters.

As an alternative to linguistically informed auxiliary tasks Srinivasan et al. (2019) uses multiple BPE vocabulary sizes to generate different segmentations. Each segmentation is treated as an individual task.

A.3 Data augmentation

Back-translation Caswell et al. (2019) shows that adding a special tag to the synthetic data improves performance. A technique that exploits this idea is training an initial translation model with synthetic data generated via BT and then finetune it with gold data (Abdulmumin et al., 2019). This simple yet effective training algorithm improves NMT for LRLs; however, it can also degrade performance on HRLs if trained without a tagging strategy (Marie et al., 2020).

Multiple improvements of BT have been proposed. Edunov et al. (2018) shows that sampling or noisy beam search can generate more effective pseudo-parallel data. However, for LRLs an optimal beam search and greedy decoding are better. A factor that influences BT's effectiveness is the quality of the initial MT systems (Hoang et al., 2018). Using back-translated data from multiple sources (Poncelas et al., 2019) or optimizing the ranking of back-translated data yields further gains (Soto et al., 2020).

BT results in gains when the parallel corpora are naturally occurring text and not translationese, as the latter would only improve automatic n metrics (Toral et al., 2018; Graham et al., 2020). **?** shows that BT produces more fluent text and is preferred by humans. Additionally, translationese and original data can be modeled as separate languages in a multilingual model (Riley et al., 2020). BT is also a central part of unsupervised MT (UMT; cf. §6.4) and zero-shot MT (Gu et al., 2019).

Sentence modification Zhu et al. (2019) proposes to replace a randomly chosen word in a sentence with a *soft-word*. That means that, instead of sampling a word from the lexical distribution of a LM like Kobayashi (2018), the authors use the hidden state vector of the LM directly. Wu et al. (2019) substitutes the RNN LMs from previous work and use BERT (Devlin et al., 2019) – a transformer trained with a masked language modeling objective – instead. The authors finetune BERT with a conditional masked language modeling objective that tries to avoid the prediction of words that do not correspond to the original sentence meaning.

Another way to augmented MT data is by paraphrasing. If a good paraphrase system exists, this can increase the number of training instances (Hu et al., 2019). Paraphrasing can also be used at training time by sampling paraphrases of the reference sentence from a paraphraser and training the MT model to predict the distribution of the paraphraser (Khayrallah et al., 2020). This helps the model to generalize. Wieting et al. (2019) propose a similar approach, using minimum risk training to optimize BLEU. To avoid BLEU's constraints to a specific reference, they use paraphrasing to diversify the given reference.

Finally, existing data can be augmented by adding noise. This noise can be continuous or discrete. In the case of applying continuous noise, noise vectors are added to the word embeddings (Cheng et al., 2018; Sano et al., 2019). Discrete noise is realized by inserting, deleting, or replacing words, BPE tokens, or characters to expand the training set in an adversarial fashion (Belinkov and Bisk, 2018; Ebrahimi et al., 2018; **?**; Cheng et al., 2019, 2020).

Pivoting While it is simple to implement and effective, pivot-based approaches suffer from error propagation. To overcome that for NMT, joint training Zheng et al. (2017); Cheng (2019) and round-trip training (Ahmadnia and Dorr, 2019) have been proposed.

Pivoting with NMT systems has been used for translating Japanese, Indonesian, and Malay into Vietnamese (Trieu et al., 2019), translation of related languages (Pourdamghani and Knight, 2019), multilingual zero-shot MT (Lakew et al., 2018), and UMT (cf. §6.4) between distant language pairs (Leng et al., 2019).

A.4 Recent low-resource Shared Tasks

First, the LoResMT 2020 shared task (Ojha et al., 2020) explores the case of language pairs which have no parallel data between them (Hindi–Bhojpuri, Hindi–Magahi, and Russian–Hindi). The winning system (Laskar et al., 2020) uses a MASS model in a zero-shot fashion with additional monolingual data (see §6.4). Second, the WMT 2020 shared tasks on UMT and very low-resource supervised MT (Fraser, 2020) provide text and 60k aligned phrases for German–Upper Sorbian., The most important technique in all tracks is transfer learning, achieving surprisingly good results. For the AmericasNLP 2021 shared task on open MT (Mager et al., 2021), 10 indigenous language languages were paired with Spanish, resulting in an extreme low-resource setting (4k to 125k paired sentences), with challenges out as domain, dialectical, and orthographic mismatches between splits and datasets. The best systems shows that data cleaning and collection (§**??**) as well as multilingual approaches (§6.1) result in the best performance in this conditions. Finally the shared task on MT in Dravidian languages (Chakravarthi et al., 2021) features 3 languages paired with English as well as Tamil–Telugu. Again, the winning system uses a multilingual approach. The best performing systems use BT (§6.3) and BPE word segmentation (§2.1).

The results from these challenges indicate that the optimal selection and combination of methods differs between cases (i.e., amount of monolingual, parallel data, cleanness of data, domain mismatch, linguistic closeness of languages). This implies that data analysis and linguistic knowledge are needed to improve a final system's performance.

A.5 Transfer learning

This helps low-resource tasks as a lower amount of data can be used for training. One application of transfer learning to MT is the usage of a pretrained RNN LM (Gulcehre et al., 2015) as the decoder in an NMT system. Zoph et al. (2016) is the first work that uses pretrained models to improve NMT systems. The authors perform two experiments with an RNN encoder–decoder architecture with an attention mechanism: the model is first pretrained on a high-resource language pair This works even better if related languages are used during pretraining (Nguyen and Chiang, 2017). Using pretrained LMs at decoding time and as priors at training time also improves vanilla models (Baziotis et al., 2020).

To avoid overfitting, models can be finetuned on both a HRLs pair and a LRLs pair in a multi-task fashion (Neubig and Hu, 2018).

However, how can we represent best the vocabulary? Zoph et al. (2016) use separate embeddings for the source and the target language. However, using tied embeddings has been shown to yield better results (Press and Wolf, 2017). Edunov et al. (2019) employs ELMO (Peters et al., 2018) representations as pretrained features in the encoder of a transformer model. Song et al. (2020) shows that it is possible to improve performance by combining monolingual texts from linguistically related languages, performing a script mapping. It is also possible to extract features from a BERT model in the source language and combining these with an NMT system (Zhu et al., 2020b), but using a BERT model pretrained with a mixed sentences from source and target languages lead to even better results (Xu et al., 2021).

Encoder-decoder pretrained models have gained popularity in the last years for low-resource MT. Conneau and Lample (2019) proposes training the encoder and the decoder separately in order to get cross-language representations (XLM). This idea has further been extended by Song et al. (2019, MASS) to masking a *sequence* of tokens from the input. Training MASS in a multilingual fashion and using monolingual data for pretraining helps to improve NMT for low-resource languages and zero-shot translation (Siddhant et al., 2020). Another approach is to train the entire transformer model as a denoising autoencoder (BART; Lewis et al., 2019). The multilingual version of BART (mBART) is more suitable for NMT tasks and yields important gains (Liu et al., 2020). It is also possible to pretrain a transformer in a multi-task, text-to-text fashion, where one of the tasks is MT (T5; Raffel et al., 2020). All four models can be finetuned for MT or used in an unsupervised fashion. Improvements to BART can be obtained by augmenting the maximum likelihood objective with an additional objective, which is a data-dependent Gaussian prior distribution (Li et al., 2020). Huge LMs can improve zero-shot and few-shot learning even further (Brown et al., 2020), but at a high computational cost. Pursuing another direction, Wang et al. (2019a) develops a hybrid architecture between a transformer and a pointer-generator network. At training time, the authors jointly train the encoder and the decoder in a denoising auto-encoding fashion.

One crucial problem for transfer-learning is minimizing catastrophic forgetting (Serra et al., 2018). Chen et al. (2021) show that it is possible to combine a pre-trained multilingual model, with fine-tuining it with one single language pair, to improve zero-shot machine translation. Another way to handle this problem is reducing the number of parameter to be updated. Gheini et al. (2021) propose to only update the cross attention parameters.

A.6 Unsupervised MT

The addition of other components such as masked LMs and denoising auto-encoding has also been tried (Stojanovski et al., 2019). Unsupervised methods are vulnerable to adversarial attacks of word substitution and order change in the input. Adversarial training can improve performance in such situations (Sun et al., 2020). Since the initialization step is crucial for UMT, Ren et al. (2020) aligns semantically similar sentences from two monolingual corpora with the help of cross-lingual embeddings. With these, an SMT system is trained to warm up an NMT system. However, UMT still has to overcome a set of challenges. Søgaard et al. (2018) shows that performance decays dramatically for languages with different typological features, since, in such situations, bilingual word embeddings (Conneau et al., 2017) are far from isomorphic. Vulić et al. (2020) finds that isomorphism is also less likely if small amounts of monolingual data are used for training bilingual word embeddings. Nooralahzadeh et al. (2020) discovers that performance quickly deteriorates for a mismatch of source and target domain and that the initialization of word embeddings can affect MT performance. All of this makes UMT for LRLs or endangered languages challenging.

Some of the described issues have been addressed: Liu et al. (2019) proposes to combine word-level and subword-level embeddings to account for morphological complexity. For the problem of distant language pairs, Leng et al. (2019) proposes pivoting (cf. §6.3). Isomorphism of bilingual word-embeddings can be improved with semi-supervised methods (Vulić et al., 2019).

Garcia et al. (2020) introduces multilingual UMT systems. The main idea consists of generalizing UMT by using a multi-way back-translation objective. Recently, pretrained multilingual transformer networks are used to improve UMT even further (cf. §6.4).

B Ethical Considerations

Ethical concerns when working on MT for endangered languages include a lack of community involvement during language documentation, data creation, and development and setup of MT systems. For more information, we refer interested readers to Bird (2020). Finally, we want to mention that publicly employing low-quality MT systems for LRLs bears a risk of translating incorrectly or in biased (e.g., sexist or racist) ways.

Community consultation and the development of an online Akuzipik-English dictionary

Benjamin Hunt
George Mason University
bhunt6@gmu.edu

Lane Schwartz
University of Alaska Fairbanks
lane.schwartz@alaska.edu

Sylvia L.R. Schreiner
George Mason University
sschrei2@gmu.edu

Emily Chen
University of Illinois at Urbana-Champaign
echen41@illinois.edu

Abstract

In this paper, we present a new online dictionary of Akuzipik, an Indigenous language of St. Lawrence Island (Alaska) and Chukotka (Russia). We discuss community desires for strengthening language use in the community and in educational settings, and present specific features of an online dictionary designed to serve these community goals.

1 Introduction

Akuzipik (ISO 639-3: ess) is a polysynthetic language on the Yupik branch of the Inuit-Yupik-Unangan language family.[1] Akuzipik is spoken in the two villages — Sivuqaq (English: Gambell) and Sivungaq (English: Savoonga) — on the island of Sivuqaq (St. Lawrence Island, Alaska), and by individuals who grew up on the island and have since moved to mainland Alaska, and on the far eastern coast of the Chukotka Peninsula of Russia.

Vakhtin (2001) estimated the total number of speakers in Russia at fewer than 200, all in their 50s or older at the time; a scholar working in Chukotka (Anastasia Panova, p.c. July 2022) estimates the current total at no more than a few dozen fluent speakers. In Alaska, the ages of fluent speakers reflect a generational divide that began in earnest in the early 1990s (Koonooka, 2005): speakers born before 1980 (now in their 40s and older) tend to have grown up with Akuzipik as their first language, learning English in school, and are essentially all fully fluent in both Akuzipik and in English. Youth under 20 are much less likely to speak Akuzipik, although varying degrees of passive fluency can be observed. Schwartz et al. (2019) estimated the total number of L1 Akuzipik speakers to be between 800 and 900 of an ethnic population of approximately 2400 individuals.

[1]Akuzipik is an in-language name for the language, meaning *authentic speech*. The language has previously been known in English as Central Siberian Yupik and St. Lawrence Island/Siberian Yupik.

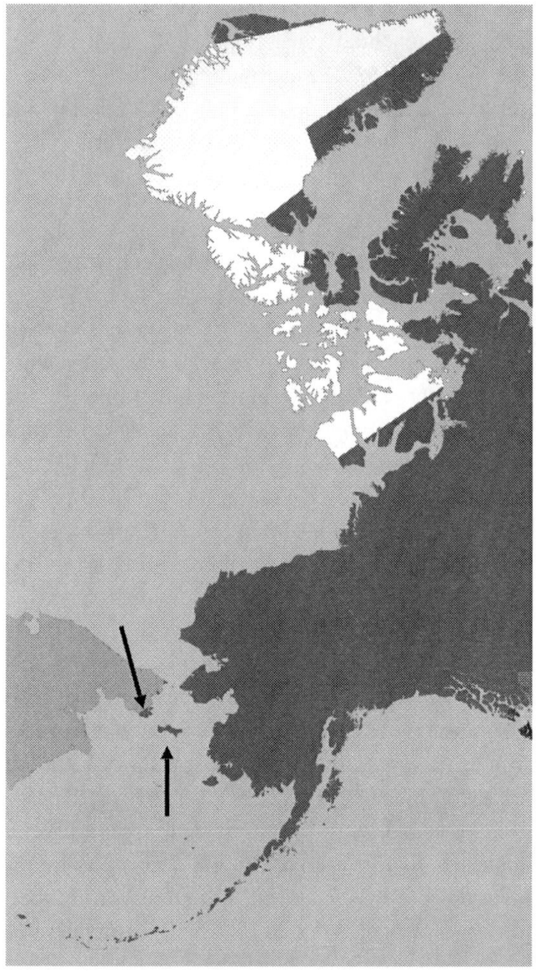

Figure 1: Traditional lands where languages in the Inuit-Yupik-Unangan language family are spoken (adapted from Krauss et al., 2010) are shown in blue. Arrows mark Sivuqaq (St. Lawrence Island, Alaska) and the Chukotka Peninsula, Russia, where Akuzipik is spoken. Other colors indicate geographically neighboring language families (Chukotkan in yellow, Dene in red).

Attitudes towards Akuzipik on Sivuqaq are generally very positive, including in younger generations, with widespread community support for language revitalization. In recent years, commu-

Proceedings of the Workshop on Natural Language Processing for Indigenous Languages of the Americas (AmericasNLP), pages 134–143
July 14, 2023

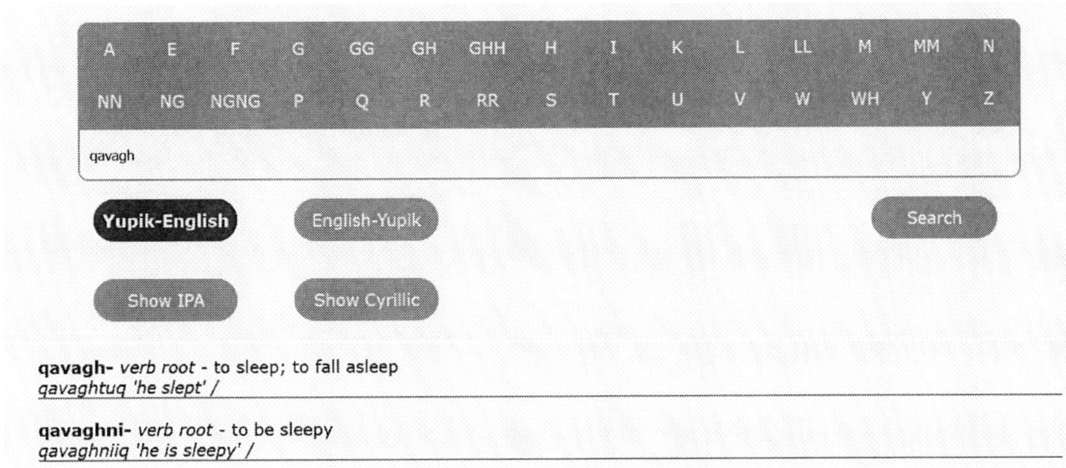

Figure 2: Example output from our 2019 Akuzipik-English online dictionary (Hunt et al., 2019)

nity members in the village of Sivuqaq established a language revitalization committee. Current goals include the short-term aim of a language nest embedding fluent Akuzipik elders within the existing pre-school program, and a long-term goal of a full Akuzipik immersion curriculum in the local school.

Over the past four years, we have conducted linguistic fieldwork in the village of Sivuqaq, both remotely (due to the COVID-19 pandemic) and more recently in person. During that time, we have consulted with community members, including the language revitalization committee and the elected tribal council, and have gathered feedback regarding community priorities and desires regarding technology in the context of language revitalization and language education. In this paper, we provide a brief overview of this feedback and present a new online dictionary that incorporates what we have learned.

2 Limitations of Prior Work: 2019 Akuzipik-English online dictionary

Despite the existence of a two-volume bilingual Akuzipik-English dictionary (Badten et al., 2008), access to this dictionary in its printed form is largely inaccessible to the average Akuzipik speaker for everyday use because of its cost and multi-volume form-factor. A small number of physical copies of the dictionary are kept in the local school, but are not generally available to residents of the village. Overall, this has meant that very few community members on the island have access to the Akuzipik-English dictionary; we believe the situation to be quite similar in Chukotka with respect to the Akuzipik-Russian print dictionary.

To address this lack of accessibility, following consultation with the Native Village of Gambell, in 2019 we released the first online Akuzipik-English dictionary (Hunt et al., 2019).[2] Our 2019 online dictionary, illustrated in Figure 2 above, enabled basic browsing and lookup of Akuzipik words from the Badten et al. (2008) bilingual print dictionary.

2.1 Limitation: Exact String Matching

Using an digitized database of the data compiled for the print dictionary, our 2019 online dictionary used a simple string match function search through the database for entries that contained the user-input string in the entry's headword. Users could also search for English words in the gloss or notes if the English-Akuzipik button was selected. One major limitation of that method was that users were required to know exactly how to spell the word they were looking for, as the string match function did not take near matches into account. When a user entered a string, the interface would return all entries where the search string matched either the entire headword or part of the headword. If the English search was enabled, entries were returned in which the search string was found in its entirety in the gloss or notes. Notably, the dictionary interface did not offer any suggestions for words that the user might be looking for based on the characters they had entered, as most modern search entries do with autocomplete/autofill.

Matching entries were then printed in a single

[2] http://computational.linguistics.illinois.edu/yupik/index_dictionary_transducer.html

list below the search bar in the order they were found (see Figure 2 on the preceding page). All available data for each entry was printed in a formatted text block followed by a horizontal rule to differentiate separate entries. This formatting strategy, while succinct and easy to produce, was not easily readable and often left entries with multiple example sentences appearing as large blocks of undifferentiated text.

2.2 Limitation: Limited morphological awareness

Given the polysynthetic nature of Akuzipik, most words are multi-morphemic and sentence-length words are relatively common (de Reuse, 1994; Jacobson, 2001). Phonological changes at morpheme boundaries are also common (Chen, 2023). As such, the simple string matching functionality described above significantly limited utility. Basic morphological analysis of searched Akuzipik words was provided through a Javascript port of our previously published finite-state morphological analyzer (Chen and Schwartz, 2018). However, results of morphological analysis were not presented to the user, and no mechanism was provided to the user to match return lexical entries identified using exact string match with specific morphemes returned by morphological analysis.

2.3 Limitation: Limited labels

Lexical entries were shown with basic part-of-speech information, most notably *noun root* and *verb root*. However, these part-of-speech labels are somewhat underspecified, merging part of speech groups that could otherwise be meaningfully differentiated, such as the types of verb roots (i.e., postural roots, emotional roots, etc. were all given the label "root" with no additional specification). Additional labels regarding such pragmatic or sociolinguistic information as dialectal variation, borrowings, archaisms, and word frequency were also lacking.

3 Community Consultation Process

Prior to the COVID-19 pandemic, we met in person with representatives of the Native Village of Gambell (the local elected tribal governing council) and other community groups, including the local language revitalization group, to discuss community priorities and desires regarding language technology in the context of language revitalization and language education. Our methodology in these fieldwork excursions are discussed in Schwartz et al. (2019) and Schreiner et al. (2020). One issue that arose consistently during discussion with the tribal council and in informal discussions with community members was a desire to support Akuzipik language use by young adults, and especially young parents. The lack of access to Akuzipik language resources (including the dictionary) was consistently raised.

Some of the most enthusiastic support we heard in favor of the development of high-quality online-accessible Akuzipik language resources was from members of the language community who had grown up in or had subsequently moved to cities such as Nome or Anchorage in mainland Alaska. Many of these we spoke with were in their 30s and 40s fluent or semi-fluent speakers of Akuzipik, and often living away from the island. Some speakers wished to consult the dictionary for words they don't know or no longer remember, or to help in their efforts to teach their children the language. Some English-speaking non-native teachers at the school also requested access the dictionary.

We continued remote consultation with various community members and organizations throughout the COVID-19 pandemic, an undertaking we present a detailed accounting of in Schreiner et al. (2022), and in doing so identified the limitations listed in Section 2 on the previous page. As we identified shortcomings of our 2019 online dictionary, we began the development of a new online dictionary designed to explicitly address these limitations and to incorporate additional community-requested features. We describe these in detail in Section 4 on the following page.

We resumed in-person visits to the island in the summer of 2022, the fall of 2022, and the spring of 2023. During these visits, we presented our resulting new online dictionary to the Native Village of Gambell, to the local language revitalization group, and to students and teachers at the local school. Overall, reception was positive, with many community members expressing their excitement to have access to the dictionary on their own devices. Members of the tribal council expressed their support for our continued work on the dictionary project and directed us to a number of community members that would be good candidates for eventual participating in audio recordings of the dictionary's content.

Our ongoing community consultation resulted in two additional specific requests that we have since implemented. In summer 2022, the community language revitalization group requested a "word of the day" to be displayed on the front page of the online dictionary. In November 2022, a community member voiced concern that the original compilers of the bilingual dictionary (Badten et al., 2008) had not been the prominence and credit on the online dictionary's main page that it deserved as a substantial documentary work. We promptly fulfilled both of these requests, adding a "word of the day" to the front page of the online dictionary and prominently crediting Badten et al. (2008) on both the front page and on all entries and data that were sourced from that work.

Dissemination of our online dictionary was initially by word of mouth up through early 2022, along with some mention through local use of social media. Later in 2022, several speakers made Facebook posts about the dictionary which garnered hundreds of responses on the social media platform. Following these posts, using basic web analytics, were were able to identify that the majority of the online dictionary's regular users are located on mainland Alaska. In November 2022, following additional local consultation, we hung posters with a QR code in public buildings, and left extra posters with tribal and city officials, at their request.

4 Resolving prior limitations and fulfilling community requests: 2023 Akuzipik-English online dictionary

In this section, we present our online Akuzipik-English bilingual dictionary.[3, 4] This dictionary is the direct result of the ongoing community consultation process described in Section 3 on the previous page. We present features that address each of the shortcomings described in Section 2 and the community requests identified in Section 3. Overall, efforts have been made to increase the visibility of dictionary entries and to make metalinguistic data and analyses more readable to non-linguists.

4.1 Morphological Parser

Perhaps the most significant improvement in our 2023 online dictionary over our earlier online dictionary is the full integration of a finite-state morphological analyzer. This integration allows users to input fully inflected Akuzipik words and receive a morpheme-by-morpheme parse and a list of search results corresponding to the word's component morphemes. This functionality was partially available in the first version of the dictionary, but improvements to the parser and the search algorithm now provide users with a clearer parse and more accurate results. An example parse is shown in Figure 3 on on the following page.

Morphological analysis is performed by a Javascript port of our Akuzipik finite-state morphological analyzer (Chen et al., 2020). In cases where the analyzer provides multiple possibly valid analyses of a word, we utilize a simple heuristic that defaults to the most parsimonious result, in this case the shortest. Following morphological analysis, the component morpheme sequence is shown, and the dictionary search algorithm returns results for each component morpheme individually, with preference given to exact matches. These features mitigate (but do not completely solve) the limitations raised in Sections 2.1 and 2.2.

We hope that in addition to enabling more robust search capabilities that morphologically aware search results will eventually be beneficial to users in educational settings, such as in the elementary and high school Akuzipik classes in the school. The integration of the morphological analyzer was an important step in targeting this use case, as it gives learners a simple way to determine the constituent parts of a word they have not encountered before.

4.2 Rich labels

Search results display a short summary of each dictionary entry (Figure 4 on the next page) that includes rich part-of-speech and etymology tags that address the limitation addressed in Section 2.3. These rich tags (Figure 5 on the following page) enable grammatical, pragmatic, and sociolinguistic aspects of each entry to be presented in a more salient manner. For example, tags for part-of-speech, root or particle class (postural, emotional, exclamatory, conjunctive, etc.), dialect usage (Chukotka, St. Lawrence Island, etc.), and productive capabilities of derivational morphemes can be easily assigned to any entry. This was in part inspired by the system used in the Yugtun (Yup'ik)

[3] https://bhunt6.github.io/akuzipigestun-sangaawa

[4] https://github.com/bhunt6/akuzipigestun-sangaawa

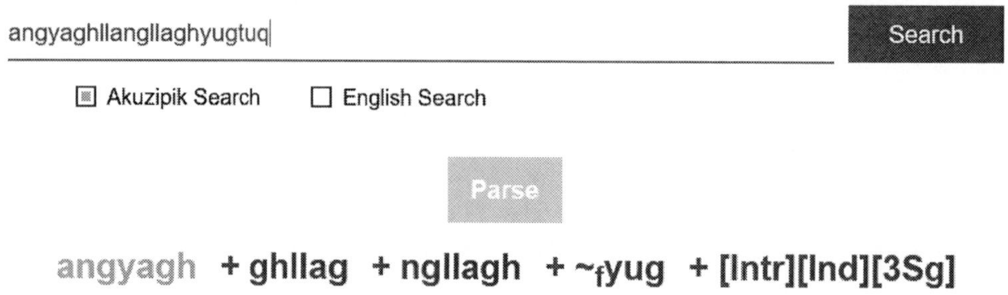

Figure 3: An example parse for *angyaghllangllaghyugtuq* (He/she wants to make a big boat).

Figure 4: Example search results with part-of-speech and etymology tags.

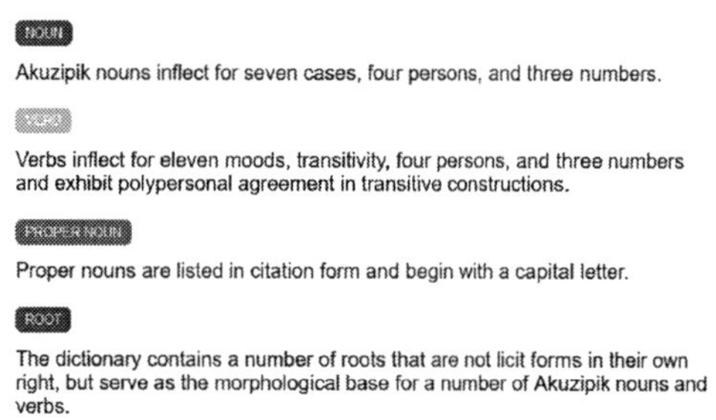

Figure 5: Some example tags

dictionary.[5]

We intend that this system will be expanded to include tags for common lexical items, archaisms, and loanwords.

4.3 Mobile-friendly with auto-complete

The dictionary user interface supports mobile device aspect ratios and an auto-complete function in the search bar. The search bar supports auto-complete functionality in both Akuzipik and English, as shown in Figure 6.

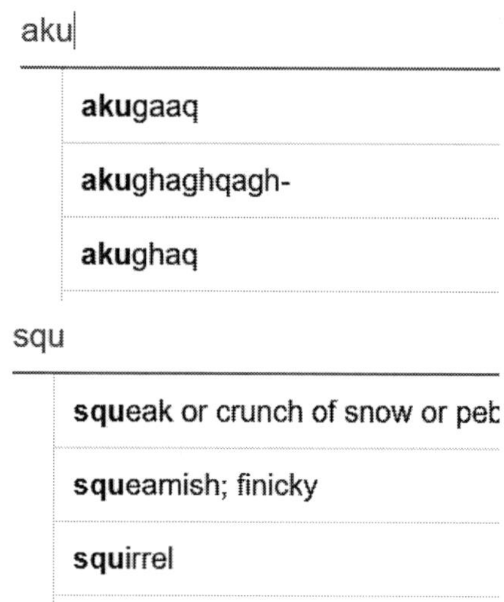

Figure 6: Autocomplete in Akuzipik and English

4.4 Word of the day

Based on feedback from the local language revitalization group, we implemented a "Word of the Day" that displays an lexical entry card on the dictionary landing page and links to the full entry page (Figure 7). The word of the day is taken from

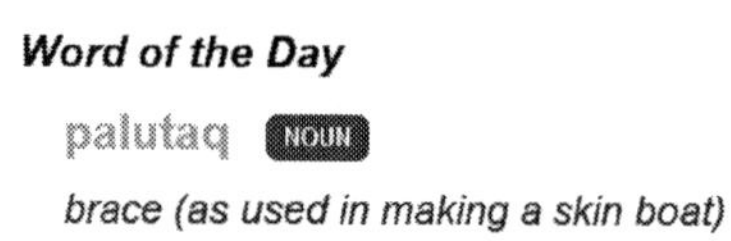

Figure 7: Word of the day section

a randomized list of the dictionary's entries, and will display a new entry daily without repeats until 2045. This was one of the first explicit requests from the community for a specific functionality, so its implementation was a priority.

[5]https://yugtun.com

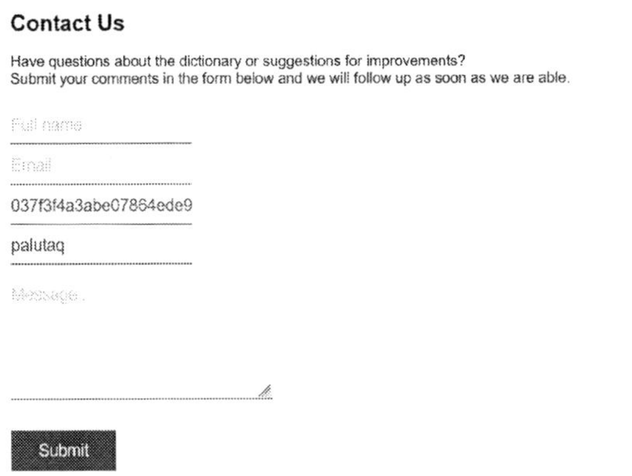

Figure 8: The contact form with entry data autofilled

4.5 Citations and feedback

An addition that has been in development since the beginning of the project is a comprehensive "About" page containing all information relevant to the navigation and use of the online dictionary, including a breakdown of how the analyzer functions, the anatomy of an entry, motivations and methodology behind the current implementation, and importantly, in-depth citations of the sources for the entries.

This page also breaks down the meanings and functions of the tags in the new tag system as well as the various symbologies used in the dictionary source material and includes a list of those contributors that have given their permission for their names to be publicly displayed.

A simple feedback form has been added to the contact page (Figure 8), allowing users to submit error reports and suggestions for improvements and edits to entries. This form can also be accessed via a report/feedback button on each entry page to allow users to more easily submit feedback related to a particular entry. The metadata specific to that entry is sent along with the report automatically so that users do not need to transfer any information to the feedback form and can focus on their suggestions.

4.6 Full entries

Each lexical entry is displayed on its own full entry page, containing all of the information available for that headword. Having a dedicated page for each entry allows us to add more entry-specific information in the future, like images, audio, additional sources, and usage examples from the corpus or user-submitted sentences. These dedicated pages are also much more readable and their appearance is more like entry pages in popular online dictionaries with which users are likely familiar such as the Yugtun dictionary and most English language dictionaries. Figure 9 show an example of a full lexical entry for a noun, while Figure 11 shows an example of a full lexical entry for a verb.

4.7 Inflection tables

The addition of inflectional tables (Figure 10 on the next page) for each entry was a large step in improving the functionality of the dictionary for Akuzipik learners. These tables are located at the bottom of each noun (and, eventually, verb) entry and display all possible inflections of the base word (not including any derivational morphology). For noun entries, each grammatical case paradigm is given its own collapsible table with layman-readable row and column headers for person, number, and possession. Verb entries will receive the same treatment for each grammatical mood, and headers for person, number, and transitivity.

4.8 Word wheel

Another addition to the online interface that was chosen to increase the visibility of entries in the dictionary is the word wheel. This is a widget on the right side of each entry page (see Figure 9 and Figure 11) that displays a handful of words that are close to the current headword alphabetically in the dictionary database. This wheel encourages exploration of the dictionary's content beyond direct searches. This may be of particular use given the polysynthetic nature of Akuzipik; in some cases there are a number of words with separate entries that employ the same root and some of the same derivational morphemes (but in some cases have distinct lexicalized meanings). A recent addition to the scroll wheel is an unlimited scroll behavior that allows users to cycle through the lexicon as much as they want, further encouraging exploration.

5 Ongoing and Future Work

A number of improvements that have not yet been implemented are currently in progress.

5.1 Lexical frequency

Taking inspiration from other online dictionaries such as the Scottish Gaelic dictionary, Am Faclair Baeg [https://www.faclair.com/], and the Yugtun dictionary, we plan to integrate an indication

Figure 9: Full dictionary entry for *palutaq*

Absolutive			
	Singular (one)	Dual (two)	Plural (3 or more)
Unpossessed	palutaq	palutak	palutat
My (1s)	palutaqa	palutagka	palutanka
Our$_2$ (1d)	palutaghpung	palutagpung	palutapung
Our$_{3+}$ (1p)	palutaghput	palutagput	palutaput
Your (2s)	palutan	palutagken	palutaten
Your$_2$ (2d)	palutaghtek	palutagtek	palutatek
Your$_{3+}$ (2p)	palutaghsi	palutagsi	palutasi
His/her/its (3s)	palutaa	palutakek	palutii
Their$_2$ (3d)	palutaak	palutagkek	palutiik
Their$_{3+}$ (3p)	palutaat	palutagket	palutiit
4s	palutani	palutagni	palutani
4d	palutaghtek	palutagtek	palutatek
4p	palutaghteng	palutagtek	palutateng

Relative +

Ablative Modalis +

Locative +

Figure 10: Nominal inflectional tables for *palutaq*

Figure 11: Full dictionary entry for *angyagh-*

of usage frequency into the entry data. Our future plans include a similar implementation to the Gaelic dictionary's user-submitted usage data and rating system. In the short term, we plan to include data on each word's frequency of occurrence in the Akuzipik written corpus. This could be accomplished using the new tag system by adding a "Common in Corpus" tag to these entries.

5.2 Improved morphological integration

In its current state, the integrated morphological parser often returns a number of possible parses for any given input word form. Our current strategy has been to display only the least morphologically complex result (often the shortest result). Active research is needed to develop robust mechanisms for improving reliability and interpretability of morphological results.

5.3 Word of the day

Currently, the "word" of the day is always an entry headword which may or may not be a licit Akuzipik surface form, depending on its part of speech. This is because of the variance in citation forms between different parts of speech; e.g. noun citation forms are given in their absolutive unpossessed singular form, while verbs are left in an underlying root form. Members of the community have suggested a system whereby speakers can submit suggestions for words of the day; those suggestions could be displayed as specialized entries with a full morphological parse and corresponding glosses. This may better enable the use of the dictionary's word-of-the-day in educational settings as a "start of class" activity, for example.

5.4 Derivational morphemes

Currently, the part of the lexicon accessible by the dictionary interface includes all noun and verb bases, particles, demonstratives, and pronouns. The inclusion of the derivational morphemes known as "postbases" is the next step in covering the contents of the print dictionary.

5.5 Audio integration

A major long-term goal is to add audio recordings of each entry to the database. The production of these recordings is a substantial undertaking given the size of the lexicon. Recording has begun, and community linguists (currently training with academic team members) will facilitate this process.

6 Conclusion: Process and Ownership

Throughout our work with the Akuzipik-speaking community, we have sought to humbly and respectfully provide the tools and expertise that we as academic researchers are able to bring to the table. We have sought to build and will continue to seek meaningful and long-lasting relationships with individuals and governing bodies on St. Lawrence

Island. And yet, it remains the case that we are not Indigenous.

As we seek to ethically engage in this work through continual relationship-building and meaningful consultation with community members and elected tribal leadership, we continue to bear in mind the moral obligations of cognizance, beneficence, accountability, and non-maleficence (Schwartz, 2022) as we work with Indigenous data.

A critically important consideration in this work is the goal of a mechanism for community input and ownership over the data contained in the dictionary. In addition to integrating feedback from users regarding word usage and glossing, indicating differences in usage between individuals, clans, and language varieties is important for demonstrating the community's ownership of the data. We hope that an eventual crowd-sourced community-governed data framework will also contribute to the tool's longevity and help to accomplish one of the core objectives of the Akuzipik reclamation project at large, namely, its self-sustainability. Ultimately, we intend feedback in the form of word frequency, clan/individual variation, and other fine-tuning of the documentary record to be received and integrated into the dictionary by a team of community linguists trained in and devoted to the upkeep of the project.

Ethics Statement

The work described in this paper, as well as the accompanying work on Akuzipik that our team has engaged in, has been undertaken with ongoing discussions with rights holders in the Akuzipik-speaking community in the village of Sivuqaq (Gambell).

Limitations

One major limitation of the current methodology is its predication on the existence of a recorded lexicon in some form that can be ported into an online format. This approach may not be ideal as a framework for the development of a new dictionary, as its express goal is to increase accessibility to existing resources and facilitate the expansion of those resources. Additionally, the development of a bespoke, dependency-free web-application for showcasing existing resources is likely low on the list of viable strategies for a community-led reclamation effort, especially if there are no community members already familiar with web-development. Any replication of the work described here is more suited for a group with a set of existing resources, access to developers, and a need to quickly get those resources into the hands of community members.

The other primary limitation of this tool and its development methodology in its current form is the potential lack of accessibility in the types of communities for which it is intended. Despite the increase in access to internet-capable smart devices in communities such as that on St. Lawrence Island, in many such places, the availability of reliable wireless internet access remains relatively low. Users are often forced to use expensive cellular data plans to conduct any amount of web-browsing. While the ultimate vision for this dictionary is for it to be packaged in a downloadable, offline format, replications of the tool in its current live-web implementation may leave many people unable to use it with the frequency that they would like. Though this is certainly a limiting factor in the effectiveness of this tool, the deployment of an offline version of the dictionary remains a preeminent goal of the project.

Akuzipik Dictionary Website

`https://bhunt6.github.io/akuzipigestun-sangaawa`

Akuzipik Dictionary Code

`https://github.com/bhunt6/akuzipigestun-sangaawa`

References

Linda Womkon Badten, (Aghnaghaghpik), Vera Oovi Kaneshiro, (Uqiitlek), Marie Oovi, (Uvegtu), and Christopher Koonooka, (Petuwaq). 2008. *St. Lawrence Island / Siberian Yupik Eskimo Dictionary*. Alaska Native Language Center, University of Alaska Fairbanks.

Emily Chen. 2023. *Modeling Saint Lawrence Island Yupik Morphology To Support Revitalization*. Ph.D. thesis, University of Illinois.

Emily Chen, Hyunji 'Hayley' Park, and Lane. Schwartz. 2020. Improving finite-state morphological analysis for St. Lawrence Island Yupik with paradigm function morphology. In *Proceedings of the 12th Language Resources and Evaluation Conference*.

Emily Chen and Lane Schwartz. 2018. A morphological analyzer for St. Lawrence Island / Central Siberian Yupik. In *Proceedings of the 11th Language Resources and Evaluation Conference (LREC'18)*, Miyazaki, Japan.

Willem J. de Reuse. 1994. *Siberian Yupik Eskimo — The Language and Its Contacts with Chukchi*. Studies in Indigenous Languages of the Americas. University of Utah Press, Salt Lake City, Utah.

Benjamin Hunt, Emily Chen, Sylvia L.R. Schreiner, and Lane Schwartz. 2019. Community lexical access for an endangered polysynthetic language: An electronic dictionary for St. Lawrence Island Yupik. In *Proceedings of the 2019 Conference of the North American Chapter of the Association for Computational Linguistics (Demonstrations)*, pages 122–126, Minneapolis, Minnesota. Association for Computational Linguistics.

Steven A. Jacobson. 2001. *A Practical Grammar of the St. Lawrence Island/Siberian Yupik Eskimo Language*, 2nd edition. Alaska Native Language Center, University of Alaska Fairbanks, Fairbanks, Alaska.

Christopher Koonooka, (Petuwaq). 2005. Yupik language instruction in Gambell (St. Lawrence Island, Alaska). *Études/Inuit/Studies*, 29(1/2):251–266.

Michael Krauss, Gary Holton, Jim Kerr, and Colin T. West. 2010. Indigenous peoples and languages of Alaska. ANLC Identifier G961K2010.

Sylvia L.R. Schreiner, Benjamin Hunt, Emily Chen, Preston Haas, and Ukaall Crystal Aningayou. 2022. Semantic fieldwork from a distance with speakers of akuzipik. *Semantic Fieldwork Methods*, 4(2).

Sylvia L.R. Schreiner, Lane Schwartz, Benjamin Hunt, and Emily Chen. 2020. Multidirectional leveraging for computational morphology and language documentation and revitalization. *Language Documentation and Conservation*, 14:69–86.

Lane Schwartz. 2022. Primum Non Nocere: Before working with Indigenous data, the ACL must confront ongoing colonialism. In *Proceedings of the 60th Annual Meeting of the Association for Computational Linguistics (Volume 2: Short Papers)*, pages 724–731, Dublin, Ireland. Association for Computational Linguistics.

Lane Schwartz, Sylvia Schreiner, and Emily Chen. 2019. Community-focused language documentation in support of language education and revitalization for St. Lawrence Island Yupik. *Études Inuit Studies*, 43(1-2):291–311.

Nikolay Vakhtin. 2001. *Iazyki Narodov Severa v XX Veke: Ocherki iazykovogo sdviga (Languages of the Peoples of the North in the XX Century: Essays on the Language Shift)*.

Finding words that aren't there: Using word embeddings to improve dictionary search for low-resource languages

Antti Arppe, Andrew Neitsch, Daniel B. Dacanay, Jolene Poulin, Daniel W. Hieber, and **Atticus G. Harrigan**
Alberta Language Technology Lab, University of Alberta
https://altlab.ualberta.ca

Abstract

Modern machine learning techniques have produced many impressive results in language technology, but these techniques generally require an amount of training data that is many orders of magnitude greater than what exists for low-resource languages in general, and endangered languages in particular. However, dictionary definitions in a comparatively much more well-resourced majority language can provide a link between low-resource languages and machine learning models trained on massive amounts of majority-language training data. Promising results have been achieved by leveraging these embeddings in the search mechanisms of bilingual dictionaries of Plains Cree (*nêhiyawêwin*), Arapaho (*Hinóno'éitíit*), Northern Haida (*X̲aad Kíl*), and Tsuut'ina (*Tsúùt'ínà*), four Indigenous languages spoken in North America. Not only are the search results in the majority language of the definitions more relevant, but they can be semantically relevant in ways not achievable with classic information retrieval techniques: users can perform successful searches for words that do not occur at all in the dictionary. Not only this, but these techniques are directly applicable to any bilingual dictionary providing translations between a high- and low-resource language.

1 Introduction

This paper presents an approach for improving the searchability of electronic dictionaries of low-resource languages, exemplified using bilingual dictionaries of Plains Cree (endonym: *nêhiyawêwin*; Glottocode: plai1258; ISO 639-3 code: crk), Arapaho (*Hinóno'éitíit*; Glottocode: arap1274; ISO 639-3 code: arp), Northern Haida (*X̲aad Kíl*; Glottocode: haida1248; ISO 639-3 code: hdn), and Tsuut'ina (*Tsúùt'ínà*; Glottocode: sars1236; ISO 639-3 code: srs), leveraging existing semantic embedding technology for majority languages in the novel context of low-resource minority languages.

Broadly speaking, search and information retrieval revolves around determining the means by which one may reliably find the most relevant discrete entries (or document(s)) from a set of multiple such documents. In the case of bilingual dictionaries, presenting entry headwords in an minority Indigenous language with definitions in a majority target language, the definitions in the majority language (in our case, English) of each entry may be considered the"documents" one searches when using target language (English) search terms. The challenge, therefore, is determining how to find the most relevant Indigenous language words (which are the headwords of the entries) for these queries. This is particularly challenging when the sought-after target language definitions do not contain the exact search terms, but instead use related target language words; in these cases, even exact search word matches do not necessarily translate to the highest relevance. For instance, Indigenous languages that have a complex morphological system can store large amounts of information and meaning within a single lexeme, which in a morphologically simpler languages (such as English) may need to be represented with multiple words or phrases. Consider, for example the Plains Cree words *nôtamiskwêw* for 's/he hunts beavers', and *êskêw* for 's/he makes a hole in the ice to hunt beaver; s/he breaks up a beaver lodge (i.e. in hunting)', which would both require a combination of the English search terms 'hunt' and 'beaver' to be accurately matched. In contrast, an entry such as *mâmawohkamâtowak*, meaning 'they do things together, they cooperate; they work (at it/him) together as a group; they assemble themselves to help one another.' would be matched with the search terms 'cooperate', or 'work' and 'together', but would be missed with the obvious synonym 'collaborate'.

Thus, the general problem remains determining the means to capture and represent the underlying

Proceedings of the Workshop on Natural Language Processing for Indigenous Languages of the Americas (AmericasNLP), pages 144–155
July 14, 2023 ©2023 Association for Computational Linguistics

meanings of both 1) the targets, the entries represented by their (English) definitions, and in 2) the (English) search terms, particularly when they may be more than the sum of the words in isolation. For endangered languages which are often also less-resourced ones, this challenge becomes greater as the vocabulary contents in their dictionaries (and definitions) are typically much more limited than those in majority languages, resulting in even fewer words to potentially match. For example, even many high-frequency English words, such as *national*, *administration*, and *network* (all within the top 1000 most frequent content words in large corpora such as COCA), have no matches whatsoever in the English definitions in any bilingual dictionaries of the four Indigenous languages named above. Searching with these words using typical methods would therefore result in "`No results`" – a discouraging outcome for a user – even when these dictionaries actually do contain relevant entries that could be shown.

Word-embeddings present one possible solution for this. Because they represent the underlying concepts that the individual words are pointing at, this allows us to represent concepts, or combinations of concepts, that individual words are pointing at. In turn, this allows for comparing the concepts referred to by the search terms and the entry definitions, rather than the individual words themselves. This paper discusses the implementation and evaluation of this solution to four bilingual dictionaries between an Indigenous language and English, all of which we have made available on-line.[1]

2 Background and previous related work

2.1 How Indigenous lexical resources are (often) limited

The majority of endangered and Indigenous languages are extremely low-resourced, with corpora and lexical databases that are a fraction of the size of even basic learner's dictionaries in major languages such as English. Often these lexical databases are the product of fieldwork conducted by just one or a small number of linguists, in projects where financial and temporal constraints prevent the kind of extensive data collection that occurs for well-resourced languages.

For example, in a survey of 284 published dictionaries and lexical databases of lesser-resourced languages (Hieber, in progress), the mean number of entries per language is 5,772 and the median is 4,321, with only 39 sources containing more than 10,000 entries, and only five having more than 20,000. Only two sources—Mundari (Glottocode: `mund1320`; ISO: `unr`) and Marwari (Glottocode: `raja1256`; ISO: `mwr`)—reach 50,000 entries. By comparison, the Cambridge Learner's Dictionary of English (O'Shea et al., 2012)—marketed as covering only vocabulary relevant to the B1–B2 (intermediate) levels of CEFR (the Common European Framework of Reference, used for assessing language proficiency)— contains over 35,000 entries. This intermediate-level dictionary therefore contains more entries than all but two dictionaries in the history of Indigenous language documentation.

In addition to the aforementioned temporal and financial limitations limiting dictionary sizes in many Indigenous languages, many such languages also suffer from lexical attrition accompanying the process of language obsolescence (or "language death") (Sands et al., 2007). The remaining speakers may simply not remember as many words as their predecessors once did. For other languages, the number of lexemes may *in fact* be smaller than speakers of major Indo-European languages are accustomed to. Words in some languages may cover a broader semantic field, on average, than their Indo-European counterparts. Jack Martin (p.c.) notes for his lexical databases on U.S. Southeastern languages that "these numbers, while low by English standards, actually reflect a very high percentage of the words that are used".

Other languages have fewer lexemes by virtue of how their grammar operates. The Tsafiki language (a.k.a. Colorado; Glottocode: `colo1256`; ISO: `cof`), for example, has 4,000 lexical entries and only 32 true verbs, but includes another 6,000 subentries formed by adding suffixes to those 4,000 base entries to create new words (Dickinson, 2000). Inuit languages are likewise renowned for possessing thousands of lexical suffixes that can derive new words, even though the number of base roots is actually rather small. If dictionaries of these languages are based on roots rather than stems (as is often the case), lookup and search can become quite difficult for dictionary users, who must first locate the relevant main entry, and then the target

[1] These on-line dictionaries are the following: *itwêwina* (Plains Cree-to-English) `https://itwewina.altlab.app`; *Nihíitono* (Arapaho-to-English) `https://nihiitono.altlab.dev`; *Gúusaaw* (Northern Haida-to-English) `https://guusaaw.altlab.dev`; and *Gūnáhà* (Tsuut'ina-to-English) `https://gunaha.altlab.dev`.

subentry.

All this is to say that, for most documentary lexical databases, the number of entries is quite small compared to well-resourced languages. This fact creates a significant problem for potential users of these databases: because there are so few entries, it can be difficult to locate the entry most relevant to the user's search term. This problem arises in primarily two ways: 1) the language may not have a specific term for the (majority language) concept the user is searching for; and 2) the language has a term for the (majority language) search query, but no definition exactly matches that query. For instance, searching the Plains Cree-to-English dictionary (`http://creedictionary.com/search/?q=collaborate`) gives no result for the English search term *collaborate*, though this resource does provide matches for the semantically synonymous word *cooperate* and as well as synonymous multi-word expression *work together* (*mâmawatoskêwak* 'they work together′). Neither does one get a match for *procrastinate*, though the same dictionary does contain many entries concerning the semantically related concept *delay*, e.g. *otamihtwâsow* 's/he delays him/herself with work′.

In the first case, it would be useful if the dictionary could display results that are semantically related to the search term, or in a neighboring semantic field, or have some sort of semantic relationship to the search term (hypernymy, meronymy, antonymy, etc.), preferably with the results sorted by relevance. Thereby, one would hope to be given the same Plains Cree result *mâmawatoskêwak* for the search term *collaborate*, as for what is already provided for *co-operate* and *work together*. This is not how most electronic dictionaries historically have worked, and those dictionaries that do incorporate some measure of semantic association rely on massive datasets to accomplish it (see §2.3) – an approach not feasible for low-resource languages.

There are many causes for the second case, wherein a lexical database contains an entry that would be considered a correct match for the user's search term, but the user is unsuccessful in locating it. It may be the case that the language has a word for the search term, but the definition of that word does not encompass the entirety of the semantic breadth of the term. This is quite common for documentary lexicons, which are often based as much on wordlist elicitation as corpus data (usually more so), often resulting in only frequent, 'core' meanings of polysemous word entries being gathered. However, documentary lexicons are also more likely to focus on what are called *basic level* terms, that is, terms which are considered the most cognitively and linguistically salient (Taylor, 2003), to the exclusion of others. As a consequence, documentary lexicons often lack entries for terms that are either very high or low in ontological specificity; for example, they are likely to contain entries for 'arm' and 'leg' but less likely to contain entries for the more abstract 'appendage' or more specific 'paw'. In the above case, one would hope to be shown the results for *delay*, when searching with *procrastinate* (if no exact matches are to be found for this search term).

Entries that are multi-word expressions (MWEs) may also lead to less-than-ideal search results. In Plains Cree, for instance, there is a verb stem *mihcêtohk-* meaning 'to work together on something'. In a non–semantically-informed dictionary, the user must search for the exact phrase "work together" to find this entry. Searching for just "work" or "together" will likely return a host of irrelevant results such as *atoskê-* 'to work' or *miyopayin-* 'to work well' before *mihcêtohk-*, and searching with a synonym such as 'collaborate' would not yield *mihcêtohk-* among the results.

The definitional conventions of a dictionary can also significantly affect searchability. Definitions may be either *intensional* (describing the properties or necessary and sufficient conditions for a concept) or *extensional* (specifying the range or types of entities that fall within the concept (Svensén, 2009, 218–222)); for example, an intensional definition of *motor vehicle* would mention the need for a motor and use for transport/transit, etc., while an extensional definition might mention cars, motorcycles, mopeds, etc. If a user searches for one type of definitional style but the database adopts the other, lookup may fail if a semantically-informed search algorithm is not used.

Idiomatic expressions also cause difficulties for lookup, since users may search for the idiomatic meaning rather than the literal one (or vice versa). For example, the West Danish (Jutlandic) word *ræv* 'fox' also means 'sly, cunning person', and this idiomatic meaning is only sometimes included in dictionaries (Arboe, 2015, 162). In a traditional dictionary, if this sense were not included, users would not be able to find it in a search for "sly" or "cunning". For a semantically-informed dictionary, however, a search for either of these terms would very likely include *ræv* as a result.

As outlined, all of these problems may be addressed by a semantically-informed search algorithm which returns results based on semantic relevance to the search string. A more general advantage of this approach is that it allows users to search using nearly any semantic relationship (meronymy, hypernymy, etc.), and facilitates searching for less canonical types of entries, such as multi-word expressions, idioms, slang, etc. This is especially important given that the majority of lexical items sought by dictionary users tend *not* to be the canonical, single-word lexical item that dictionaries are often designed around. Research has found that users hardly ever look up common words; most searches are for idioms, encyclopedic-like information, culture-specific words, abbreviations, and slang (Svensén, 2009, 466).

As mentioned, however, implementing semantically-informed search has historically been no easy task for low-resource languages. In §3, we show how we implemented such a semantically-informed search algorithm for several low-resource languages.

2.2 Quantifying the challenge

The small size of most low resource language dictionaries inevitably results in a large number of high frequency majority language lemmata simply not occurring in any entries, resulting in a significant portion of even fairly innocuous majority language search queries returning no exact matches using traditional search methods. For Plains Cree, for example, only 88% of the top 1000 most frequent English lemmata are present within the definitions of the current dictionary, and for languages such as Tsuut'ina (Glottocode: `sars1236`; ISO 639-3 code: `srs`), this proportion is as low as 44.7% (Table 1).

The nature of the high-frequency vocabulary which tends to be missing in these four dictionaries is variable, but follows some general patterns, with common words relating to government, legislature, technology, and abstract concepts often being absent (such as 'national', 'policy', 'data', and 'theory', ranked by frequency in COCA at positions 311, 406, and 417, and 896 respectively). In total, 26 of the top 1000 most frequent English content lemmata did not occur in any of the four dictionaries mentioned in Table 1 (see Appendix A).

Top Lemmata	Plains Cree	Arapaho	Northern Haida	Tsuut'ina
100	99	100	93	91
200	194	198	174	145
300	287	295	249	197
400	374	393	315	237
500	462	486	378	280
600	554	578	441	325
700	639	668	494	348
800	719	759	543	385
900	809	853	598	418
1000	880	939	641	447

Table 1: Counts among the 1000 top most frequent English lemmata (as per COCA – the one-billion word Corpus of Contemporary American English), excluding function words (Davies, 2008)) not found in any definitions in dictionaries of Plains Cree (~23 000 entries), Arapaho (~25 000 entries, with some repeated lemmata (Cowell, 2012)), Northern Haida (~5500 entries (Lachler, 2010)), and Tsuut'ina (~12 500 entries, but primarily inflectional wordforms and paradigms, with a total lemma count in the low thousands)

As Table 1 demonstrates, lacunae such as aforementioned become markedly more prevalent as less frequent terms are used as search queries. However, even in instances where an exact match can be found, it may be useful for users (particularly learners) for semantically related terms to be returned as well. For instance, if a user searches for "yellow hat", it may be of use for them to also receive entries such as "orange toque". However, this strategy poses the further problem of sorting and presenting results in terms of relevance, as well as of determining the relative relevance of individual words in multi-word searches.

2.3 Previous approaches to expanding search

General search engines sort their search results using what is typically a proprietary sorting algorithm, making it difficult to build off of widely accepted forms of search relevance (Sullivan, 2002). Instead, it is best to examine other approaches to search retrieval and ranking, innovating and adapting these practices for the task at hand. This section outlines a number of prior approaches for search and ranking.

2.3.1 The Boolean model

The earliest approach to search result ranking is the Boolean retrieval model. This model creates a weight for each entry given the query terms, using the sum of all individual query term weights as the document weight. If a query term is in the entry, the model represents that with a 1, and with a 0 otherwise (Larson, 2012). The method then returns all entries marked as 1, with no ranking system for the results

2.3.2 Machine-learning-aided search

A more complex approach to sorting relevant search results is to use deep learning or some form of matrix to determine how alike a search result is to the query entered (McDonald et al., 2018). However, these approaches require large amounts of training data, often more than exists in a given low-resource language. These models can still be leveraged by training them on the definitions in a bilingual dictionary, which are entered in a majority language, and providing a relevance ranking from majority language query terms to majority language definitions. This process is explained in further detail below.

2.3.3 Search by translation

In one previous description of multilingual information access, texts were translated from one source language into another target language for easier querying by the end user. This translation process was at first done manually and eventually automatically (Oard, 2012). This method presents some challenges, such as determining the original language of a text, that do not apply to the dictionary use case as the source and target languages of the dictionary are known. Applying this method to an online dictionary would mean translating each source language headword into its target language counterpart, or translating all query terms to match the dictionary entry language. However, since the dictionary already has definitions provided in the majority language, this work would be redundant. Thus, the information retrieval system should instead query on the definitions, as our approach does.

2.3.4 Search by synonym expansion

One successful example of improving search results through defining synonyms for entries may be seen in Shi et al. (2005). In their study, which specifically concerned biological terminology, they used pre-existing databases of similar terms for all biology-related entries to generate a network of synonyms, but relied on manual classification (using the Princeton WordNet (Miller, 1995; Fellbaum, 1998)) for general words and phrases, i.e. the non-medical information, in the database texts.

To circumvent the need for manual synonym classification, Zhang et al. (2017) derived a method for automatically determining synonymy. This approach, however, is only available for languages with large corpora, as it relies on creating a machine learning model in the source language to create a synonym web. This approach was successful in improving how results are clustered; as such, we used a tool based on the same word vector model below (namely, `word2vec`).

2.3.5 Semantic expansion

A final approach, would involve starting with a large pre-existing database, such as WordNet, and pairing it down to only the relevant terms for efficiency and ease of use, as was done by Turcato et al. (2000). However, this approach assumes that each low resource language entry has at least one direct synonym in the high resource language, and that the semantic hierarchies and relationships of a majority language WordNet would be applicable outright to the target language, two facts which are often untrue.

In the absence of pre-existing models to leverage for the creation of a synonym table, creating a synonym network for a low-resource language dictionary would require many hours of manual input while consulting a pre-existing word network database, such as WordNet. This has been done before for Plains Cree with some success (Dacanay et al., 2021a); however, in addition to being highly time-consuming, this method also relies on the aforementioned, typically incorrect assumption that majority language semantic categories can be applied uncritically to target language vocabulary.

2.3.6 Issues with previous approaches

While these approaches suffice for a variety of search-based problems, they do not tackle the problem in the context of a bilingual dictionary with minority language headwords. The last four approaches assume that users will only ever use majority language search terms, which is an unfair assumption. Furthermore, the data required to train any sort of neural network or to automatically classify entries into a word net or a group of synonyms is much larger than the data available for low resource languages, such as Plains Cree. As such, a new approach was required to adequately solve this search and ranking scenario.

3 Our approach

We will present our approach primarily with examples from *itwêwina* (`itwêwina.altlab.app`), an online intelligent bilingual dictionary application, making use of our *morphodict* platform[2] for Plains Cree – English, although we have implemented this feature also for bilingual on-line dictionaries for Arapaho, Northern Haida, and Tsuut'ina, and will present examples from the first two languages in the evaluation section further below.[3] *itwêwina* is freely accessible to the public and receives roughly 20,000 searches per month. It combines multiple dictionary sources (Wolvengrey; Maskwachees Cultural College, 2009; LeClaire and Cardinal, 1998), and has approximately 22,000 headwords[4], of which only about 10,000 appear in any Plains Cree corpus that we know of. Through modeling with finite-state transducers (FST) (Snoek et al., 2014; Harrigan et al., 2017), it can dynamically recognize wordforms and display paradigm tables for millions of additional inflected word-forms.

Searches can be entered in either English or Plains Cree. We break the search process into two phases: retrieval, and ranking. The goal of retrieval is to find potentially relevant definitions for the input query. For Cree-language searches, a spell-relaxed finite state transducer identifies potential matching headwords. For English-language searches, the application uses classical information retrieval techniques of matching stemmed keywords between queries and definitions. Ranking is necessary because an unsorted list of matches would provide a poor user experience: there may be many hundreds of potentially matching words. Therefore, results returned by the finite-state transducer analyzer or classical information retrieval methods are ranked using a combination of result features[5] (Turnbull and Berryman, 2016) such as corpus or dictionary frequency, or edit distance.

In an attempt to improve the relevance of the top search results returned by *itwêwina*, we added in spring of 2021 a new result feature to feed into the relevance ranking function: a semantic distance measure, based on word embeddings, between input queries and resultant definitions. While this did improve relevance, the most novel and surprising feature which this revealed was the ability of word embeddings to allow the retrieval of useful search results for words that are not even in the dictionary (target language definitions), in addition to improving the search results for multi-word phrases.

4 Method

4.1 Word embeddings

A word embedding is a dimensionality reduction technique that assigns a relatively low-dimensional vector to each element of a set of words, in a way that captures relationships between words. The vector typically consists of first-layer model weights learned during the training of a neural network. For example, the 2013 `word2vec` model of Mikolov et al. (2013a,b) provides for each of 3 million words and phrases, not a 3-million-dimensional vector without semantic relationships, but instead a 300-dimensional vector with semantic relationships. The word embedding model is trained on a portion of a corpus of approximately 100 billion words[6] of Google News articles. The training process attempts to minimize the errors in predicting which words are most likely to occur surrounding any given input word. This necessarily assigns similar vectors to words that frequently occur in similar contexts in the corpus; thus, words corresponding to similar vectors are semantically related. Furthermore, these semantic relations are often seemingly algebraic in nature, allowing (in some instances (Ethayarajh et al., 2019) (Rogers et al., 2017)) for the automated solving of word analogy equations.

4.2 Application to low-resource languages

We do not have 100 billion words of Plains Cree text to train an equivalent model on, or for any of the three other Indigenous languages discussed in this paper. The largest Cree corpus has some 150 thousand word tokens (Arppe et al., 2020). However, we can use the vectors for English, and their algebraic nature, to compute vectors for every English definition as an average of their constituent individual English words, and compare those to the input query; this has the additional benefit of working for bilingual dictionaries for *any* low-resource language for which there are pre-trained

[2]The codebase which implements this ranking feature for all these languages is publicly available: `https://github.com/UALbertaALTLab/morphodict`

[3]Tsuu'ina examples have been left out, as its bilingual dictionary source is only a glossary based on a small collection of texts with a relatively restricted and skewed vocabulary.

[4]This was the value in 2021 when the the quantitative study presented in this paper was done, after which this number has grown to more than 25,000 entries.

[5]`https://web.stanford.edu/class/cs276/`

[6]`https://code.google.com/archive/p/word2vec/`

word embeddings for the language used in the definitions; indeed, as mentioned, we have already implemented this search feature for bilingual online dictionaries of Arapaho, Northern Haida, and Tsuut'ina, all with definitions in English.

When the dictionary data is loaded into the system, we use the Google News vectors to compute a vector for the English definition of every Plains Cree entry by adding up vectors for each word of the definition (Harrigan and Arppe, 2021; Dacanay et al., 2021a,b). For example, for the definition "yellow hat" of *osâwastotin*, we compute $v(\texttt{yellow hat}) := v(\texttt{yellow}) + v(\texttt{hat})$ and save that. This yields a vector for the definition overall, $v(\texttt{osâwastotin}_1) := v(\texttt{yellow hat})$. When there are multiple definitions for a Plains Cree word, we save a vector for each one so that we can show the word as a result if any definition is a good match.

When someone searches for "yellow hat," we again use the news vectors to compute a vector for the input query, $v(\texttt{yellow}) + v(\texttt{hat})$, and measure its distance to every definition in the dictionary (as the cosine between the two vectors). This is one instance in which the small available lexicons of these language is actually an advantage, as it is much faster to compare the search query vector to each of the over 22,000 Plains Cree definitions than it would be for the much larger number of definitions in a more comprehensive dictionary. In this case, while classical information retrieval techniques would have had little difficulty finding results for 'yellow' or 'hat' individually, the word embedding-based model retrieves not only 'yellow' and 'hat', but also other combinations of colour and clothing not specified in the search:

1. *osâwastotin*: yellow hat
2. *nîpâmâyâtastotin*: purple hat
3. *astotin*: hat, cap, headgear
4. *osâwêkin*: yellow material, yellow cloth
5. *osâwasâkay*: yellow dress, coat

However, as mentioned, this search method can also return relevant results for queries entirely absent from the database. For example, despite having no definition for 'freighter' (indeed, no definition even containing that word), using the word embeddings, a search for 'freighter' turns up *nâpihkwân* "ship, large boat" as the top result. This is because the word embeddings of the definition suggest semantically related concepts: 'boat,' 'ship.' Our approach is similar to the reverse dictionary lookup for Wolastoqey (Passamaquoddy-Maliseet) evaluated by Bear and Cook (2022).

This word embedding method can also be used to automatically cluster words into semantic classes. In its most basic form, this can be done simply by making use of hierarchical agglomerative clustering based on a distance matrix of the word vectors. While this technique produces useful and valuable clusters out-of-box, further manual adjustment significantly improves results (Harrigan and Arppe, 2021).

5 Results and evaluation

5.1 Qualitative assessment

In practice, our semantic search functionality returns results for 'missing' words (in the English definitions) with varying degrees of quality; for the sake of qualitative assessment, we may divide these result qualities into three (subjective) categories: high, moderate, and poor. A high quality result describes an instance in which the top search result for a missing word is either synonymous with, or highly semantically related to, the query word in question. Examples of missing words with high quality top matches include 'policy', which returns the Cree entry *wiyasiwêwin* ("law, rule, decision, council, band council, office"), 'attorney', which returns *oyasiwêwiyiniw* ("band councillor, court judge, lawyer"), and 'pdf', which returns *masinahikan* ("book, letter, mail, written document, ..."). Among the top 26 highest frequency English lemmata from COCA which do not appear in any of the low-resource language dictionaries previously mentioned in section 1.1, Anglophone manual annotators evaluated 18 of the top results for Plains Cree and Arapaho, and 5 of the top results for Northern Haida as being of high quality.

Moderate quality results describe those in which the top match is broadly, but not precisely, semantically related to the query word; examples of this include 'international', which returns the Cree entry for *opîtatowêw* "Ukrainian, European", a related, but decidedly non-synonymous term. Three of the top 26 missing words for Plains Cree and Arapaho, and 11 for Northern Haida were evaluated as having top matches of moderate quality.

Poor quality results are those in which the top match is either entirely semantically unrelated, or sufficiently irrelevant to be of no use. Examples of poor quality results include 'percent', which returns the Cree entry for *nisto-sôniyâs* "three quarters, seventy-five cents". For a term such as 'percent', the most appropriate match in current Plains Cree dictionaries would be one relating either to portions (such as *pahki-* "portion of") or relating to the number one-hundred (*mitâtahtomitanaw*), however, neither of these results are returned. Another example is 'career', for which the top match is the Cree entry for *ispîhtaskîwin* "season", rather than the more fitting *atoskêwin* "work, labour, employment, job, contract, industry". 5 of the top 26 missing words for Plains Cree and Arapaho, and 10 for Northern Haida were evaluated as having poor quality top matches.

In total, for the two larger bilingual dictionaries (for Plains Cree and Arapaho), a substantial majority of top results for missing words were of high or moderate quality (21 out of 26 in both cases), with the smaller Haida dictionary performing more poorly outright (likely because of its reduced semantic coverage by virtue of size; if no entries corresponding even to the basic semantic domain of a search query are to be found, then even a theoretically perfect semantic search would not return semantically relevant results). However, even with the Haida dictionary, a majority (16 out of 26) of top results for missing words were of high or moderate quality. Results for the mean number of high, moderate, and poor matches in the top ten search results of the top 26 highest frequency missing English lemmata for these three dictionaries are detailed in Table 2.

When considering the position among all returned results of the single most semantically relevant match for these 26 missing word search queries (as per a manual annotator), the median position of this match was 2 for Plains Cree, 3 for Arapaho, and 4.5 for Haida. As such, even for the relatively small Haida dictionary, a user would typically only need to scroll through the top five search results when searching for a missing word to find the most relevant match.

	High	Moderate	Poor
Plains Cree	3.08	3.23	3.08
Arapaho	3.65	3.15	3.19
Northern Haida	0.54	3.23	6.23

Table 2: Mean number of *high*, *moderate*, and *poor* quality results in the top ten matches for missing English lemma search queries.

5.2 Search terms with metaphorical meaning

As mentioned in section 1, this search method also allows for the use of (English) metaphorical terms as search queries; for example, when searching the English term 'soapbox' in Plains Cree, the top two results are *kakêskihkêmowinâhtik* "pulpit, lecturn" and *kîhkâwitaskiw* "s/he likes to scold, s/he is always cross and scolding in a loud voice", and the top result for 'snowballing' is *asascikêwin* "piling things together", with *kîpikin* "it grows quickly" being in 7th. However, the success of these metaphorical search queries remains inconsistent. For example, the top ten results for 'snake' contain only entries related to reptiles, and none related to deceitful, malicious humans. Similarly, multi-word metaphors tended to return results relating to the literal meaning of their constituent elements (for example, "cabin fever" returns only results relating to cabins, e.g. *wâskâhikanis* "small house, cabin", and fevers, e.g. *sîkwâspinêwin* "spring fever", rather than to loneliness or boredom).

5.3 Polysemous search terms

On a related note, one of the most notable errors in general with our semantic search method concerns polysemous English search queries, this being largely a product of `word2vec` generating embeddings on the level of the individual word, rather than the sentence. In addition to affecting the accuracy of metaphorical search terms, this also has the effect of semantically grouping target language words based on irrelevant English collocations. For example, when given the search term 'administration', all three dictionaries returned entries containing the word 'bush' within their top ten results (such as *hlk'awáng* "for S to clear C [land] of bush or trees" in Northern Haida) due to the frequent occurrence of the collocation 'Bush administration' in news corpora, and matches for the search query 'reality' contained the word 'television' (such as *wó3onikúu3o.o* "movie, television show, picture, photograph" in Arapaho) within the top ten results of all three dictionaries.

5.4 Multi-word search terms

The quality of search results for multi-word expressions tended to vary depending on the semantic transparency of the expression's constituent elements. For example, when searching for the expression 'simmer down' (in which all of the constituent words are transparently related to the end meaning of the expression), the top result in the Northern Haida dictionary is *sahl ts'asäláng* 'for S to let C boil without stirring it [said of fish only]'. However, when searching for an expression such as 'blow up' (whose constituent words are only idiosyncratically related to the action described), the top results (shown here in the Plains Cree dictionary) relate to the more conventional meanings of both words individually (*pôtâtam* "s/he blows at s.t. ...", *matwêtahikêw* "s/he strikes blow"), rather than to the more fitting meaning of the full phrase (which might rather best be expressed through *pahkitêw* "it explodes"). Similarly, idiomatic multi-word phrases behaved in much the same way as idiomatic expressions in general, overwhelmingly returning results relating to the literal meanings of their constituent elements; for example, 'see eye to eye' returns top results relating to eyes and sight (e.g. *miskîsikos* "eye, small eye, little eye", but no results related to the phrasal meaning of understanding.

These results are perhaps unsurprising, given the means by which our word embeddings were generated; `word2vec` being a tool which creates embeddings for individual words with their context taken only as a bag-of-words, rather than for creating them for whole phrases, it is to be expected that the isolated meanings of each individual word in a multi-word expression would take precedence over the meaning of the phrase as a whole. One possible means of addressing this would be the use of a sentence-based language model such as `BERT` ((Devlin et al., 2019)), which is able to generate contextualised word embeddings based on specific sentential surroundings, possibly allowing for a better modelling of common, semantically opaque multi-word phrases.

5.5 Preliminary quantitative assessment

In addition to its ability to return useful results for entries not present in the dictionary, the use of word embeddings can also improve relevance ranking for results which *are* present. Although more rigorous analysis is needed, preliminary results indicate that use of word embedding distance increases one of our key search quality metrics from 0.61 to 0.70 (this metric being a measure of the frequency with which certain desirable results appear as a top-10 result on a test set of 549 sample core vocabulary item queries).

6 Future work and conclusion

One potentially promising research theme to explore is the improvement of multi-word vector creation methods for definitions and search strings, perhaps through the use of term-frequency—inverse-document-frequency weights when adding word vectors to form definition vectors. Similarly, investigating whether newer pre-trained word embedding models (Pennington et al., 2014; Speer et al., 2017) could produce higher-quality results. Advances in the use of word embeddings for other NLP tasks in low-resource languages (e.g. Adams et al. 2017) may also translate to improved dictionary search.

7 Limitations

When a dictionary for a low-resource language lacks a word, but has several related ones in terms of synonymy or semantic similarity, it is a definite benefit to be able to provide those to the dictionary user instead of merely saying, "No results found." However, there are some potential drawbacks here: for example, this could increase the rate at which words acquire connotations by analogy with English. 'Locomotive' and 'train' are closely related concepts in English; but that does not necessarily hold for every language, and there is some risk in implying that it does.

Language instructors will be all too familiar with students using tools like Google Translate to do their homework for them instead of doing the hard work of learning the language. On a larger scale, Google Translate itself was formerly available as a free service that software developers could use to do automated machine translation in bulk; this was abruptly discontinued in 2011. Industry rumour[7] held that the bulk service was being used to generate so much of the parallel text appearing on the internet—parallel text needed to train machine translation models—that those models could no longer improve sufficiently if they continued to inadvertently be fed primarily their own outputs. This highlights the possible risk that applying machine learning tools like word embeddings can end up distorting language. To this end, we believe that the use of word embeddings to provide analogous words to dictionary users is beneficial, but does not and cannot replace actual lexicography.

[7]https://kv-emptypages.blogspot.com/2011/06/analysis-of-shutdown-announcements-of.html

8 Ethics Statement

The on-line dictionaries described in this manuscript have been developed in order to support the explicit objectives of the language communities in question, to support their language instruction, maintenance, and revitalization activities.

9 Acknowledgements

We thank the Social Sciences and Humanities Research Council (SSHRC) for their Partnership Grant (#895-2019-1012) that has supported this project during the last several years. Earlier stages of the software development of *morphodict*, our morphologically intelligent on-line dictionary platform that we make use of, were implemented by Eddie Antonio Santos. We would also want to recognize the extensive documentation work by Arok Wolvengrey (Plains Cree), Andy Cowell (Arapaho), Jordan Lachler (Northern Haida), Chris Cox (Tsuut'ina), and Bruce Starlight (Tsuut'ina), not to mention the significant contributions of Elders, knowledge keepers, and speakers in the various Indigenous language communities, in compiling together the lexicographical resources incorporated in the intelligent dictionaries discussed in this paper.

References

Oliver Adams, Adam Makarucha, Graham Neubig, Steven Bird, and Trevor Cohn. 2017. Cross-lingual word embeddings for low-resource language modeling. In *Proceedings of the 15th Conference of the European Chapter of the Association for Computational Linguistics: Volume 1, Long Papers*, pages 937–947.

Torben Arboe. 2015. Receding idioms in West Danish (Jutlandic). In Elisabeth Piirainen and Ari Sherris, editors, *Language endangerment: Disappearing metaphors and shifting conceptualizations*, pages 155–173. John Benjamins, Amsterdam.

Antti Arppe, Katherine Schmirler, Atticus G Harrigan, and Arok Wolvengrey. 2020. A morphosyntactically tagged corpus for Plains Cree. In *Papers of the 49th Algonquian Conference (PAC49)*, volume 49, pages 1–16.

Diego Bear and Paul Cook. 2022. Leveraging a bilingual dictionary to learn Wolastoqey word representations. In *Proceedings of the Thirteenth Language Resources and Evaluation Conference*, pages 1159–1166, Marseille, France. European Language Resources Association.

Andy Cowell, editor. 2012. *English-Arapaho Dictionary, 4th ed.* Center for the Study of the Indigenous Languages of the West.

Daniel Dacanay, Atticus Harrigan, and Antti Arppe. 2021a. Computational analysis versus human intuition: A critical comparison of vector semantics with manual semantic classification in the context of Plains Cree. In *Proceedings of the 4th Workshop on the Use of Computational Methods in the Study of Endangered Languages Volume 1 (Papers)*, pages 33–43.

Daniel Dacanay, Atticus Harrigan, Arok Wolvengrey, and Antti Arppe. 2021b. The more detail, the better? –investigating the effects of semantic ontology specificity on vector semantic classification with a Plains Cree/*nêhiyawêwin* dictionary. In *Proceedings of the First Workshop on Natural Language Processing for Indigenous Languages of the Americas*, pages 143–152.

Mark Davies. 2008. The Corpus of Contemporary American English (COCA).

Jacob Devlin, Ming-Wei Chang, Kenton Lee, and Kristina Toutanova. 2019. BERT: Pre-training of deep bidirectional transformers for language understanding. In *Proceedings of the 2019 Conference of the North American Chapter of the Association for Computational Linguistics: Human Language Technologies, Volume 1 (Long and Short Papers)*, pages 4171–4186, Minneapolis, Minnesota. Association for Computational Linguistics.

Connie Dickinson. 2000. Complex predicates in Tsafiki. *Proceedings of the Annual Meeting of the Berkeley Linguistics Society*, 26(2):27–37.

Kawin Ethayarajh, David Duvenaud, and Graeme Hirst. 2019. Towards understanding linear word analogies. In *Proceedings of the 57th Annual Meeting of the Association for Computational Linguistics*, pages 3253–3262, Florence, Italy. Association for Computational Linguistics.

Christiane Fellbaum, editor. 1998. *WordNet: An Electronic Lexical Database.* MIT Press, Cambridge, MA.

Atticus Harrigan and Antti Arppe. 2021. Leveraging English word embeddings for semi-automatic semantic classification in *Nêhiyawêwin* (Plains Cree). In *Proceedings of the First Workshop on Natural Language Processing for Indigenous Languages of the Americas*, pages 113–121.

Atticus G Harrigan, Katherine Schmirler, Antti Arppe, Lene Antonsen, Trond Trosterud, and Arok Wolvenengrey. 2017. Learning from the computational modelling of Plains Cree verbs. *Morphology*, 27(4):565–598.

Daniel W. Hieber. in progress. A survey of lexical resources in low-resource languages.

Jordan Lachler, editor. 2010. *Dictionary of Alaskan Haida*. Sealaska Heritage Institute.

Ray R. Larson. 2012. *Understanding Information Retrieval Systems*, chapter Information Retrieval Systems. Auerbach Publications.

Nancy LeClaire and George Cardinal, editors. 1998. *Alberta Elders' Cree Dictionary*. Duval Publishing House Ltd.

Maskwachees Cultural College. 2009. *Maskwacîs dictionary of Cree words / nêhiyaw pîkiskwêwinisa*.

Ryan T. McDonald, Georgios-Ioannis Brokos, and Ion Androutsopoulos. 2018. Deep relevance ranking using enhanced document-query interactions. *CoRR*, abs/1809.01682.

Tomás Mikolov, Kai Chen, Greg Corrado, and Jeffrey Dean. 2013a. Efficient estimation of word representations in vector space. In *International Conference on Learning Representations*, Scottsdale, Arizona, USA.

Tomas Mikolov, Ilya Sutskever, Kai Chen, Greg S Corrado, and Jeff Dean. 2013b. Distributed representations of words and phrases and their compositionality. In *Advances in Neural Information Processing Systems*, pages 3111–3119.

George A. Miller. 1995. Wordnet: A lexical database for English. *Communications of the ACM*, 38(11):39–41.

Douglas W. Oard. 2012. *Understanding Information Retrieval Systems*, chapter Multilingual Information Access. Auerbach Publications.

Stella O'Shea, Helen Waterhouse, et al., editors. 2012. *Cambridge learner's dictionary*, 4 edition. Cambridge University Press, Cambridge.

Jeffrey Pennington, Richard Socher, and Christopher D Manning. 2014. Glove: Global vectors for word representation. In *Proceedings of the 2014 conference on empirical methods in natural language processing (EMNLP)*, pages 1532–1543.

Anna Rogers, Aleksandr Drozd, and Bofang Li. 2017. The (too many) problems of analogical reasoning with word vectors. In *Proceedings of the 6th Joint Conference on Lexical and Computational Semantics (*SEM 2017)*, pages 135–148, Vancouver, Canada. Association for Computational Linguistics.

Bonny Sands, Amanda L. Miller, and Johanna Brugman. 2007. The lexicon in language attrition: The case of Nǀuu. In *Selected Proceedings of the 37th Annual Conference on African Linguistics*, pages 55–65, Somerville, MA. Cascadilla Proceedings Project.

Zhongmin Shi, Baohua Gu, Fred Popowich, and Anoop Sarkar. 2005. Synonym-based expansion and boosting-based re-ranking: A two-phase approach for genomic information retrieval. In *Text Retrieval Conference (TREC)*.

Conor Snoek, Dorothy Thunder, Kaidi Lõo, Antti Arppe, Jordan Lachler, Sjur Moshagen, and Trond Trosterud. 2014. Modeling the noun morphology of Plains Cree. In *Proceedings of the 2014 Workshop on the Use of Computational Methods in the Study of Endangered Languages*, pages 34–42.

Robyn Speer, Joshua Chin, and Catherine Havasi. 2017. Conceptnet 5.5: An open multilingual graph of general knowledge. In *Proceedings of the Thirty-First AAAI Conference on Artificial Intelligence, February 4-9, 2017, San Francisco, California, USA*, pages 4444–4451. AAAI Press.

Danny Sullivan. 2002. How search engines work.

Bo Svensén. 2009. *A handbook of lexicography: The theory and practice of dictionary-making*. Cambridge University Press, Cambridge.

John R. Taylor. 2003. *Linguistic categorization*, 3 edition. Oxford Textbooks in Linguistics. Oxford University Press, Oxford.

Davide Turcato, Fred Popowich, Janine Toole, Dan Fass, Devlan Nicholson, and Gordon Tisher. 2000. Adapting a synonym database to specific domains. In *Proceedings of the ACL-2000 Workshop on Recent Advances in Natural Language Processing and Information Retrieval: Held in Conjunction with the 38th Annual Meeting of the Association for Computational Linguistics - Volume 11*, RANLPIR '00, page 1–11, USA. Association for Computational Linguistics.

Doug Turnbull and John Berryman. 2016. *Relevant Search: With Applications for Solr and Elasticsearch*. Manning.

Arok Wolvengrey, editor. *nēhiýawēwin: itwēwina / Cree: Words*. University of Regina Press.

Li Zhang, Jun Li, and Chao Wang. 2017. Automatic synonym extraction using word2vec and spectral clustering. In *2017 36th Chinese Control Conference (CCC)*, pages 5629–5632.

A Appendix

The following is a list of all 26 English lemmas within the top 1000 most common content lemmas in COCA (Davies, 2008) which are not present in the definitions of any of entries in the consulted dictionaries of Plains Cree, Arapaho, Northern Haida, and Tsuut'ina, along with their frequency rank in COCA overall (including function words).

1. percent (265)
2. national (311)
3. policy (406)
4. data (417)
5. international (616)
6. campaign (634)
7. author (680)

8. administration (744)
9. career (796)
10. candidate (830)
11. network (882)
12. district (885)
13. theory (896)
14. reality (956)
15. democratic (1020)
16. democratic (1028)
17. politics (1059)
18. user (1081)
19. attorney (1102)
20. budget (1107)
21. senator (1144)
22. Senate (1155)
23. violence (1156)
24. civil (1171)
25. institution (1190)
26. professional (1192)

Enhancing Spanish-Quechua Machine Translation with Pre-Trained Models and Diverse Data Sources: LCT-EHU at AmericasNLP Shared Task

Nouman Ahmed, Natalia Flechas Manrique, and **Antonije Petrović**
University of the Basque Country (UPV/EHU)
{anouman001, nflechas001, apetrovic001}@ikasle.ehu.eus

Abstract

We present the LCT-EHU submission to the AmericasNLP 2023 low-resource machine translation shared task. We focus on the Spanish-Quechua language pair and explore the usage of different approaches: (1) Obtain new parallel corpora from the literature and legal domains, (2) Compare a high-resource Spanish-English pre-trained MT model with a Spanish-Finnish pre-trained model (with Finnish being chosen as a target language due to its morphological similarity to Quechua), and (3) Explore additional techniques such as copied corpus and back-translation. Overall, we show that the Spanish-Finnish pre-trained model outperforms other setups, while low-quality synthetic data reduces the performance.

1 Introduction

The LCT-EHU team participated in the AmericasNLP 2023 low-resource machine translation shared task. The task involved machine translation from Spanish to 11 different indigenous languages. The languages in question are very much low-resource, with the number of speakers spanning from a few tens of thousands to a few million and with limited availability of parallel data. Monolingual data is not easily obtained either - Wikipedia is available only in a few of these languages, with the number of articles not being very high. Our team focused on Spanish-Quechua language pair with the approach consisting in:

- Finding and aligning new parallel data. We obtained bilingual legal documents of the Government of Ecuador (the constitution and some laws); the novel "The Little Prince", and the UN Declaration of Human Rights.
- Using pre-trained machine translation models trained on other language pairs. We experimented with Spanish-English, as a high-resource language pair, and Spanish-Finnish, with the linguistic intuition that using an agglutinative language on the target side would provide a closer set-up to the problem we were working on, as previously explored by Ortega and Pillaipakkamnatt (2018) and Ortega et al. (2020).
- Synthetic and monolingual data. We experimented with a copied corpus approach and synthetic parallel corpus creation from monolingual Spanish data.

The official metric used in the shared task is chrF++ (Popović, 2017). In the previous edition of the AmericasNLP shared task, the chrF score of 34.6 was obtained by the REPUcs team (Moreno, 2021) for the Spanish-Quechua language pair. However, this year's shared task takes the second-best result of 34.3 as a baseline.

All of the source code and newly collected data are available in the Github repository [1].

2 Related Work

Some previous work and approaches that were important for our experiments are explained in the following sub-sections.

2.1 AmericasNLP 2021 Shared Task

In the first edition of the AmericasNLP low-resource MT shared task, various contributions to the field of machine translation of American indigenous languages were published. The organizers provided training data collected from various sources, alongside manually translated development and test data. Two tracks were available: (1) development set used for training, and (2) development set not used for training.

Helsinki team (Vázquez et al., 2021) won the task in the majority of language pairs in both tracks,

[1] `https://github.com/nouman-10/MT-SharedTask`

Proceedings of the Workshop on Natural Language Processing for Indigenous Languages of the Americas (AmericasNLP), pages 156–162
July 14, 2023

using a two-phase transformer training. They also obtained additional parallel and monolingual data for Spanish-Quechua. Their Model A was a multilingual model with 11 languages, trained for 200 000 steps, which was then trained independently for each of the target indigenous languages for additional 2 500 steps. Model B was a multilingual model with Spanish as the only source language, and with 11 target languages (10 indigenous languages + English). The two-phase training was performed again. In the first phase, they trained the model with 90% of Spanish-English data, while the remaining 10% was divided between 10 indigenous languages, each taking 1% . In the second phase, the proportion of Spanish-English data is reduced to 50%, while including backtranslated data as well. Different versions of both Model A and Model B were trained, depending on whether the development data was used during training or not.

2.2 Synthetic translations and copied corpus

The use of synthetic translation approaches is born out of a common concern in machine translation: the lack of high-quality parallel data for many language pairs. To solve this, various solutions have been proposed. One of the most common ones is known as back-translation (Sennrich et al., 2016), which involves creating a synthetic parallel corpus by translating monolingual data from the target language into the source language (or source to target, in other approaches) and using this to augment the existing parallel data for training models. Another approach (Currey et al., 2017) involves using monolingual data from the target and aligning it with itself, to mimic parallel data (this is known as *copied corpus*). The authors try to explain the success of this approach by stating that there might be an improved accuracy on named entities and words that are identical in both source and target texts.

3 Data

In this section, we will describe the data used in the experiments.

3.1 Original parallel data

The following corpora were provided by the organizers of the competition (Agić and Vulić (2019) and Tiedemann (2012):

- **JW300 (quz & quy)** A collection of Jehovah's Witnesses Texts, both in Cuzco and Ayacucho Quechua.
- **MINEDU (quy)**: Sentences extracted from the official dictionary of the Ministry of Education (MINEDU) in Peru for Quechua Ayacucho.
- **Dict_misc (quy)**: Dictionary entries and samples collected by Diego Huarcaya.

The counts of sentences and domain information are presented in Table 1. The column *Count* refers to the number of sentences in this table and all subsequent ones.

Name	Domain	Count
JW300	Religious	121064
MINEDU	Dictionary	643
Dict misc	Dictionary	8998

Table 1: Original data of the AmericasNLP 2023 competition.

3.2 Additional resources

We also used resources that were introduced by some of the teams that participated in the 2021 competition. Details of the data introduced by the Helsinki-NLP team (Vázquez et al., 2021) are presented in Table 2.

Name	Domain	Count
Peruvian Constitution	Legal	1276
Bolivian Constitution	Legal	2193
Tatoeba (OPUS)	Misc.	163
Bible	Religious	31102

Table 2: Data introduced by the Helsinki-NLP 2021 team.

In Table 3 the details of the corpora used by the REPUcs-AmericasNLP2021 (Moreno, 2021) team are shown.

Name	Domain	Count
Web Misc	Misc.	985
Lexicon	Dictionary	6161
Handbook	Educational	2296
Peruvian Constitution	Legal	999
Regulations of the Amazon Parliament	Legal	287

Table 3: Data introduced by the REPUcs-AmericasNLP2021 team.

In addition to the data collected in the previous AmericasNLP task, we found some parallel data that was used to build *A Basic Language Technology Toolkit for Quechua* (Rios, 2016) [2]. The parallel data was used to create a multilingual treebank in the three languages of the machine translation systems, Spanish-German and Spanish-Cuzco Quechua. The majority of the corpus was Spanish-German, with the Quechua counterpart being translated by several native speakers in Peru. There were multiple aligned documents available here but most of them needed further cleaning and alignment. The three documents that were selected are:

- Strategy paper of the Swiss Agency for Development and Cooperation on the cooperation with Peru [3]
- 2009 Annual report of the Deutsche Welle Academy about Development and the Media [4]
- 2008 Annual report of a private foundation dedicated to education [5]

The sentence count of the documents is also shown in Table 4.

Name	Count
Cosude	529
DW	856
Fundeducation	440

Table 4: Additional resources of Cuzco Quechua

3.3 New resources

Apart from using the already existing resources, we have gathered, processed, and aligned publicly available documents found around the web. The summary of these resources is shown in Table 5. It is important to emphasize that, theoretically, Quechua should be regarded as a linguistic family rather than a single language, given that its various varieties exhibit limited mutual intelligibility when they are geographically distant. Within the specialized literature, the term "Quechua" is employed to refer to the varieties spoken in Bolivia and Peru, while the term "Quichua" is preferred for those spoken in Ecuador and Argentina, as indicated by Avellana (Avellana). For the sake of simplicity, when uncertainty arises regarding the specific Quechua variety being discussed, we adopt the `que` code as a macrolanguage identifier.

The documents were found in pdf format and were transformed into plain text using the `pdftotext` [6] tool, trying to keep the layout of the original pdf as intact as possible. Since most of the documents contained word wrapping to keep the fixed width of the document, we performed the unwrapping in such cases by joining the words at the ends of the lines which ended with the - sign. In this step, we made an effort to preserve the original document structure whenever feasible. For instance, with "The Little Prince," we maintained the chapter arrangement of the novel. Similarly, when dealing with the Ecuadorian constitution and laws [7], we retained the individual article divisions.

In the subsequent stage, we performed sentence segmentation at the chapter level while preserving the chapter boundaries. Our team experimented with several sentence segmenters such as `NLTK`, `spaCy`, and `stanza`. Following careful consideration, we ultimately chose `stanza` based on a higher alignment score, as explained in the next paragraph. For `stanza`, we opted for the Spanish sentence segmentation model for both Spanish and Quechua texts.

The `HunAlign` (Varga et al., 2007) tool was utilized to align the sentences. Additionally, we used a dictionary provided by AmericasNLP organizers as an input to the tool to improve the alignments. Overall, the legal document alignments were quite accurate, whereas the alignments of "The Little Prince" were slightly less precise. This could be attributed to the greater freedom often allowed in translations of literary works compared to the strict and rigid translations necessary in legal contexts. Even though `HunAlign` gives a confidence score for each alignment, we did not perform any filtering of the aligned sentences and decided to use all obtained alignments.

3.4 Synthetic translations

We collected three history books in Spanish. Specifically, old Chronicles of the Indies about the Incan empire and the subsequent colonial period. We hypothesized that because these books have plenty

[2] https://github.com/a-rios/squoia

[3] https://www.cooperacionsuiza.pe/cosude/

[4] http://www.dw.de/

[5] http://www.fundeducation.org/

[6] https://www.xpdfreader.com/

[7] https://www.asambleanacional.gob.ec/es/contenido/publicaciones

Name	Domain	Quechua variety	Count
The Little Prince	Literature	que	1312
UN Human Rights Declaration	Legal	qus	91
The Constitution of Ecuador	Legal	que	2243
Ley Soberania Alimentaria	Legal	que	174
Ley Consumo Drogas	Legal	que	69
Ley Organica Alimentacion	Legal	que	186

Table 5: Description of the gathered new parallel data

of words in Quechua language, they would be from a suitable domain. The three books were turned into plain text files and their sentences were segmented in the way described in the previous section. After that, the texts were translated into Quechua with the Spanish-Finnish model we fine-tuned on the original datasets and the additional resources introduced by participating teams in the 2021 competition (`train + extra`). Table 6 shows the final sentence counts of these books after being processed.

Name	Domain	Count
Comentarios Reales	History	1032
Nueva Cronica y Buen Gobierno	History	3578
Cronica del Peru	History	1798

Table 6: Chronicles of the Indies description.

3.5 Monolingual (Copied Corpus)

Following the approach in (Currey et al., 2017), we decided to add some monolingual Quechua data and copy it as is to create a parallel corpus. We used publicly available datasets on Huggingface and segmented the sentences based on line breaks, without any post-processing. The datasets included data cc100 (Conneau et al. (2020) and Wenzek et al. (2020) which was an attempt to recreate the dataset used for training XLM-R, and data from (Zevallos et al., 2022), which is a monolingual corpus of Southern Quechua and includes the Wiki and OSCAR corpora. Table 7 shows the sentence counts of these datasets

Name	Count
cc100	113931
Llamacha	182669

Table 7: Description of monolingual data used for Copied Corpus Approach

4 Models & Results

We experimented with 2 major model setups and 5 different kinds of dataset combinations. The two setups were based on fine-tuned machine translation models of Spanish-English and Spanish-Finnish (Tiedemann and Thottingal, 2020). On the one hand, the reason behind using a fine-tuned Spanish-English model was that both of them are high-resource languages, and thus the model has been trained on large amounts of data. This probably means that the model has learned a good Spanish encoder, and thus could be useful for further fine-tuning. On the other hand, the reasoning behind choosing a Spanish-Finnish model and fine-tuning on Spanish-Quechua was the similarity between Finnish and Quechua (specifically the agglutinative morphology of both languages), and Finnish having comparably more data than Quechua. All models were trained for 20 epochs, with evaluation being done after every 1000 steps. The best model was selected based on the chrF score on the development set. Here, we will define the different combinations of datasets used for our experiments:

- `train` : The original parallel-data provided in the AmericasNLP-2023 Shared Task (as mentioned in Table 1).
- `train + extra`: This includes the combination of original parallel data and extra Ayacucho Quechua (Quy) data gathered from different sources.
- `train + extra + aligned`: This includes the data above plus our newly gathered parallel data (as mentioned in Table 5).
- `train + extra + aligned + copied`: In addition to the above data, it also includes the monolingual copied corpus, (Table 7).

Model name	Pre-trained model	Data	Dev		Test		Sub
			chrF	BLEU	chrF	BLEU	
baseline			33.80	3.47	34.3	3.63	-
es_en_orig		train	36.70	3.11	-	-	-
es_en_extra		train+extra	36.57	2.42	-	-	-
es_en_aligned	es-en	train+extra+aligned	36.96	2.81	37.71	**3.47**	4
es_en_copied		train+extra+aligned+copied	31.48	1.22	-	-	-
es_en_quz		train+extra+quz	36.86	2.72	-	-	-
es_fi_orig		train	36.93	2.86	-	-	-
es_fi_extra		train+extra	37.51	3.04	38.21	3.11	2
es_fi_aligned	es-fi	train+extra+aligned	37.34	2.90	**38.59**	3.45	3
es_fi_copied		train+extra+aligned+copied	32.01	1.66	-	-	-
es_fi_quz		train+extra+quz	**37.70**	**3.36**	38.40	3.08	1
es_fi_all		all	36.40	2.54	37.26	3.06	5

Table 8: Results of the experiments on the development data, and official results on test data of Spanish-Quechua language pair. Column "Sub" describes the submission number to the official shared task evaluation.

- `train + extra + aligned + quz`: It includes all the data above excluding copied corpus, but also includes the additional data gathered from different sources pertaining to Cuzco Quechua (Quz). The reason for removing copied corpus was that it resulted in a decrease of the chrF score in all the experiments.
- `all`: It includes all the data above excluding the copied corpus, but includes the synthetic translations, as mentioned in Section 3.4.

4.1 Fine-tuned Spanish to English

Following (Vázquez et al., 2021), where including a majority of Spanish-English parallel data while building an MT system for low-resource languages improved the performance across all the languages, we decided to use an already fine-tuned Spanish-English MT model and fine-tune it again on our Spanish-Quechua parallel corpus. Concretely, we used the `opus-mt-es-en` model available at Huggingface [8]. As expected, we can see that these models perform quite close to the baseline system. Including more data seems to help as well, with the exception of copied corpus. The reason for this, we suspect, is due to the quantity of the data being higher than our total Spanish-Quechua parallel corpora (no analysis was done on the quality of the data). The best model in this case was fine-tuned on `train + extra + aligned` achieving a chrF score of 36.96 and 37.71 on the development and test set respectively with the `train + extra + quz` performing quite similarly as well.

4.2 Fine-tuned Spanish to Finnish

Lastly, we tried using a fine-tuned version of the Spanish-Finnish MT model. The model we used was `opus-mt-es-fi`, available at Huggingface [9]. The reason for choosing this specific model was firstly because of the similarity between Finnish and Quechua, i.e, both being agglutinative languages, and secondly, Finnish being a relatively high-resource language as compared to Quechua. This proved to be the best model among our experiments, which we believe is due to the reasons mentioned above. We can see in Table 8 that adding aligned data from Ayacucho Quechua seems to help more than adding Cuzco Quechua parallel sources. The best model among the experiments was trained on `train + extra + aligned` and achieved a chrF score of 37.34 and 38.59 on the development and test set respectively.

One final experiment was conducted on all of the collected data meaning `train + extra + aligned + quz + bcktr`. The model was able to achieve a chrF score of 36.40 and 37.26 on the Spanish-Quechua development and test set respectively. All the models are available on Huggingface [10]

[8] `https://huggingface.co/Helsinki-NLP/opus-mt-es-en`

[9] `https://huggingface.co/Helsinki-NLP/opus-mt-es-fi`

[10] `https://huggingface.co/americasnlp-lct-ehu`

5 Conclusion

To summarize our findings, in our submission to the AmericasNLP 2023 low-resource machine translation shared task for the Spanish-Quechua language pair, we have explored fine-tuning existing models in different language pairs, combining them with different data setups. We have collected and aligned new parallel data, created synthetic translations, and made use of copied corpus approach. The highest-performing model on the development data achieved 37.70 chrF. This model was obtained by fine-tuning OPUS MT's Spanish-Finnish model on the original training data, augmented with additional data presented by previous year's teams, both for Ayacucho and Cuzco Quechua. In the test set, however, the highest performing model was different, obtaining a chrF score of 38.59. This model was the same as the previous one, but the data consisted of the original training data, data from previous year's submissions (excluding Cuzco Quechua) and the novel alignments introduced in this work.

6 Acknowledgements

The authors would like to thank Erasmus Mundus European Masters Program in Language and Communication Technologies for its support. We would also like to thank the Center for Information Technology of the University of Groningen for their support and for providing access to the Hábrók high performance computing cluster.

References

Željko Agić and Ivan Vulić. 2019. JW300: A wide-coverage parallel corpus for low-resource languages. In *Proceedings of the 57th Annual Meeting of the Association for Computational Linguistics*, pages 3204–3210, Florence, Italy. Association for Computational Linguistics.

Alicia Avellana. *Las Categorías Funcionales en el Español en Contacto con Lenguas Indígenas de la Argentina: Tiempo, Aspecto y Modo*. Ph.D. thesis, Universidad de Buenos Aires, year =.

Alexis Conneau, Kartikay Khandelwal, Naman Goyal, Vishrav Chaudhary, Guillaume Wenzek, Francisco Guzmán, Edouard Grave, Myle Ott, Luke Zettlemoyer, and Veselin Stoyanov. 2020. Unsupervised cross-lingual representation learning at scale. In *Proceedings of the 58th Annual Meeting of the Association for Computational Linguistics*, pages 8440–8451, Online. Association for Computational Linguistics.

Anna Currey, Antonio Valerio Miceli Barone, and Kenneth Heafield. 2017. Copied monolingual data improves low-resource neural machine translation. In *Proceedings of the Second Conference on Machine Translation*, pages 148–156, Copenhagen, Denmark. Association for Computational Linguistics.

Oscar Moreno. 2021. The REPU CS' Spanish–Quechua submission to the AmericasNLP 2021 shared task on open machine translation. In *Proceedings of the First Workshop on Natural Language Processing for Indigenous Languages of the Americas*, pages 241–247, Online. Association for Computational Linguistics.

John Ortega and Krishnan Pillaipakkamnatt. 2018. Using morphemes from agglutinative languages like Quechua and Finnish to aid in low-resource translation. In *Proceedings of the AMTA 2018 Workshop on Technologies for MT of Low Resource Languages (LoResMT 2018)*, pages 1–11, Boston, MA. Association for Machine Translation in the Americas.

John E. Ortega, Richard Alexander Castro Mamani, and Kyunghyun Cho. 2020. Neural machine translation with a polysynthetic low resource language. *Machine Translation*, 34:325 – 346.

Maja Popović. 2017. chrF++: words helping character n-grams. In *Proceedings of the Second Conference on Machine Translation*, pages 612–618, Copenhagen, Denmark. Association for Computational Linguistics.

Annette Rios. 2016. *A Basic Language Technology Toolkit for Quechua*. Ph.D. thesis.

Rico Sennrich, Barry Haddow, and Alexandra Birch. 2016. Improving neural machine translation models with monolingual data. In *Proceedings of the 54th Annual Meeting of the Association for Computational Linguistics (Volume 1: Long Papers)*, pages 86–96, Berlin, Germany. Association for Computational Linguistics.

Jörg Tiedemann. 2012. Parallel data, tools and interfaces in OPUS. In *Proceedings of the Eighth International Conference on Language Resources and Evaluation (LREC'12)*, pages 2214–2218, Istanbul, Turkey. European Language Resources Association (ELRA).

Jörg Tiedemann and Santhosh Thottingal. 2020. OPUS-MT — Building open translation services for the World. In *Proceedings of the 22nd Annual Conferenec of the European Association for Machine Translation (EAMT)*, Lisbon, Portugal.

Daniel Varga, Peter Halacsy, Andras Kornai, Viktor Nagy, Laszlo Nemeth, and Viktor Tron. 2007. Parallel corpora for medium density languages. In *Recent Advances in Natural Language Processing IV. Selected papers from RANLP-05*, pages 247–258. Benjamins, Amsterdam.

Raúl Vázquez, Yves Scherrer, Sami Virpioja, and Jörg Tiedemann. 2021. The Helsinki submission to the AmericasNLP shared task. In *Proceedings of the First Workshop on Natural Language Processing for Indigenous Languages of the Americas*, pages 255–264, Online. Association for Computational Linguistics.

Guillaume Wenzek, Marie-Anne Lachaux, Alexis Conneau, Vishrav Chaudhary, Francisco Guzmán, Armand Joulin, and Edouard Grave. 2020. CCNet: Extracting high quality monolingual datasets from web crawl data. In *Proceedings of the Twelfth Language Resources and Evaluation Conference*, pages 4003–4012, Marseille, France. European Language Resources Association.

Rodolfo Zevallos, John Ortega, William Chen, Richard Castro, Nuria Bel, Cesar Toshio, Renzo Venturas, Hilario Aradiel, and Nelsi Melgarejo. 2022. Introducing qubert: A large monolingual corpus and bert model for southern quechua. In *Proceedings of the Third Workshop on Deep Learning for Low-Resource Natural Language Processing*, pages 1–13.

ChatGPT is not a good indigenous translator

David Stap **Ali Araabi**
Language Technology Lab
University of Amsterdam
{d.stap, a.araabi}@uva.nl

Abstract

This report investigates the continuous challenges of Machine Translation (MT) systems on indigenous and extremely low-resource language pairs. Despite the notable achievements of Large Language Models (LLMs) that excel in various tasks, their applicability to low-resource languages remains questionable. In this study, we leveraged the AmericasNLP competition to evaluate the translation performance of different systems for Spanish to 11 indigenous languages from South America. Our team, LTLAmsterdam, submitted a total of four systems including GPT-4, a bilingual model, fine-tuned M2M100, and a combination of fine-tuned M2M100 with kNN-MT. We found that even large language models like GPT-4 are not well-suited for extremely low-resource languages. Our results suggest that fine-tuning M2M100 models can offer significantly better performance for extremely low-resource translation.

1 Introduction

This paper presents the participation of the Language Technology Lab (LTL) from the University of Amsterdam in the AmericasNLP 2023 Shared Task, which aims to develop Machine Translation (MT) systems for indigenous languages of the Americas. We submitted translation results for Spanish into all indigenous languages: Hñähñu (oto), Wixarika (hch), Nahuatl (nah), Guaraní (gn), Bribri (bzd), Rarámuri (tar), Quechua (quy), Aymara (aym), Shipibo-Konibo (shp), Asháninka (cni), and Chatino (czn). In the face of limited parallel and monolingual data, our approaches focus on maximizing the potential of available resources and models. Specifically, our objectives include: 1) evaluating the performance of GPT-4, a state-of-the-art language model, in extremely low-resource settings; 2) utilizing a carefully optimized transformer setting for low-resource NMT (Araabi and Monz, 2020; Zwennicker and Stap); 3) exploring the effectiveness of a fine-tuned version of the multilingual M2M100 (Fan et al., 2021) model; and 4) investigating the potential of augmenting a neural model with a k-nearest-neighbor machine translation (kNN-MT) (Khandelwal et al., 2021) component. Our experiments show that, while GPT-4 demonstrates comparable performance to bilingual models trained from scratch, it significantly lags behind the fine-tuned M2M100 models. Notably, our M2M100+kNN-MT system emerged as our top-performing approach.

2 Data and preprocessing

2.1 Data

We used the parallel data provided by the shared task organizers for training across all South American languages (Ebrahimi et al., 2023). For Chatino, we used the Chatino Speech Corpus Archive Dataset.[1]

2.2 Pre-processing

We apply punctuation normalization, tokenization, data cleaning, and true-casing using the Moses scripts (Koehn et al., 2007). The sentence length is limited to a maximum of 175 tokens during training. After replacing phrases with variables, we also apply BPE segmentation (Sennrich et al., 2016) with the BPE parameter effective for each data size (Araabi and Monz, 2020). Table 2 presents the number of training samples following preprocessing.

3 Models and experiments

3.1 GPT-4

Large Language Models (LLM) such as ChatGPT are strong translation models for high-resource languages (Jiao et al., 2023). For low-resource languages, ChatGPT produces relatively few halluci-

[1] https://scholarworks.iu.edu/dspace/handle/2022/21028

Proceedings of the Workshop on Natural Language Processing for Indigenous Languages of the Americas (AmericasNLP), pages 163–167
July 14, 2023

The translations provided may not be entirely accurate but are the closest possible translations using available resources.
Here is the translation for [TGT]
(Note: The provided text does not contain correct Ashaninka punctuation.)
The 10th sentence cannot be translated since it goes against Bribri cultural values, as the language has certain rules that may prevent imperative structures or indications that may go against tribal communication.
These translations are based on the Mezquital Ñahñu dialect.
(Note: Nahuatl is an indigenous language spoken in Mexico and there exists variation in vocabulary and grammar across different dialects, regions and time periods, so these translations may differ from other possible versions)
(Seq items above included due to impossibility of translating Mary Todd, Abe Lincoln, Illinois, and A Christmas Carol.)
The translations provided are approximations based on the Bribri language structure and available lexical resources.
(Note: Unfortunately, there isn't much appropriate vocabulary available online for Hnahnu/Ñähñu Language, which is an indigenous language of Mexico. I tried my best to give some translations, but the result may not be accurate.)

Table 1: Some examples of unwanted output produced by ChatGPT during translation.

Language	code	#sentences	#subwords
Asháninka	cni	3869	5k
Aymara	aym	13000	10k
Bribri	bzd	7502	5k
Guaraní	gn	26011	20k
Nahuatl	nah	15898	20k
Hñähñu	oto	4838	$5k$
Quechua	quy	250709	$20k$
Rarámuri	tar	13754	$10k$
Shipibo	shp	29126	$20k$
Wixarika	hch	8963	$10k$
Chatino	czn	310	$5k$

Table 2: Number of training samples and vocabulary size after preprocessing.

nations under perturbation, and its hallucinations are qualitatively different from conventional translation models (Guerreiro et al., 2023). It remains unclear how well LLMs perform when translating into *extremely* low-resource languages.

We use the ChatGPT (`gpt-4`) API[2] to translate Spanish source languages into the indigenous target languages. Following (Jiao et al., 2023) we use the following translation prompt: "*Please provide the* [TGT] *translation for these sentences:*". We add the following role content: "*You are a machine translation system.*" (Peng et al., 2023). Initial experiments with Temperature set to 0 (Peng et al., 2023) produce results that are inferior to the default Temperature value, so we stick to the latter. During translation, ChatGPT frequently added boilerplate text to translations such as "*Feel free to make adjustments if you have a better understanding of the language.*". See Table 1 for additional examples of unwanted ChatGPT boilerplate outputs. While some of these outputs, such as the warnings about inaccurate translations, can be valuable to machine translation users, we remove this boilerplate text in a post-processing step before evaluating the translations.

[2]`https://platform.openai.com/docs/api-reference/chat`

3.2 Bilingual

To conduct our bilingual experiments, we employ Transformer models (Vaswani et al., 2017) with parameters proposed by Araabi and Monz (2020), specifically tailored to extremely low-resource data regime. We use the Fairseq library (Ott et al., 2019) for our experiments.

3.3 Finetuned M2M100

Following Adelani et al. (2022), we fine-tuned the multilingual M2M100 model (Fan et al., 2021) for translations from Spanish to Indigenous languages.

M2M100 necessitates specifying the target language tag during decoding. Given that the Indigenous languages of interest are not part of M2M100, we adopted the approach suggested by Adelani et al. (2022) and selected a language tag that *is* represented in the pre-trained model. Preliminary results indicated that the translation quality remained unaffected by the choice of the target language tag, so we chose Swahili as the target language.

We used the 418M parameter version of M2M100 and trained individual models for each of the 11 target languages. These models were finetuned using the HuggingFace toolkit (Wolf et al., 2020). We employed the default learning rate of

model	oto	hch	nah	gn	bzd	tar	quy	aym	shp	cni	czn	avg
GPT-4	0.119	0.169	0.161	0.160	0.106	0.141	0.264	0.203	0.180	0.194	–	0.170
bilingual	0.073	0.185	0.072	0.120	0.113	0.113	0.133	0.146	0.129	0.217	**0.293**	0.145
M2M100	0.131	0.287	0.299	0.301	0.198	0.141	0.360	0.295	0.203	0.262	0.146	0.238
+kNN	**0.178**	**0.458**	**0.527**	**0.402**	**0.401**	**0.292**	**0.475**	**0.459**	**0.470**	**0.425**	0.158	**0.386**
GPT-4	0.117	0.157	0.159	0.155	0.094	0.130	0.258	0.183	0.162	0.189	–	0.160
bilingual	0.078	0.210	0.070	0.119	0.123	0.114	0.150	0.140	0.124	0.216	**0.366**	0.155
M2M100	0.139	0.304	0.260	0.329	0.214	0.151	0.368	0.252	0.198	0.260	0.144	0.238
+ kNN	**0.145**	**0.319**	**0.273**	**0.341**	**0.261**	**0.180**	**0.370**	**0.276**	**0.279**	**0.300**	0.152	**0.263**

Table 3: Chrf++ scores for Spanish→X directions on the development set (top rows) and test set (bottom rows). Best results are depicted in **bold**, and best results that do not encode the development set are underlined.

5e−5, set the maximum source and target length to 200, and stop training after 3 epochs.

3.4 Finetuned M2M100 + *k*NN-MT

We made the decision to withdraw this model from the competition track due to its encoding of the development set. Although it does not technically violate the competition rule (which states: "*The only limitation is that we ask participants to not have the test input translated by hand or train on the development or test sets*"), our solution operates in a grey area and confers an unfair advantage over other submissions. That said, we describe the approach below.

We operated under the assumption that the provided development data is similar to the test data. Using the development data during training or an additional fine-tuning step is a clear strategy for leveraging this similarity when aiming for enhanced performance on the development and test set domains. However, we opted for an alternative approach that permits more fine-grained control over the degree to which the resulting model depends on the development data as opposed to the training data. Furthermore, we explicitly sought to prevent encoding information about the development set within the resulting model weights, as this could potentially lead to overfitting and reduced generalization capabilities. Such an outcome would undermine the primary objective of creating a robust and versatile MT system that can effectively handle a wide range of input data in the context of Indigenous languages.

k-nearest-neighbor machine translation (*k*NN-MT) is a semi-parametric model that combines a parametric component with a nearest neighbor retrieval mechanism that allows direct access to a datastore of cached examples (Khandelwal et al., 2021). The datastore consists of key-value pairs, where each key is a decoder output representation, and the value is the corresponding target token. At inference time, the model searches the datastore to retrieve the set of k nearest neighbors, and combines the resulting distribution with the NMT distribution through interpolation.

For our submissions, we encoded the development sets of all Spanish to X directions in separate datastores. We do a grid search over *k*NN hyperparameters $\lambda \in \{0.2, 0.3, ...0.7\}$, $k \in \{8, 16, 32\}$ and $T \in \{50, 100\}$ on oto and hch. Based on these results we fix λ to 0.3, k to 32, and T to 50 and report results for those. We use the *k*NN-transformers library (Alon et al., 2022) for our experiments.

4 Results

We report Chrf++ scores (Popović, 2017) in Table 3. In general, we observe similar patterns for the development and test sets. Comparing GPT-4 and our bilingual models, we conclude that GPT-4 is better for 7/10 directions on both the development and test set. Scores for both models are very low; neither ChatGPT nor bilingual NMT are good indigenous translators.

Our *k*NN approach yields best results for 10/11 language directions, and the fine-tuned M2M100 is the best model that does not encode the development set.

Compared to other submissions, our *k*NN model ranks first for Spanish-Bribri, Spanish-Asháninka, and Spanish-Nahuatl, but we decided to withdraw this model (see Section 3.4).

5 Conclusion

In this paper, we describe our submissions to the AmericasNLP 2023 Shared Task on Machine Translation into Indigenous Languages. We submitted translations for all 11 languages. Our best system is the result of finetuning M2M100 on an unseen indigenous language, and augmenting this model with a k-nearest-neighbor datastore based on the development set.

This model ranked first in the Spanish-Bribri, Spanish-Asháninka, and Spanish-Nahuatl language pairs in the competition. However, we have made the decision to withdraw this model due to its operation in a grey area with respect to the competition rules. The uncertainty surrounding its compliance raises concerns about fairness among all participants, prompting us to take this action after discussion with the organizers.

References

David Adelani, Jesujoba Alabi, Angela Fan, Julia Kreutzer, Xiaoyu Shen, Machel Reid, Dana Ruiter, Dietrich Klakow, Peter Nabende, Ernie Chang, Tajuddeen Gwadabe, Freshia Sackey, Bonaventure F. P. Dossou, Chris Emezue, Colin Leong, Michael Beukman, Shamsuddeen Muhammad, Guyo Jarso, Oreen Yousuf, Andre Niyongabo Rubungo, Gilles Hacheme, Eric Peter Wairagala, Muhammad Umair Nasir, Benjamin Ajibade, Tunde Ajayi, Yvonne Gitau, Jade Abbott, Mohamed Ahmed, Millicent Ochieng, Anuoluwapo Aremu, Perez Ogayo, Jonathan Mukiibi, Fatoumata Ouoba Kabore, Godson Kalipe, Derguene Mbaye, Allahsera Auguste Tapo, Victoire Memdjokam Koagne, Edwin Munkoh-Buabeng, Valencia Wagner, Idris Abdulmumin, Ayodele Awokoya, Happy Buzaaba, Blessing Sibanda, Andiswa Bukula, and Sam Manthalu. 2022. A Few Thousand Translations Go a Long Way! Leveraging Pre-trained Models for African News Translation. In *Proceedings of the 2022 Conference of the North American Chapter of the Association for Computational Linguistics: Human Language Technologies*, pages 3053–3070, Seattle, United States. Association for Computational Linguistics.

Uri Alon, Frank Xu, Junxian He, Sudipta Sengupta, Dan Roth, and Graham Neubig. 2022. Neuro-symbolic language modeling with automaton-augmented retrieval. In *International conference on machine learning*, pages 468–485. PMLR.

Ali Araabi and Christof Monz. 2020. Optimizing Transformer for low-resource neural machine translation. In *Proceedings of the 28th International Conference on Computational Linguistics*, pages 3429–3435, Barcelona, Spain (Online). International Committee on Computational Linguistics.

Abteen Ebrahimi, Manuel Mager, Arturo Oncevay, Enora Rice, Cynthia Montaño, John Ortega, Shruti Rijhwani, Alexis Palmer, Rolando Coto-Solano, Hilaria Cruz, and Katharina Kann. 2023. Findings of the AmericasNLP 2023 shared task on machine translation into indigenous languages. In *Proceedings of the Third Workshop on Natural Language Processing for Indigenous Languages of the Americas*. Association for Computational Linguistics.

Angela Fan, Shruti Bhosale, Holger Schwenk, Zhiyi Ma, Ahmed El-Kishky, Siddharth Goyal, Mandeep Baines, Onur Celebi, Guillaume Wenzek, Vishrav Chaudhary, Naman Goyal, Tom Birch, Vitaliy Liptchinsky, Sergey Edunov, Edouard Grave, Michael Auli, and Armand Joulin. 2021. Beyond English-centric multilingual machine translation. *Journal of Machine Learning Research*, 22(107):1–48.

Nuno M. Guerreiro, Duarte Alves, Jonas Waldendorf, Barry Haddow, Alexandra Birch, Pierre Colombo, and André F. T. Martins. 2023. Hallucinations in Large Multilingual Translation Models. ArXiv:2303.16104 [cs].

Wenxiang Jiao, Wenxuan Wang, Jen-tse Huang, Xing Wang, and Zhaopeng Tu. 2023. Is ChatGPT A Good Translator? Yes With GPT-4 As The Engine. ArXiv:2301.08745 [cs].

Urvashi Khandelwal, Angela Fan, Dan Jurafsky, Luke Zettlemoyer, and Mike Lewis. 2021. Nearest Neighbor Machine Translation. ArXiv:2010.00710 [cs].

Philipp Koehn, Hieu Hoang, Alexandra Birch, Chris Callison-Burch, Marcello Federico, Nicola Bertoldi, Brooke Cowan, Wade Shen, Christine Moran, Richard Zens, Chris Dyer, Ondrej Bojar, Alexandra Constantin, and Evan Herbst. 2007. Moses: Open source toolkit for statistical machine translation. In *ACL 2007, Proceedings of the 45th Annual Meeting of the Association for Computational Linguistics, June 23-30, 2007, Prague, Czech Republic*. The Association for Computational Linguistics.

Myle Ott, Sergey Edunov, Alexei Baevski, Angela Fan, Sam Gross, Nathan Ng, David Grangier, and Michael Auli. 2019. fairseq: A fast, extensible toolkit for sequence modeling. In *Proceedings of the 2019 Conference of the North American Chapter of the Association for Computational Linguistics: Human Language Technologies, NAACL-HLT 2019, Minneapolis, MN, USA, June 2-7, 2019, Demonstrations*, pages 48–53. Association for Computational Linguistics.

Keqin Peng, Liang Ding, Qihuang Zhong, Li Shen, Xuebo Liu, Min Zhang, Yuanxin Ouyang, and Dacheng Tao. 2023. Towards Making the Most of ChatGPT for Machine Translation. ArXiv:2303.13780 [cs].

Maja Popović. 2017. chrF++: words helping character n-grams. In *Proceedings of the Second Conference on Machine Translation*, pages 612–618, Copenhagen, Denmark. Association for Computational Linguistics.

Rico Sennrich, Barry Haddow, and Alexandra Birch. 2016. Neural machine translation of rare words with subword units. In *Proceedings of the 54th Annual Meeting of the Association for Computational Linguistics*, pages 1715–1725, Berlin, Germany. Association for Computational Linguistics.

Ashish Vaswani, Noam Shazeer, Niki Parmar, Jakob Uszkoreit, Llion Jones, Aidan N. Gomez, Łukasz

Kaiser, and Illia Polosukhin. 2017. Attention is all you need. In *Advances in Neural Information Processing Systems (NIPS)*, Long Beach, California. Neural Information Processing Systems (NIPS). ArXiv: 1706.03762.

Thomas Wolf, Lysandre Debut, Victor Sanh, Julien Chaumond, Clement Delangue, Anthony Moi, Pierric Cistac, Tim Rault, Remi Louf, Morgan Funtowicz, Joe Davison, Sam Shleifer, Patrick Von Platen, Clara Ma, Yacine Jernite, Julien Plu, Canwen Xu, Teven Le Scao, Sylvain Gugger, Mariama Drame, Quentin Lhoest, and Alexander Rush. 2020. Transformers: State-of-the-Art Natural Language Processing. In *Proceedings of the 2020 Conference on Empirical Methods in Natural Language Processing: System Demonstrations*, pages 38–45, Online. Association for Computational Linguistics.

Just Zwennicker and David Stap. Towards a general purpose machine translation system for sranantongo. In *Proceedings of the 2022 EMNLP Workshop WiNLP*, Abu Dhabi, United Arab Emirates (Hybrid).

Few-shot Spanish-Aymara Machine Translation Using English-Aymara Lexicon

Nat Gillin
nat.gillin@gmail.com

Brian Gummibaerhausen
brian.gbh@gmail.com

Abstract

This paper presents the experiments to train a Spanish-Aymara machine translation model for the AmericasNLP 2023 Machine Translation shared task. We included the English-Aymara GlobalVoices corpus and an English-Aymara lexicon to train the model and limit our training resources to train the model in a *few-shot* manner.

1 Introduction

Aymara is a language spoken in Bolivia, Peru and Chile. It is one of the larger languages in the Americas, and has more than 2 million speakers[1], yet it has received worryingly little attention from NLP researchers. The development of language technologies encourage potential work in the documentation, promotion, preservation and revitalization of the languages (Galla, 2016; Mager et al., 2018). Recent initiatives to promote research on languages of the Americas brings NLP researchers closer to the Americas languages communities and activists (Fernández et al., 2013; Coler and Homola, 2014; Hois and Ruiz, 2018; Kann et al., 2018; Zhang et al., 2020; Ortega et al., 2020). Particularly, machine translation is a useful tool that encourages more research in the languages as it bridges the communication gaps in NLP researchers' understanding of the models' capabilities and limitations.

The AmericasNLP 2021 workshop hosted the Open Machine Translation (OMT) shared task focusing on indigenous and endangered Americas languages (Mager et al., 2021). The organizers provided a seed collection of publicly available corpora and highlighted the various nuances and variability of the translations due to the geographical and linguistic diversity between the language varieties. The Spanish data for development and test sets created in the AmericasNLP 2021 shared task are translated into the Aymara La Paz jilata variant, which is the same variant used in the Global Voices corpus (Tiedemann, 2012; Prokopidis et al., 2016). While Aymara is mutually intelligible across different dialects, they might differ in specific terminologies and minor grammatical preferences.

This paper presents our submission to the AmericasNLP 2023 machine translation shared task (Ebrahimi et al., 2023). We submitted our system that focuses only on translating from Spanish into Aymara. We fine-tuned a multilingual T5 model (Xue et al., 2021) by adding an Aymara-English lexicon[2] to the existing Spanish-Aymara and English-Aymara Global Voices corpus and the Spanish-Aymara shared task training data (Conneau et al., 2018; Ebrahimi et al., 2022).

Other than presenting the results of our AmericasNLP shared task submission, parts of this paper will also serve as a demonstration of how the model was modified from typical model training using HuggingFace suite of libraries (Wolf et al., 2020; Lhoest et al., 2021; McMillan-Major et al., 2021), this is especially useful for low-resource sequence-to-sequence tasks.

2 Pre-trained Tokenizer and New Languages

While the current state of vogue in using massively multilingual pre-trained models on low-resource languages allows researchers to extend the models' sub-word tokenizers, the models implicitly re-use the tokens from how it was previously pre-trained and simply ignore the new tokens by labelling them as `[UNKNOWN]`. In cases where the character set of the low-resource languages' orthography matches the languages that the models were pre-trained on,

[1] Statistics retrieved from Catalogue of Endangered Languages (2023)

[2] The lexicon is created from the notes of a student learning Aymara as a foreign-language, it is hosted on HuggingFace dataset hub. The original sources of the lexicon attributes to Parker (2008) *Webster Aymara-English thesaurus* and Peace Corps (1967) *Beginning Aymara* book.

Proceedings of the Workshop on Natural Language Processing for Indigenous Languages of the Americas (AmericasNLP), pages 168–172

it is possible that the models repurpose the sub-words to learn new parameter behaviors given sufficient computes and hyperparameter tuning experiments.

```
from transformers import AutoTokenizer
from datasets import load_dataset

lexicon_dataset = load_dataset(
    "alvations/aymara-english", on_bad_lines='skip')

tokenizer = AutoTokenizer.from_pretrained('google/mt5-base')

# Train a new tokenizer using the new dataset
# and the old tokenizer object.
new_tokenizer = tokenizer.train_new_from_iterator(
    lexicon_dataset, vocab_size=50_000)
new_tokens = set(new_tokenizer.vocab).difference(tokenizer.vocab)

# Before: 250100
print('Before:', len(tokenizer))
tokenizer.add_tokens(list(new_tokens))

# After (adding vocab): 251152
tokenizer.add_tokens(
    lexicon_dataset['train']['Aymara'] +
    lexicon_dataset['train']['English'])
print('After (adding vocab):', len(tokenizer))
```

To preserve the learned model parameters, a researcher using the multilingual model can extend its tokenizer's sub-word vocabulary by relearning the sub-word tokenizer from scratch, then apply it to dataset with the new language and finally extending the new sub-words to the pre-trained vocabulary. To assign new parameters in the model for these new sub-words tokens, the embedding layer of the model needs to be extended. The code snippet above demonstrates the function to extend the new language's vocabulary to existing pre-trained mT5 model.

The following snippet below presents the differences of the input token indices depending on how the tokenizer was extended for a new language.

```
from transformers import AutoTokenizer

tokenizer_old = AutoTokenizer.from_pretrained('google/mt5-base')
tokenizer_new = AutoTokenizer.from_pretrained('alvations/mt5-aym-lex')

sent = "1899n ahuicha yuriwayi"

tokenized_old_ids = tokenizer_old(sent)['input_ids']
tokenized_new_ids = tokenizer_new(sent)['input_ids']

tokens_old = [tokenizer.decode([s]) for s in tokenized_old_ids]
tokens_new = [tokenizer.decode([s]) for s in tokenized_new_ids]

print(tokens_old)
# Ouputs: ['1899', 'n', '', 'ahu', 'icha', 'yuri', 'way', 'i', '</s>']

print(tokens_new)
# Outputs: ['1899', 'n', '', 'ahuicha', 'yuri', 'way', 'i', '</s>']
```

Instead of using the subword tokenizer, users can pre-tokenize the new language data using a linguistic motivated rule-based tokenizer and add the tokens without further splitting these tokens into subwords to the models' vocabulary. However the tokenizer does not automatically recognize/determine spelling variants, e.g. "*ahuicha*" (i.e. "*grandma*" in English and "*abuela*" in Spanish) can also be spelled as "*awichajax*" in Aymara.

3 Experimental Setup

All models fine-tuned in this paper uses the mT5 architecture using A100 GPUs with 40GB RAM. We use the all default hyperparameters of the HuggingFace's `Seq2SeqTrainingArguments` except:

- `warmup_steps`[3] was set to 500, instead of the default 0
- `auto_find_batch_size` is enabled with the default algorithm to determine batch size automatically
- `max_steps` is set at 200,000. We cap the maximum number of model updates to 200K to limit the computing resources used for our experiments to approximately 24 hours per model, vis-a-vis *'few-shot'* training.

We fine-tuned a zero-shot lexicon-enriched system mT5 model with Aymara-English lexicon, the Spanish-Aymara and English-Aymara Global Voices corpus and Spanish-Aymara XNLI training data split for the training data. And we use the Spanish-Aymara XNLI development data split provided by the shared task organizers to select the best performing model.

Training Data	`mt5-base`	`mt5-zero`	`mt5-lex`
XNLI Train (spa-aym)	✓	✓	✓
Global Voices (spa-aym)	✓	✓	✓
Global Voices (eng-aym)		✓	✓
Lexicon (eng-aym)			✓

Table 1: Training Datasets used by the mT5 Variants

Our official submission to the shared task is selected from the best-performing system that scored the lowest perplexity loss and highest BLEU score. Other than the best performing zero-shot lexicon-enriched system (`mT5-lex`), we experimented and a baseline model that only fine-tuned Spanish-Aymara Global Voice and XNLI

[3]This hyperparameter is used to gradually increased the learning rate to make training more stable (Huang et al., 2020). The original transformer (Vaswani et al., 2017) set the warmup to 4,000.

dataset (`mT5-base`) and a second baseline that adds on the English-Aymara Global Voices data to Spanish-Aymara Global Voices and XNLI dataset (`mT5-zero`). Table 1 summarizes the datasets used to train the corresponding mT5 models.

4 Results

Our official submission to the shared-task scored a measly 0.12 BLEU (Papineni et al., 2002) and 9.22 ChrF score (Popović, 2015) on the AmericasNLP 2023 shared task test set. The best performing team in the shared task achieved 4.45 BLEU and 36.24 ChrF. The target Aymara text from the test set was not released publicly, hence we present the results of our model variants on the development set.

System	ChrF	BLEU
`mt5-base`	**30.59**	2.78
`mt5-zero`	23.98	**2.99**
`mt5-lex`	22.01	1.38

Table 2: Results on AmericasNLP 2023 Spanish-Aymara Development Set

We note the oracle effect of selecting the best model during training based on the development set, thus the results from Table 2 might be inflated.

As a sanity check, we translated the lexicon used to train `mt5-lex` from English into Spanish using the NLLB machine translation model (Costa-jussà et al., 2022) and count the tokens from the lexicon that matches the development texts. We found that the lexicon has little matches to the tokens in the development sets, see Appendix A for more details.

5 Conclusion

In this paper we present our participation in the AmericasNLP 2023 Spanish-Aymara machine translation shared task. We experimented with adding an English-Aymara lexicon and training

We share the follow resources created in our participation for future researchers to improve English/Spanish-Aymara translations.

- English-Aymara Lexicon
- `mt-base` model
- `mt-zero` model
- `mt-lex` model
- Model training script

References

Catalogue of Endangered Languages. 2023. University of Hawaii at Manoa.

Matthew Coler and Petr Homola. 2014. Rule-based machine translation for aymara. *Endangered Languages and New Technologies*, pages 67–80.

Alexis Conneau, Ruty Rinott, Guillaume Lample, Adina Williams, Samuel Bowman, Holger Schwenk, and Veselin Stoyanov. 2018. XNLI: Evaluating cross-lingual sentence representations. In *Proceedings of the 2018 Conference on Empirical Methods in Natural Language Processing*, pages 2475–2485, Brussels, Belgium. Association for Computational Linguistics.

Marta R Costa-jussà, James Cross, Onur Çelebi, Maha Elbayad, Kenneth Heafield, Kevin Heffernan, Elahe Kalbassi, Janice Lam, Daniel Licht, Jean Maillard, et al. 2022. No language left behind: Scaling human-centered machine translation. *arXiv preprint arXiv:2207.04672*.

Abteen Ebrahimi, Manuel Mager, Arturo Oncevay, Vishrav Chaudhary, Luis Chiruzzo, Angela Fan, John Ortega, Ricardo Ramos, Annette Rios, Ivan Vladimir Meza Ruiz, Gustavo Giménez-Lugo, Elisabeth Mager, Graham Neubig, Alexis Palmer, Rolando Coto-Solano, Thang Vu, and Katharina Kann. 2022. AmericasNLI: Evaluating zero-shot natural language understanding of pretrained multilingual models in truly low-resource languages. In *Proceedings of the 60th Annual Meeting of the Association for Computational Linguistics (Volume 1: Long Papers)*, pages 6279–6299, Dublin, Ireland. Association for Computational Linguistics.

Abteen Ebrahimi, Manuel Mager, Arturo Oncevay, Enora Rice, Cynthia Montaño, John Ortega, Shruti Rijhwani, Alexis Palmer, Rolando Coto-Solano, Hilaria Cruz, and Katharina Kann. 2023. Findings of the AmericasNLP 2023 shared task on machine translation into indigenous languages. In *Proceedings of the Third Workshop on Natural Language Processing for Indigenous Languages of the Americas*. Association for Computational Linguistics.

Dayana Iguarán Fernández, Ornela Quintero Gamboa, Jose Molina Atencia, and Oscar Elías Bedoya. 2013. Design and implementation of an "web api" for the automatic translation colombia's language pairs: Spanish-wayuunaiki case. In *2013 IEEE Colombian Conference on Communications and Computing (COLCOM)*, pages 1–9. IEEE.

Candace Kaleimamoowahinekapu Galla. 2016. Indigenous language revitalization, promotion, and education: Function of digital technology. *Computer Assisted Language Learning*, 29(7):1137–1151.

Jesús Manuel Mager Hois and Ivan Vladimir Meza Ruiz. 2018. Hacia la traducción automática de las lenguas indígenas de méxico. *Digital Humanities 2018: Book of Abstracts/Libro de resúmenes*.

Xiao Shi Huang, Felipe Perez, Jimmy Ba, and Maksims Volkovs. 2020. Improving transformer optimization through better initialization. In *International Conference on Machine Learning*, pages 4475–4483. PMLR.

Katharina Kann, Jesus Manuel Mager Hois, Ivan Vladimir Meza-Ruiz, and Hinrich Schütze. 2018. Fortification of neural morphological segmentation models for polysynthetic minimal-resource languages. In *Proceedings of the 2018 Conference of the North American Chapter of the Association for Computational Linguistics: Human Language Technologies, Volume 1 (Long Papers)*, pages 47–57, New Orleans, Louisiana. Association for Computational Linguistics.

Quentin Lhoest, Albert Villanova del Moral, Yacine Jernite, Abhishek Thakur, Patrick von Platen, Suraj Patil, Julien Chaumond, Mariama Drame, Julien Plu, Lewis Tunstall, Joe Davison, Mario Šaško, Gunjan Chhablani, Bhavitvya Malik, Simon Brandeis, Teven Le Scao, Victor Sanh, Canwen Xu, Nicolas Patry, Angelina McMillan-Major, Philipp Schmid, Sylvain Gugger, Clément Delangue, Théo Matussière, Lysandre Debut, Stas Bekman, Pierric Cistac, Thibault Goehringer, Victor Mustar, François Lagunas, Alexander Rush, and Thomas Wolf. 2021. Datasets: A community library for natural language processing. In *Proceedings of the 2021 Conference on Empirical Methods in Natural Language Processing: System Demonstrations*, pages 175–184, Online and Punta Cana, Dominican Republic. Association for Computational Linguistics.

Manuel Mager, Ximena Gutierrez-Vasques, Gerardo Sierra, and Ivan Meza-Ruiz. 2018. Challenges of language technologies for the indigenous languages of the Americas. In *Proceedings of the 27th International Conference on Computational Linguistics*, pages 55–69, Santa Fe, New Mexico, USA. Association for Computational Linguistics.

Manuel Mager, Arturo Oncevay, Abteen Ebrahimi, John Ortega, Annette Rios, Angela Fan, Ximena Gutierrez-Vasques, Luis Chiruzzo, Gustavo Giménez-Lugo, Ricardo Ramos, Ivan Vladimir Meza Ruiz, Rolando Coto-Solano, Alexis Palmer, Elisabeth Mager-Hois, Vishrav Chaudhary, Graham Neubig, Ngoc Thang Vu, and Katharina Kann. 2021. Findings of the AmericasNLP 2021 shared task on open machine translation for indigenous languages of the Americas. In *Proceedings of the First Workshop on Natural Language Processing for Indigenous Languages of the Americas*, pages 202–217, Online. Association for Computational Linguistics.

Angelina McMillan-Major, Salomey Osei, Juan Diego Rodriguez, Pawan Sasanka Ammanamanchi, Sebastian Gehrmann, and Yacine Jernite. 2021. Reusable templates and guides for documenting datasets and models for natural language processing and generation: A case study of the HuggingFace and GEM data and model cards. In *Proceedings of the 1st Workshop on Natural Language Generation, Evaluation, and Metrics (GEM 2021)*, pages 121–135, Online. Association for Computational Linguistics.

John E Ortega, Richard Alexander Castro-Mamani, and Jaime Rafael Montoya Samame. 2020. Overcoming resistance: The normalization of an Amazonian tribal language. In *Proceedings of the 3rd Workshop on Technologies for MT of Low Resource Languages*, pages 1–13, Suzhou, China. Association for Computational Linguistics.

Kishore Papineni, Salim Roukos, Todd Ward, and Wei-Jing Zhu. 2002. Bleu: a method for automatic evaluation of machine translation. In *Proceedings of the 40th Annual Meeting of the Association for Computational Linguistics*, pages 311–318, Philadelphia, Pennsylvania, USA. Association for Computational Linguistics.

Philip M. Parker. 2008. *Webster's Aymara - English Thesaurus Dictionary*. ICON Group International.

Peace Corps. 1967. *Beginning Aymara: A course for English speakers*. Peace Corps.

Maja Popović. 2015. chrF: character n-gram F-score for automatic MT evaluation. In *Proceedings of the Tenth Workshop on Statistical Machine Translation*, pages 392–395, Lisbon, Portugal. Association for Computational Linguistics.

Prokopis Prokopidis, Vassilis Papavassiliou, and Stelios Piperidis. 2016. Parallel Global Voices: a collection of multilingual corpora with citizen media stories. In *Proceedings of the Tenth International Conference on Language Resources and Evaluation (LREC'16)*, pages 900–905, Portorož, Slovenia. European Language Resources Association (ELRA).

Liling Tan, Josef van Genabith, and Francis Bond. 2015. Passive and pervasive use of bilingual dictionary in statistical machine translation. In *Proceedings of the Fourth Workshop on Hybrid Approaches to Translation (HyTra)*, pages 30–34, Beijing. Association for Computational Linguistics.

Jörg Tiedemann. 2012. Parallel data, tools and interfaces in OPUS. In *Proceedings of the Eighth International Conference on Language Resources and Evaluation (LREC'12)*, pages 2214–2218, Istanbul, Turkey. European Language Resources Association (ELRA).

Ashish Vaswani, Noam Shazeer, Niki Parmar, Jakob Uszkoreit, Llion Jones, Aidan N Gomez, Łukasz Kaiser, and Illia Polosukhin. 2017. Attention is all you need. *Advances in neural information processing systems*, 30.

Thomas Wolf, Lysandre Debut, Victor Sanh, Julien Chaumond, Clement Delangue, Anthony Moi, Pierric Cistac, Tim Rault, Remi Louf, Morgan Funtowicz, Joe Davison, Sam Shleifer, Patrick von Platen, Clara Ma, Yacine Jernite, Julien Plu, Canwen Xu, Teven Le Scao, Sylvain Gugger, Mariama Drame,

Quentin Lhoest, and Alexander Rush. 2020. Transformers: State-of-the-art natural language processing. In *Proceedings of the 2020 Conference on Empirical Methods in Natural Language Processing: System Demonstrations*, pages 38–45, Online. Association for Computational Linguistics.

Linting Xue, Noah Constant, Adam Roberts, Mihir Kale, Rami Al-Rfou, Aditya Siddhant, Aditya Barua, and Colin Raffel. 2021. mT5: A massively multilingual pre-trained text-to-text transformer. In *Proceedings of the 2021 Conference of the North American Chapter of the Association for Computational Linguistics: Human Language Technologies*, pages 483–498, Online. Association for Computational Linguistics.

François Yvon and Sadaf Abdul Rauf. 2020. *Using lexical and terminological resources in neural machine translation*. Ph.D. thesis, LIMSI-CNRS.

Shiyue Zhang, Benjamin Frey, and Mohit Bansal. 2020. ChrEn: Cherokee-English machine translation for endangered language revitalization. In *Proceedings of the 2020 Conference on Empirical Methods in Natural Language Processing (EMNLP)*, pages 577–595, Online. Association for Computational Linguistics.

A Lexicon Matches in Development Set

There are 81 unique words that matches the Spanish translated lexicon to the tokens in the development set. The matches sum up to a frequency of 373 out of a total number of 53,135 in the development set on the Spanish source. However when we match the target Aymara text with the lexicon and we find only 4 unique words matches that occurred 9 times in the development set. Looking at the sentences that contains the Aymara word matches to the lexicon, the Aymara sentences from the development set contains loan words either from Spanish or English,

The 4 unique Spanish - Aymara lexicon matches are:

- *el vuelo -> fly*
- *mayo -> may*
- *firme -> firm*
- *hijo -> son*

The sentences that contains the target side matches are:

- *The firm Uk* ullartatï.
- Tamax may maya temanakanw yatiñ munapxchixa.
- Aka jan walt'awix may may lup'iypachatamxa, ukampis samart'awim suyt'am.
- Jichhurux awkixan nayra jakawipat arst'awaya ukatx kunawsatix Estados Unidos markar sarawayjix may may kast sarawinak utjirinakaw uñicht'ayätani
- *I'll fly away* uk ajlliristxa.
- Aruskipt'aw Hilbert, *Las mariposas son libres, El mago de Oz, Tierra de juguetes* y Vuelos ukanakatx purt'anirinakax uñjtawayapxaniwa.
- Ukampirus, niyapunix may uñjiristwa, uh, V6 inas.

We note that the underlined loan phrases matches contributes to the matching counts in the lexicon. And when it comes to the Aymara lexicon entry '*may*', it is a false-friend match, in both development setences that contains '*may may*', it phrase seems to be a grammatical/syntactic construct.

With the above anecdote, we find that lexicon effects in machine translation might not be evident in metrics scores if the lexicon matches in the test set is low, unlike previous studies of using lexicon in high resource languages (Tan et al., 2015; Yvon and Rauf, 2020).

PlayGround Low Resource Machine Translation System for the 2023 AmericasNLP Shared Task

Tianrui Gu, Kaie Chen, Siqi Ouyang, Lei Li
University of California, Santa Barbara
{tianruigu, kaiechen, siqiouyang, leili}@ucsb.edu

Abstract

This paper presents PlayGround's submission to the AmericasNLP 2023 shared task on machine translation (MT) into indigenous languages. We finetuned NLLB-600M, a multilingual MT model pre-trained on Flores-200, on 10 low-resource language directions and examined the effectiveness of weight averaging and back translation. Our experiments showed that weight averaging, on average, led to a 0.0169 improvement in the ChrF++ score. Additionally, we found that back translation resulted in a 0.008 improvement in the ChrF++ score.

1 Introduction

We participated in the AmericasNLP 2023 (Ebrahimi et al., 2023) shared task with the goal of advancing previous studies (Mager et al., 2021) on indigenous American languages. The task is to translate Spanish into 10 indigenous languages, including Ashaninka, Aymara, Bribri, Guarani, Hñähñu, Nahuatl, Quechua, Raramuri, Shipibo-Konibo, and Wixarika. Additionally, there was another language, Chatino[1], for which we did not participate in.

We started with the monolingual and bilingual data from Mager et al. (2021) and finetuned NLLB-600M, a multilingual pre-trained MT model from Meta's No Language Left Behind (NLLB) project (NLLBTeam et al., 2022) both bilingually and multilingually. On top of that, we employed weight averaging and back translation. For back translation, we additionally filtered the back translated sentence pairs to improve the data quality.

We demonstrate that training on model weights averaged from multiple checkpoints improves translation quality, as indicated by a 0.0169 increase in the ChrF++ score on average, without requiring additional computation resources. Additionally, we found that back translation can enhance translation quality for low-resource languages, although it is sensitive to the quality of synthetic data. To address this, we introduced a data filtering technique to improve the quality of synthetic data. With filtered back translation, our system achieved an average improvement of 0.008 in the ChrF++ score. Furthermore, our study reveals that multilingual fine-tuning achieves comparable translation quality to bilingual fine-tuning for low-resource languages.

We selected the bilingual model with weight averaging and back translation as our final submission. The implementation of this study is available in our Git repository[2].

2 Methods

2.1 Data

We adopted the data preparation method described by the University of Helsinki's submission to AmericasNLP 2021 (Vázquez et al., 2021) for our system. The details of the dataset can be found in Table 1. Our model training utilized the filtered parallel data (referred to as parallel data), which consisted of the training data provided by the organizers as well as additional data collected by the University of Helsinki (Vázquez et al., 2021). In order to generate synthetic parallel data (referred to as synthetic data), we employed monolingual data and applied back translation techniques (refer to Section 2.3). The development data was used for model selection purposes.

2.2 Pre-trained Model

Our models are based on the NLLB-600M Seq2Seq pre-training scheme introduced by the NLLB team (NLLBTeam et al., 2022). For tokenization, we utilize the SentencePiece tokenizer (Kudo and Richardson, 2018), following the NLLB configuration. The NLLB model was initially trained on

[1] https://scholarworks.iu.edu/dspace/handle/2022/21028

[2] https://github.com/KaieChen/ameircasnlp2023

Proceedings of the Workshop on Natural Language Processing for Indigenous Languages of the Americas (AmericasNLP), pages 173–176
July 14, 2023 ©2023 Association for Computational Linguistics

Lang	Filtered	Monoling	Dev
Ashaninka	3858	13195	883
Aymara	8352	16750	996
Bribri	7303	0	996
Guarani	14483	40516	995
Hñähñu	7049	537	599
Nahuatl	17431	9222	672
Quechua	228624	60399	996
Raramuri	16529	0	995
Shipibo-Konibo	28854	23595	996
Wixarika	11525	511	994

Table 1: Number of segments in dataset. Filtered data and monolingual data are collected and filtered by University of Helsinki team (Vázquez et al., 2021) from AmericasNLP 2021.

the Flores-200 dataset, which consists of Aymara, Guarani, Quechua, and Spanish.

2.3 Fine-tuned Models

We fine-tune NLLB-600M using the data mentioned in Table 1. For both X-to-Spanish and Spanish-to-X directions, we fine-tune NLLB-600M using filtered parallel data in both bilingual and multilingual way. This produces 20 bilingual models and 2 multilingual models.

We leverage the above X-to-Spanish models to generate back translated data to enrich the training corpus. Then we further fine-tune the Spanish-to-X models with parallel dataset extended with back translated sentence pairs.

The final models are obtained with weight averaging since the training can be unstable with insufficient data.

2.3.1 Back Translation

In order to make use of monolingual data in indigenous languages, we employed back translation. Specifically, we froze the decoder layers of NLLB model and performed fine-tuning of an X-to-Spanish model using parallel data. Then, we utilized this model to generate synthetic sentences.

Data filtering: Synthetic sentences may contain noise. To address this issue, we implement a data filter to select a subset of synthetic sentences that will expand the original parallel dataset (Ranathunga et al., 2023). In our task, we initially fine-tuned a Spanish-to-X model using the parallel data. Subsequently, we evaluated this model on the synthetic sentences and selected the top N samples with the lowest cross-entropy loss. The value of N is determined by the following:

$$N = \min(|Y_{par}|, |Y_{syn}|) \qquad (1)$$

where $|Y_{par}|$ represents the number of segments in the parallel dataset, and $|Y_{syn}|$ represents the number of segments in the synthetic dataset.

Finally, we combined the selected synthetic data with the parallel data and proceeded to perform additional fine-tuning of the NLLB model.

2.3.2 Weight Averaging

Studies have shown that averaging the weights of multiple finetuned models can enhance accuracy (Wortsman et al., 2022). In our training approach, the weights of the next epoch are trained based on the average of the model weights from the previous K epochs. For inference, we compute the final model by averaging the model weights from the last K epochs. The model can be defined as follows:

$$\textbf{NLLB}(x; \Theta_t) = \textbf{NLLB}(x; \frac{1}{K}\sum_{k=1}^{K}\Theta_{t-k}) \qquad (2)$$

where Θ_t represents the model parameters at epoch t.

This technique shares similarities with training different models using various hyperparameters (Wortsman et al., 2022; Xu et al., 2020). However, as we only need to train a single model, this technique can be particularly efficient for large language models. The effectiveness of this approach is further discussed in Section 3.

2.3.3 Hyperparameters

In the fine-tuning process, we froze the encoder layers of the NLLB model, considering its prior training on a vast amount of Spanish sentences. We optimized the model using AdamW (Loshchilov and Hutter, 2017) with hyperparameters $\beta = (0.9, 0.999)$, $\epsilon = 10^{-6}$. We employed a learning rate of 3×10^{-4} for a total of $10,000$ iterations. For regularization, we utilized the same dropout rate as the original NLLB model and a weight decay of 0.01. Furthermore, for weight averaging, we set the value of K to be 5.

2.4 Evaluation

We report the results using ChrF++ (Popović, 2017), following the evaluation script[3] provided by the AmericasNLP 2023 shared task. ChrF++

[3]https://github.com/AmericasNLP/americasnlp2023

Target language	Baseline (Test)	Multi	Multi+	Multi++	Bi	Bi++	Bi++ (Test)
Wixarika	**0.304**	0.277	0.294	0.294	0.266	0.279	0.288
Hñähñu	0.147	0.129	0.133	0.138	0.144	0.141	**0.148**
Aymara	0.283	0.291	0.328	0.326	0.336	0.326	**0.300**
Shipibo-Konibo	**0.329**	0.224	0.238	0.253	0.261	0.283	0.277
Nahuatl	**0.266**	0.241	0.252	0.275	0.282	0.283	0.237
Guarani	**0.336**	0.304	0.316	0.321	0.315	0.303	0.331
Asháninka	0.258	0.222	0.238	0.272	0.269	0.286	**0.280**
Quechua	0.343	0.324	0.341	-	0.337	-	**0.344**
Rarámuri	**0.184**	0.161	0.175	-	0.184	-	0.145
Bribri	**0.165**	0.210	0.237	-	0.231	-	0.148

Table 2: Result in ChrF++ on develop dataset, except for baseline and Bi++(test). Baseline model is the best submission for AmericasNLP 2021. The effectiveness of weight averaging (Multi+ and Bi+) and back translation is compared (Multi++ and Bi++). We also compared the performance of bilingual (Bi) and multilingual (Multi).

captures the character-level performance, making it particularly suitable for evaluating the polysynthetic properties observed in many indigenous languages (Zheng et al., 2021).

3 Results

The results are presented in Table 2 for both the development and test datasets. Our **Bi++** model demonstrates improvements in four languages: Hñähñu, Aymara, Asháninka, and Quechua, compared to the **Baseline** model provided by the organizer. In general, the trends in results for the development and training datasets are similar, except for Rarámuri and Bribri. This discrepancy may be attributed to the test dataset containing more unknown tokens, to which our model is sensitive.

Previous study (Mager et al., 2021) has primarily focused on fine-tuning bilingual machine translation models. However, the results from our **Multi++** and **Bi++** models demonstrate the promising potential of multilingual fine-tuning (Tang et al., 2020). On average, the ChrF++ score for **Multi++** is only 0.0012 lower than that of **Bi++**.

We also compared the effectiveness of weight averaging and back translation. Weight averaging improved translations for all target languages. On average, **Multi+** achieved a ChrF++ score that was 0.0169 higher than **Multi**. These results indicate that our simple technique can enhance low-resource machine translation without requiring additional computational resources.

However, the impact of back translation varied across languages, as observed in the results for **Multi+** and **Multi++**. On average, the implementation of back translation resulted in a 0.008 improvement in the ChrF++ metric. For Wixarika and Aymara, there was a slight drop in the ChrF++ scores after back translation. Despite performing data filtering, the quality of synthetic data largely depends on the performance of the X-to-Spanish model.

In summary, our fine-tuning technique has shown improvements in performance. However, with further refinements and design enhancements, there is potential for our model to achieve higher levels of performance.

4 Conclusion

In this paper, we presented our submission to the AmericasNLP 2023 shared task. Our system utilized the NLLB-600M pre-trained model to translate Spanish into 10 indigenous languages. We also investigated the potential of multilingual translation models, which showed promising results. Additionally, we found that averaging model weights from previous epochs proved to be an efficient and effective approach. While back translation demonstrated performance improvements, further methods are necessary to address noisy data. These findings highlight the positive outcomes of our study and provide valuable insights for future advancements in low-resource machine translation techniques.

References

Abteen Ebrahimi, Manuel Mager, Arturo Oncevay, Enora Rice, Cynthia Montaño, John Ortega, Shruti Rijhwani, Alexis Palmer, Rolando Coto-Solano, Hilaria Cruz, and Katharina Kann. 2023. Findings of the AmericasNLP 2023 shared task on machine translation into indigenous languages. In *Proceedings of the Third Workshop on Natural Language Processing for Indigenous Languages of the Americas*. Association for Computational Linguistics.

Taku Kudo and John Richardson. 2018. SentencePiece: A simple and language independent subword tokenizer and detokenizer for neural text processing. In *Proceedings of the 2018 Conference on Empirical Methods in Natural Language Processing: System Demonstrations*, pages 66–71, Brussels, Belgium. Association for Computational Linguistics.

Ilya Loshchilov and Frank Hutter. 2017. Fixing weight decay regularization in adam. *CoRR*, abs/1711.05101.

Manuel Mager, Arturo Oncevay, Abteen Ebrahimi, John Ortega, Annette Rios, Angela Fan, Ximena Gutierrez-Vasques, Luis Chiruzzo, Gustavo Giménez-Lugo, Ricardo Ramos, Ivan Vladimir Meza Ruiz, Rolando Coto-Solano, Alexis Palmer, Elisabeth Mager-Hois, Vishrav Chaudhary, Graham Neubig, Ngoc Thang Vu, and Katharina Kann. 2021. Findings of the AmericasNLP 2021 shared task on open machine translation for indigenous languages of the Americas. In *Proceedings of the First Workshop on Natural Language Processing for Indigenous Languages of the Americas*, pages 202–217, Online. Association for Computational Linguistics.

NLLBTeam, Marta R. Costa-jussà, James Cross, Onur Çelebi, Maha Elbayad, Kenneth Heafield, Kevin Heffernan, Elahe Kalbassi, Janice Lam, Daniel Licht, Jean Maillard, Anna Sun, Skyler Wang, Guillaume Wenzek, Al Youngblood, Bapi Akula, Loic Barrault, Gabriel Mejia Gonzalez, Prangthip Hansanti, John Hoffman, Semarley Jarrett, Kaushik Ram Sadagopan, Dirk Rowe, Shannon Spruit, Chau Tran, Pierre Andrews, Necip Fazil Ayan, Shruti Bhosale, Sergey Edunov, Angela Fan, Cynthia Gao, Vedanuj Goswami, Francisco Guzmán, Philipp Koehn, Alexandre Mourachko, Christophe Ropers, Safiyyah Saleem, Holger Schwenk, and Jeff Wang. 2022. No language left behind: Scaling human-centered machine translation.

Maja Popović. 2017. chrF++: words helping character n-grams. In *Proceedings of the Second Conference on Machine Translation*, pages 612–618, Copenhagen, Denmark. Association for Computational Linguistics.

Surangika Ranathunga, En-Shiun Annie Lee, Marjana Prifti Skenduli, Ravi Shekhar, Mehreen Alam, and Rishemjit Kaur. 2023. Neural machine translation for low-resource languages: A survey. *ACM Comput. Surv.*, 55(11).

Yuqing Tang, Chau Tran, Xian Li, Peng-Jen Chen, Naman Goyal, Vishrav Chaudhary, Jiatao Gu, and Angela Fan. 2020. Multilingual translation with extensible multilingual pretraining and finetuning. *CoRR*, abs/2008.00401.

Raúl Vázquez, Yves Scherrer, Sami Virpioja, and Jörg Tiedemann. 2021. The Helsinki submission to the AmericasNLP shared task. In *Proceedings of the First Workshop on Natural Language Processing for Indigenous Languages of the Americas*, pages 255–264, Online. Association for Computational Linguistics.

Mitchell Wortsman, Gabriel Ilharco, Samir Ya Gadre, Rebecca Roelofs, Raphael Gontijo-Lopes, Ari S Morcos, Hongseok Namkoong, Ali Farhadi, Yair Carmon, Simon Kornblith, and Ludwig Schmidt. 2022. Model soups: averaging weights of multiple fine-tuned models improves accuracy without increasing inference time. In *Proceedings of the 39th International Conference on Machine Learning*, volume 162 of *Proceedings of Machine Learning Research*, pages 23965–23998. PMLR.

Yige Xu, Xipeng Qiu, Ligao Zhou, and Xuanjing Huang. 2020. Improving BERT fine-tuning via self-ensemble and self-distillation. *CoRR*, abs/2002.10345.

Francis Zheng, Machel Reid, Edison Marrese-Taylor, and Yutaka Matsuo. 2021. Low-resource machine translation using cross-lingual language model pretraining. In *Proceedings of the First Workshop on Natural Language Processing for Indigenous Languages of the Americas*, pages 234–240, Online. Association for Computational Linguistics.

Four Approaches to Low-Resource Multilingual NMT: The Helsinki Submission to the AmericasNLP 2023 Shared Task

Ona de Gibert Raúl Vázquez Mikko Aulamo
Yves Scherrer Sami Virpioja Jörg Tiedemann
University of Helsinki, Dept. of Digital Humanities
{firstname.lastname}@helsinki.fi

Abstract

The Helsinki-NLP team participated in the AmericasNLP 2023 Shared Task with 6 submissions for all 11 language pairs arising from 4 different multilingual systems. We provide a detailed look at the work that went into collecting and preprocessing the data that led to our submissions. We explore various setups for multilingual Neural Machine Translation (NMT), namely knowledge distillation and transfer learning, multilingual NMT including a high-resource language (English), language-specific fine-tuning, and a system with a modular architecture. Our multilingual Model B ranks first in 4 out of the 11 language pairs.

1 Introduction

This paper presents the submission of the Helsinki-NLP team to the AmericasNLP 2023 Shared Task. The task consisted in developing Machine Translation (MT) systems for 11 indigenous languages of the Americas: Aymara (aym), Bribri (bzd), Asháninka (cni), Chatino (czn), Guarani (gn), Wixarika (hch), Nahuatl (nah), Hñähñu (oto), Quechua (Quy), Shipibo-Konibo (shp), and Rarámuri (tar). The AmericasNLP task has been running for two years: in 2021 (Mager et al., 2021) it was first introduced, and in 2022 it consisted of Speech-to-Text Translation (STT).[1] This year's task is similar to the one held in 2021, but it includes an additional language (Chatino) and the use of the development set in training is not allowed. Our 2021 submission (Vázquez et al., 2021) reached the first rank in nine out of ten languages and serves as the baseline for this year's task.

The 11 target languages involved in the task vary a lot in terms of "resourcedness". On one side of the spectrum, there are languages like Quechua and Guarani with millions of native speakers, whereas on the other end, the variety of Hñähñu used in the development and test sets only has about 100 elder speakers.[2] Many of the target languages show dialectal variation, and some have different spelling norms and conventions. Furthermore, some datasets contain instances of code-switching with Spanish, and some of the languages are polysynthetic. All these factors make the task at hand particularly challenging.

A large part of our effort focuses on increasing the amount of parallel data for training. Building on our work for the 2021 shared task, we employ several strategies: mining, extraction and alignment of publicly available parallel resources, backtranslation of monolingual data (Sennrich et al., 2016), and data augmentation by pivoting through English (Xia et al., 2019).

On the modelling side, our winning 2021 submission was based on a multilingual (one-to-many) model that was pretrained mostly on the Spanish-to-English task and later fine-tuned on the low-resource indigenous languages. We keep this general approach in most of this year's submissions, but provide some variations to this theme:

Model A uses knowledge distillation and transfer learning instead of training from scratch. In this context, we also experiment with different data labeling schemes.

Model B reproduces our 2021 setup with updated data.

Model C reimplements Model B's strategy using OpusTrainer[3] and introduces a language-specific fine-tuning step.

Model D uses a modular architecture in a multilingual setting with language-specific decoder modules.

[1] http://turing.iimas.unam.mx/americasnlp/st.html

[2] https://github.com/AmericasNLP/americasnlp2023/blob/main/data/information_datasets.pdf

[3] https://github.com/hplt-project/OpusTrainer

Proceedings of the Workshop on Natural Language Processing for Indigenous Languages of the Americas (AmericasNLP), pages 177–191
July 14, 2023 ©2023 Association for Computational Linguistics

Our best-performing model is Model B. The collected data and our code are publicly available on our fork of the organizers' Git repository.[4]

The rest of the paper is organised as follows. Section 2 provides a detailed description of our data collection and preparation efforts. Section 3 describes in detail the models presented. Section 4 outlines the results and, finally, section 5 concludes our work.

2 Data collection and preparation

Similar to our 2021 submission, we worked on finding relevant corpora from additional sources and cleaning and filtering them. We utilised the OpusFilter toolbox[5] (Aulamo et al., 2020), which provides both ready-made and extensible methods for combining, cleaning, and filtering parallel and monolingual corpora. OpusFilter uses a configuration file that lists all the steps for processing the data; in order to make quick changes and extensions programmatically, we generated the configuration file with a Python script.

2.1 Data collection

We combined the data previously collected for our 2021 participation with some new resources. An overview of the resources, including references and URLs, is given in Table 4 in the appendix.

Organizer-provided resources The shared task organizers provided parallel datasets for training for all 11 languages. These datasets are referred to as *train* in this paper. For some of the languages (e.g., Ashaninka, Wixarika and Shipibo-Konibo), the organizers pointed participants to repositories containing additional data. We refer to these resources as *extra*. Furthermore, the organizers provided development (*dev*) and test (*test*) sets for all 11 language pairs of the shared task (Ebrahimi et al., 2023).

OPUS The OPUS corpus collection (Tiedemann, 2012) provides only few datasets for the relevant languages. We utilized the *GNOME, Mozilla10n* and *Ubuntu* corpora, which consist of localization files. Additionally, we made use of the *Tatoeba* and *Wikimedia* corpora, which have been recently updated on the OPUS website.[6] These bitexts contain 384 sentence pairs for Aymara, 25233 for Guarani, 169 for Nahuatl and 1187 for Quechua parallel with Spanish.

To ensure collecting data only for the relevant languages, we ran language detection on the corpora. For language identification we used HeLI-OTS (Jauhiainen et al., 2022), which includes language models for Guarani, Nahuatl and Quechua. We kept only pairs where both the source and the target sentences are detected to be in the correct language. For the Spanish side, we also accepted sentences identified as other Romance languages, namely Catalan, Galician, French, Portuguese, Extremaduran and Occitan. For Aymara and Nahuatl, we chose to accept sentences where the detected language is not English or Spanish, as Aymara is not included in the language model and only a small proportion of sentences were detected to be Nahuatl. The language identification filtering leaves 320 sentence pairs for Aymara, 19751 for Guarani, 153 for Nahuatl and 718 for Quechua.

FLORES The FLORES-200 development and test sets (NLLB Team et al., 2022) cover Aymara, Guarani and Quechua. Since this is a multiparallel dataset, we paired the indigenous languages with their corresponding Spanish sentences. We concatenated the development and test sets and added them to our training data.

Bibles The JHU Bible corpus (McCarthy et al., 2020) covers all languages of the shared task with at least one Bible translation. When several Bibles were available for a given indigenous language, we scored them with a character 6-gram language model trained on the development sets and chose the Bible(s) with the lowest average cross-entropy scores. We paired them with the available Spanish Bibles using the `product` method in OpusFilter to randomly take at most 3 different versions of the same sentence (skipping empty and duplicate lines).[7]

Legal texts, educational material and news In 2021, we collected constitutions and laws of various Latin American countries with their translations into indigenous languages. We expanded this collection by adding the Chatino–Spanish Mexican constitution. We also added the Universal Declaration of Human Rights (UDHR) where avail-

[4]`https://github.com/Helsinki-NLP/americasnlp2023-st`

[5]`https://github.com/Helsinki-NLP/OpusFilter`, version 2.6.

[6]`https://opus.nlpl.eu/`

[7]We sampled three Spanish sentences when there was a single Bible version for the the indigenous language, two for 2–3 versions, and one for more than three versions.

able in the Universal Declaration of Human Rights Translation Project.[8] Furthermore, we extracted Nahuatl and Bribri educational material as well as Guaraní parallel news items from PDF documents and websites. The document and sentence alignment was done semi-automatically using source-specific heuristics and the hunalign[9] (Varga et al., 2005) tool. We provide a script in our repository to replicate these data gathering and alignment procedures.[10]

Spanish–English data All submitted models take advantage of abundant parallel data for Spanish–English. The resources come from OPUS (Tiedemann, 2012) and include the following sources: *OpenSubtitles, Europarl, GlobalVoices, News-Commentary, TED2020, Tatoeba, bible-uedin*. The Spanish–English *WMT-News* corpus, also from OPUS, is used for validation.

2.2 Back-translations of monolingual data

The organizers also provided some monolingual resources for some indigenous languages. We also obtained monolingual Wikipedia dumps for some languages through the Tatoeba Translation Challenge project (Tiedemann, 2020). We used the 2021 reverse Model B to translate these resources to Spanish (thereby fixing the processing for Quechua reported in the 2021 paper).

2.3 Pivot translations of English-aligned data

Some parallel datasets provided by the organizers or available on OPUS were aligned with English. Furthermore, the No Language Left Behind (Costa-jussà et al., 2022) project released training data for Aymara–English and Guarani–English. We used a publicly available English-to-Spanish MT system from the OPUS-MT project[11] to translate the English side to Spanish in order to constitute additional Spanish–Indigenous data.

2.4 Data normalization, cleaning and filtering

We noticed that some of the corpora in the same language used different orthographic conventions and had other issues that would hinder NMT model training. We applied various data normalization and cleaning steps to improve the quality of the data, with the goal of making the training data more similar to the development data (which we expected to be similar to the test data).

For Bribri, Raramuri and Wixarika, we found normalization scripts or guidelines on the organizers' Github page or sources referenced therein (cf. ⚙ entries in Table 4). We reimplemented them as custom OpusFilter preprocessors. For Chatino, we implemented a preprocessor that normalized the tone characters variations in the different datasets.

The organizer-provided training sets for Bribri, Hñähñu, Nahuatl, and Raramuri were originally tokenized. We detokenized these corpora with the Moses detokenizer supported by OpusFilter, using the English patterns. Finally, for all datasets, we applied OpusFilter's WhitespaceNormalizer preprocessor, which replaces all sequences of whitespace characters with a single space.

We filtered some of the datasets using predefined filters from OpusFilter. Not all filters were applied to all languages; instead, we selected the appropriate filters based on manual observation of the data and the proportion of sentences removed by the filter. Appendix A describes the filters in detail.

2.5 Data tagging

Since all our models are multilingual models with several target languages, we include a **target language tag** at the beginning of the source sentence. Furthermore, we add two more tags: variant tags and quality tags.

Variant tags represent the different variants of a particular language and they were inferred either from the documentation of the data source or from a manual inspection focusing on the character set of the specific text. In the end, we only used variant tags for two languages: Chatino and Quechua. The `<default>` variant is always the variant of the development and test sets. Besides the `<default>` variant, for Chatino we define the `<plain>` variant, which does not use tones. It is important to mention that 95% of our training data for Chatino belongs to the `<plain>` variant. For Quechua, the development and test data is in Ayacucho Quechua (quy), whereas other data are in Cuzco Quechua or a Bolivian variety of Quechua. We define the variant labels <quz> and <quh> for the latter two.

Quality tags refer to the origin of the data:

[8] https://www.ohchr.org/en/human-rights/universal-declaration/universal-declaration-human-rights/about-universal-declaration-human-rights-translation-project

[9] https://github.com/danielvarga/hunalign

[10] under `data/getdata2023.py`

[11] We used the `opusTCv20210807+bt_transformer-big_2022-03-13` model from https://github.com/Helsinki-NLP/Tatoeba-Challenge/tree/master/models/eng-spa.

`<default>` for relatively clean data sources, `<noisy>` for unreliable data sources or with noisy sentence alignment, `<bt>` for back-translations, and `<bible>` for Bibles. The statistics of the quality tags for the training corpora are provided in subsection 2.8.

If not specified otherwise, all tags are used during the training phase. When generating test translations, we use the language tag, followed by the default variant and quality tags.

2.6 Concatenation and deduplication

After tagging, the different training sets were concatenated, and all exact duplicates were removed from the data using OpusFilter's duplicate removal step. Note that because of the language variant tags, some duplicates marked as different variants may have remained.

For the Spanish–English data, duplicates were removed separately from the OpenSubtitles part and the rest of the data.

2.7 Data postprocessing

We apply data postprocessing steps for two target languages: Chatino and Hñähñu.

Chatino has a tonal structure, where each word is tagged at the end with a superscript tone character (^{ABcEfGHIJK}), for example: *Kyqya*^{A} *no*^{A} *shtya*^{H} *renq*^{J} *2/2022-CC qo*^{E} *4/2022-CC*. Sometimes, the character ^{J} can also be found within a word. A manual inspection of the results allowed us to see that our models were not producing the superscript characters, presumably due to Unicode normalization performed during subword segmentation with SentencePiece. Therefore, we opted for substituting the characters in the character set mentioned above by their superscript counterparts if they were found at the end of a token. For ^{J}, we replaced all occurrences regardless of their position.

Regarding **Hñähñu**, organizers already acknowledge that the training variant (Valle del Mezquital) is a different one from the development and test sets (Ñûhmû de Itxenco), a severely endangered variant spoken by less than 100 people. The training data did not contain any sample from the development and test set variant, having some characters in the training data that never appear in the development set. In consequence, we chose to substitute all occurrences of the character set that only appear in the training data, by their non-diacritic counterpart. For example, *ë* becomes *e*, *è* becomes *e* and *ě* becomes *e*. The full character substitution can be consulted in our GitHub repository.

2.8 Data sizes

Table 1 shows the sizes of the used datasets. *train* refers to the official training data and *extra* to all other datasets except the Bibles. The data sizes are listed separately before and after filtering, as well as after concatenation and duplicate removal (*combined*). There is a difference of almost two orders of magnitude between the smallest (czn) and largest (quy) combined training data sets. Including the Bibles data (*bibles*) evens out the situation a bit, but Quechua has still significantly more data than any of the other languages. The development sets comprise 500–1000 sentences for each of the languages.

As discussed in subsection 2.5, we use different quality tags for different data sources. Table 1 also shows the amount of the different tags in the *combined* set. In addition, `<bible>` was used always for *bibles*.

Finally, Table 2 shows the sizes of the Spanish–English datasets before and after filtering. Model A uses different data than models B, C and D; see section 3 for details.

3 Models

We tested four major model configurations, which we refer to as A, B, C and D. All models are multilingual neural MT (NMT) models and include the Spanish–English translation task in some form. Models B and C also include language-specific finetuning steps. All models are based on the Transformer architecture (Vaswani et al., 2017). Models A and C are trained using the MarianNMT Toolkit (Junczys-Dowmunt et al., 2018), while B and D are implemented with OpenNMT-py 2.0 (Klein et al., 2020). All models were trained on a single GPU, except Model D, which was trained on 4 GPUs.

We use subword SentencePiece segmentation (Kudo and Richardson, 2018) for the training data. We train a shared vocabulary for all languages with size 32k that is used in all the models. Further details of the configurations are listed in Appendix B.

3.1 Model A

Model A is a multilingual one-to-many model based on knowledge distillation (Kim and Rush, 2016), where you distill a smaller student model from a powerful teacher; and transfer learning (Zoph et al., 2016), where you train a parent model

Data type		train		extra		combined (train+extra)				bibles
Processing		none	filtered	none	filtered	filtered+deduplicated				filtered
Quality tag						all	<default>	<noisy>	<bt>	<bible>
Ashaninka	cni	3,883	3,878	13,195	8,593	12,448	3,855	–	8,593	23,321
Aymara	aym	6,531	6,039	34,551	27,265	33,136	22,380	288	10,468	92,082
Bribri	bzd	7,508	7,490	659	588	7,853	7,519	334	–	23,103
Chatino	czn	357	354	4,841	4,798	4,804	4,804	–	–	47,570
Guarani	gn	26,032	26,012	82,703	72,597	86,698	36,435	16,833	33,430	23,687
Hñähñu	oto	4,889	4,888	9,013	8,593	13,401	13,331	70	–	23,849
Nahuatl	nah	16,145	15,863	26,892	22,558	35,360	27,839	1,473	6,048	47,674
Quechua	quy	125,008	109,372	261,055	209,814	306,999	268,020	617	38,362	123,829
Raramuri	tar	14,720	14,495	2,255	2,194	16,529	16,529	–	–	23,678
Shipibo-Konibo	shp	14,592	14,553	40,317	36,029	49,428	29,977	78	19,373	47,638
Wixarika	hch	8,966	8,960	3,165	2,932	11,784	11,518	–	266	23,867

Table 1: Numbers of segment pairs used for training (*train*: official training set provided by the organizers; *extra*: additional training data collected by the organizers and us, including back-translations and pivoted data but excluding Bibles; *bibles*: generated Bible data segments). The table also shows the effect of filtering and deduplication, as well as the repartition of data over the different quality tags (<default> for relatively clean data sources, <noisy> for unreliable data sources or with noisy sentence alignment, and <bt> for back-translations).

	news		opensubs		bibles	dev
Processing	none	filtered+deduped	none	filtered+deduped	filtered	none
Quality tag		<default>		<noisy>	<bible>	<default>
Model A	–	–	61,434,251	26,158,993	–	9,122
Models B, C, D	3,761,249	3,346,060	61,447,674	20,343,327	61,198	14,522

Table 2: Spanish–English dataset sizes: *news* is the combination of other training corpora (Europarl, GlobalVoices, News-Commentary, TED2020, Tatoeba) than OpenSubtitles and Bibles. The *dev* set for Model A consists of Spanish side of the official development sets machine-translated to English, and the WMT-News corpus for the other models.

on a high-resource pair and then continue training a child model on the low-resource data.

Regarding transfer learning, we train a parent model on a high-resource language pair (*es–en*) and then we continue training on the indigenous languages' data. Furthermore, for the *es–en* parent model, we apply knowledge distillation. We distill a *es–en* system from the No Language Left Behind (NLLB) model[12] (Costa-jussà et al., 2022) by simply training a new model on NLLB translated data from Spanish into English. The rationale behind this decision is to benefit from the advantages of a large pretrained NMT model while optimizing its size to enable effective fine-tuning.

In contrast to the other models, we exclusively use the OpenSubtitles dataset for Spanish–English training. This dataset consists of relatively brief sentences discussing general subjects. The motivation to use only this dataset was based on an examination of the development sets, which exhibited similar content characteristics. For development, we translate the source Spanish counterpart of the development sets provided by the organizers into English with the NLLB model with the hope that the distilled model will overfit to its teacher's distributions.

For the child model, we experiment with different data labeling schemes and submit three different versions:

- A.1: Parent model fine-tuned on indigenous data with all tags.
- A.2: Parent model fine-tuned on indigenous data without quality tags (keeping only the language and variant tags)
- A.3: Ensemble model of A.1 and A.2

3.2 Model B

Model B is a multilingual one-to-many model that reproduces the Model B setup from 2021 with updated training data.

The training takes place in three phases. In the first phase, the model is trained on 91% of Spanish–English data and 9% of data coming from the indigenous languages. The two English sets, *news* and *opensubs*, were assigned the same weight to avoid overfitting on subtitle data. In the second phase, the proportion of Spanish–English data is reduced to 37%, with the remainder sampled to equal amounts from the indigenous languages.

We train the first phase for 100k steps and pick the best intermediate savepoint according to the English validation set, which occurred after 80k steps. We initialize phase 2 with this savepoint and continue training until 200k steps. We then pick the five most promising savepoints based on the accuracy of the concatenated development sets, and select the best out of these five for each target language separately.

Starting from these savepoints, we added a third phase with language-specific finetuning, using 40% of English data and 60% of the individual target-language data. We trained these models for an additional 12k steps and selected the best intermediate savepoint. However, language-specific finetuning only increased the results for Ashaninka, Guarani and Raramuri. For the other languages, we used the best model savepoint from the second phase.

3.3 Model C

Model C is a set of 11 different language-specific models following the same strategy as Model B, trained with OpusTrainer.[13] OpusTrainer is a tool for curriculum learning, especially designed for multilingual scenarios, since it allows to specify the desired mixture of datasets from different language sources.

Similarly to Model B, the training takes place in three phases. We train our models with all the available data for all language pairs with the following configuration: (1) First, we train for one epoch with 90% of the *es–en* data and 10% of indigenous data, coming from each of the 11 indigenous languages. (2) Then, we train two epochs with a 50/50 distribution. Finally, (3) we add a language-specific fine-tuning step, where we train with a distribution of 10% of *es–en* data, 10% of *es–indigenous* and 80% of the desired language until convergence with early-stopping.

For inference, we ensemble the last four checkpoints with different combinations (1, 1-2, 1-2-3, 1-2-3-4) for each model. We select the best ensemble approach for each language pair based on the development set scores.

3.4 Model D

Model D is a multilingual modular sequence-to-sequence Transformer model (Vázquez et al., 2020;

[12]We use the NLLB-200's 3.3B variant as the teacher. https:/huggingface.co/facebook/nllb-200-3.3B

[13]https://github.com/hplt-project/OpusTrainer

Escolano et al., 2021). It is trained to perform Spanish-to-many translation, as well as a denoising auto-encoding objective (Lewis et al., 2020) for each of the 11 indigenous languages as well as English. Each model consists of 12 layers: a 6-layer Spanish encoder and decoders that share s layers followed by $6 - s$ language-specific layers. We trained distinct models with $s = 1, 2, 3$. Model D is set to $s = 1$ since it outperformed the others with respect to ChrF scores in the development set. Training details are given in Appendix B.

4 Results

Our results are shown in Table 3 with the official automatic evaluation metric, ChrF (Popović, 2015). We also include the results of this year's baseline and the best of the contenders for each of the target languages.

The baseline turned out to be quite hard to beat: for five languages (*hch, nah, oto, shp, tar*), the best submission was less than 2 ChrF points above the baseline. The competition among participants was also very tight this year: for the same five languages, there is less than 1 ChrF point difference between the first and second participant. Differences of less than 2 ChrF points can be observed for two additional languages (*cni, gn*). We believe that conducting significance testing to compare the participants' results would be beneficial in this scenario.

Regarding our models, Model B is our clear best-performing system. It reached first rank on 4 out of the 11 language pairs and third rank on two other occasions. Model B consistently outperformed all our other models. Its good performance can be attributed to its pre-training phase on Spanish-English data including a small percentage of the indigenous data. For this model, we also focused our efforts in checkpoints' selection. Further analysis will be required to investigate the performance differences between our models B and C, which used the same overall setup but show various minor differences in terms of toolkits, hyperparameters and curriculum definition.

The variants of Model A perform very similarly to each other, although removing the quality tags (A.2) leads to a significant increase for *es–shp*. Comparing models A and model B, our results indicate that training a multilingual model jointly from scratch is more beneficial than transfer learning approaches.

Model C seems to be on par with models A, although it works particularly well for *es–czn*. With Model C, we expected that language-specific fine-tuning would boost results. If we compare models B and C, our results match previous research, where it is stated that low-resource translation benefits from jointly-trained multilingual models (Johnson et al., 2017).

Finally, while Model D works well for *es–shp*, outperforming models C and A.2, we observe that in general it yields poor results. Nonetheless, we decided to use it anyway to test it in a real use case. Specifically for Model D, we were interested in testing the knowledge transfer capabilities of modular systems in low-resource multilingual scenarios. Indeed, these systems have demonstrated efficient transfer learning properties (Escolano Peinado, 2022). However, in this set of experiments, Model D lags behind our other non-modular systems for all other languages, indicating that perhaps the data available to train the language-specific modules was insufficient or that the parameter sharing strategies we chose were not optimal. In our experiments we also noticed that the modular systems ignore the variant and quality tags, which hampers their performance due to the imbalance of training resources. This can be seen in the case of *es-czn*, where the model is unable to learn the variant of the test set due to the unbalanced amount of that variant in the training data (only 5%).

5 Conclusions

In this paper, we have presented our contribution to the AmericasNLP 2023 Shared Task. We have described our efforts in terms of data collection and processing. We presented our 6 submissions to the task for all language pairs. We explore various setups for multilingual NMT, including knowledge distillation, transfer learning, multilingual NMT with English, language-specific fine-tuning, and a multilingual modular system.

Our strongest system follows the same architecture as our winning submission in 2021, which was used as the baseline for this year. There are two main differences between our current submission and the baseline:

- Additional training data: the amount of added resources varies across the languages, and not all of our collection efforts seem to have paid off. While results improved substantially for Guarani, no significant improvements could

Data	Model	Run	aym	bzd	cni	czn	gn	hch	nah	oto	quy	shp	tar	Average
dev	baseline		32.7	23.8	26.8	–	31.1	29.9	29.8	14.7	33.8	31.7	19.6	27.39
	A.1	1	36.0	19.6	26.0	13.5	34.8	29.3	27.6	13.1	35.9	22.4	18.4	25.15
	A.2	2	35.3	18.2	26.9	13.0	34.8	28.8	27.8	13.1	35.9	27.2	18.1	25.37
	A.3	4	36.4	19.7	26.0	13.5	36.0	29.3	29.0	13.2	36.4	23.7	18.0	25.56
	B	6	37.2	21.9	29.2	17.0	38.3	31.7	31.2	14.5	34.0	34.3	20.3	28.15
	C	3	34.8	18.9	26.5	14.4	35.1	29.0	27.3	13.2	33.9	21.5	18.6	24.84
	D	5	23.1	10.4	20.5	7.0	29.7	19.8	21.4	9.4	26.5	22.5	13.3	18.51
test	baseline		28.30	16.50	25.80	–	33.60	30.40	26.60	14.70	34.30	32.90	18.40	26.15
	best contender		**36.24**	**26.08**	**29.98**	**39.97**	39.34	32.25	**27.33**	14.81	**39.52**	**33.43**	18.74	–
	A.1	1	32.31	20.18	25.18	21.89	37.23	29.47	23.96	13.93	36.22	19.66	17.67	25.25
	A.2	2	31.98	19.19	25.99	21.67	36.60	29.48	25.61	14.23	36.49	25.41	17.45	25.83
	A.3	4	32.52	20.28	25.14	22.61	37.97	29.90	25.82	14.11	37.19	20.51	17.04	25.74
	B	6	33.44	22.45	28.41	32.07	**40.42**	**32.34**	26.87	**15.30**	33.29	33.35	**19.15**	28.83
	C	3	32.34	20.06	25.62	26.73	37.38	30.76	23.72	13.92	34.97	19.68	18.43	25.78
	D	5	21.86	11.16	19.60	7.17	31.15	21.01	19.87	10.66	27.72	22.85	12.92	18.72

Table 3: ChrF scores for the six submissions, computed on the development and test set. The Run column provides the numeric IDs with which our submissions are listed in the overview paper. In addition, we provide the baseline and the best competitor scores for each target language.

be observed for Nahuatl and Quechua. For Bribri, the model generalizes better to the test set than in 2021, but is still far behind the best contender.

- Inclusion of variant and quality tags: the experiments with Model A suggest that variant and quality tags can help, but that our current attribution of tags was not optimal. It could be promising to base the tags on more objective criteria like character and word overlap or alignment quality.

These two additions have allowed us to beat our own baseline.

Acknowledgements

This work was supported by the FoTran project, funded by the European Research Council (ERC) under the European Union's Horizon 2020 research and innovation programme under grant agreement No 771113.

This work was also supported by the HPLT project which has received funding from the European Union's Horizon Europe research and innovation programme under grant agreement No 101070350.

References

Željko Agić and Ivan Vulić. 2019. JW300: A wide-coverage parallel corpus for low-resource languages. In *Proceedings of the 57th Annual Meeting of the Association for Computational Linguistics*, pages 3204–3210, Florence, Italy. Association for Computational Linguistics.

Mikko Aulamo, Sami Virpioja, and Jörg Tiedemann. 2020. OpusFilter: A configurable parallel corpus filtering toolbox. In *Proceedings of the 58th Annual Meeting of the Association for Computational Linguistics: System Demonstrations*, pages 150–156, Online. Association for Computational Linguistics.

David Brambila. 1976. *Diccionario Raramuri – Castellano (Tarahumara).* Obra Nacional de la Buena Prensa, México.

Gina Bustamante, Arturo Oncevay, and Roberto Zariquiey. 2020. No data to crawl? monolingual corpus creation from PDF files of truly low-resource languages in Peru. In *Proceedings of the Twelfth Language Resources and Evaluation Conference*, pages 2914–2923, Marseille, France. European Language Resources Association.

Luis Chiruzzo, Pedro Amarilla, Adolfo Ríos, and Gustavo Giménez Lugo. 2020. Development of a Guarani - Spanish parallel corpus. In *Proceedings of the Twelfth Language Resources and Evaluation Conference*, pages 2629–2633, Marseille, France. European Language Resources Association.

Christos Christodoulopoulos and Mark Steedman. 2015. A massively parallel corpus: the Bible in 100 languages. *Language Resources and Evaluation*, 49:375–395.

Marta R Costa-jussà, James Cross, Onur Çelebi, Maha Elbayad, Kenneth Heafield, Kevin Heffernan, Elahe Kalbassi, Janice Lam, Daniel Licht, Jean Maillard, et al. 2022. No language left behind: Scaling human-centered machine translation. *arXiv preprint arXiv:2207.04672*.

Rubén Cushimariano Romano and Richer C. Sebastián Q. 2008. Ñaantsipeta asháninkaki birakochaki. diccionario asháninka-castellano. versión preliminar. http://www.lengamer.org/publicaciones/diccionarios/.

Abteen Ebrahimi, Manuel Mager, Arturo Oncevay, Enora Rice, Cynthia Montaño, John Ortega, Shruti Rijhwani, Alexis Palmer, Rolando Coto-Solano, Hilaria Cruz, and Katharina Kann. 2023. Findings of the AmericasNLP 2023 shared task on machine translation into indigenous languages. In *Proceedings of the Third Workshop on Natural Language Processing for Indigenous Languages of the Americas*. Association for Computational Linguistics.

Carlos Escolano, Marta R. Costa-jussà, José A. R. Fonollosa, and Mikel Artetxe. 2021. Multilingual machine translation: Closing the gap between shared and language-specific encoder-decoders. In *Proceedings of the 16th Conference of the European Chapter of the Association for Computational Linguistics: Main Volume*, pages 944–948, Online. Association for Computational Linguistics.

Carlos Escolano Peinado. 2022. Learning multilingual and multimodal representations with language-specific encoders and decoders for machine translation. *Ph.D. Thesis*, UPC, Departament de Teoria del Senyal i Comunicacions.

Isaac Feldman and Rolando Coto-Solano. 2020. Neural machine translation models with back-translation for the extremely low-resource indigenous language Bribri. In *Proceedings of the 28th International Conference on Computational Linguistics*, pages 3965–3976, Barcelona, Spain (Online). International Committee on Computational Linguistics.

Ana-Paula Galarreta, Andrés Melgar, and Arturo Oncevay. 2017. Corpus creation and initial SMT experiments between Spanish and Shipibo-konibo. In *Proceedings of the International Conference Recent Advances in Natural Language Processing, RANLP 2017*, pages 238–244, Varna, Bulgaria. INCOMA Ltd.

Ximena Gutierrez-Vasques, Gerardo Sierra, and Isaac Hernandez Pompa. 2016. Axolotl: a web accessible parallel corpus for Spanish-Nahuatl. In *Proceedings of the Tenth International Conference on Language Resources and Evaluation (LREC'16)*, pages 4210–4214, Portorož, Slovenia. European Language Resources Association (ELRA).

Tommi Jauhiainen, Heidi Jauhiainen, and Krister Lindén. 2022. HeLI-OTS, off-the-shelf language identifier for text. In *Proceedings of the 13th Conference on Language Resources and Evaluation*, pages 3912–3922, Marseille, France. European Language Resources Association.

Melvin Johnson, Mike Schuster, Quoc V. Le, Maxim Krikun, Yonghui Wu, Zhifeng Chen, Nikhil Thorat, Fernanda Viégas, Martin Wattenberg, Greg Corrado, Macduff Hughes, and Jeffrey Dean. 2017. Google's multilingual neural machine translation system: Enabling zero-shot translation. *Transactions of the Association for Computational Linguistics*, 5:339–351.

Marcin Junczys-Dowmunt, Roman Grundkiewicz, Tomasz Dwojak, Hieu Hoang, Kenneth Heafield, Tom Neckermann, Frank Seide, Ulrich Germann, Alham Fikri Aji, Nikolay Bogoychev, André F. T. Martins, and Alexandra Birch. 2018. Marian: Fast neural machine translation in C++. In *Proceedings of ACL 2018, System Demonstrations*, pages 116–121, Melbourne, Australia. Association for Computational Linguistics.

Yoon Kim and Alexander M. Rush. 2016. Sequence-level knowledge distillation. In *Proceedings of the 2016 Conference on Empirical Methods in Natural Language Processing*, pages 1317–1327, Austin, Texas. Association for Computational Linguistics.

Guillaume Klein, François Hernandez, Vincent Nguyen, and Jean Senellart. 2020. The OpenNMT neural machine translation toolkit: 2020 edition. In *Proceedings of the 14th Conference of the Association for Machine Translation in the Americas (Volume 1: Research Track)*, pages 102–109, Virtual. Association for Machine Translation in the Americas.

Taku Kudo and John Richardson. 2018. SentencePiece: A simple and language independent subword tokenizer and detokenizer for neural text processing. In *Proceedings of the 2018 Conference on Empirical Methods in Natural Language Processing: System Demonstrations*, pages 66–71, Brussels, Belgium. Association for Computational Linguistics.

Mike Lewis, Yinhan Liu, Naman Goyal, Marjan Ghazvininejad, Abdelrahman Mohamed, Omer Levy, Veselin Stoyanov, and Luke Zettlemoyer. 2020. BART: Denoising sequence-to-sequence pre-training for natural language generation, translation, and comprehension. In *Proceedings of the 58th Annual Meeting of the Association for Computational Linguistics*, pages 7871–7880, Online. Association for Computational Linguistics.

Manuel Mager, Diónico Carrillo, and Ivan Meza. 2018. Probabilistic finite-state morphological segmenter for wixarika (huichol) language. *Journal of Intelligent & Fuzzy Systems*, 34(5):3081–3087.

Manuel Mager, Arturo Oncevay, Abteen Ebrahimi, John Ortega, Annette Rios, Angela Fan, Ximena Gutierrez-Vasques, Luis Chiruzzo, Gustavo Giménez-Lugo, Ricardo Ramos, Ivan Vladimir Meza Ruiz, Rolando Coto-Solano, Alexis Palmer, Elisabeth Mager-Hois, Vishrav Chaudhary, Graham Neubig, Ngoc Thang Vu, and Katharina Kann. 2021. Findings of the AmericasNLP 2021 shared task on open machine translation for indigenous languages of the Americas. In

Proceedings of the First Workshop on Natural Language Processing for Indigenous Languages of the Americas, pages 202–217, Online. Association for Computational Linguistics.

Jesús Manuel Mager Hois, Carlos Barron Romero, and Ivan Vladimir Meza Ruíz. 2016. Traductor estadístico wixarika - español usando descomposición morfológica. *COMTEL*, 6.

Arya D. McCarthy, Rachel Wicks, Dylan Lewis, Aaron Mueller, Winston Wu, Oliver Adams, Garrett Nicolai, Matt Post, and David Yarowsky. 2020. The Johns Hopkins University Bible corpus: 1600+ tongues for typological exploration. In *Proceedings of the 12th Language Resources and Evaluation Conference*, pages 2884–2892, Marseille, France. European Language Resources Association.

Elena Mihas. 2011. *Añaani katonkosatzi parenini, El idioma del alto Perené*. Milwaukee, WI: Clarks Graphics.

Héctor Erasmo Gómez Montoya, Kervy Dante Rivas Rojas, and Arturo Oncevay. 2019. A continuous improvement framework of machine translation for Shipibo-konibo. In *Proceedings of the 2nd Workshop on Technologies for MT of Low Resource Languages*, pages 17–23, Dublin, Ireland. European Association for Machine Translation.

NLLB Team, Marta R. Costa-jussà, James Cross, Onur Çelebi, Maha Elbayad, Kenneth Heafield, Kevin Heffernan, Elahe Kalbassi, Janice Lam, Daniel Licht, Jean Maillard, Anna Sun, Skyler Wang, Guillaume Wenzek, Al Youngblood, Bapi Akula, Loic Barrault, Gabriel Mejia Gonzalez, Prangthip Hansanti, John Hoffman, Semarley Jarrett, Kaushik Ram Sadagopan, Dirk Rowe, Shannon Spruit, Chau Tran, Pierre Andrews, Necip Fazil Ayan, Shruti Bhosale, Sergey Edunov, Angela Fan, Cynthia Gao, Vedanuj Goswami, Francisco Guzmán, Philipp Koehn, Alexandre Mourachko, Christophe Ropers, Safiyyah Saleem, Holger Schwenk, and Jeff Wang. 2022. No language left behind: Scaling human-centered machine translation.

John E Ortega, Richard Alexander Castro-Mamani, and Jaime Rafael Montoya Samame. 2020. Overcoming resistance: The normalization of an Amazonian tribal language. In *Proceedings of the 3rd Workshop on Technologies for MT of Low Resource Languages*, pages 1–13, Suzhou, China. Association for Computational Linguistics.

Maja Popović. 2015. chrF: character n-gram F-score for automatic MT evaluation. In *Proceedings of the Tenth Workshop on Statistical Machine Translation*, pages 392–395, Lisbon, Portugal. Association for Computational Linguistics.

Prokopis Prokopidis, Vassilis Papavassiliou, and Stelios Piperidis. 2016. Parallel Global Voices: a collection of multilingual corpora with citizen media stories. In *Proceedings of the Tenth International Conference on Language Resources and Evaluation (LREC'16)*, pages 900–905, Portorož, Slovenia. European Language Resources Association (ELRA).

Rico Sennrich, Barry Haddow, and Alexandra Birch. 2016. Improving neural machine translation models with monolingual data. In *Proceedings of the 54th Annual Meeting of the Association for Computational Linguistics (Volume 1: Long Papers)*, pages 86–96, Berlin, Germany. Association for Computational Linguistics.

Noam Shazeer and Mitchell Stern. 2018. Adafactor: Adaptive learning rates with sublinear memory cost. In *Proceedings of the 35th International Conference on Machine Learning*, volume 80 of *Proceedings of Machine Learning Research*, pages 4596–4604. PMLR.

Jörg Tiedemann. 2020. The tatoeba translation challenge – realistic data sets for low resource and multilingual MT. In *Proceedings of the Fifth Conference on Machine Translation*, pages 1174–1182, Online. Association for Computational Linguistics.

Jörg Tiedemann. 2012. Parallel data, tools and interfaces in OPUS. In *Proceedings of the Eight International Conference on Language Resources and Evaluation (LREC'12)*, Istanbul, Turkey. European Language Resources Association (ELRA).

D. Varga, L. Németh, P. Halácsy, A. Kornai, V. Trón, and V. Nagy. 2005. Parallel corpora for medium density languages. In *Proceedings of Recent Advances in Natural Language Processing (RANLP-2005)*, pages 590–596.

Ashish Vaswani, Noam Shazeer, Niki Parmar, Jakob Uszkoreit, Llion Jones, Aidan N Gomez, Łukasz Kaiser, and Illia Polosukhin. 2017. Attention is all you need. *Advances in neural information processing systems*, 30.

Raúl Vázquez, Alessandro Raganato, Mathias Creutz, and Jörg Tiedemann. 2020. A systematic study of inner-attention-based sentence representations in multilingual neural machine translation. *Computational Linguistics*, 46(2):387–424.

Raúl Vázquez, Yves Scherrer, Sami Virpioja, and Jörg Tiedemann. 2021. The Helsinki submission to the AmericasNLP shared task. In *Proceedings of the First Workshop on Natural Language Processing for Indigenous Languages of the Americas*, pages 255–264, Online. Association for Computational Linguistics.

Raúl Vázquez, Umut Sulubacak, and Jörg Tiedemann. 2019. The University of Helsinki submission to the WMT19 parallel corpus filtering task. In *Proceedings of the Fourth Conference on Machine Translation (Volume 3: Shared Task Papers, Day 2)*, pages 294–300, Florence, Italy. Association for Computational Linguistics.

Mengzhou Xia, Xiang Kong, Antonios Anastasopoulos, and Graham Neubig. 2019. Generalized data augmentation for low-resource translation. In *Proceedings of the 57th Annual Meeting of the Association for Computational Linguistics*, pages 5786–5796, Florence, Italy. Association for Computational Linguistics.

Barret Zoph, Deniz Yuret, Jonathan May, and Kevin Knight. 2016. Transfer learning for low-resource neural machine translation. In *Proceedings of the 2016 Conference on Empirical Methods in Natural Language Processing*, pages 1568–1575, Austin, Texas. Association for Computational Linguistics.

A OpusFilter settings

The following filters were used for the training data except for back-translated data, Bibles and the OpenSubtitles data for Model A:

- LengthFilter: Remove sentences longer than 1000 characters. Applied to Aymara, Chatino, Nahuatl, Quechua, Raramuri.
- LengthRatioFilter: Remove sentences with character length ratio of 4 or more. Applied to Ashaninka, Aymara, Chatino, Guarani, Hñähñu, Nahuatl, Quechua, Raramuri, Wixarika.
- CharacterScoreFilter: Remove sentences for which less than 90% characters are from the Latin alphabet. Applied to Aymara, Quechua, Raramuri.
- TerminalPunctuationFilter: Remove sentences with dissimilar punctuation; threshold -2 (Vázquez et al., 2019). Applied to Aymara, Quechua.
- NonZeroNumeralsFilter: Remove sentences with dissimilar numerals; threshold 0.5 (Vázquez et al., 2019). Applied to Aymara, Quechua, Raramuri, Wixarika.

The Bribri and Shipibo-Konibo corpora seemed clean enough that we did not apply any filters for them.

After generating the Bible data, we noticed that some of the lines contained only a single 'BLANK' string. The segments with these lines were removed afterwards.

From the provided monolingual datasets, we filtered out sentences with more than 500 words.

The back-translated data was filtered with the following filters:

- LengthRatioFilter with threshold 2 and word units
- CharacterScoreFilter with Latin script and threshold 0.9 on the Spanish side and 0.7 on the other side
- LanguageIDFilter with a threshold of 0.8 for the Spanish side only.

The OpenSubtitles data for Model A was filtered with the following filters:

- LengthRatioFilter with threshold of 3 and word units.
- CharacterScoreFilter with Latin script and threshold 0.75 on both sides.
- AlphabetRatioFilter with a default threshold of 0.75.
- LongWordFilter with a default maximum length of 40.
- AverageWordLengthFilter with default values of minimum length of 2 and maximum length of 20.

B Hyperparameters

Models A use a 6-layered Transformer with 8 heads, 512 dimensions in the embeddings and 2,048 dimensions in the feed-forward layers. The batch size is 1,000 sentence-pairs. The Adam optimizer is used with β_1=0.9 and β_2=0.98. The models are trained until convergence with early-stopping on development data after ChrF has stalled 10 times.

Model B uses a 8-layered Transformer with 16 heads, 1,024 dimensions in the embeddings and 4,096 dimensions in the feed-forward layers. The batch size is 9,200 tokens in phase 1 and 4,600 tokens in phase 2, with an accumulation count of 4. The Adam optimizer is used with $beta_1$=0.9 and β_2=0.997. The Noam decay method is used with a learning rate of 2.0 and 16000 warm-up steps. Subword sampling is applied during training (20 samples, $\alpha = 0.1$). As a post-processing step, we removed the <unk> tokens from the outputs of Model B.

Model C uses a 6-layered Transformer with 8 heads, 512 dimensions in the embeddings and 2,048 dimensions in the feed-forward layers. The batch size is 1,000 sentence-pairs. The Adam optimizer is used with β_1=0.9 and β_2=0.98.

Model D was trained for a total of 150K steps to minimize the negative log-likelihood of the target translation. We accumulate gradients over all translation directions before back-propagation, using AdaFactor (Shazeer and Stern, 2018) with learning rate of 3.0. We trained the model on 4 AMD MI100 GPUs for $\sim$48hrs. The 8-headed Transformer layers have 512 dimensions in the self attention and 2,048 in the feed forward sub-layers.

Language		Resource
Aymara aym	✹	GlobalVoices (Tiedemann, 2012; Prokopidis et al., 2016)
	☆	BOconst: `https://www.kas.de/c/document_library/get_file?uuid=8b51d469-63d2-f001-ef6f-9b561eb65ed4&groupId=288373`
	★	FLORES-200: `https://github.com/facebookresearch/flores`
	★ ♻	NLLB-MD: `https://github.com/facebookresearch/flores`
	★	OPUS: Mozilla-I10n, wikimedia (Tiedemann, 2012)
	★	UDHR: `https://searchlibrary.ohchr.org/search?ln=en&cc=UDHR+Translation+Collection`
	★ ♻	GlobalVoices (en-aym) (Tiedemann, 2012; Prokopidis et al., 2016)
	☆ ↺	OPUS: Wikipedia (Tiedemann, 2020)
	▤	*ayr-x-bible-2011-v1*
Bribri bzd	✹	(Feldman and Coto-Solano, 2020)
	★	MEP: `https://mep.go.cr/educatico/minienciclopedias-pueblos-indigenas`
	★	IUCN: `https://portals.iucn.org/library/sites/library/files/documents/2016-071.pdf`
	▤	*bzd-x-bible-bzd-v1*
	⚙	`https://github.com/AmericasNLP/americasnlp2021/blob/main/data/bribri-spanish/orthographic-conversion.csv`
Ashaninka cni	✹	`https://github.com/hinantin/AshaninkaMT` (Ortega et al., 2020; Cushimariano Romano and Sebastián Q., 2008; Mihas, 2011)
	☆ ↺	ShaShiYaYi (Bustamante et al., 2020): `https://github.com/iapucp/multilingual-data-peru`
	▤	*cni-x-bible-cni-v1*
Chatino czn	✹	`https://scholarworks.iu.edu/dspace/handle/2022/21028`
	★	MXconst: `https://constitucionenlenguas.inali.gob.mx/`
	★ ♻	CTP-ENG: `https://github.com/AmericasNLP/americasnlp2023`
	▤	*cta-x-bible-cta-v1, ctp-x-bible-ctp-v1, cya-x-bible-cya-v1*
Guarani gn	✹	(Chiruzzo et al., 2020)
	★	PYconst: `http://ej.org.py/principal/constitucion-nacional-en-guarani/`
	★	News: `https://spl.gov.py/es/index.php/noticias` & `https://www.spl.gov.py/gn/index.php/marandukuera`
	★	Jojajovai: `https://github.com/pln-fing-udelar/jojajovai`
	★	FLORES-200: `https://github.com/facebookresearch/flores`
	★ ♻	NLLB-seed: `https://github.com/facebookresearch/flores`
	★	UDHR: `https://searchlibrary.ohchr.org/search?ln=en&cc=UDHR+Translation+Collection`

(Continues on next page)

Language		Resource
Guarani *(cont.)*	★	OPUS: GNOME, Mozilla-I10n, Tatoeba, Ubuntu, wikimedia (Tiedemann, 2012)
	☆ ↺	OPUS: Wikipedia (Tiedemann, 2020)
	📕	*gug-x-bible-gug-v1*
Wixarika hch	✹	`https://github.com/pywirrarika/wixarikacorpora` (Mager et al., 2018)
	☆	MXconst: `https://constitucionenlenguas.inali.gob.mx/`
	☆	corpora.wixes, paral_own, segcorpus.wixes: `https://github.com/pywirrarika/wixarikacorpora`
	☆ ↺	social.wix: `https://github.com/pywirrarika/wixarikacorpora`
	📕	*hch-x-bible-hch-v1*
	⚙	`https://github.com/pywirrarika/wixnlp/blob/master/normwix.py` (Mager Hois et al., 2016)
Nahuatl nah	✹	Axolotl (Gutierrez-Vasques et al., 2016)
	☆	MXConst: `https://constitucionenlenguas.inali.gob.mx/`
	★	Educational: `https://nawatl.com/category/textos/`
	★	Dict: `https://nahuatl.wired-humanities.org/`
	★	Short stories: `https://nahuatl.org.mx/cuentos-nahuatl-14-ejemplares-para-descargar/`
	★	INPImonograph: `https://www.gob.mx/inpi/documentos/monografia-nacional-los-pueblos-indigenas-de-mexico` & `https://www.gob.mx/inpi/documentos/libros-en-lenguas-indigenas`
	★	UDHR: `https://searchlibrary.ohchr.org/search?ln=en&cc=UDHR+Translation+Collection`
	★	OPUS: Tatoeba, wikimedia (Tiedemann, 2012)
	☆ ↺	OPUS: Wikipedia (Tiedemann, 2020)
	📕	*azz-x-bible-azz-v1, ncj-x-bible-ncj-v1, nhi-x-bible-nhi-v1*
Hnähñu oto	✹	Tsunkua: `https://tsunkua.elotl.mx/about/`
	☆	MXConst: `https://constitucionenlenguas.inali.gob.mx/`
	★	Dictionary: `http://xixona.dlsi.ua.es/~fran/ote-spa.tsv`
	★	UDHR: `https://searchlibrary.ohchr.org/search?ln=en&cc=UDHR+Translation+Collection`
	📕	*ote-x-bible-ote-v1*
Quechua quy	✹	JW300 (quy+quz) (Agić and Vulić, 2019)
	☆	MINEDU, dict_misc: `https://github.com/AmericasNLP/americasnlp2021/tree/main/data/quechua-spanish`
	☆	PEconst: `https://www.wipo.int/edocs/lexdocs/laws/qu/pe/pe035qu.pdf`

(Continues on next page)

Quechua *(cont.)*	☆	BOconst: https://www.kas.de/documents/252038/253252/7_dokument_dok_pdf_33453_4.pdf/9e3dfb1f-0e05-523f-5352-d2f9a44a21de?version=1.0&t=1539656169513
	★	UDHR (3 versions): https://searchlibrary.ohchr.org/search?ln=en&cc=UDHR+Translation+Collection
	★	FLORES-200: https://github.com/facebookresearch/flores
	★ ♻	JW300 (en–quy, en–quz) (Agić and Vulić, 2019)
	★	OPUS: GNOME, Mozilla-I10n, Tatoeba, Ubuntu, wikimedia (Tiedemann, 2012)
	☆ ↺	OPUS: Wikipedia (Tiedemann, 2020)
	📖	*quy-x-bible-quy-v1, quz-x-bible-quz-v1*
Shipibo-Konibo shp	✹	(Galarreta et al., 2017; Montoya et al., 2019)
	☆	Educational, Religious: http://chana.inf.pucp.edu.pe/resources/parallel-corpus/
	★	LeyArtesano: https://cdn.www.gob.pe/uploads/document/file/579690/Ley_Artesano_Shipibo_Konibo_baja__1_.pdf
	★	Tsanas: http://chana.inf.pucp.edu.pe
	★	Covid19: https://github.com/iapucp/covid19-multilingue-peru
	★	UDHR: https://searchlibrary.ohchr.org/search?ln=en&cc=UDHR+Translation+Collection
	☆ ↺	ShaShiYaYi (Bustamante et al., 2020): https://github.com/iapucp/multilingual-data-peru
	📖	*shp-SHPTBL*
Raramuri tar	✹	(Brambila, 1976)
	☆	MXConst: https://constitucionenlenguas.inali.gob.mx/
	📖	*tac-x-bible-tac-v1*
	⚙	https://github.com/AmericasNLP/americasnlp2021/pull/5
English en	☆	OPUS: Europarl, GlobalVoices, News-Commentary, TED2020, Tatoeba, OpenSubtitles (Tiedemann, 2012)
	📖	OPUS: bible-uedin (Christodoulopoulos and Steedman, 2015)
Spanish	📖	*spa-x-bible-americas, spa-x-bible-hablahoi-latina, spa-x-bible-lapalabra, spa-x-bible-newworld, spa-x-bible-nuevadehoi, spa-x-bible-nuevaviviente, spa-x-bible-nuevointernacional, spa-x-bible-reinavaleracontemporanea*

Table 4: Data resources used for training. ✹ refers to the official training data provided by the organizers. ☆ marks datasets from the *extra* categories already used in 2021, and ★ refers to new *extra* data. 📖 designates Bible identifiers from the JHUBC. Datasets marked with ↺ are created using backtranslation, datasets marked with ♻ using pivot translation from English to Spanish. Conversion tables and scripts are listed under ⚙.

Sheffield's Submission to the AmericasNLP Shared Task on Machine Translation into Indigenous Languages

Edward Gow-Smith, Danae Sánchez Villegas

Computer Science Department, University of Sheffield, UK

{egow-smith1, dsanchezvillegas1}@sheffield.ac.uk

Abstract

In this paper we describe the University of Sheffield's submission to the AmericasNLP 2023 Shared Task on Machine Translation into Indigenous Languages which comprises the translation from Spanish to eleven indigenous languages. Our approach consists of extending, training, and ensembling different variations of NLLB-200. We use data provided by the organizers and data from various other sources such as constitutions, handbooks, news articles, and backtranslations generated from monolingual data. On the dev set, our best submission outperforms the baseline by 11% average chrF across all languages, with substantial improvements particularly for Aymara, Guarani and Quechua. On the test set, we achieve the highest average chrF of all the submissions, we rank first in four of the eleven languages, and at least one of our submissions ranks in the top 3 for all languages.[1]

1 Introduction

The 2023 AmericasNLP Shared Task (Ebrahimi et al., 2023) involves developing machine translation systems for translating from Spanish to eleven low resource indigenous languages: Aymara (*aym*), Bribri (*bzd*), Asháninka (*cni*), Chatino (*czn*), Guarani (*gn*), Wixarika (*hch*), Nahuatl (*nah*), Hñähñu (*oto*), Quechua (*quy*), Shipibo-Konibo (*shp*), and Rarámuri (*tar*). Developing machine translation systems for these languages is challenging since many of them are polysynthetic (i.e., words are composed of several morphemes) and word boundaries are not standardized; they present different orthographic variations (e.g., classical vs. modern Nahuatl variations); presence of code-switching is common, among other difficulties of low resource settings.

Previous work has explored the effectiveness of pretrained machine translation models in low resource settings (Haddow et al., 2022) showing their impact on improving translation quality and addressing data scarcity challenges. Following this approach, our submissions to the 2023 AmericasNLP shared task consist of extending and finetuning various versions of NLLB-200 (Costa-jussà et al., 2022), a state-of-the-art machine translation model specifically designed for low resource settings. NLLB-200 is trained on 202 languages across 1 220 language pairs, including three of the languages present in the AmericasNLP shared task: *aym*, *gn*, and *quy*.[2] We further train our models on data from various sources such as constitutions and news articles, and we leverage multilingual training and ensembling to improve their performance. Models are evaluated using chrF (Popović, 2015), the official metric of the task. On the test set, we achieve the highest average chrF across all languages, and the best chrF for four of the languages.

The rest of the paper is organised as follows: Section 2 describes the data sources for training our models, Section 3 explains our three submissions in detail, Section 4 presents the results on the dev and test sets, Section 5 analyses the impact of different factors to the model's performance, Section 6 looks at zero-shot capabilities, and we draw conclusions in Section 7.

2 Data

2.1 Data Collection

We collect data from a variety of data sources, including training data provided by the organisers (AmericasNLP 2023), data from prior submissions to the AmericasNLP shared task (Helsinski and REPUcs) and relevant datasets specific to the in-

[1]We release code for training our models here: https://github.com/edwardgowsmith/americasnlp-2023-sheffield

[2]We present inference results on the dev set for these models in Table 4.

Proceedings of the Workshop on Natural Language Processing for Indigenous Languages of the Americas (AmericasNLP), pages 192–199
July 14, 2023 ©2023 Association for Computational Linguistics

Language	AmericasNLP 2023	Helsinki	REPUcs	NLLB	Train Total	Backtranslations	Bibles
aym	15,586	149,225	10,729	8,809	173,620	16,750	154,520
bzd	7,508				7,508		38,502
cni	3,883				3,883	13,192	38,846
czn	3,118				3,118		
gn	26,032	1,713		7,906	33,938	40,515	39,457
hch	8,966	2,404			11,370	510	39,756
nah	16,145				19,993	8,703	39,772
oto	4,889	3,834			8,723	537	39,726
quy	542,914	3,634			557,277		154,825
shp	14,592	14,656			29,248	23,592	79,341
tar	14,721	3,856			18,577		39,444

Table 1: Amount of parallel data collected for each language. AmericasNLP 2023: parallel training data provided by the organizers, Helsinki: data taken from Vázquez et al. (2021), REPUcs: data taken from Moreno (2021), NLLB: data from Costa-jussà et al. (2022), Backtranslations: back-translations created from monolingual data, Bibles: data from The JHU Bible corpus (McCarthy et al., 2020).

digenous languages included in the task (NLLB). Table 1 shows the size of the training data for each language. The total amount of training data is unevenly distributed among datasets, with Quechua (557 277), Aymara (173 620), and Guarani (33 938) having the greatest amount of training data.

AmericasNLP 2023 Data provided by the organisers of the 2023 AmericasNLP Shared Task includes parallel datasets for training the eleven languages. Table 8 contains all datasets and references.

Helsinki We take data from OPUS (Tiedemann, 2012) and other sources (including constitutions) provided by the University of Helsinki's submission (Vázquez et al., 2021) to the AmericasNLP 2021 Shared Task (Mager et al., 2021). The collected data from constitutions includes translations of the Mexican constitution into Hñähñu, Nahuatl, Raramuri and Wixarika, of the Bolivian constitution into Aymara and Quechua, and of the Peruvian constitution into Quechua.

REPUcs We use data collected for the REPUcs' submission to the 2021 AmericasNLP shared task (Moreno, 2021). They introduce a new parallel corpus with Quechua data from three sources: (1) Duran (2010), which contains poems, stories, riddles, songs, phrases and a vocabulary for Quechua; (2) Lyrics translate (2008) which provides different lyrics of poems and songs; and (3) a Quechua handbook (Iter and Ortiz Cárdenas, 2019).

NLLB We use two datasets introduced by Costa-jussà et al. (2022) as part of the training and evaluation for NLLB-200: (1) the NLLB Multi-Domain dataset, which provides 8 809 English-Aymara examples in the news, health, and unscripted chat domains and (2) the NLLB Seed dataset, which contains 6 193 English-Guarani examples consisting of professionally-translated sentences.

Bibles We also collect translations from the JHU Bible corpus (McCarthy et al., 2020), which provides translations of the bible for all languages of the Shared Task except for Chatino. However, we do not observe performance improvements from using this data in our experiments (Section 5).

2.2 Backtranslations

We generate backtranslations using the monolingual data sourced by Vázquez et al. (2021) for seven languages. This data comes from Bustamante et al. (2020), Tiedemann (2020), Mager et al. (2018), Tiedemann (2012), and Agić and Vulić (2019). We train NLLB-200 3.3B on X-*es* for all 11 languages, X, in the task. We take two checkpoints of this model at different stages of training (**backtrans 1** and **backtrans 2**). We find this data improve performance for two of the languages in the task (*gn* and *shp*, see Section 4).

2.3 Data Overlap

We note that NLLB-200, the pretrained machine translation model we base our experiments on (see Section 3) is trained on a portion of the collected data. Specifically, Spanish-Aymara and English-Aymara data from GlobalVoices, and Spanish-Quechua data from Tatoeba, both as part of OPUS. We believe that the inclusion of this data will still be beneficial to the model, since NLLB-200 is not optimised for the languages we are interested in as part of this task.

Model	aym	bzd	cni	czn	gn	hch	nah	oto	quy	shp	tar	mean
Baseline												
(Vázquez et al., 2021)	32.7	23.8	26.8	-	31.1	29.9	29.8	14.7	33.8	31.7	19.6	27.4
Submission 3												
NLLB-1.3B (single best)	39.1	24.5	30.5	40.1	35.5	31.8	30.1	14.7	35.8	32.2	19.4	29.4
Submission 2												
NLLB-1.3B (best per lang)		24.6										
NLLB-3.3B									38.8			
NLLB-1.3B (- NLLB Seed)	41.1											30.3
NLLB-1.3B (+ backtrans 1)					36.9							
NLLB-1.3B (+ backtrans 2)										35.4		
Submission 1												
Ensemble 1		25.1										
Ensemble 2				40.2								
Ensemble 3						31.8						30.5
Ensemble 4									39.1			
Ensemble 5											20.0	

Table 2: Dev set chrF scores for our three submissions. Here, the mean excludes *czn*.

2.4 Data Processing

The training data provided by the organisers is tokenised for *nah* and *oto*. We detokenise it to put it in line with the rest of the training data. We replace punctuation not included in NLLB-200's vocabulary. For *oto*, we find that 7% of the dev set contains characters not in the vocabulary, since these characters do not occur in the training sets, we don't take steps to handle them. For *czn*, we replace all superscript tone markings at the end of words with their standard counterparts, and then replace them naively back at inference.

3 Models

To tackle the 2023 AmericasNLP task on automatic translation of eleven low resource indigenous languages, we use NLLB-200 (Costa-jussà et al., 2022), a state-of-the-art machine translation model specifically designed for low resource settings. We experiment with different distilled versions of NLLB-200 with 600M and 1.3B parameters, and the version with 3.3B parameters. Although inference results on three languages[3] show that the largest version, NLLB-3.3B, performs better than smaller versions (see Table 4), due to the large computational cost of using NLLB-3.3B we run most of our experiments with the 1.3B distilled version. Models are fine-tuned on all the training data (Train Total), i.e. all data sources in Section 2 excluding Bibles and backtranslations, unless indicated. Moreover, we look at ensembling as an approach to improve the overall performance.

Submission 3 We train NLLB-200 1.3B distilled on the training data[4] and we choose the best checkpoint based on average chrF across all languages. We submit translations for all languages using this model (**NLLB-1.3B (single best)**).

Submission 2 We take the best-performing single model per language, excluding ensembles. We find that for the majority of languages, the best single model (by dev chrF) is the same as Submission 3, so we only submit additional translations for five languages:

- **NLLB-1.3B (- NLLB Seed) - *aym*** NLLB-1.3B trained on all data (Train Total) except for NLLB Seed.
- **NLLB-1.3B (best per lang) - *bzd*** NLLB-1.3B trained on all data.
- **NLLB-1.3B (+ backtrans 1) - *gn*** NLLB-1.3B trained on all data plus backtranslations from checkpoint 1.
- **NLLB-3.3B - *quy*** NLLB-3.3B trained on all data.
- **NLLB-1.3B (+ backtrans 2) - *shp*** NLLB-1.3B trained on all data plus backtranslations from checkpoint 2.

Submission 1 We experiment with various ensembles of models in attempt to improve performance further – we only find improvements over Submission 2 through ensembling for five of the

[3]NLLB-200 training data includes *aym*, *gn* and *quy*.

[4]We exclude Bibles data and backtranslations.

Submission	aym	bzd	cni	czn	gn	hch	nah	oto	quy	shp	tar	mean
3	35.3	24.5	28.5	39.9	39.1	32.0	27.3	14.8	37.2	28.6	18.4	29.6
2	36.2	24.4			39.3				39.3	33.4		30.3
1		25.0		40.0		32.3			39.5		18.7	30.5

Table 3: Test set chrF scores for our three submissions. Here, the mean includes all languages.

Model	quy	aym	gn
Baseline			
(Vázquez et al., 2021)	33.8	32.7	31.1
Inference			
600M distilled	30.0	34.2	32.5
1.3B distilled	31.0	35.2	35.2
1.3B	31.2	34.5	34.3
3.3B	32.9	35.4	35.6
Submission			
3	35.8	39.1	35.5
2	38.8	41.1	36.9
1	39.1	-	-

Table 4: Dev set chrF results for various NLLB-200 models, compared to the baseline and our submissions.

languages in the task. These selected ensembles are as follows:

- **Ensemble 1 - *bzd*** The best NLLB-1.3B model for *bzd* and an NLLB-600M model trained on all languages.
- **Ensemble 2 - *czn*** The best average NLLB-1.3B model and an NLLB-3.3B model trained on all languages.
- **Ensemble 3 - *hch*** The best average NLLB-1.3B model and an NLLB-600M model trained on all languages.
- **Ensemble 4 - *quy*** NLLB-3.3B trained on all languages, NLLB-3.3B trained on just the three supported languages (*aym*, *gn*, and *quy*), and NLLB-1.3B trained on all languages.
- **Ensemble 5 - *tar*** NLLB-1.3B trained on all languages, NLLB-600M trained on all languages, and NLLB-1.3B trained on all languages with a label smoothing of 0.2 (rather than 0.1).

3.1 Experimental Setup

We train the models in a multilingual fashion across all 11 language pairs present in the task, extending the embedding matrix to cover the tags for the new languages. We experiment with freezing various parameters, but find best results from training everything. We run our experiments on a single A100 GPU with batch sizes of 64, 16, and 2 for the 600M-, 1.3B-, and 3.3B-parameter models, respectively. We run our experiments in fairseq (Ott et al., 2019). Full hyperparameters for all of our runs are provided in Table 7. To evaluate our models, following the official evaluation, we use chrF (Popović, 2015) computed using SacreBLEU (Post, 2018) with signature: `nrefs:1|case:mixed|eff:yes|nc:6|nw:0|space:no|version:2.1.0`.

4 Results

4.1 Dev Set Results

Table 2 presents the results of our models on the dev set. We observe that for all languages, at least one of our models outperforms the baseline (Vázquez et al., 2021), with the exception of *oto* where we obtain comparable performance. The greatest improvements over the baseline model are on the three NLLB supported languages: *aym* (41.1 compared to 32.7), *gn* (36.9 compared to 31.1) and *quy* (39.1 compared to 33.8). We note that backtranslations only lead to improved performance on *gn* and *shp*, which are the two languages with the greatest amount of available monolingual data.

Inference results NLLB-200 is trained on data from three of the languages in this shared task: *quy*, *aym*, *gn*. Table 4 shows the inference results for these languages on the dev set for different variations of NLLB-200 models, along with our submissions. We observe a considerable improvement from the distilled 600M to 1.3B distilled models, with the greatest improvement over the baseline model for *gn*. We note that the 1.3B and 3.3B models outperform the baseline model for *aym* and *gn*. For *quy*, the inference results are worse than the baseline, likely due to the large amount of training data available in the task. We are able to improve substantially upon the inference results for *quy* and *aym*, but much less so for *gn* – this may be due to much less training data being available for *gn* compared to the other two languages.

Model	aym	bzd	cni	czn	gn	hch	nah	oto	quy	shp	tar	mean
NLLB-1.3B (single best)	39.1	24.5	30.5	40.1	35.5	31.8	30.1	14.7	35.8	32.2	19.4	30.3
NLLB-3.3B only quy									35.3			
NLLB-3.3B all langs									38.3			
1.3B random initialisation	21.9	17.6	24.2	33.7	22.8	25.1	24.3	13.7	22.9	22.2	16.9	22.3
NLLB-1.3B + bibles	38.3	24.1	30.0	38.0	35.5	30.0	28.0	14.7	35.2	31.9	18.9	28.7

Table 5: Dev set chrF scores for our additional experiments. For comparison, we reproduce the best single model as the first row.

4.2 Test Set Results

Results on the test set are shown in Table 3. Overall, our best submission achieves the highest average chrF across all languages from all submissions to the task (the second-best average is 29.4, compared to our 30.5). We also rank first for four of the eleven languages: *aym*, *czn*, *quy*, and *shp*. Our biggest improvement upon the second-place team is for *czn*, where we achieve 40.0 compared to 36.6. Submissions 1 and 2 rank in the top 3 for all languages. Surprisingly, the best chrF score was obtained on *czn* (40.0), the language with the least amount of training data (3 118 examples), followed by *quy* (39.5), and *aym* (36.5).

5 Additional Experiments

We provide the results of additional experiments to better understand the impact of various factors to our model's performance. The results of these experiments are shown in Table 5.

Multilingual training We look into whether multilingual training is beneficial to the model. For this, we train a 3.3B-parameter model on the *quy* data only, and compare this version (NLLB-3.3B only quy) to the one trained on all languages (NLLB-3.3B all langs) at the same number of updates (480 000). We find that multilingual training greatly improves the performance on *quy*, suggesting the model benefits from transfer learning across the languages. We suspect the benefit of the multilingual approach is related to the fact that although the languages included in the task are from different linguistic families, they share linguistic properties (e.g., polysynthetic or agglutinative).

Random initialization To analyse the benefit of starting from NLLB-200, we train an equivalent model to the 1.3B parameter version with randomly-initialised parameters. We see that this model performs much worse than the equivalent NLLB-200 model. As expected, we observe the greatest differences on the languages supported by NLLB-200 (*aym*, *gn*, *quy*).

	es-shp	quy-shp	aym-shp	gn-shp
NLLB-1.3B (+ backtrans 2)	35.4	30.5	29.3	26.7

Table 6: Dev set chrF scores for three zero-shot translation directions with our best model for *es-shp*.

Bibles data Similar to findings of Vázquez et al. (2021), we observe a drop in average performance through training on the Bibles data for the majority of languages except for *gn* and *oto*, where we obtain comparable performance.

6 Zero-shot Performance

We investigate whether our models have any zero-shot capabilities, i.e. translating a language pair for which the model has not seen any training data. For this, we take the best-performing model for *es-shp* (NLLB-1.3B + backtrans 2), and evaluate it on translating *quy-shp*, *aym-shp*, and *gn-shp*.[5] The results of these experiments are shown in Table 6. We find that our model is able to retain decent performance for these three zero-shot directions (maximum 25% drop in chrF), despite training all of the parameters of the machine translation model.

7 Conclusions

In this paper we describe our submissions to the AmericasNLP 2023 Shared Task. We participated with three submissions which consist of training different versions of the NLLB-200 model on publicly available data from different sources. Models are trained in a multilingual fashion and we experiment with different ensembles of models to further improve performance. We improve upon the inference scores for NLLB-200 3.3B for its three supported languages, and our best submission achieved the highest average chrF across all languages of any submission to the task.

[5]This is possible due to multiparallel dev sets across all languages.

Acknowledgments

This work is supported by the Centre for Doctoral Training in Speech and Language Technologies (SLT) and their Applications funded by the UK Research and Innovation grant EP/S023062/1.

References

Constenla Umaña Adolfo, F Elizondo Figueroa, and F Pereira Mora. 1998. Curso básico de bribri.

Željko Agić and Ivan Vulić. 2019. JW300: A wide-coverage parallel corpus for low-resource languages. In *Proceedings of the 57th Annual Meeting of the Association for Computational Linguistics*, pages 3204–3210, Florence, Italy. Association for Computational Linguistics.

David Brambila. 1976. *Diccionario rarámuri-castellano (tarahumar)*. Obra Nacional de la buena Prensa.

Gina Bustamante, Arturo Oncevay, and Roberto Zariquiey. 2020. No data to crawl? monolingual corpus creation from PDF files of truly low-resource languages in Peru. In *Proceedings of the Twelfth Language Resources and Evaluation Conference*, pages 2914–2923, Marseille, France. European Language Resources Association.

Luis Chiruzzo, Pedro Amarilla, Adolfo Ríos, and Gustavo Giménez Lugo. 2020. Development of a Guarani - Spanish parallel corpus. In *Proceedings of the Twelfth Language Resources and Evaluation Conference*, pages 2629–2633, Marseille, France. European Language Resources Association.

Marta R Costa-jussà, James Cross, Onur Çelebi, Maha Elbayad, Kenneth Heafield, Kevin Heffernan, Elahe Kalbassi, Janice Lam, Daniel Licht, Jean Maillard, et al. 2022. No language left behind: Scaling human-centered machine translation. *arXiv preprint arXiv:2207.04672*.

Rubén Cushimariano Romano and Richer C. Sebastián Q. 2008. Ñaantsipeta asháninkaki birakochaki. diccionario asháninka-castellano. versión preliminar. `http://www.lengamer.org/publicaciones/diccionarios/`.

Maximiliano Duran. 2010. La lengua general de los incas. Accessed: : 2023-05-25.

Abteen Ebrahimi, Manuel Mager, Arturo Oncevay, Enora Rice, Cynthia Montaño, John Ortega, Shruti Rijhwani, Alexis Palmer, Rolando Coto-Solano, Hilaria Cruz, and Katharina Kann. 2023. Findings of the AmericasNLP 2023 shared task on machine translation into indigenous languages. In *Proceedings of the Third Workshop on Natural Language Processing for Indigenous Languages of the Americas*. Association for Computational Linguistics.

Margery Peña Enrique. 2005. Diccionario fraseológico bribri-espanol˜ espanol-bribri, 2nd edn˜. *San Jose: Editorial de la Universidad de Costa Rica.[Google Scholar]*.

Ana-Paula Galarreta, Andrés Melgar, and Arturo Oncevay. 2017. Corpus creation and initial SMT experiments between Spanish and Shipibo-konibo. In *Proceedings of the International Conference Recent Advances in Natural Language Processing, RANLP 2017*, pages 238–244, Varna, Bulgaria. INCOMA Ltd.

Ximena Gutierrez-Vasques, Gerardo Sierra, and Isaac Hernandez Pompa. 2016. Axolotl: a web accessible parallel corpus for Spanish-Nahuatl. In *Proceedings of the Tenth International Conference on Language Resources and Evaluation (LREC'16)*, pages 4210–4214, Portorož, Slovenia. European Language Resources Association (ELRA).

Barry Haddow, Rachel Bawden, Antonio Valerio Miceli Barone, Jindřich Helcl, and Alexandra Birch. 2022. Survey of low-resource machine translation. *Computational Linguistics*, 48(3):673–732.

Cesar Iter and Zenobio Ortiz Cárdenas. 2019. Runasimita yachasun.

Carla Victoria Jara Murillo. 1993. I ttè. historias bribris. *San José: Editorial Universidad de Costa Rica*.

Carla Victoria Jara Murillo. 2018. *Gramática de la lengua bribri*.

Lyrics translate. 2008. Lyrics translate. Accessed: : 2023-05-25.

Manuel Mager, Diónico Carrillo, and Ivan Meza. 2018. Probabilistic finite-state morphological segmenter for wixarika (huichol) language. *Journal of Intelligent & Fuzzy Systems*, 34(5):3081–3087.

Manuel Mager, Carrillo Dionico, and Ivan Meza. 2020. The wixarika-spanish parallel corpus the wixarika-spanish parallel corpus.(august 2018).

Manuel Mager, Arturo Oncevay, Abteen Ebrahimi, John Ortega, Annette Rios, Angela Fan, Ximena Gutierrez-Vasques, Luis Chiruzzo, Gustavo Giménez-Lugo, Ricardo Ramos, Ivan Vladimir Meza Ruiz, Rolando Coto-Solano, Alexis Palmer, Elisabeth Mager-Hois, Vishrav Chaudhary, Graham Neubig, Ngoc Thang Vu, and Katharina Kann. 2021. Findings of the AmericasNLP 2021 shared task on open machine translation for indigenous languages of the Americas. In *Proceedings of the First Workshop on Natural Language Processing for Indigenous Languages of the Americas*, pages 202–217, Online. Association for Computational Linguistics.

Arya D. McCarthy, Rachel Wicks, Dylan Lewis, Aaron Mueller, Winston Wu, Oliver Adams, Garrett Nicolai, Matt Post, and David Yarowsky. 2020. The Johns Hopkins University Bible corpus: 1600+ tongues for typological exploration. In *Proceedings of the*

Twelfth Language Resources and Evaluation Conference, pages 2884–2892, Marseille, France. European Language Resources Association.

Elena Mihas. 2011. *Añaani katonkosatzi parenini, El idioma del alto Perené*. Milwaukee, WI: Clarks Graphics.

Héctor Erasmo Gómez Montoya, Kervy Dante Rivas Rojas, and Arturo Oncevay. 2019. A continuous improvement framework of machine translation for Shipibo-konibo. In *Proceedings of the 2nd Workshop on Technologies for MT of Low Resource Languages*, pages 17–23, Dublin, Ireland. European Association for Machine Translation.

Oscar Moreno. 2021. The REPU CS' Spanish–Quechua submission to the AmericasNLP 2021 shared task on open machine translation. In *Proceedings of the First Workshop on Natural Language Processing for Indigenous Languages of the Americas*, pages 241–247, Online. Association for Computational Linguistics.

Carla Victoria Jara Murillo and Alí García Segura. 2013. *Se'ttö bribri ie: Hablemos en bribri*. Programa de Regionalización Interuniversitaria CONARE.

John E Ortega, Richard Alexander Castro-Mamani, and Jaime Rafael Montoya Samame. 2020. Overcoming resistance: The normalization of an Amazonian tribal language. In *Proceedings of the 3rd Workshop on Technologies for MT of Low Resource Languages*, pages 1–13, Suzhou, China. Association for Computational Linguistics.

Myle Ott, Sergey Edunov, Alexei Baevski, Angela Fan, Sam Gross, Nathan Ng, David Grangier, and Michael Auli. 2019. fairseq: A fast, extensible toolkit for sequence modeling. In *Proceedings of NAACL-HLT 2019: Demonstrations*.

Maja Popović. 2015. chrF: character n-gram F-score for automatic MT evaluation. In *Proceedings of the Tenth Workshop on Statistical Machine Translation*, pages 392–395, Lisbon, Portugal. Association for Computational Linguistics.

Matt Post. 2018. A call for clarity in reporting BLEU scores. In *Proceedings of the Third Conference on Machine Translation: Research Papers*, pages 186–191, Brussels, Belgium. Association for Computational Linguistics.

Sofía Flores Solórzano. 2017. Corpus oral pandialectal de la lengua bribri.

Jörg Tiedemann. 2012. Parallel data, tools and interfaces in OPUS. In *Proceedings of the Eighth International Conference on Language Resources and Evaluation (LREC'12)*, pages 2214–2218, Istanbul, Turkey. European Language Resources Association (ELRA).

Jörg Tiedemann. 2020. The tatoeba translation challenge–realistic data sets for low resource and multilingual mt. *arXiv preprint arXiv:2010.06354*.

Raúl Vázquez, Yves Scherrer, Sami Virpioja, and Jörg Tiedemann. 2021. The Helsinki submission to the AmericasNLP shared task. In *Proceedings of the First Workshop on Natural Language Processing for Indigenous Languages of the Americas*, pages 255–264, Online. Association for Computational Linguistics.

A Hyperparameters

Hyper-parameter	Value
Batch size	16†
Update freq	1
Max learning rate	0.01
Schedule	inverse square root
Warmup steps	10 000
Adam betas	0.9, 0.98
Label smoothing	0.1‡
Weight decay	0.0001
Dropout	0.3
Clip norm	1e-6
Language pair temperature	3⋆
Number of updates	1M
Valid freq	40K updates + every epoch
Beam size	5

Table 7: Hyper-parameters used to train our models.
†: 64 for NLLB-600M, 2 for NLLB-3.3B.
‡: 0.2 for one of our models, used in Ensemble 5.
⋆: 1 for NLLB-3.3B models (including for backtranslations)

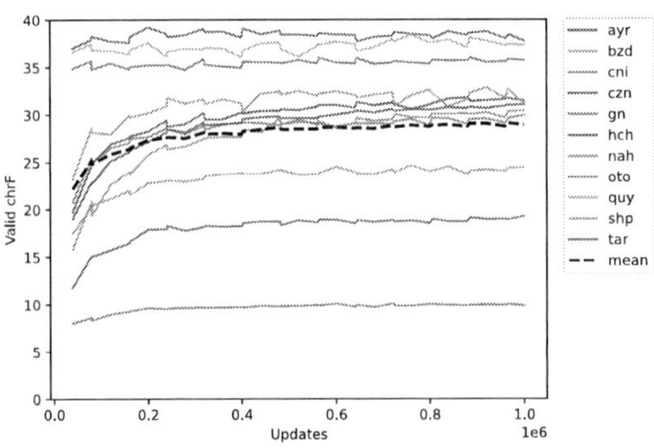

Figure 1: Valid chrF scores during training of our best single model (Submission 3).

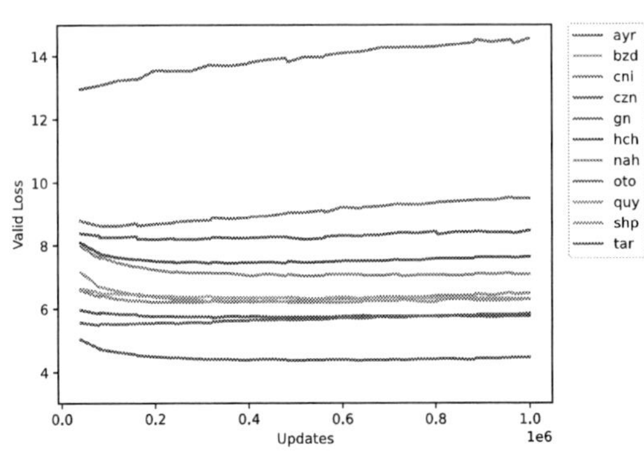

Figure 2: Valid losses during training of our best single model (Submission 3).

Dataset	Source
ashaninka-spanish	Ortega et al. (2020) Cushimariano Romano and Sebastián Q. (2008) Mihas (2011)
aymara-spanish	GlobalVoices (Tiedemann, 2012)
bribri-spanish	Adolfo et al. (1998) Solórzano (2017) Jara Murillo (2018) Murillo and Segura (2013) Jara Murillo (1993) Enrique (2005)
guarani-spanish	Chiruzzo et al. (2020)
hñähñu-spanish	Tsunkua `https://tsunkua.elotl.mx/about/`
wixarika-spanish	Mager et al. (2020)
shipibo_konibo-spanish	Montoya et al. (2019) Galarreta et al. (2017)
raramuri-spanish	Brambila (1976)
quechua-spanish	JW300 (Agić and Vulić, 2019) GlobalVoices (Tiedemann, 2012)
nahuatl-spanish	Axolotl (Gutierrez-Vasques et al., 2016)
chatino-spanish	IUScholar Works `https://scholarworks.iu.edu/dspace/handle/2022/21028`

Table 8: Data provided by the organisers of the 2023 AmericasNLP

Enhancing Translation for Indigenous Languages: Experiments with Multilingual Models

Atnafu Lambebo Tonja[1], **Hellina Hailu Nigatu**[2], **Olga Kolesnikova**[1], **Grigori Sidorov**[1], **Alexander Gelbukh**[1], **Jugal Kalita**[3]

[1]Instituto Politécnico Nacional (IPN), Mexico,

[2]University of California, Berkeley, USA,

[3]University of Colorado, Colorado Springs, USA

Abstract

This paper describes CIC NLP's submission to the AmericasNLP 2023 Shared Task on machine translation systems for indigenous languages of the Americas. We present the system descriptions for three methods. We used two multilingual models, namely M2M-100 and mBART50, and one bilingual (one-to-one) — Helsinki NLP Spanish-English translation model, and experimented with different transfer learning setups. We experimented with 11 languages from America and report the setups we used as well as the results we achieved. Overall, the mBART setup was able to improve upon the baseline for three out of the eleven languages.

1 Introduction

While machine translation systems have shown commendable performance in recent years, the performance is lagging for low-resource languages (Hadgu et al., 2022; Tonja et al., 2023). Since low-resource languages suffer from a lack of sufficient data (Siddhant et al., 2022; Haddow et al., 2022), most models and methods that are developed for high-resource languages do not work well in low-resource settings. Additionally, low-resource languages are linguistically diverse and have divergent properties from the mainstream languages in NLP studies (Zheng et al., 2021).

Though low-resource languages lack sufficient data to train large models, some such languages still have a large number of native speakers (Zheng et al., 2021). While the availability of language technologies such as machine translation systems can be helpful for such linguistic communities, they could also bring harm and exposure to exploitation (Hovy and Spruit, 2016). Borrowing from human-computer interaction (HCI) studies (Schneider et al., 2018), we want to acknowledge our belief that low-resource language speakers should be empowered to create technologies that benefit their communities. Many indigenous communities have community-rooted efforts for preserving their languages and building language technologies for their communities [1] and we hope that methods from Shared Tasks like this will contribute to their efforts.

Improving machine translation systems for low-resource languages is an active research area and different approaches (Zoph et al., 2016; Karakanta et al., 2018; Ortega et al., 2020a; Goyal et al., 2020; Tonja et al., 2022; Imankulova et al., 2017) have been to improve the performance of systems geared forward low-resource languages. We participated in the AmericasNLP 2023 Shared Task in hopes of contributing new approaches for low-resource machine translation that are likely to be helpful for community members interested in developing and adapting these technologies for their languages.

In recent years, large pre-trained models have been used for downstream NLP tasks, including machine translation (Brants et al., 2007) because of the higher performance in downstream tasks compared to traditional approaches (Han et al., 2021). One trend is to use these pre-trained models and fine-tune them on smaller data sets for specific tasks (Sun et al., 2019). This method has shown promising results in downstream NLP tasks for languages with low or limited resources (Tars et al., 2022; Zhao and Zhang, 2022). In our experiments, we used multilingual and bilingual models and employed different fine-tuning strategies for the eleven languages in the 2023 Shared Task (Ebrahimi et al., 2023).

In this paper, we describe the system setups we used and the results we obtained from our experiments. One of our systems improves upon the baseline for three languages. We also reflect on the setups we experimented with but ended up not submitting in hopes that future work could improve upon them.

[1]https://papareo.nz/

Proceedings of the Workshop on Natural Language Processing for Indigenous Languages of the Americas (AmericasNLP), pages 200–205
July 14, 2023

2 Languages and Datasets

In this section, we present the languages and datasets used in our shared task submission. Table 1 provides an overview of the languages, their linguistic families, and the numbers of parallel sentences.

Language	ISO	Family	Train	Dev	Test
Aymara	aym	Aymaran	6,531	996	1,003
Bribri	bzd	Chibchan	7,508	996	1,003
Asháninka	cni	Arawak	3,883	883	1002
Chatino	czn	Zapotecan	357	499	1,000
Guarani	gn	Tupi-Guarani	26,032	995	1,003
Wixarika	hch	Uto-Aztecan	8,966	994	1003
Nahuatl	nah	Uto-Aztecan	410,000	672	996
Hñähñu	oto	Oto-Manguean	4,889	599	1,001
Quechua	quy	Quechuan	125,008	996	1,003
Shipibo-Konibo	shp	Panoan	14,592	996	1,002
Rarámuri	tar	Uto-Aztecan	14721	995	1002

Table 1: This table provides information about the languages with which we experimented including ISO language code and language family as well as the number of sentences in training, development, and test sets for each language.

Aymara is an Aymaran language spoken by the Aymara people of the Bolivian Andes. It is one of only a handful of Native American languages with over one million speakers (Homola, 2012). Aymara, along with Spanish and Quechua, is an official language in Bolivia and Peru. The data for the Aymara-Spanish come from the Global Voices (Tiedemann, 2012).

Bribri The Bribri language is spoken in Southern Costa Rica. Bribri has two major orthographies: Jara[2] and Constenla[3] and the writing is not standardized which results in spelling variations across documents. In this case, the sentences use an intermediate representation to unify existing orthographies. The Bribri-Spanish data (Feldman, 2020) came from six different sources.

Asháninka Asháninka is an Arawakan language spoken by the Asháninka people of Peru and Acre, Brazil[4]. It is primarily spoken in the Satipo Province located in the Amazon forest. The parallel data for Asháninka-Spanish come mainly from three sources (Cushimariano Romano and Sebastián Q., 2008; Ortega et al., 2020b; Mihas, 2011) and translations by Richard Castro.

Chatino Chatino is a group of indigenous Mesoamerican languages. These languages are a branch of the Zapotecan family within the Oto-Manguean language family. They are natively spoken by 45,000 Chatino people (Cruz and Woodbury, 2006) whose communities are located in the southern portion of the Mexican state of Oaxaca. The parallel data for Chatino-Spanish can be accessed here[5].

Guarani Guarani is a South American language that belongs to the Tupi-Guarani family (Britton, 2005) of the Tupian languages. It is one of the official languages of Paraguay (along with Spanish), where it is spoken by the majority of the population, and where half of the rural population are monolingual speakers of the language (Mortimer, 2006).

Wixarika Wixarika is an indigenous language of Mexico that belongs to the Uto-Aztecan language family (de la Federación, 2003). It is spoken by the ethnic group widely known as the Huichol (self-designation Wixaritari), whose mountainous territory extends over portions of the Mexican states of Jalisco, San Luis Potosí, Nayarit, Zacatecas, and Durango, but mostly in Jalisco. United States: La Habra, California; Houston, Texas.

Nahuatl Nahuatl is a Uto-Aztecan language and was spoken by the Aztec and Toltec civilizations of Mexico[6]. The Nahuatl language has no standard orthography and has wide dialectical variations (Zheng et al., 2021).

Hñähñu Hñähñu, also known as Otomí, belongs to the Oto-Pamean family and lived in central Mexico for many centuries (Lastra, 2001). Otomí is a tonal language with a Subject-Verb-Object (SVO) word order (Ebrahimi et al., 2022). It is spoken in several states across Mexico.

Quechua The Quechua-Spanish data (Agić and Vulić, 2019; Tiedemann, 2012) has three different sources: the Jehova's Witnesses texts, the Peru Minister of Education, and dictionary entries and samples collected by Diego Huarcaya. The Quechua language, also known as Runasimi is spoken in Peru and is the most widely spoken pre-Columbian language family of the Americas (Ebrahimi et al., 2022).

[2]https://www.lenguabribri.com/se-tt%C3%B6-bribri-ie-hablemos-en-bribri

[3]https://editorial.ucr.ac.cr/index.php

[4]https://www.everyculture.com/wc/Norway-to-Russia/Ash-ninka.html

[5]`https://scholarworks.iu.edu/dspace/handle/2022/21028`

[6]www.elalliance.org/languages/nahuatl

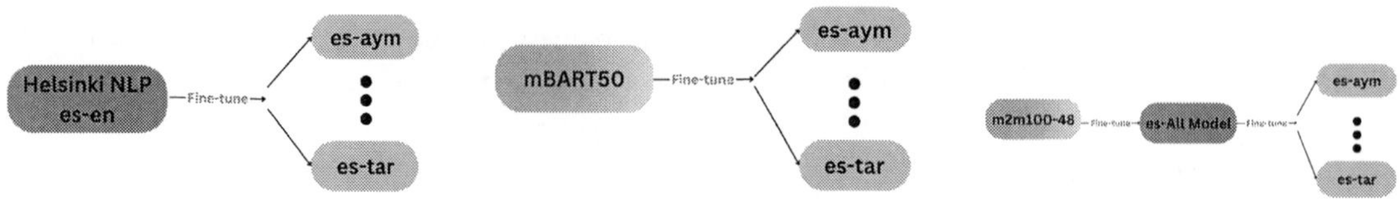

(a) Spanish-English (Helsinki) model (b) mBART50 model (c) m2m100-48$_{inter}$ model

Figure 1: Experiments on **(a)** fine-tuning bilingual model, **(b)** and **(c)** fine-tuning multilingual models. For **(a)** we fine-tuned the bilingual Spanish-English model on Spanish-Indigenous pairs, for **(b)** we fine-tuned the multilingual mBART50 model on Spanish-Indigenous pairs, and for **(c)** we fine-tuned the multilingual m2m100-48 model first on Spanish-All to produce m2m100-48$_{inter}$ model and then fine-tuned the m2m100-48$_{inter}$ model on Spanish-Indigenous pairs.

Shipibo-Konibo Shipibo-Konibo - Spanish data (Montoya et al., 2019; Galarreta et al., 2017) come from three different sources: samples from flashcards translated to Shipibo-Konibo, sentences translated from books for bilingual education, and dictionary entries.

Rarámuri Rarámuri, also known as Tarahumara is a Uto-Azetcan language spoken in Northern Mexico (Caballero, 2017). Rarámuri is a polysynthetic and agglutinative language spoken mainly in the Sierra Madre Occidental region of Mexico (Ebrahimi et al., 2022).

3 Models

We experimented with two multilingual and one bilingual translation model with different transfer learning setups. We used M2M-100 and mBART50 for the multilingual experiment and the Helsinki-NLP Spanish-English model for the bilingual experiment. Figure 1 shows the models used in this experiment.

3.1 Bilingual models

For the bilingual model, as shown in Figure 1a, we use a publicly available Spanish - English[7] pre-trained model from Huggingface[8] trained by Helsinki-NLP. The pre-trained MT models released by Helsinki-NLP are trained on OPUS, an open-source parallel corpus for covering 500 languages (Tiedemann and Thottingal, 2020; Tiedemann, 2020). This model is trained using the framework of Marian NMT (Junczys-Dowmunt et al., 2018). Each model has six self-attention layers in the encoder and decoder parts, and each layer has eight attention heads.

We used this model with the intention that the model trained with high-resource languages will improve the translation performance of low-resource indigenous languages when using a model trained with high-resource languages. We fine-tuned the Spanish-English model for each of the Spanish-to-Indigenous language pairs.

3.2 Multilingual models

For multilingual models, we used the Many-to-Many multilingual translation model that can translate directly between any pair of 100 languages (M2M100) (Fan et al., 2021) with 48M parameters and a sequence-to-sequence denoising auto-encoder pre-trained on large-scale monolingual corpora in 50 languages (mBART50) (Tang et al., 2020). We fine-tuned multilingual models in two ways:

1. We fine-tuned two multilingual models on each Spanish-Indigenous language pair for 5 epochs and evaluated their performance using the development data before training the final submission system. As shown in Figure 1b, for the final system, we only fine-tuned mBART50 on Spanish-indigenous data based on the development set evaluation performance.

2. Fine-tuning multilingual models first on the Spanish - All (mixture of all indigenous language data) dataset to produce an intermediate model and then fine-tuning the intermediate model for each of the Spanish-Indigenous language pairs as shown in Figure 1c. For this experiment, we combined all language pairs' training data to form a Spanish - all parallel corpus, and then we first fine-tuned m2m100-48 using a combined dataset for five

[7]https://huggingface.co/Helsinki-NLP/opus-mt-es-en
[8]https://huggingface.co/

Data	Model	aym	bzd	cni	czn	gn	hch	nah	oto	quy	shp	tar	Average
Baseline		28.3	16.5	25.8	-	33.6	30.4	26.6	14.7	34.3	32.9	18.4	-
Dev	M1	12.25	20.3	26.65	-	23.83	11.09	29.55	6.57	35.04	20.99	14.12	20.03
	M2	20.65	18.59	20.63	-	20.40	12.7	18.66	10.17	33.53	21.03	13.54	18.99
	M3	14.70	19.9	25.62	-	23.62	11.82	29.94	7.94	35.3	21.32	14.19	**20.43**
	M4	20.89	12.17	23.59	-	20.84	13.51	22.63	7.16	30.86	18.02	12.60	18.22
Test	M2	**19.05**	19.90	23.50	14.41	19.35	12.05	21.88	**9.22**	34.15	20.43	13.86	18.89
	M3	18.52	**21.17**	**25.85**	**15.61**	**21.75**	13.88	**26.57**	7.40	**35.62**	**21.26**	**14.87**	**20.22**
	M4	18.59	13.24	23.79	13.64	20.94	**14.67**	22.60	7.28	32.75	18.13	12.07	17.97

Table 2: chrF2 scores for the three submissions, computed on the development and test sets. M1, M2, M3, and M4 represent M2M100-48, M2M100-48$_{inter}$, mBART50 and Helsinki-NLP models respectively. The development set evaluations are used to select the best-performing model before working on submission data. The development set was not trained when evaluating the dev set, but we included the dev set during training for the final submission. The **bold** results show the models that out-preforms the baseline (Vázquez et al., 2021) results. The **bold** results show out-preforming models from our three model setups(excluding the baseline) for each individual language.

epochs and saved the model, here referred to as m2m100-48$_{inter}$ model. We fine-tuned the m2m100-48$_{inter}$ model again on each Spanish-Indigenous language pair for another 5 epochs and evaluated the performance on the development set before training the final submission system.

Evaluation We used chrF2 (Popović, 2017) evaluation metric to evaluate our MT systems.

4 Results

We submitted three (two multilingual and one bilingual) systems, as shown in Table 2, namely m2m100-48$_{inter}$, mBART50, and Helsinki-NLP. We included the dev set performance for all the models we trained before the final model to compare the results with the final model evaluated by using test set data. From the dev set result, it can be seen that fine-tuning the multilingual model on the Spanish-Indigenous language pair outperforms the fine-tuned result of the bilingual and m2m100-48$_{inter}$ models. From all the models evaluated using the dev set, mBART50 outperformed the others on average.

Our test results show comparable results when compared to the strongest baseline shared by the AmericasNLP 2023, and our model outperformed the baseline for Spanish-Bribri (es-bzd), Spanish-Asháninka (es-cni), and Spanish-Quechua (es-quy) pairs. Similarly, mBART50 outperformed the other models on average on the test set.

5 Conclusion

In this work, we present the system descriptions and results for our submission to the 2023 AmericasNLP Shared Task on Machine Translation into Indigenous Languages. We used pre-trained models and tested different fine-tuning strategies for the eleven languages provided for the shared task. We used one bilingual (Helsinki NLP English-Spanish model) and two multilingual (M2M-100 and mBART50) models for our experiments. In addition to fine-tuning the individual languages' data, we concatenated the data from all eleven languages to create a Spanish-All dataset and fine-tuned the M2M-100 model before fine-tuning for the individual languages. Our mBAERT50 model beat the strong baseline in three languages.

Acknowledgements

References

Željko Agić and Ivan Vulić. 2019. JW300: A wide-coverage parallel corpus for low-resource languages. In *Proceedings of the 57th Annual Meeting of the Association for Computational Linguistics*, pages 3204–3210, Florence, Italy. Association for Computational Linguistics.

Thorsten Brants, Ashok C. Popat, Peng Xu, Franz J. Och, and Jeffrey Dean. 2007. Large language models in machine translation. In *Proceedings of the 2007 Joint Conference on Empirical Methods in Natural Language Processing and Computational Natural Language Learning (EMNLP-CoNLL)*, pages 858–867, Prague, Czech Republic. Association for Computational Linguistics.

A Scott Britton. 2005. Guaraní-english/english-guaraní: Concise dictionary. *New York: Hippocrene*.

Gabriela Caballero. 2017. Choguita rarámuri (tarahumara) language description and documentation: a guide to the deposited collection and associated materials. language documentation conservation.

Emiliana Cruz and Anthony C Woodbury. 2006. The sandhi of tones in the chatino de quiahije. In *Memoirs of the Congress of Indigenous Languages of Latin Americaírica-II.*

Rubén Cushimariano Romano and Richer C. Sebastián Q. 2008. Ñaantsipeta asháninkaki birakochaki. diccionario asháninka-castellano. versión preliminar. `http://www.lengamer.org/publicaciones/diccionarios/`.

Diario Oficial de la Federación. 2003. Ley general de derechos lingüísticos de los pueblos indígenas. *Dirección General de Bibliotecas.*

Abteen Ebrahimi, Manuel Mager, Arturo Oncevay, Vishrav Chaudhary, Luis Chiruzzo, Angela Fan, John Ortega, Ricardo Ramos, Annette Rios, Ivan Meza-Ruiz, Gustavo A. Giménez-Lugo, Elisabeth Mager, Graham Neubig, Alexis Palmer, Rolando Coto-Solano, Ngoc Thang Vu, and Katharina Kann. 2022. Americasnli: Evaluating zero-shot natural language understanding of pretrained multilingual models in truly low-resource languages.

Abteen Ebrahimi, Manuel Mager, Arturo Oncevay, Enora Rice, Cynthia Montaño, John Ortega, Shruti Rijhwani, Alexis Palmer, Rolando Coto-Solano, Hilaria Cruz, and Katharina Kann. 2023. Findings of the AmericasNLP 2023 shared task on machine translation into indigenous languages. In *Proceedings of the Third Workshop on Natural Language Processing for Indigenous Languages of the Americas*. Association for Computational Linguistics.

Angela Fan, Shruti Bhosale, Holger Schwenk, Zhiyi Ma, Ahmed El-Kishky, Siddharth Goyal, Mandeep Baines, Onur Celebi, Guillaume Wenzek, Vishrav Chaudhary, et al. 2021. Beyond english-centric multilingual machine translation. *The Journal of Machine Learning Research*, 22(1):4839–4886.

Coto-Solano R Feldman, I. 2020. Neural Machine Translation Models with Back-Translation for the Extremely Low-Resource Indigenous Language Bribri. In *Proceedings of the 28th International Conference on Computational Linguistics*, pages 3965–3976.

Ana-Paula Galarreta, Andrés Melgar, and Arturo Oncevay. 2017. Corpus creation and initial SMT experiments between Spanish and Shipibo-konibo. In *Proceedings of the International Conference Recent Advances in Natural Language Processing, RANLP 2017*, pages 238–244, Varna, Bulgaria. INCOMA Ltd.

Vikrant Goyal, Sourav Kumar, and Dipti Misra Sharma. 2020. Efficient neural machine translation for low-resource languages via exploiting related languages. In *Proceedings of the 58th annual meeting of the association for computational linguistics: student research workshop*, pages 162–168.

Barry Haddow, Rachel Bawden, Antonio Valerio Miceli Barone, Jindřich Helcl, and Alexandra Birch. 2022. Survey of Low-Resource Machine Translation. *Computational Linguistics*, 48(3):673–732.

Asmelash Teka Hadgu, Abel Aregawi, and Adam Beaudoin. 2022. Lesan – machine translation for low resource languages. In *Proceedings of the NeurIPS 2021 Competitions and Demonstrations Track*, volume 176 of *Proceedings of Machine Learning Research*, pages 297–301. PMLR.

Xu Han, Zhengyan Zhang, Ning Ding, Yuxian Gu, Xiao Liu, Yuqi Huo, Jiezhong Qiu, Yuan Yao, Ao Zhang, Liang Zhang, et al. 2021. Pre-trained models: Past, present and future. *AI Open*, 2:225–250.

Petr Homola. 2012. Building a formal grammar for a polysynthetic language. In *Formal Grammar: 15th and 16th International Conferences, FG 2010, Copenhagen, Denmark, August 2010, FG 2011, Ljubljana, Slovenia, August 2011, Revised Selected Papers*, pages 228–242. Springer.

Dirk Hovy and Shannon L. Spruit. 2016. The social impact of natural language processing. In *Proceedings of the 54th Annual Meeting of the Association for Computational Linguistics (Volume 2: Short Papers)*, pages 591–598, Berlin, Germany. Association for Computational Linguistics.

Aizhan Imankulova, Takayuki Sato, and Mamoru Komachi. 2017. Improving low-resource neural machine translation with filtered pseudo-parallel corpus. In *Proceedings of the 4th Workshop on Asian Translation (WAT2017)*, pages 70–78.

Marcin Junczys-Dowmunt, Roman Grundkiewicz, Tomasz Dwojak, Hieu Hoang, Kenneth Heafield, Tom Neckermann, Frank Seide, Ulrich Germann, Alham Fikri Aji, Nikolay Bogoychev, André F. T. Martins, and Alexandra Birch. 2018. Marian: Fast neural machine translation in C++. In *Proceedings of ACL 2018, System Demonstrations*, pages 116–121, Melbourne, Australia. Association for Computational Linguistics.

Alina Karakanta, Jon Dehdari, and Josef van Genabith. 2018. Neural machine translation for low-resource languages without parallel corpora. *Machine Translation*, 32:167–189.

Y. Lastra. 2001. *Chapter 6. Otomí Language Shift and Some Recent Efforts to Reverse It*, pages 142–165. Multilingual Matters, Bristol, Blue Ridge Summit.

Elena Mihas. 2011. *Añaani katonkosatzi parenini, El idioma del alto Perené.* Milwaukee, WI: Clarks Graphics.

Héctor Erasmo Gómez Montoya, Kervy Dante Rivas Rojas, and Arturo Oncevay. 2019. A continuous improvement framework of machine translation for Shipibo-konibo. In *Proceedings of the 2nd Workshop on Technologies for MT of Low Resource Languages*, pages 17–23, Dublin, Ireland. European Association for Machine Translation.

Katherine Mortimer. 2006. Guaraní académico or jopará? educator perspectives and ideological debate in paraguayan bilingual education. *Working Papers in Educational Linguistics (WPEL)*, 21(2):3.

John E Ortega, Richard Castro Mamani, and Kyunghyun Cho. 2020a. Neural machine translation with a polysynthetic low resource language. *Machine Translation*, 34(4):325–346.

John E Ortega, Richard Alexander Castro-Mamani, and Jaime Rafael Montoya Samame. 2020b. Overcoming resistance: The normalization of an Amazonian tribal language. In *Proceedings of the 3rd Workshop on Technologies for MT of Low Resource Languages*, pages 1–13, Suzhou, China. Association for Computational Linguistics.

Maja Popović. 2017. chrf++: words helping character n-grams. In *Proceedings of the second conference on machine translation*, pages 612–618.

Hanna Schneider, Malin Eiband, Daniel Ullrich, and Andreas Butz. 2018. Empowerment in hci - a survey and framework. CHI '18, page 1–14, New York, NY, USA. Association for Computing Machinery.

Aditya Siddhant, Ankur Bapna, Orhan Firat, Yuan Cao, Mia Xu Chen, Isaac Caswell, and Xavier Garcia. 2022. Towards the next 1000 languages in multilingual machine translation: Exploring the synergy between supervised and self-supervised learning.

Chi Sun, Xipeng Qiu, Yige Xu, and Xuanjing Huang. 2019. How to fine-tune bert for text classification? In *Chinese Computational Linguistics: 18th China National Conference, CCL 2019, Kunming, China, October 18–20, 2019, Proceedings 18*, pages 194–206. Springer.

Yuqing Tang, Chau Tran, Xian Li, Peng-Jen Chen, Naman Goyal, Vishrav Chaudhary, Jiatao Gu, and Angela Fan. 2020. Multilingual translation with extensible multilingual pretraining and finetuning. *arXiv preprint arXiv:2008.00401*.

Maali Tars, Taido Purason, and Andre Tättar. 2022. Teaching unseen low-resource languages to large translation models. In *Proceedings of the Seventh Conference on Machine Translation (WMT)*, pages 375–380.

Jörg Tiedemann. 2012. Parallel data, tools and interfaces in OPUS. In *Proceedings of the Eighth International Conference on Language Resources and Evaluation (LREC'12)*, pages 2214–2218, Istanbul, Turkey. European Language Resources Association (ELRA).

Jörg Tiedemann. 2020. The tatoeba translation challenge – realistic data sets for low resource and multilingual MT. In *Proceedings of the Fifth Conference on Machine Translation*, pages 1174–1182, Online. Association for Computational Linguistics.

Jörg Tiedemann and Santhosh Thottingal. 2020. OPUS-MT – building open translation services for the world. In *Proceedings of the 22nd Annual Conference of the European Association for Machine Translation*, pages 479–480, Lisboa, Portugal. European Association for Machine Translation.

Atnafu Lambebo Tonja, Olga Kolesnikova, Muhammad Arif, Alexander Gelbukh, and Grigori Sidorov. 2022. Improving neural machine translation for low resource languages using mixed training: The case of ethiopian languages. In *Advances in Computational Intelligence: 21st Mexican International Conference on Artificial Intelligence, MICAI 2022, Monterrey, Mexico, October 24–29, 2022, Proceedings, Part II*, pages 30–40. Springer.

Atnafu Lambebo Tonja, Olga Kolesnikova, Alexander Gelbukh, and Grigori Sidorov. 2023. Low-resource neural machine translation improvement using source-side monolingual data. *Applied Sciences*, 13(2).

Raúl Vázquez, Yves Scherrer, Sami Virpioja, and Jörg Tiedemann. 2021. The helsinki submission to the americasnlp shared task. In *Proceedings of the First Workshop on Natural Language Processing for Indigenous Languages of the Americas*. The Association for Computational Linguistics.

Jing Zhao and Wei-Qiang Zhang. 2022. Improving automatic speech recognition performance for low-resource languages with self-supervised models. *IEEE Journal of Selected Topics in Signal Processing*, 16(6):1227–1241.

Francis Zheng, Machel Reid, Edison Marrese-Taylor, and Yutaka Matsuo. 2021. Low-resource machine translation using cross-lingual language model pretraining. In *Proceedings of the First Workshop on Natural Language Processing for Indigenous Languages of the Americas*, pages 234–240.

Barret Zoph, Deniz Yuret, Jonathan May, and Kevin Knight. 2016. Transfer learning for low-resource neural machine translation. *arXiv preprint arXiv:1604.02201*.

Findings of the AmericasNLP 2023 Shared Task on Machine Translation into Indigenous Languages

Abteen Ebrahimi[◇] Manuel Mager[♠] Shruti Rijhwani[♡]
Enora Rice[◇] Arturo Oncevay[▽] Claudia Garcia Baltazar
María Elena Méndez Cortés Cynthia Montaño[♣] John E. Ortega[ψ]
Rolando Coto-Solano[Ω] Hilaria Cruz[♯] Alexis Palmer[◇] Katharina Kann[◇]
[◇]University of Colorado Boulder [♠]AWS AI Labs [♡]Google DeepMind
[▽]University of Edinburgh [♣]University of California, Berkeley [ψ]Notheastern University
[Ω]Dartmouth College [♯]University of Louisville

Abstract

In this work, we present the results of the AmericasNLP 2023 Shared Task on Machine Translation into Indigenous Languages. This edition of the shared task features eleven language pairs, one of which – Chatino–Spanish – uses a newly collected evaluation dataset, consisting of professionally translated text from the legal domain. Seven teams participated in the shared task, with a total of 181 submissions. Additionally, we conduct a human evaluation of the best system outputs and compare them to the best submissions from the 2021 shared task. We find that this analysis agrees with the quantitative measure we use to rank submissions, ChrF, which itself shows an improvement of 9.64 points on average across all languages, compared to the prior winning system.

1 Introduction

The majority of Indigenous languages, including those native to the Americas, are under-represented in modern natural language processing (NLP), as technological advances are often concentrated on the small set of languages that have large amounts of easily available data (Joshi et al., 2020). Beyond the lack of data, linguistic factors like morphological complexity, non-standard orthographies, and language isolates make it even more challenging to adapt existing NLP methods to Indigenous languages (Mager et al., 2018; Schwartz et al., 2020).

However, there are multiple benefits of developing technologies that support Indigenous languages – building NLP models for under-represented languages can bring equitable access to information and technology to speakers of these languages (Mager et al., 2018). Additionally, several Indigenous languages in the Americas are endangered, and language technologies have proven to be beneficial to Indigenous communities and linguistic researchers in the documentation, preservation, and revitalization of endangered languages (Galla, 2016; Anastasopoulos, 2019; Zhang et al., 2022; Rijhwani, 2023). The AmericasNLP workshop seeks to highlight NLP and linguistic research on Indigenous languages spoken across the Americas, and promote the development of computational approaches which work well for these languages. The AmericasNLP Shared Task on Machine Translation into Indigenous Languages is hosted as part of the workshop to specifically focus on improvements in machine translation (MT) systems for these languages. In this work, we describe the third edition of the shared task. For this year, a new gold-standard parallel dataset for translation evaluation, between Spanish and Chatino, was developed. This dataset uses text from the legal domain, with source sentences taken from press releases of the Supreme Court of Mexico. This allows for evaluation on technical and challenging text, which are likely to be relevant to speakers of the language.

This work is structured as follows: in Section 2, we present a brief overview of related work on MT and Indigenous languages; in Section 3 and 4, we provide details on the shared task rules, and newly collected data; in Section 5, we summarize the submitted systems; and, in Sections 6 and 7, we provide an analysis of the main results and further

Language	ISO	Family	Train	Dev	Test
Asháninka	cni	Arawak	3883	883	1002
Aymara	aym	Aymaran	6531	996	1003
Bribri	bzd	Chibchan	7508	996	1003
Chatino	**ctp**	**Oto-Manguean**	**357**	**499**	**1000**
Guarani	gn	Tupi-Guarani	26032	995	1003
Nahuatl	nah	Uto-Aztecan	16145	672	996
Otomí	oto	Oto-Manguean	4889	599	1001
Quechua	quy	Quechuan	125008	996	1003
Rarámuri	tar	Uto-Aztecan	14721	995	1002
Shipibo-Konibo	shp	Panoan	14592	996	1002
Wixarika	hch	Uto-Aztecan	8966	994	1003

Table 1: The languages in the AmericasNLP 2023 shared task. Chatino (bolded) is the new language for this edition of the competition.

Proceedings of the Workshop on Natural Language Processing for Indigenous Languages of the Americas (AmericasNLP), pages 206–219
July 14, 2023

	Team	Andes	CIC-NLP	Helsinki-NLP*	LCT-EHU	LTLAmsterdam	Playground	Sheffield*
	Langs	1	11	11	1	11	10	11
	Subs	1	33	66	5	33	10	33
Data	Crawl			✓	✓			
	Ext. Bilingual	✓		✓	✓			
	Opus			✓				
	Religous			✓	✓			✓
	Wikipedia			✓				
	Prior Year			✓	✓		✓	✓
	No Addtl.		✓					
	Monolingual Trans			✓	✓		✓	✓
	Pivot Trans.			✓				
	Cleaning/Norm			✓		✓		✓
Pretraining	ChatGPT					✓		
	Encoder-Decoder		✓	✓	✓	✓		
	M2M-100		✓			✓		
	mBART		✓					
	mT5	✓						
	NLLB						✓	✓
Train	Ensemble							✓
	Multistage		✓	✓			✓	✓
	Multilingual		✓	✓			✓	✓

Table 2: Participating teams (*Team*) with system description paper. The information contained in this table is as follows: number of languages with a corresponding submission (*Langs.*), total number of submissions (*Sub.*). (*Data*) presents a summary of any external data collection, or *No Add.* if no external data was used, as well as if preprocessing steps are described. The *Pretraining* section describes if a pretrained translation model, or from-scratch encoder-decoder architecture was used. The *Train* section provides a summary of the training process for submissions. For more details we refer to the system description paper of each system, and note that certain external datasets or preprocessing steps may have been used within a system and not described in the description paper. We describe how each feature is defined in Appendix A.2.

experiments.

2 Related Work

2.1 NLP for Indigenous Languages

Low-resource languages are often referred to as 'less studied', 'resource-scarce', 'less computerized', 'less privileged', 'less commonly taught', or 'low-density' (Magueresse et al., 2020). Indigenous languages are largely included under this umbrella term, and they represent a unique challenge when dealing with NLP tasks.

First, most of the Indigenous languages worldwide are generally understudied, which means that even though we can grasp some of their general grammatical features based on other previously studied languages from the same linguistic families, there are still particular traits which haven't been described. Second, Indigenous languages are typologically different: some of them are polysynthetic, such as the languages belonging to Uto-Aztecan family (e.g. Nahuatl, Wixarika) with rich morphophonemics and a large number of inflections (Mithun, 2001). Other languages are highly analytic with simpler morphology, but with complex tonal systems such as Chatino and Chinantec, from the Oto-Manguean family. Due to the lack of prior study, it becomes challenging to even define what constitutes a language versus a language variety among Indigenous languages.

Finally, another major challenge is the diversification of orthographies and the scarcity of written corpora in such languages. However, in lieu of these challenges, there has been a substantial increase in NLP applications for Indigenous languages (Mohanty et al., 2023). For example, Hedderich et al. (2020) survey common methods used in low-resource scenarios, such as data augmentation, distant supervision, and cross-lingual language models. Mager et al. (2018) provide an overview of research in NLP related to the Indigenous languages of the Americas, with an accompanying, and continually-updated,repository of research works and other resources for Indigenous languages. Recently, ACL 2022 featured a theme track on *Language Diversity: from Low-Resource to Endangered Languages*, which highlights papers

RANK	TEAM	VERSION	COUNT	TOT. CHRF	TOT. BLEU	AVG. BLEU	AVG. CHRF	AVG. BLEU ALL	AVG. CHRF ALL
1	Sheffield	1	11	335.04	61.29	5.57	30.46	5.57	30.46
2	Sheffield	2	11	333.57	60.35	5.49	30.32	5.49	30.32
3	Sheffield	3	11	325.51	57.59	5.24	29.59	5.24	29.59
4	Helsinki-NLP	6	11	317.09	56.17	5.11	28.83	5.11	28.83
5	Helsinki-NLP	2	11	284.11	43.60	3.96	25.83	3.96	25.83
6	Helsinki-NLP	3	11	283.62	40.57	3.69	25.78	3.69	25.78
7	Helsinki-NLP	4	11	283.09	47.19	4.29	25.74	4.29	25.74
8	Helsinki-NLP	1	11	277.71	44.22	4.02	25.25	4.02	25.25
10	LTLAmsterdam	3	11	261.83	35.53	3.23	23.80	3.23	23.80
11	PlayGround	1	10	249.71	30.52	3.05	24.97	2.77	22.70
12	CIC-NLP	2	11	222.50	17.38	1.58	20.23	1.58	20.23
13	CIC-NLP	1	11	207.80	18.49	1.68	18.89	1.68	18.89
14	Helsinki-NLP	5	11	205.96	15.63	1.42	18.72	1.42	18.72
15	CIC-NLP	3	11	197.69	14.46	1.31	17.97	1.31	17.97
16	LTLAmsterdam	2	11	171.11	18.70	1.70	15.56	1.70	15.56
17	LTLAmsterdam	1	10	160.42	12.68	1.27	16.04	1.15	14.58
18	LCT-EHU	3	1	38.59	3.45	3.45	38.59	0.31	3.51
19	LCT-EHU	1	1	38.40	3.08	3.08	38.40	0.28	3.49
20	LCT-EHU	2	1	38.21	3.11	3.11	38.21	0.28	3.47
21	LCT-EHU	4	1	37.71	3.47	3.47	37.71	0.32	3.43
22	LCT-EHU	5	1	37.26	3.06	3.06	37.26	0.28	3.39
23	Andes	1	1	9.22	0.12	0.12	9.22	0.01	0.84

Table 3: Ranking of the submissions to the shared task. For each team and submission version, COUNT represents the number of languages supported with TOT. CHRF and TOT. BLEU representing the sum ChrF and BLEU scores over all supported languages by a submission. While AVG. BLEU and AVG. CHRF represent the average of all supported languages by a submission, the AVG*ALL columns represent the average over all 11 shared task languages, with AVG. CHRF ALL determining the final ranking of the submissions.

focusing on Indigenous languages, and featured a keynote discussion on how to best support linguistic diversity (Muresan et al., 2022).

2.2 Low-Resource MT

Low-Resource MT (LRMT) tackles the challenge of developing translation systems for language pairs with limited parallel data. Traditional neural machine translation approaches struggle in such scenarios due to data scarcity.

Multilingual transfer learning has been successful in enhancing translation quality in LRMT by leveraging knowledge from related languages (Zoph et al., 2016; Nguyen and Chiang, 2017; Aharoni et al., 2019). By utilizing shared representations across languages, multilingual models can generalize well to unseen language pairs with limited data.

One effective LRMT approach using transfer learning is finetuning large multilingual language models on specific language pairs. This involves adapting pretrained models like mBART, M2M-100, and NLLB-200 to target specific language pairs or domains of interest (Liu et al., 2020; Fan et al., 2020; Team et al., 2022). Refining the model's parameters through this technique enhances translation quality for low-resource languages (Thillainathan et al., 2021; Liu et al., 2020).

Back-translation is another effective technique employed in LRMT, which generates synthetic parallel data by translating and re-translating monolingual data (Sennrich et al., 2016; Feldman and Coto-Solano, 2020; Lample et al., 2018). By incorporating this technique, LRMT systems can benefit from additional training examples, leading to improved translation performance.

3 Task and Evaluation

The shared task focuses on *open* machine translation: outside of the development set and any prohibited datasets, teams are allowed to collect and train on an unlimited amount of external data. As translation performance for low-resource Indigenous languages is generally low, we choose this setting to allow models to achieve the best possible performance, in hopes that usable translation models become more quickly developed.

Metrics Translation evaluation is done with ChrF (Popović, 2015), as implemented in SCAREBLEU (Post, 2018), as the target languages are morphologically rich. While teams are not required to submit a system for all languages, the final score for each submission is calculated by taking an average over all eleven languages; if there is no model output for a given language, the score is taken as 0.

4 Languages and Data

For development and evaluation, the AmericasNLP 2021 shared task used multi-way parallel translations of the Spanish XNLI test set across 10 languages: Asháninka, Aymara, Bribri, Guarani, Nahuatl, Otomí, Quechua, Rarámuri, Shipibo-Konibo and Wixarika (Ebrahimi et al., 2022). For this edition of the shared task, we use the same evaluation set and additionally introduce a new evaluation dataset, created from Mexican court proceedings, for Spanish–Chatino. This set was released as a surprise language near the end of the competition, along with a small amount of Spanish–Chatino and English–Chatino data for training. In this section, we describe the Chatino language, Spanish source data, and translation process. For a detailed overview of the ten other evaluation languages, we refer the reader to Ebrahimi et al. (2022) and Mager et al. (2021).

4.1 Chatino

San Juan Quiahije Chatino (SJQ, ISO 639-3 ctp), spoken by about 5000 people, is an Oto-Manguean language spoken in Oaxaca, Mexico and by Chatinos who live in many cities throughout the United States, with a high concentration in the Southeastern United States in the states of North Carolina, Alabama, and Georgia. The Chatino languages are some of the most complex tonal languages in the world. SJQ has 10 tonemes and 15 morphological tonal categories. In the created corpus, tones are represented as superscripts.

4.2 Evaluation Dataset

Source Data A main motivation for this dataset is to create a resource which could be more directly applicable to the real life needs of the communities involved, while at the same time limiting negative ethical implications (Mager et al., 2023). As such, we choose to use legal text as the source domain. The Mexican Constitution and the General Law of Linguistic Rights of Indigenous Peoples (*Ley General De Derechos Lingüísticos de los Pueblos Indígenas*[1]) states that the 68 Indigenous languages spoken in the country before the Spanish conquest are National Languages. This gives all people the right to perform bureaucratic and legal actions in their native language. As a first approximation of this text, we gather press releases from the Mexican Supreme Court.[2] This allows us to avoid the potential harms of directly generating low-quality translations of written laws and court decisions, while still allowing for insights into the issues and challenges of translating legal terms and text. Furthermore, the text generated by the Mexican Supreme Court is public domain, allowing for free usage.

Translation Process To create the dataset, we crawl 10,000 instances from the Supreme Court press releases, and randomly select a subset for translation. Translations are jointly done by two professional translators, who are native San Juan Quiahije Chatino speakers. Legal terms in Spanish are translated into Chatino, in order to reduce code-switching and borrowed words. This translation of domain-specific terms represents the most challenging aspect of the translation process, with translators investigating the context and meaning of specific words in order to create accurate translations. For more difficult cases, translators consulted with lawyers to clarify the meaning of certain texts. For all translations, both translators worked together to reach an agreement on the translated text. Examples of difficult to translate words and entities include "dismissal, approval, jurisprudence, regulations among others and Chamber of Deputies, the nation's Supreme Court of Justice and Magistrate."

5 Baseline and Submitted Systems

In this section, we describe the 2023 baseline system and each team's approach. We present a summary of all approaches in Table 2.

5.1 Baseline

The AmericasNLP 2021 shared task used a transformer encoder–decoder model (Vaswani et al., 2017) along with hyperparameters shown to work well for low-resource settings (Guzmán et al., 2019). For this year's edition of the shared task, we use the winning 2021 system (Vázquez et al., 2021) as the baseline, as it greatly outperformed the previous baseline and other submissions on all languages.

5.2 Andes

The Andes team (Gillin and Gummibaerhausen, 2023) submitted a translation system for Spanish–Aymara. The system is based on mT5 (Xue et al.,

[1] https://www.diputados.gob.mx/LeyesBiblio/pdf/LGDLPI.pdf

[2] https://www.scjn.gob.mx/multimedia/comunicados

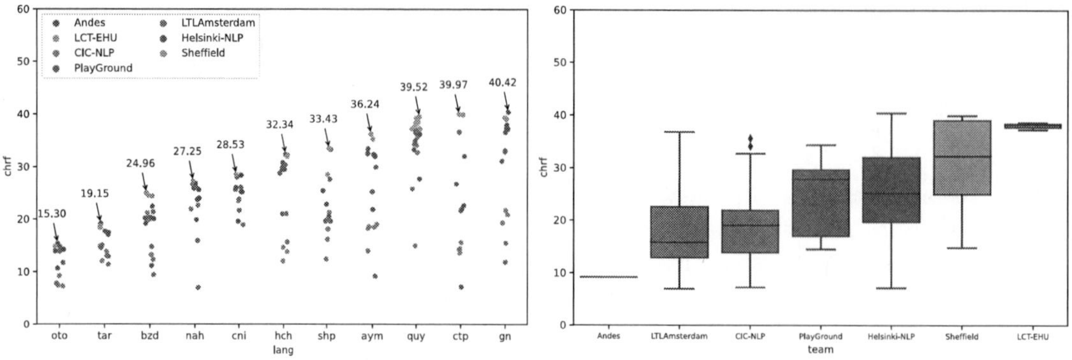

Figure 1: Main results of the shared task, in ChrF. In the left chart, we plot the performance of every submission, for each language. On the right, we show the distribution of per-team performance, across all submissions and languages. We note that distributions may not be directly comparable depending on the number of submissions from each team.

2021) and is further finetuned on English–Aymara data, in addition to the provided Spanish–Aymara data. The English parallel data consists of a lexicon, collected from books meant for language learning (Wexler and Programs, 1967; Parker, 2008)

5.3 CIC-NLP

The CIC-NLP team (Tonja et al., 2023) submitted three different models across all languages, based on either mBART50 (Tang et al., 2021) and M2M100 (Fan et al., 2020) or a publicly released English–Spanish translation model.[3] The multilingual models were first optionally finetuned on a concatenation of the es-XX training data across all languages. Language-specific models were then created by further finetuning on data for a specific target language. The English–Spanish model was only finetuned on data for a specific language pair.

5.4 Helsinki-NLP

The Helsinki-NLP team (Vázquez et al., 2023) submitted six different models across all languages, following four main modeling approaches. Model B is a copy of the team's winning multilingual one-to-many 2021 model, and Model C is a reimplementation of this approach using OpusTrainer and a language specific-finetuning step. Model A focuses on knowledge distillation and transfer learning: a parent English–Spanish model is distilled from the NLLB model, and is then further finetuned on target-language data. Model D uses language-specific decoders as part of a modular architecture: a specified number of decoder layers are shared across languages, while others are trained separately per language. The team also focused heavily on data collection and cleaning. In addition to the data provided by the shared task, the team collected data from OPUS (Tiedemann, 2012), the FLORES-200 (Team et al., 2022) evaluation sets, the Bible (McCarthy et al., 2020), the Universal Declaration of Human Rights, and various texts extracted from websites or PDFs of educational materials and news. MT was also used to leverage monolingual Wikipedia data as well as parallel data between the target languages and English. Texts were detokenized and whitespace normalized if necessary. Data from all sources was concatenated and deduplicated to create the final training data, and special tags denoting the quality and language variety of the source material were added to each example.

5.5 LCT-EHU

The LCT-EHU team (Ahmed et al., 2023) focused on the Spanish–Quechua language pair and submitted five different models to the competition. Among their contributions, they collected new parallel corpora, experimented with high-resource bilingual systems as pretrained models, such as Spanish–English and Spanish–Finnish, and generated synthetic parallel data from monolingual texts using back-translation and the copied corpus technique (Currey et al., 2017). The best result on the test set was obtained by using a model pretrained on Spanish–Finnish and by including new parallel data from the literature and legal domains, despite originating from different variants of Quechua Ayacucho.

[3] https://huggingface.co/Helsinki-NLP/opus-mt-es-en

Team	AYM	BZD	CNI	CTP	GN	HCH	NAH	OTO	QUY	SHP	TAR
2021 Baseline	15.70	6.80	10.20	-	19.30	12.60	15.70	5.40	30.40	12.10	3.90
2021 Best	28.30	16.50	25.80	-	33.60	30.40	26.60	14.70	34.30	32.90	18.40
Andes	9.22	-	-	-	-	-	-	-	-	-	-
CIC-NLP	19.05	21.17	25.85	15.61	21.75	14.67	26.57	9.22	35.62	21.26	14.87
Helsinki-NLP	33.44	22.45	28.41	32.07	**40.42**	**32.34**	26.87	**15.30**	37.19	33.35	**19.15**
LCT-EHU	-	-	-	-	-	-	-	-	38.59	-	-
LTLAmsterdam	25.23	21.36	26.04	36.61	32.89	30.38	26.03	13.85	36.81	19.8	15.06
PlayGround	29.98	14.80	28.01	-	33.17	28.75	23.68	14.75	34.38	27.66	14.53
Sheffield	**36.24**	**24.96**	**28.53**	**39.97**	39.34	32.25	**27.25**	14.81	**39.52**	**33.43**	18.74
↑ 2021	12.60	9.70	15.60	-	14.30	17.80	10.90	9.30	3.90	20.80	14.50
↑ 2023	7.94	8.46	2.73	-	6.82	1.94	0.73	0.60	5.22	0.53	0.75

Table 4: Summary of best performing submission from each team per language. Note that values can come from multiple submissions, making these scores different than what is used to calculate the overall shared task ranking. ↑2021 marks the difference between the 2021 Baseline and 2021 winning system. ↑2023 marks the difference between the 2021 best (i.e., 2023 baseline) system and the best 2023 system.

5.6 LTLAmsterdam

The LTLAmsterdam team (Stap and Araabi, 2023) submitted four different models for all language pairs. Their approaches included a bilingual system, an off-the-shelf commercial large language model used for translation, and a finetuned multilingual model with additional adaptation. The bilingual systems were trained using transformer models with parameters specifically tailored for low-resource languages (Araabi and Monz, 2020). For the large language model, they utilized the ChatGPT API[4] and followed the prompts proposed by Jiao et al. (2023). Additionally, they finetuned the M2M100 multilingual model (Fan et al., 2021), specifically choosing the 418M parameter version and training a model for each language pair. It is important to highlight that none of the target languages in the shared task were originally included in the set of languages of M2M100. Finally, they augmented the finetuned M2M100 model with a k-nearest neighbor (kNN) datastore for inference (Khandelwal et al., 2021), effectively creating a semi-parametric model that combines the parametric M2M100 model with a nearest neighbor retrieval mechanism.

5.7 PlayGround

The PlayGround team (Gu et al., 2023) submitted one model for each language pair, except for Spanish–Chatino. Their approach focused on utilizing the pretrained NLBB-200 model (Team et al., 2022), which they finetuned using the available monolingual and parallel data for the shared task. They conducted a comparison between bilingual and multilingual finetuned models, incorporating back-translated data through finetuning the NLBB-200 model with Spanish as the target language. Additionally, they adopted a weight-averaging approach (Wortsman et al., 2022).

5.8 Sheffield

The Sheffield team (Gow-Smith and Villegas) submitted three models for all languages. Approaches were based off various versions of the NLLB-200 model (Team et al., 2022). In addition to the provided training data, the team used data from teams which participated in prior editions of the shared task (Moreno, 2021; Vázquez et al., 2021). Data from other sources, such as the Bible (McCarthy et al., 2020) and NLLB project were also considered, however the authors found that Bible data did not improve performance on the development set, and did not include it in the final systems. Back-translation was also used to create additional parallel data. The submissions include specific preprocessing steps to prepare the data, such as detokenization and replacement of tone markings for Chatino. The team experimented with the distilled 600M, 1.3B and 3.3B versions of NLLB, and models were first finetuned on a concatenation of all available training data. The checkpoint with best average ChrF across all languages was considered as Submission 3. For Submission 2, the best check-

[4] `https://platform.openai.com/docs/api-reference/chat`

point per language was used. Submission 1 consists of ensembles of the various NLLB models. As NLLB relies on specific tags to denote the target languages, the embedding matrix was extended and new languages tags were created for the shared task languages which are unsupported.

6 Results

We present the overall ranking of submissions to the shared task in Table 3 and the best score per language for each team across all submissions in Table 4.

The overall winner of the shared task, the Sheffield Submission 1, achieves the best performance for 7 languages: Aymara, Bribri, Asháninka, Chatino, Nahuatl, Quechua, and Shipibo-Konibo. The Helsinki Submission 6 (i.e., Model B) has the highest performance for 4 languages: Guarani, Wixarika, Otomí, and Rarámuri. Systems are much more competitive than prior competitions, achieving extremely close ChrF scores for many languages, such as Asháninka, Guarani, Wixarika, and Shipibo-Konibo. The Sheffield and Helsinki teams both collect additional data, and train models in a multilingual and multi-stage fashion. Both also mention data cleaning and preprocessing in their pipeline, and we hypothesize that this step is likely vital for good performance, due to noise, domain mismatch, and differences in variants between the training and evaluation sets. For all languages except for Aymara, all teams have at least one submission which improves (often by a large margin) over the original 2021 baseline.

Comparison with Prior Years As the evaluation set for 10 of the languages is the same as for 2021, we can analyze the performance of submitted MT systems over time. In this year's shared task, we see improvements over the best 2021 system, the 2021 Helsinki submission (Vázquez et al., 2021), for all languages, but to varying degree. The largest improvements are for Bribri, Aymara, Guarani and Quechua. We also see small improvements for Asháninka and Wixarika. However, improvements for Nahuatl, Otomí, and Shipibo-Konibo are marginal. Overall, the improvements over Vázquez et al. (2021) are smaller in magnitude, compared to the improvements in 2021. This can be expected, however, as the baseline for this year's shared task represents a much stronger lower bound. Of the four languages with largest improvement, three are achieved by a Sheffield submission: Aymara, Bribri, and Quechua. This may be attributed, in part, to the use of the NLLB model by the team, which supports Aymara and Quechua in its original set of pretraining languages. On average across the 10 shared languages, we see a further 9.63 improvement in ChrF over 2021 results by the best submitted systems.

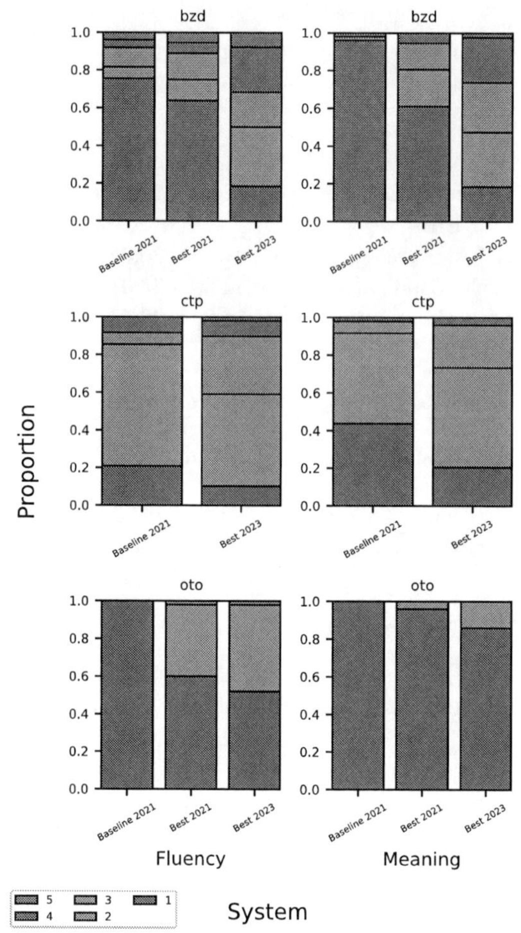

Figure 2: Results of the qualitative human evaluation. Ratings of *fluency* are displayed in the left column, and *meaning* in the right. Results are shown as a proportion of all evaluated sentences.

7 Additional Experiments

7.1 Qualitative Analysis

As quantitative measures of translation performance do not paint a complete picture, we also conduct a qualitative analysis of the system outputs for Bribri, Chatino, and Otomí. We randomly sample 50 parallel examples across the 2021 baseline, the 2021 winning system (Vázquez et al., 2021), and the 2023 submission with best performance for each language: Sheffield Submission 1 for Bribri and Chatino, and Helsinki Submission 6 for Otomí. Examples are shuffled and presented to a native speaker of each language, along with the Spanish source and gold reference. Annotations are done across two dimensions: *meaning* and *fluency*, using a categorical 1-5 scale. The guidelines given to annotators can be found in Appendix A.1.

The results of this analysis are shown in Figure 2. Similar to the trend of improvement in ChrF, we also see improvements in the rating of meaning and fluency across the three systems in this analysis. For Bribri, a strong majority of translations from the original 2021 baseline has a score of 1 across both dimensions. While we see some improvements from the Helsinki 2021 system, the 2023 system provides a considerable increase in translation quality; ratings of between 2-4 are now assigned to the majority of examples. For Chatino, the baseline system is stronger than for Bribri, and the improvement between the two systems is smaller when considering the proportion of examples rated as 1. For the 2023 system, we see the largest increase in quantity for ratings of 3. Otomí sees the worst performance of the three languages, with the majority of examples being rated as 1, across all three systems. Fluency does improve slightly, with an increase in the number of 2 ratings. However, examples with higher ratings are effectively non-existent. We also see a difference in improvement across *fluency* and *meaning*, with the former showing higher improvement. For all languages, even if we see an increase in the proportion of higher rated examples, the number of near-perfect (i.e., rating of 5) remains consistently small.

7.2 Impact of In-domain Data

The LTLAmsterdam team (Stap and Araabi, 2023) describes systems which make use of kNN and an external data store (Khandelwal et al., 2021) during decoding. It was jointly decided in a discussion between the organizers and team that submissions which use this approach – Submissions 4,5,6,7, and 8 – fall in a grey area with respect to the competition rules and would not be included in the main results, due to the fact that development set examples were included in the data store. However, these submissions can give insights into the potential improvements one can expect if there is access to parallel examples which are in-domain with respect to an expected test set. If we consider these submissions, they achieve the best performance for three languages: Bribri, Asháninka, and Nahuatl. Improvements over the next best team submission is 0.88 ChrF on average over the three languages. As such, given that systems still struggle with producing outputs with the highest qualitative rating (§7.1), this approach may be beneficial for producing more constrained and higher-quality outputs, given that access to high-quality parallel data is available.

8 Conclusion

In this paper we present the results of the AmericasNLP 2023 shared task. For this iteration, we collect a new dataset for translation evaluation between Spanish and Chatino, consisting of legal text from court press releases. Additionally, we keep the prior 10 evaluation languages used in 2021. Overall, 7 teams participated in the shared task. For all languages, multiple submissions improve over the previous best ChrF, but the magnitude varies per language. The best results were achieved by either finetuned versions of NLLB or a from-scratch transformer encoder–decoder model. To confirm the improvement in ChrF from the previous shared task, we conduct a human evaluation of system outputs, which, although it supports the quantitative improvement, highlights the fact that systems are still not able to produce translations of the highest quality. Furthermore, there is still variability in the absolute performance across languages. As such, while the results of the shared task mark a promising trend in increasing translation quality for Indigenous languages, there are still improvements which can be made in order to create usable translation systems for Indigenous languages.

Acknowledgments

We would like to thank all teams that submitted systems to this year's AmericasNLP shared task! We would also like to thank Eric Ramos Aguilar for their help with the qualitative annotation of system outputs.

References

Roee Aharoni, Melvin Johnson, and Orhan Firat. 2019. Massively multilingual neural machine translation. In *Proceedings of the 2019 Conference of the North American Chapter of the Association for Computational Linguistics: Human Language Technologies, Volume 1 (Long and Short Papers)*, pages 3874–3884, Minneapolis, Minnesota. Association for Computational Linguistics.

Nouman Ahmed, Natalia Flechas Manrique, and Antonije Petrović. 2023. Enhancing Spanish-Quechua Machine Translation with Pre-Trained Models and Diverse Data Sources: LCT-EHU at AmericasNLP Shared Task. In *"Proceedings of the Third Workshop on Natural Language Processing for Indigenous Languages of the Americas"*. Association for Computational Linguistics.

Antonios Anastasopoulos. 2019. *Computational tools for endangered language documentation*. University of Notre Dame.

Ali Araabi and Christof Monz. 2020. Optimizing transformer for low-resource neural machine translation. In *Proceedings of the 28th International Conference on Computational Linguistics*, pages 3429–3435, Barcelona, Spain (Online). International Committee on Computational Linguistics.

Anna Currey, Antonio Valerio Miceli Barone, and Kenneth Heafield. 2017. Copied monolingual data improves low-resource neural machine translation. In *Proceedings of the Second Conference on Machine Translation*, pages 148–156, Copenhagen, Denmark. Association for Computational Linguistics.

Abteen Ebrahimi, Manuel Mager, Arturo Oncevay, Vishrav Chaudhary, Luis Chiruzzo, Angela Fan, John Ortega, Ricardo Ramos, Annette Rios, Ivan Vladimir Meza Ruiz, Gustavo Giménez-Lugo, Elisabeth Mager, Graham Neubig, Alexis Palmer, Rolando Coto-Solano, Thang Vu, and Katharina Kann. 2022. AmericasNLI: Evaluating Zero-shot Natural Language Understanding of Pretrained Multilingual Models in Truly Low-resource Languages. In *Proceedings of the 60th Annual Meeting of the Association for Computational Linguistics (Volume 1: Long Papers)*, pages 6279–6299, Dublin, Ireland. Association for Computational Linguistics.

Angela Fan, Shruti Bhosale, Holger Schwenk, Zhiyi Ma, Ahmed El-Kishky, Siddharth Goyal, Mandeep Baines, Onur Celebi, Guillaume Wenzek, Vishrav Chaudhary, Naman Goyal, Tom Birch, Vitaliy Liptchinsky, Sergey Edunov, Michael Auli, and Armand Joulin. 2021. Beyond english-centric multilingual machine translation. *Journal of Machine Learning Research*, 22(107):1–48.

Angela Fan, Shruti Bhosale, Holger Schwenk, Zhiyi Ma, Ahmed El-Kishky, Siddharth Goyal, Mandeep Baines, Onur Celebi, Guillaume Wenzek, Vishrav Chaudhary, Naman Goyal, Tom Birch, Vitaliy Liptchinsky, Sergey Edunov, Edouard Grave, Michael Auli, and Armand Joulin. 2020. Beyond English-Centric Multilingual Machine Translation.

Isaac Feldman and Rolando Coto-Solano. 2020. Neural machine translation models with back-translation for the extremely low-resource indigenous language bribri. In *Proceedings of the 28th International Conference on Computational Linguistics*, page 3965–3976, Barcelona, Spain (Online). International Committee on Computational Linguistics.

Candace Kaleimamoowahinekapu Galla. 2016. Indigenous language revitalization, promotion, and education: Function of digital technology. *Computer Assisted Language Learning*, 29(7):1137–1151.

Nat Gillin and Brian Gummibaerhausen. 2023. Few-shot Spanish-Aymara Machine Translation Using English-Aymara Lexicon.

Edward Gow-Smith and Danae Sánchez Villegas. Sheffield's Submission to the AmericasNLP Shared Task on Machine Translation into Indigenous Languages.

Tianrui Gu, Kaie Chen, Siqi Ouyang, and Lei Li. 2023. PlayGround Low Resource Machine Translation System for the 2023 AmericasNLP Shared Task. In *"Proceedings of the Third Workshop on Natural Language Processing for Indigenous Languages of the Americas"*. Association for Computational Linguistics.

Francisco Guzmán, Peng-Jen Chen, Myle Ott, Juan Pino, Guillaume Lample, Philipp Koehn, Vishrav Chaudhary, and Marc'Aurelio Ranzato. 2019. The FLORES Evaluation Datasets for Low-Resource Machine Translation: Nepali–English and Sinhala–English. In *Proceedings of the 2019 Conference on Empirical Methods in Natural Language Processing and the 9th International Joint Conference on Natural Language Processing (EMNLP-IJCNLP)*, pages 6098–6111, Hong Kong, China. Association for Computational Linguistics.

Michael A Hedderich, Lukas Lange, Heike Adel, Jannik Strötgen, and Dietrich Klakow. 2020. A survey on recent approaches for natural language processing in low-resource scenarios. *arXiv preprint arXiv:2010.12309*.

Wenxiang Jiao, Wenxuan Wang, Jen tse Huang, Xing Wang, and Zhaopeng Tu. 2023. Is chatgpt a good translator? yes with gpt-4 as the engine.

Pratik Joshi, Sebastin Santy, Amar Budhiraja, Kalika Bali, and Monojit Choudhury. 2020. The state and fate of linguistic diversity and inclusion in the NLP world. In *Proceedings of the 58th Annual Meeting of the Association for Computational Linguistics*, pages 6282–6293, Online. Association for Computational Linguistics.

Urvashi Khandelwal, Angela Fan, Dan Jurafsky, Luke Zettlemoyer, and Mike Lewis. 2021. Nearest neighbor machine translation. In *International Conference on Learning Representations*.

Guillaume Lample, Myle Ott, Alexis Conneau, Ludovic Denoyer, and Marc'Aurelio Ranzato. 2018. Phrase-based &amp neural unsupervised machine translation. In *Proceedings of the 2018 Conference on Empirical Methods in Natural Language Processing*. Association for Computational Linguistics.

Yinhan Liu, Jiatao Gu, Naman Goyal, Xian Li, Sergey Edunov, Marjan Ghazvininejad, Mike Lewis, and Luke Zettlemoyer. 2020. Multilingual denoising pre-training for neural machine translation. *Transactions of the Association for Computational Linguistics*, 8:726–742.

Manuel Mager, Ximena Gutierrez-Vasques, Gerardo Sierra, and Ivan Meza-Ruiz. 2018. Challenges of language technologies for the indigenous languages of the Americas. In *Proceedings of the 27th International Conference on Computational Linguistics*, pages 55–69, Santa Fe, New Mexico, USA. Association for Computational Linguistics.

Manuel Mager, Elisabeth Mager, Katharina Kann, and Ngoc Thang Vu. 2023. Ethical considerations for machine translation of indigenous languages: Giving a voice to the speakers. *arXiv preprint arXiv:2305.19474*.

Manuel Mager, Arturo Oncevay, Abteen Ebrahimi, John Ortega, Annette Rios, Angela Fan, Ximena Gutierrez-Vasques, Luis Chiruzzo, Gustavo Giménez-Lugo, Ricardo Ramos, Ivan Vladimir Meza Ruiz, Rolando Coto-Solano, Alexis Palmer, Elisabeth Mager-Hois, Vishrav Chaudhary, Graham Neubig, Ngoc Thang Vu, and Katharina Kann. 2021. Findings of the AmericasNLP 2021 Shared Task on Open Machine Translation for Indigenous Languages of the Americas. In *Proceedings of the First Workshop on Natural Language Processing for Indigenous Languages of the Americas*, pages 202–217, Online. Association for Computational Linguistics.

Alexandre Magueresse, Vincent Carles, and Evan Heetderks. 2020. Low-resource languages: A review of past work and future challenges.

Arya D. McCarthy, Rachel Wicks, Dylan Lewis, Aaron Mueller, Winston Wu, Oliver Adams, Garrett Nicolai, Matt Post, and David Yarowsky. 2020. The Johns Hopkins University Bible Corpus: 1600+ Tongues for Typological Exploration. In *Proceedings of the Twelfth Language Resources and Evaluation Conference*, pages 2884–2892, Marseille, France. European Language Resources Association.

Marianne Mithun. 2001. *The languages of native North America*. Cambridge University Press.

Sushree Mohanty, Shantipriya Parida, and Satya Dash. 2023. Role of nlp for corpus development of endangered languages.

Oscar Moreno. 2021. The REPU CS' Spanish–Quechua Submission to the AmericasNLP 2021 Shared Task on Open Machine Translation. In *Proceedings of the First Workshop on Natural Language Processing for Indigenous Languages of the Americas*, pages 241–247, Online. Association for Computational Linguistics.

Smaranda Muresan, Preslav Nakov, and Aline Villavicencio, editors. 2022. *Proceedings of the 60th Annual Meeting of the Association for Computational Linguistics (Volume 1: Long Papers)*. Association for Computational Linguistics, Dublin, Ireland.

Toan Q. Nguyen and David Chiang. 2017. Transfer learning across low-resource, related languages for neural machine translation. In *Proceedings of the Eighth International Joint Conference on Natural Language Processing (Volume 2: Short Papers)*, pages 296–301, Taipei, Taiwan. Asian Federation of Natural Language Processing.

Philip M. Parker. 2008. *Webster's Aymara - English Thesaurus Dictionary*. ICON Group International, Inc.

Maja Popović. 2015. chrF: Character n-gram F-score for automatic MT evaluation. In *Proceedings of the Tenth Workshop on Statistical Machine Translation*, pages 392–395, Lisbon, Portugal. Association for Computational Linguistics.

Matt Post. 2018. A Call for Clarity in Reporting BLEU Scores. In *Proceedings of the Third Conference on Machine Translation: Research Papers*, pages 186–191, Brussels, Belgium. Association for Computational Linguistics.

Shruti Rijhwani. 2023. Improving Optical Character Recognition for Endangered Languages.

Lane Schwartz, Francis Tyers, Lori Levin, Christo Kirov, Patrick Littell, Chi-kiu Lo, Emily Prud'hommeaux, Hyunji Hayley Park, Kenneth Steimel, Rebecca Knowles, et al. 2020. Neural polysynthetic language modelling. *arXiv preprint arXiv:2005.05477*.

Rico Sennrich, Barry Haddow, and Alexandra Birch. 2016. Improving neural machine translation models with monolingual data.

David Stap and Ali Araabi. 2023. Chatgpt is not a good indigenous translator. In *"Proceedings of the Third Workshop on Natural Language Processing for Indigenous Languages of the Americas"*. Association for Computational Linguistics.

Yuqing Tang, Chau Tran, Xian Li, Peng-Jen Chen, Naman Goyal, Vishrav Chaudhary, Jiatao Gu, and Angela Fan. 2021. Multilingual Translation from Denoising Pre-Training. In *Findings of the Association for Computational Linguistics: ACL-IJCNLP 2021*, pages 3450–3466, Online. Association for Computational Linguistics.

NLLB Team, Marta R. Costa-jussà, James Cross, Onur Çelebi, Maha Elbayad, Kenneth Heafield, Kevin Heffernan, Elahe Kalbassi, Janice Lam, Daniel Licht, Jean Maillard, Anna Sun, Skyler Wang, Guillaume

Wenzek, Al Youngblood, Bapi Akula, Loic Barrault, Gabriel Mejia Gonzalez, Prangthip Hansanti, John Hoffman, Semarley Jarrett, Kaushik Ram Sadagopan, Dirk Rowe, Shannon Spruit, Chau Tran, Pierre Andrews, Necip Fazil Ayan, Shruti Bhosale, Sergey Edunov, Angela Fan, Cynthia Gao, Vedanuj Goswami, Francisco Guzmán, Philipp Koehn, Alexandre Mourachko, Christophe Ropers, Safiyyah Saleem, Holger Schwenk, and Jeff Wang. 2022. No Language Left Behind: Scaling Human-Centered Machine Translation.

Sarubi Thillainathan, Surangika Ranathunga, and Sanath Jayasena. 2021. Fine-tuning self-supervised multilingual sequence-to-sequence models for extremely low-resource nmt. In *2021 Moratuwa Engineering Research Conference (MERCon)*, page 432–437.

Jorg Tiedemann. 2012. Parallel Data, Tools and Interfaces in OPUS.

Atnafu Lambebo Tonja, Hellina Hailu Nigatu, Olga Kolesnikova, Grigori Sidorov, Alexander Gelbukh, and Jugal Kalita. 2023. Enhancing Translation for Indigenous Languages: Experiments with Multilingual Models.

Ashish Vaswani, Noam Shazeer, Niki Parmar, Jakob Uszkoreit, Llion Jones, Aidan N Gomez, Łukasz Kaiser, and Illia Polosukhin. 2017. Attention is All you Need. In *Advances in Neural Information Processing Systems*, volume 30. Curran Associates, Inc.

Raúl Vázquez, Yves Scherrer, Sami Virpioja, and Jörg Tiedemann. 2021. The Helsinki submission to the AmericasNLP shared task. In *Proceedings of the First Workshop on Natural Language Processing for Indigenous Languages of the Americas*, pages 255–264, Online. Association for Computational Linguistics.

Raúl Vázquez, Yves Scherrer, Sami Virpioja, and Jörg Tiedemann. 2023. The Helsinki submission to the AmericasNLP shared task. pages 255–264. Association for Computational Linguistics.

Paul Wexler and Washington State University Peace Corps Training Programs. 1967. *Beginning Aymara: A Course for English Speakers*. The Programs.

Mitchell Wortsman, Gabriel Ilharco, Samir Ya Gadre, Rebecca Roelofs, Raphael Gontijo-Lopes, Ari S Morcos, Hongseok Namkoong, Ali Farhadi, Yair Carmon, Simon Kornblith, and Ludwig Schmidt. 2022. Model soups: averaging weights of multiple fine-tuned models improves accuracy without increasing inference time. In *Proceedings of the 39th International Conference on Machine Learning*, volume 162 of *Proceedings of Machine Learning Research*, pages 23965–23998. PMLR.

Linting Xue, Noah Constant, Adam Roberts, Mihir Kale, Rami Al-Rfou, Aditya Siddhant, Aditya Barua, and Colin Raffel. 2021. mT5: A massively multilingual pre-trained text-to-text transformer.

Shiyue Zhang, Ben Frey, and Mohit Bansal. 2022. How can NLP help revitalize endangered languages? a case study and roadmap for the Cherokee language. In *Proceedings of the 60th Annual Meeting of the Association for Computational Linguistics (Volume 1: Long Papers)*, pages 1529–1541, Dublin, Ireland. Association for Computational Linguistics.

Barret Zoph, Deniz Yuret, Jonathan May, and Kevin Knight. 2016. Transfer learning for low-resource neural machine translation. In *Proceedings of the 2016 Conference on Empirical Methods in Natural Language Processing*, page 1568–1575, Austin, Texas. Association for Computational Linguistics.

Appendix

Lang.	Team	Ver.	ChrF	BLEU
aym	Sheffield	1	36.24	4.45
aym	Sheffield	3	35.27	4.03
aym	Helsinki-NLP	6	33.44	3.37
aym	Helsinki-NLP	4	32.52	3.15
aym	Helsinki-NLP	3	32.34	3.04
aym	Helsinki-NLP	1	32.31	3.30
aym	Helsinki-NLP	2	31.98	2.44
aym	PlayGround	1	29.98	1.96
aym	LTLAmsterdam	3	25.23	1.68
aym	Helsinki-NLP	5	21.86	1.10
aym	CIC-NLP	1	19.05	1.13
aym	CIC-NLP	3	18.59	0.56
aym	CIC-NLP	2	18.52	0.84
aym	LTLAmsterdam	1	18.28	0.96
aym	LTLAmsterdam	2	14.00	0.09
aym	Andes	1	9.22	0.12
bzd	Sheffield	1	24.96	6.35
bzd	Sheffield	3	24.49	6.21
bzd	Sheffield	2	24.38	6.18
bzd	Helsinki-NLP	6	22.45	5.64
bzd	LTLAmsterdam	3	21.36	5.23
bzd	CIC-NLP	2	21.17	4.72
bzd	Helsinki-NLP	4	20.28	5.02
bzd	Helsinki-NLP	1	20.18	4.66
bzd	Helsinki-NLP	3	20.06	4.44
bzd	CIC-NLP	1	19.90	3.92
bzd	Helsinki-NLP	2	19.19	4.36
bzd	PlayGround	1	14.80	2.04
bzd	CIC-NLP	3	13.24	1.66
bzd	LTLAmsterdam	2	12.32	0.97
bzd	Helsinki-NLP	5	11.16	1.10
bzd	LTLAmsterdam	1	9.44	1.38
cni	Sheffield	1	28.53	3.23
cni	Helsinki-NLP	6	28.41	4.45
cni	PlayGround	1	28.01	3.53
cni	LTLAmsterdam	3	26.04	3.03
cni	Helsinki-NLP	2	25.99	3.39
cni	CIC-NLP	2	25.85	2.72
cni	Helsinki-NLP	3	25.62	2.31
cni	Helsinki-NLP	1	25.18	3.40
cni	Helsinki-NLP	4	25.14	3.44
cni	CIC-NLP	3	23.79	3.28
cni	CIC-NLP	1	23.50	2.84
cni	LTLAmsterdam	2	21.63	0.59
cni	Helsinki-NLP	5	19.60	0.13
cni	LTLAmsterdam	1	18.91	2.35
ctp	Sheffield	1	39.97	12.33
ctp	Sheffield	3	39.90	12.26

Lang.	Team	Ver.	ChrF	BLEU
ctp	LTLAmsterdam	2	36.61	8.45
ctp	Helsinki-NLP	6	32.07	8.59
ctp	Helsinki-NLP	3	26.73	3.75
ctp	Helsinki-NLP	4	22.61	4.01
ctp	Helsinki-NLP	1	21.89	3.49
ctp	Helsinki-NLP	2	21.67	3.73
ctp	CIC-NLP	2	15.61	1.20
ctp	CIC-NLP	1	14.41	1.09
ctp	LTLAmsterdam	3	14.37	0.98
ctp	CIC-NLP	3	13.64	0.87
ctp	Helsinki-NLP	5	7.17	0.00
gn	Helsinki-NLP	6	40.42	8.40
gn	Sheffield	1	39.34	6.96
gn	Sheffield	3	39.07	7.18
gn	Helsinki-NLP	4	37.97	7.99
gn	Helsinki-NLP	3	37.38	7.49
gn	Helsinki-NLP	1	37.23	7.55
gn	Helsinki-NLP	2	36.60	6.90
gn	PlayGround	1	33.17	5.56
gn	LTLAmsterdam	3	32.89	5.43
gn	Helsinki-NLP	5	31.15	4.69
gn	CIC-NLP	2	21.75	1.84
gn	CIC-NLP	3	20.94	1.54
gn	CIC-NLP	1	19.35	1.34
gn	LTLAmsterdam	1	15.50	1.21
gn	LTLAmsterdam	2	11.91	0.10
hch	Helsinki-NLP	6	32.34	11.49
hch	Sheffield	1	32.25	12.04
hch	Sheffield	2	31.98	11.43
hch	Helsinki-NLP	3	30.76	10.98
hch	LTLAmsterdam	3	30.38	11.56
hch	Helsinki-NLP	4	29.90	12.59
hch	Helsinki-NLP	2	29.48	11.30
hch	Helsinki-NLP	1	29.47	12.30
hch	PlayGround	1	28.75	9.90
hch	LTLAmsterdam	2	21.04	7.69
hch	Helsinki-NLP	5	21.01	6.24
hch	LTLAmsterdam	1	15.66	0.71
hch	CIC-NLP	3	14.67	1.46
hch	CIC-NLP	2	13.88	0.08
hch	CIC-NLP	1	12.05	1.58
nah	Sheffield	1	27.25	2.33
nah	Helsinki-NLP	6	26.87	2.05
nah	CIC-NLP	2	26.57	1.36
nah	LTLAmsterdam	3	26.03	1.33
nah	Helsinki-NLP	4	25.82	1.75
nah	Helsinki-NLP	2	25.61	2.00
nah	Helsinki-NLP	1	23.96	1.41
nah	Helsinki-NLP	3	23.72	1.75
nah	PlayGround	1	23.68	0.90

Lang.	Team	Ver.	ChrF	BLEU
nah	CIC-NLP	3	22.60	1.22
nah	CIC-NLP	1	21.88	1.07
nah	Helsinki-NLP	5	19.87	0.14
nah	LTLAmsterdam	1	15.93	0.96
nah	LTLAmsterdam	2	7.02	0.03
oto	Helsinki-NLP	6	15.30	1.95
oto	Sheffield	1	14.81	1.71
oto	PlayGround	1	14.75	1.07
oto	Helsinki-NLP	2	14.23	1.45
oto	Helsinki-NLP	4	14.11	1.51
oto	Helsinki-NLP	1	13.93	1.41
oto	Helsinki-NLP	3	13.92	1.43
oto	LTLAmsterdam	3	13.85	1.25
oto	LTLAmsterdam	1	11.70	1.34
oto	Helsinki-NLP	5	10.66	0.12
oto	CIC-NLP	1	9.22	0.26
oto	LTLAmsterdam	2	7.77	0.02
oto	CIC-NLP	2	7.40	0.07
oto	CIC-NLP	3	7.28	0.05
quy	Sheffield	1	39.52	4.61
quy	Sheffield	2	39.26	4.54
quy	LCT-EHU	3	38.59	3.45
quy	LCT-EHU	1	38.40	3.08
quy	LCT-EHU	2	38.21	3.11
quy	LCT-EHU	4	37.71	3.47
quy	LCT-EHU	5	37.26	3.06
quy	Sheffield	3	37.24	4.33
quy	Helsinki-NLP	4	37.19	4.28
quy	LTLAmsterdam	3	36.81	3.00
quy	Helsinki-NLP	2	36.49	3.77
quy	Helsinki-NLP	1	36.22	3.49
quy	CIC-NLP	2	35.62	2.55
quy	Helsinki-NLP	3	34.97	2.74
quy	PlayGround	1	34.38	2.53
quy	CIC-NLP	1	34.15	2.59
quy	Helsinki-NLP	6	33.29	2.99
quy	CIC-NLP	3	32.75	2.05
quy	Helsinki-NLP	5	27.72	0.91
quy	LTLAmsterdam	1	25.75	1.47
quy	LTLAmsterdam	2	14.97	0.33
shp	Sheffield	1	33.43	6.32
shp	Helsinki-NLP	6	33.35	6.10
shp	Sheffield	3	28.57	4.00
shp	PlayGround	1	27.66	2.81
shp	Helsinki-NLP	2	25.41	3.13
shp	Helsinki-NLP	5	22.85	1.05
shp	CIC-NLP	2	21.26	1.83
shp	Helsinki-NLP	4	20.51	2.25
shp	CIC-NLP	1	20.43	2.28
shp	LTLAmsterdam	3	19.80	1.83
shp	Helsinki-NLP	3	19.68	2.04
shp	Helsinki-NLP	1	19.66	2.03
shp	CIC-NLP	3	18.13	1.66
shp	LTLAmsterdam	1	16.20	1.59
shp	LTLAmsterdam	2	12.42	0.34
tar	Helsinki-NLP	6	19.15	1.16
tar	Sheffield	1	18.74	0.95
tar	Helsinki-NLP	3	18.43	0.60
tar	Sheffield	2	18.39	0.88
tar	Helsinki-NLP	1	17.67	1.18
tar	Helsinki-NLP	2	17.45	1.13
tar	Helsinki-NLP	4	17.04	1.21
tar	LTLAmsterdam	3	15.06	0.22
tar	CIC-NLP	2	14.87	0.17
tar	PlayGround	1	14.53	0.23
tar	CIC-NLP	1	13.86	0.38
tar	LTLAmsterdam	1	13.04	0.72
tar	Helsinki-NLP	5	12.92	0.14
tar	CIC-NLP	3	12.07	0.09
tar	LTLAmsterdam	2	11.42	0.09

Table 5: Main results of the AmericasNLP 2023 shared task.

A Annotation and Table Guidelines

A.1 Human Evaluation Guidelines

Annotators were given the following guidelines for their evaluation:

Fluency: Is the output sentence easily readable and similar to a human-produced text?

1. *Extremely bad*: The output contains mainly repetitions or hallucinations [> 80%], and is largely illegible. The text is clearly not produced by a human.
2. *Bad*: The output may contain repetitions or erroneous characters [> 60%], but also some correct words or phrases.
3. *Acceptable*: The output does not contain a significant number of repetitions, and mainly contains correct words, however may still have grammatical errors.
4. *Sufficiently good*: The output seems like a human-produced text in the target language, without repetitions or erroneous characters, but may still contain some grammatical errors.
5. *Excellent*: The output seems like a human produced text in the target language, and is readable without issues.

Meaning: How well does the translation reflect the meaning of the reference?

1. *Extremely bad*: The meaning of the source sentence can not be inferred at all.
2. *Bad*: A small number of words or phrases allow the reader to guess the meaning or semantic content of the sentence
3. *Acceptable*: A larger number of correctly translated phrases and words allow a stronger understanding of the meaning.
4. *Sufficiently good*: The general meaning of the source sentence is conveyed, while some details may be missing.
5. *Excellent*: The meaning of the source sentence, along with all relevant details, is conveyed completely.

A.2 Guidelines for System Summary

Data

- Crawl: Does the team collect additional data from websites, PDFs, documents, books, etc.
- External Bilingual: Does the team leverage existing parallel data for language pairs not used for evaluation?
- Opus/Religious/Wikipedia: Does the team use additional data from the respective resource?
- Prior Year: Does the team use data collected from the 2021 or 2022 Shared Tasks?
- Monolingual Translation: Does the team create synthetic training data by translating a monolingual dataset?
- Pivot Translation: Does the team leverage exiting parallel data, between an unsupported language pair, through translation?
- Cleaning/Normalization: Does the team specifically describe any cleaning or normalization steps?
- No Additional: Does the team solely use the data provided from the competition?

Pretraining: A check is given if the team describes a submission which uses one of the pretrained systems. Encoder-Decoder represents a vanilla encoder-decoder transformer model trained from scratch.

Train

- Ensemble: Does the team describe a submission which makes use of multiple models for translation?
- Multistage: Does the team describe the training procedure as multiple stages, with variations in hyperparameters or training data?
- Multilingual: Does the team describe the training as multilingual, or create models which are trained on multiple language pairs?

Author Index